The Delegated Welfare State

The Delegated Welfare State: Medicare, Markets, and
the Governance of Social Policy
Kimberly J. Morgan and Andrea Louise Campbell

Rule and Ruin: The Downfall of Moderation and the Destruction
of the Republican Party, From Eisenhower to the Tea Party
Geoffrey Kabaservice

The Delegated Welfare State

Medicare, Markets, and the Governance of Social Policy

KIMBERLY J. MORGAN

and

ANDREA LOUISE CAMPBELL

OXFORD
UNIVERSITY PRESS

OXFORD
UNIVERSITY PRESS

Oxford University Press, Inc., publishes works that further
Oxford University's objective of excellence
in research, scholarship, and education.

Oxford   New York
Auckland   Cape Town   Dar es Salaam   Hong Kong   Karachi
Kuala Lumpur   Madrid   Melbourne   Mexico City   Nairobi
New Delhi   Shanghai   Taipei   Toronto

With offices in
Argentina   Austria   Brazil   Chile   Czech Republic   France   Greece
Guatemala   Hungary   Italy   Japan   Poland   Portugal   Singapore
South Korea   Switzerland   Thailand   Turkey   Ukraine   Vietnam

Published by Oxford University Press, Inc.
198 Madison Avenue, New York, New York 10016

www.oup.com

Oxford is a registered trademark of Oxford University Press

Library of Congress Cataloging-in-Publication Data
Morgan, Kimberly J., 1970-
The delegated welfare state : medicare, markets, and the governance of social policy /
Kimberly J. Morgan and Andrea Louise Campbell.
p.   cm.
Includes bibliographical references and index.
ISBN 978-0-19-973034-6 (alk. paper) — ISBN 978-0-19-973035-3 (alk. paper)
1. Human services—Contracting out—United States. 2. Privatization—United States.
3. Welfare state—United States. 4. United States—Social policy. I. Campbell, Andrea Louise, 1966- II. Title.
HV95.M657   2011
361.6'50973—dc22   2011005662

TABLE OF CONTENTS

List of Figures   ix
List of Tables   xi
Acknowledgments   xiii
Abbreviations   xv

1. Introduction   3
   THE CONCEPT OF DELEGATED GOVERNANCE   4
   THE CASE STUDY OF MEDICARE   10
   THE METHODOLOGY AND ORGANIZATION OF THIS BOOK   13

2. Exploring the Delegated Welfare State   18
   CONCEPTUALIZING THE DELEGATED WELFARE STATE   19
   WHAT DOES THE DELEGATED WELFARE STATE LOOK LIKE?   22
   A CROSS-NATIONAL PERSPECTIVE ON DELEGATED GOVERNANCE   28
   WHY DID THE DELEGATED WELFARE STATE EMERGE IN THE UNITED
      STATES?   35
   DOES IT MATTER HOW SOCIAL PROGRAMS ARE ADMINISTERED?   48
   CONCLUSION   55

3. Medicare and the Delegated Welfare State in the Postwar Era   56
   THE EMERGENCE OF THE DELEGATED WELFARE STATE   57
   DELEGATING SOCIAL WELFARE DELIVERY TO THE NONPROFIT SECTOR   63
   DELEGATING THE GOVERNANCE OF MEDICARE   66
   CONCLUSION   77

4. The Rise of the Market Reform Movement   79
   THE COMPLEX POLITICS OF WELFARE STATE REFORM   80
   THE FREE MARKET MOVEMENT IN HEALTH CARE   88

THE POLITICS OF MARKET REFORM 94

CONCLUSION 105

5. Crafting the Medicare Modernization Act of 2003   107

DELEGATED GOVERNANCE IN THE MMA 108

THE POLITICAL CONTEXT: POLARIZATION, ELECTORAL COMPETITION, AND PARTISAN CONFLICT 112

PROGRAM DESIGN: THE TURN TO DELEGATED GOVERNANCE 116

PASSING THE MMA IN 2003 132

THE POLITICS OF DELEGATED GOVERNANCE 141

6. Administering the Delegated Welfare State: The Cases of Medicare and the 2003 Medicare Modernization Act   144

DELEGATED GOVERNANCE IN TRADITIONAL MEDICARE: A MIXED PICTURE 146

CREATING A SOCIAL WELFARE MARKETPLACE: THE 2003 MMA 154

CONCLUSION 165

7. The Delegated Welfare State and Policy Feedbacks   168

STUDYING FEEDBACKS AT THE MASS LEVEL: THE MMA PANEL SURVEY 170

THE FEEDBACKS THAT HAVE NOT HAPPENED (YET) 172

THE FEEDBACKS THAT DID HAPPEN: PUBLIC DEMOBILIZATION AND ISSUE PREEMPTION 190

CONCLUSION 198

8. Citizens, Consumers, and the Market Model   200

CONSUMERS AND THE REQUIREMENTS OF THE MARKET MODEL 201

SENIOR CONSUMERS AND PART D DECISION-MAKING 204

PART D EFFECTIVENESS AND SENIOR WELFARE: MIXED EVIDENCE 207

VULNERABLE POPULATIONS AND REDISTRIBUTIVE ISSUES 212

CONCLUSION 216

9. Conclusion: Delegated Governance, Past, Present, and Future   218

IMPLICATIONS FOR THINKING ABOUT THE AMERICAN STATE 222

THE POLITICS OF ENTITLEMENTS: OFF-CENTER OR CATERING TO THE MUSHY MIDDLE? 226

THE 2010 HEALTH CARE REFORM: MORE DELEGATED GOVERNANCE 227

IMPROVING THE DELEGATED WELFARE STATE 235

Appendix A. Data Sources　237

    INTERVIEWS　237

    MMA PANEL SURVEY　237

    WISCONSIN ADVERTISING PROJECT DATA　238

Appendix B. Supplementary Tables　243

Notes　253

Index　299

LIST OF FIGURES

Figure 2.1   Ideological and Operational Ambivalence: Social Security 40
Figure 2.2   Ideological and Operational Ambivalence: The Poor 41
Figure 2.3   Proportions of Government Skeptics over Time 42
Figure 4.1   Biggest Threat to the Country in the Future   83
Figure 5.1   Most Important Health Problem 1997–2006, 65+   116
Figure 5.2   Top Ten Themes in Congressional Ads, 2000   119
Figure 5.3   MMA Final Vote and Average Health Service/HMO Contributions
             to House Members, 1999–2003   138
Figure 5.4   MMA Final Vote and Average Pharmacuetical Manufacturer
             Contributions to House Members, 1999–2003   138
Figure 5.5   MMA Final Vote and Average Health Service/HMO Contributions
             to Senators, 1999–2003   139
Figure 5.6   MMA Final Vote and Average Pharmaceutical Manufacturer
             Contributions to Senators, 1999–2003   139
Figure 7.1   Issue Ownership: Parties on Health Care and Prescription Drugs,
             2003–2007   177
Figure 7.2   Issue Ownership: Handling the Prescription Drug Issue,
             1999–2007   178
Figure 7.3   Medicare-Related Participatory Acts by Program Enrollment   192
Figure 7.4   Percent of House/Senate Campaign Ads Mentioning Prescription
             Drugs and Other Topics, 2002 and 2004 195
Figure 7.5   Number of House/Senate Campaign Ads Mentioning Medicare
             Prescription Drugs, by Party 196
Figure 7.6   Opinions about Pharmaceutical Companies, 2000–2009   197
Figure 8.1   Favorability toward Prescription Drug Benefit   207
Figure 8.2   Satisfaction with Drug Plan   208
Figure 8.3   Mean Number of Problems with Drug Plan   209

LIST OF TABLES

Table 2.1   Forms of Delegated Governance   24

Table 2.2   Desire for Increased Government Spending among All Respondents, Conservatives, Republicans, and Government Skeptics, 2008   39

Table 2.3   Government Spending Preferences among Government Skeptics in Low and High Government Trust Years   44

Table 7.1   Effects of Part D or Medicare Advantage Enrollment on Group Consciousness and Attitudes toward State and Market Roles, December 2005 to May 2007   174

Table 7.2   Issue Ownership, December 2005 (Baseline) and May 2007 (Follow-up)   179

Table 7.3   Predicting Who Gives the Republican Party Credit for the New Drug Benefit, May 2007   181

Table 7.4   Predicting Pro-Republican Attitudes on Prescription Drugs and Making Right Decisions on Medicare and Government, May 2007   184

Table 7.5   Medicare-Option versus Private Drug Plans, May 2007   193

Table 8.1   Part D Experiences of Vulnerable Populations   215

Table A.1   Knowledge Networks 65+ Year-Old Panel vs. Current Population Survey   239

Table A.2   MMA Panel Survey (Internet) vs. Kaiser Family Foundation Survey (Telephone)   240

Table B.1   Effects of Part D or Medicare Advantage Enrollment on Group Consciousness and Attitudes toward State and Market Roles, December 2005, May 2007, February 2009, among Respondents Who Remained in Third Wave   243

Table B.2   Effects of Part D or Medicare Advantage Enrollment on Group Consciousness and Attitudes toward State and Market Roles: Multivariate Analysis   246

Table B.3   Issue Ownership among Wave 3 Respondents   250

Table B.4   Medicare-Related Participatory Acts among Wave 3 Respondents   252

Table B.5   Predicting Drug Plan Switching, Problems, Affordability, and Financial Security, May 2007   252

ACKNOWLEDGMENTS

This book is the result of a shared intellectual trajectory that began during our participation in the Robert Wood Johnson Foundation's Scholars in Health Policy Research program at Yale University. We cannot find sufficient words to thank the Robert Wood Johnson Foundation (RWJF) and express our profound gratitude for all that the Scholars program has done to promote the study of health policy within the social sciences. Without this fellowship we are unlikely to have had the time and resources to embark on studying such a complex yet important policy area as health care. The faculty triumvirate that ran the program at Yale—Robert Burt, Ted Marmor, and Mark Schlesinger—fostered a climate that encouraged creative intellectual inquiry and collaborative research. We are deeply grateful to them and all the other participants in the Scholars program.

The project gained further sustenance from the RWJF through a generous Investigator Award ("The Medicare Modernization Act of 2003: Ideologies, Interests, and Policy Feedbacks in the Contemporary Politics of Medicare," June 1, 2006–May 31, 2009). In addition to this financial support, we benefited from the opportunity to share our work with the many brilliant scholars attending the Investigator Award program's annual meetings. We also gratefully acknowledge financial support from the National Science Foundation ("Do Policies Shape Mass Politics? The Impact of Medicare Reform on Senior Citizens' Attitudes and Political Participation," February 2007–January 2010, SES-0647857); the George Washington Institute of Public Policy, which provided financial assistance for the writing of subsequent grant proposals; and the Massachusetts Institute of Technology and then Political Science department head Charles Stewart, who made the baseline survey of Medicare beneficiaries possible. We especially want to thank some very helpful administrators—Kim Rykoff at George Washington University, Paula Kreutzer and Maria DiMauro at MIT, and Lynn Rogut at the RWJF—who helped us navigate the shoals of grant administration. Finally, Kimberly spent a wonderful year at the Woodrow Wilson International Center for Scholars, which provided her with the time to write, support for a research assistant, and access to the many intellectual resources of Center.

We are especially grateful to the many people who read drafts of these chapters along the way, including Jacob Hacker, Jan-Kees Helderman, Sonya Michel, Ann Shola Orloff, Eric Patashnik, Mark Peterson, Gretchen Ritter, Mark Schlesinger, and seminar participants at the College of William & Mary; Columbia; George Washington; Harvard University (both the Government Department and RWJF Health Policy Scholars program); Johns Hopkins; Northwestern; Radboud Universiteit Nijmegen; SUNY Albany; University of Massachusetts, Boston; University of South Florida; UC Berkeley; UT Austin; Woodrow Wilson International Center for Scholars; and Yale (both the Political Science Department and the School of Epidemiology and Public Health). We thank discussants and participants who commented on our work at various forums and conferences, including those of the American Political Science Association, Midwest Political Science Association, International Sociological Association, Law and Society Association, and Social Science History Association; several cohorts of students in the core seminar of Harvard's Health Policy Ph.D. program; and Jim Mahoney and participants in Wolfgang Streeck and Kathy Thelen's Working Group on Institutional Change. Informal conversations with Ed Berkowitz, Sarah Binder, Bob Blendon, Dan Carpenter, Colleen Grogan, Larry Jacobs, Gabe Lenz, Julie Lynch, Jennifer Mittelstadt, Susan Moffitt, Mark Peterson, Thomas Stanton, Patty Strach, Erik Voeten, and Julian Zelizer also were enormously helpful. We are indebted to Jake Bowers and Dan Hopkins for invaluable methodological advice and to David Cutler and Kathy Swartz for their wise counsel. Many thanks also to those who helped us develop our MMA panel survey: Adam Berinsky, Robert Binstock, Fay Lomax Cook, Sunshine Hillygus, Rob Hudson, and Mark Schlesinger.

We were extremely fortunate to have some excellent research assistants along the way, and we want to extend a hardy thanks to them for all their work on our behalf: Morgan Lyon Cotti, Karen Miranda, Tara Sussman Oakman, Mike Sances, and Morgan Wimberley.

Finally, no book manuscript sees the light of day without the support of an editor, and in this case we were fortunate to have two skilled editors embrace our project—Steve Teles and David McBride. Many thanks for your support, the speedy review and production process, and the soliciting of extremely probing, thoughtful, and constructive reviews.

ABBREVIATIONS

AAPCC	Adjusted Average per Capita Cost
AARP	American Association of Retired Persons
AEI	American Enterprise Institute
AFDC	Aid to Families with Dependent Children
AHA	American Hospital Association
AMA	American Medical Association
ANES	American National Election Study
BBA	Balanced Budget Act (1995 and 1997)
BCA	Blue Cross Association
BCBS	Blue Cross Blue Shield
BOB	Bureau of the Budget
CBO	Congressional Budget Office
CHIP	Children's Health Insurance Program
CMS	Centers for Medicare and Medicaid Services
CPI	Consumer Price Index
DG	Delegated Governance
DHEW	Department of Health, Education, and Welfare
DTC	Direct-to-Consumer
FAR	Federal Acquisition Regulations
FDR	Franklin Delano Roosevelt
FEHBP	Federal Employees Health Benefits Program
FDA	Food and Drug Administration
FERA	Federal Emergency Relief Administration
FFS	Fee-for-Service
FTE	Full-Time Employee
FY	Fiscal Year
GAO	Government Accountability Office
HCFA	Health Care Financing Agency
HEW	Health, Education and Welfare
HFCA	Health Care Financing Administration

HHS	Department of Health and Human Services
HIAA	Health Insurance Association of America
HIPAA	Health Insurance Portability and Accountability Act
HMO	Health Maintenance Organization
HSA	Health Saving Account
IRA	Individual Retirement Account
JC	Joint Commission
JCAH	Joint Commission on Accreditation of Hospitals
JCAHO	Joint Commission on Accreditation of Healthcare Organizations
JOBS	Job Opportunities and Basic Skills
LIS	Low-Income Subsidy Program
MA	Medicare Advantage
MCO	Managed Care Option
MedPAC	Medicare Payment Advisory Commission
MMA	Medicare Modernization Act of 2003
MSA	Medical Savings Account
MSP	Medicare Savings Program
NAACP	National Association for the Advancement of Colored People
NASI	National Academy of Social Insurance
NBER	National Bureau of Economic Research
NES	National Election Study
NHI	National Health Insurance
NHS	National Health Service
OECD	Organisation for Economic Co-operation and Development
OIG	Office of Inspector General
OLS	Ordinary Least Squares
OMB	Office of Management and Budget
PBM	Pharmacy Benefit Manager
PDP	Prescription Drug Plan
PFFS	Private-Fee-for-Service
PhRMA	Pharmaceutical Research and Manufacturers of America
PPO	Preferred Payment Organization
PPS	Prospective Payment System
PSRO	Professional Standards Review Organization
QIO	Quality Improvement Organization
SSA	Social Security Administration
SSI	Supplemental Security Income
TANF	Temporary Assistance to Needy Families
TSA	Transportation Security Administration
VA	U.S. Department of Veterans Affairs

The Delegated Welfare State

‖ 1 ‖

Introduction

On March 23, 2010, President Barack Obama signed into law a health care reform bill that had as its centerpiece an expansion of coverage to the uninsured. The bill was hotly contested and, despite large Democratic majorities in Congress, difficult to pass. One of the mostly vividly debated issues was the extension of federal authority over the health care system. Republican critics charged that the Democrats' reform proposals were "socialism," would create "death panels . . . that give the government the power to deny care based on budgetary concerns," and would lead to a "massive government takeover of health care."[1] In fact, the law did little to directly increase federal power over the health care system. Building upon the existing system of employer-sponsored insurance, the law subsidizes coverage for the uninsured through private insurers or state Medicaid programs, and many of the latter already contract with private managed care firms to provide insurance. State governments will set up health plan exchanges for individuals and small businesses and are responsible for enforcing new federal standards for insurer policies. Beyond paying the bills, the role of federal agencies is to write regulations, oversee the actions of state governments, and serve as a fallback if states fail or refuse to perform their assigned tasks. Although the 2010 health care bill was a major piece of social legislation, it did not move the United States any closer to socialized medicine or federal government domination of the health care system.

Instead, the law followed a well-established template in American social policy-making of delegating responsibility for publicly funded social welfare programs to private entities and state governments. Repeatedly, policy-makers have discovered that using private actors or lower levels of government to deliver services or administer programs enables them to respond to pressing social demands without seeming to expand the size of the federal government. It also allows them to cut private interests into the deal, channeling public dollars to a host of nongovernmental entities, including charitable organizations, banks (student loans)[2], landlords (housing vouchers), HMOs and other health insurance companies (Medicare and Medicaid), and others. A third advantage lies in the ability of policy-makers to shift potential conflicts away from the public arena, letting private

3

actors and market arrangements resolve questions about the distribution of scarce resources. The end result is a Rube Goldberg welfare state—a complex hybrid of public and private actors engaged in social welfare provision, convoluted lines of authority and accountability, and a blurring of boundaries between public and private.[3]

This book is about the delegation of governing authority over U.S. social programs to the private sector. We focus on one example of delegated governance—the 2003 Medicare Modernization Act (MMA), which added a prescription drug benefit to Medicare that is delivered by competing, private insurance companies. The MMA also augmented the role of commercial insurers in providing overall Medicare coverage. Placing the MMA in broad historical and cross-policy context, we show that delegated governance is a long-standing phenomenon, one that predated the rise of the free market reform movement in the 1980s. The characteristics of delegated governance have changed over time, however, shifting from an initial emphasis on nonprofit organizations to delegation to for-profits and consumers themselves. The recurring use of delegated governance results from attitudinal and institutional constraints in the United States: ambiguities in public opinion about the role of the state in American society; the often powerful role of interest groups in the policy-making process, and the preeminence of Congress in crafting social programs. Delegating governance to private actors has been a way to pass social policies in a process fraught with obstacles and hemmed in by the conflicting signals sent by the mass public. These governing arrangements have a variety of consequences, from how individuals actually fare under delegated governance to how scholars should think about the nature of the American state.

The Concept of Delegated Governance

Delegated governance refers to the delegation of responsibility for publicly funded social welfare programs to non-state actors. In contrast to directly governed programs—in which bureaucratic agencies assume full responsibility for distributing benefits or providing public services—collective goals are realized through private entities that include nonprofit organizations and profit-making firms. This is both a long-standing phenomenon in American politics and one that changes form over time, although we utilize a single term to refer to the larger phenomenon both for the sake of parsimony and because each form of delegation arises from a similar set of factors. Students of bureaucracy and public administration have long noted the existence of delegated governing arrangements, labeling them "third party government," "government by proxy," "privatization," or "the hollow state,"[4] but have paid less attention to how these arrangements have evolved over time.

We focus solely on the social welfare arena, although one could certainly extend the analysis to other policy areas, including the pervasive contracting out of federal environmental policy, reliance by state governments upon private firms to manage prisons, and the growing use of private security firms to supplement conventional military forces. We limit ourselves to the study of the welfare state for reasons of intellectual coherence and because there are no comprehensive treatments of delegated governance in redistributive programs, although there have been important studies of specific social policies[5] and overarching treatments of the "contracting out" phenomenon.[6] It should also be noted that we give only limited treatment to the delegation of authority from the federal to state and local governments. In part, this reflects the fact that an already extensive literature exists on intergovernmental relations, but also that our main case study is an entirely federal program—Medicare. Nonetheless, we do note where similar political dynamics have been at work in the intergovernmental shifting of responsibilities, and that this shifting (and inadequacy of accompanying federal funds) often produces further delegation to private actors.

Evolution of a Long-Standing Phenomenon

Contrary to the commonly held view that the contracting out of government programs simply reflects the ascent of neo-liberal thought in American politics, we see delegated governance as an older phenomenon—one that enabled the tremendous growth of federal social programs in the post-1945 period. At a time of growing national security imperatives and political pressures for government involvement in a host of domestic policy areas, conservatives mounted fierce resistance against what they saw as the unstoppable growth of a governmental leviathan. Allied with sympathetic interest groups, taking advantage of institutional veto points, and drawing on anti-statist currents in public opinion, conservatives were able to stymie the formal growth of the federal government, but not its reach. Through the contracting out of public functions to private actors, and the heaping of mandates and program responsibilities upon state and local governments, politicians were able to square the circle: to claim they were addressing a wide array of public needs and demands without increasing the size of government. Medicare, the national health insurance program for senior citizens, was one of the earliest, most extensive examples of this practice in social policy, as from its inception in 1965 the program used private intermediaries to administer Medicare benefits, relied upon private accreditation organizations to assure the quality of care provided, and paid private providers to deliver care. The practice spread to other social welfare programs during the 1960s and 1970s, fueled by mostly conservative, but at times also liberal, critiques of government.

The character of delegated governance began to change in the 1980s with the ascendance of free market ideas in American politics. Previously, conservatives in both parties viewed delegated governance as a way to preempt the growth of federal governing power and rarely saw it as a way to introduce market forces into public programs. In fact, nonprofit organizations were often the preferred vehicles for the delivery of social programs—being viewed by both the Left and the Right as government-like in their concern for public welfare—as were professional-norm-driven providers, such as physicians. Moreover, there was no overarching theoretical framework that was used to justify delegation; rather, the practice was a pragmatic response to a difficult political climate and was used to help build broader coalitions around public policies.

The situation changed by the 1980s when centrists and conservatives embraced the ideas of market-based reform but also recognized how politically treacherous welfare state retrenchment would be. Realizing that strong public support for most social programs precluded a direct attack upon them, some market-oriented conservatives reinvented the old strategy of delegating responsibility to private actors but they were now guided by a more cohesive free market philosophy. To stimulate competitive market forces, new forms of delegated governance pur-ported to shift risk onto both private firms—putting their profits at stake in the hope of generating improved efficiency and quality—and onto individual benefi-ciaries, who were tasked with purchasing their benefits or services in social wel-fare marketplaces. The Republican-crafted MMA was the apotheosis of this strategy, as it responded to strong mass demand for a new drug benefit—thus putting Republicans on the side of a significant expansion in a federal entitlement program—yet also increased the role of private insurers in delivering program benefits and required senior citizens to purchase this new benefit from a market of competing prescription drug plans. To cut government, it first had to grow, planting the seeds (some hoped) for enduring changes in the shape and nature of public programs down the road.

Hence delegated governance in the United States is a perennial but also an evolving phenomenon. We could devise separate terms for each policy design, as delegation changes over time with responsibility for social welfare programs granted variously to nonprofit organizations, for-profit firms, and individuals themselves under the market-oriented consumer choice model, but we prefer to use a single label in a field already replete with jargon. More importantly, although the particular consequences of delegation differ depending on the en-tity to which responsibility is delegated, all of these forms arise from similar at-titudinal and institutional constraints that have shaped American state-building for half a century.

Factors behind Delegated Governance

Delegated governance has its origins in three characteristics of the American polity. First, delegated governance, in all its forms, helps policy-makers navigate a fundamental ambiguity at the heart of public opinion in the United States: that Americans want government programs but dislike government. In the abstract, many Americans profess a desire for small government and low taxes, and are skeptical about government. However, when asked about specific programs and whether they wish for greater protections against life's vagaries, most are much more enthusiastic about government involvement. Delegating public programs to non-state actors satisfies both of these impulses by meeting the public's demands for security without increasing the apparent size and scope of government.

Second is the role of private interests in facilitating and encouraging delegated governance. Across the forms of delegated governance, private interests have not only stymied the growth of direct federal administration but have enriched themselves by delivering publicly funded benefits and services. Private groups—such as medical providers in the case of Medicare, and pharmaceutical companies in the case of the MMA—favored the use of non-state entities to administer these programs because this would disperse power that otherwise might have been a threat to their interests. We show how permissive federal policy has repeatedly sustained private social welfare providers, at times fueling the growth of actors that would then fiercely resist incursions of governmental authority over their "private" domain.

Yet there is more going on than simply the effective deployment of campaign donations and lobbying power by these groups. First, organized interests usually have not had enough power to "call the shots"; rather, politicians frequently have sought out their assistance in constructing political coalitions around particular social policy initiatives. Interest groups certainly have had leverage and have been able to attain many of their objectives, but in large measure this is because they have been useful to politicians in power. In addition, and somewhat ironically, some advocates of delegated governance have seen it as a way to *diminish* the influence of organized interests over government decision-making. Shifting decisions about social welfare to markets and consumers, it was argued, would reduce the opportunities for rent-seeking lobbyists to influence policy-makers. Instead, private interests could fight out their battles in the marketplace, and consumer choice would be the ultimate arbiter of quality and efficiency in publicly funded programs.

Third, we emphasize the role of Congress in shaping U.S. social policy, and how this has facilitated the use of delegated governance. Unlike most advanced industrialized countries, in which executives and bureaucrats dominate the policy-making process, the United States has a powerful, independent, and distinctively organized legislative branch that plays a crucial role in crafting social programs. There are several, interlocking reasons why delegated governance is likely in this institutional context. First, the many veto points in the Congress make policy change slow and difficult, creating ample opportunities for both conservatives and opposing interest groups to block the creation of new policy initiatives. Yet, when the demand for change proves overwhelming—as it at times does, given the public's appetite for social programs—Congress will finally act but will do so through laboriously constructed political coalitions that require many deals to be cut and interests to be appeased. Delegating authority to private actors has been one way to create such coalitions, satisfying opponents who otherwise can use the levers of power to block change, bringing private interests along, and deferring often difficult decision-making about how a program will be run by shifting those decisions to private authorities. The result has been a distinctive form of "anti-bureaucratic statebuilding"[7] that enabled the growth of the modern American state in the post-1945 period.

We might wonder how unique a phenomenon American delegated governance is. Certainly, policy-makers in other nations have been bitten by the bug of privatization, and countries such as Australia, New Zealand, the Netherlands, and the United Kingdom have enacted market-based reforms that employ commercial firms to deliver public services. The older form of delegated governance can be found in some of the continental European welfare states, where publicly funded nonprofit entities have long delivered many health, educational, and social services, and nonprofit insurance funds are charged with providing social benefits. What distinguishes the United States is the truncated regulation or supervision of these private actors and the zeal with which consumer-choice reforms have been embraced in recent years (although considerable zeal can be found in some other countries as well). The United States especially differs from other countries in its willingness to delegate the administration of *health insurance* to private firms in the hope that they are best able to impose painful austerity on health care providers and to achieve cost savings. Even in countries such as the Netherlands, where private insurers play a significant role in providing coverage, the state extends a heavy regulatory hand over the health care system and does not leave cost control to private insurers.

Practical and Theoretical Consequences of Delegated Governance

Delegating the governance of social programs to non-state actors has profound effects on government functioning, the political environment, policy outcomes, and the nature of the American state. Policy-makers often resort to delegation to provide social protections without appearing to increase the size of government. But the stunted administrative apparatus that results often creates problems of its own. Delegation empowers private interests and deliberately truncates the state actors that are supposed to oversee these agents. The result can be higher costs, inefficient delivery systems, and lower quality services. Thus, although delegated governance is utilized to alleviate public skepticism toward government, the ironic effect can be to create more frustration with the tangled administrative apparatus that results. Delegated governance thus creates a self-perpetuating cycle in which deliberate administrative weakness and inadequate regulation produce unsatisfying outcomes, further fueling the public's distrust of government.

The most recent variant of delegation—consumer choice reforms that require people to select their welfare benefits from private markets—also purports to replace uncertain democratic accountability with market discipline. However, we find that the functioning of market-based accountability—in which consumers are supposed to employ exit or voice to discipline inadequate providers—is undermined by the lack of informed, "rational" decision-making by citizen-consumers. There are also important redistributive consequences, as the most vulnerable beneficiaries are often the least able to navigate complex social welfare marketplaces. And the market is not necessarily more efficient than government provision. Insufficiently regulated private actors sometimes engage in fraud and abuse, and the heavy subsidies needed to foster private actor participation in some programmatic areas drive up costs as well.

Delegated governance also has larger political consequences, although we find that they differ somewhat from what is often claimed. Opponents of delegated governance have argued that it obscures the role of the federal government in enabling social welfare needs to be met, fosters distrust in government's ability to act, and builds support for non-state forms of social provision. In addition, some conservatives have argued that market-based provision and consumer-choice reforms could work to shift loyalties from Democratic defenders of the welfare state to Republican champions of market-based reform. In the case of the MMA, however, we do not find that marketizing reforms created support for the party that brought them to fruition, nor do we find evidence of a changed view of beneficiaries about what the government's role in social welfare policy should be. However, we do find evidence for another policy feedback effect, in that delegated governance often delivers half solutions that preempt the drive for more generous public solutions by simultaneously demobilizing the forces for reform while mobilizing interest groups with a stake in the status quo. Such "issue preemption" often has been the explicit strategy of conservative policy-makers and it can work to stunt the growth of the welfare state. Delegated governance can also create policy legacies, a "new normal" of private provision that can provide a precedent for further privatization and diminution of an overt role for government. Finally, the phenomenon of delegated governance has theoretical implications for how scholars think about the nature of the American state. In recent years, a number of scholars have advanced our understanding of the nature and workings of the American state. As Elisabeth Clemens has pointed out, the American state functions less like the Weberian ideal-type and more like one of the complex machines dreamed up by Rube Goldberg. Other scholars have highlighted the varying and sometimes surprising ways in which the American state has achieved its aims, including regulatory initiatives, legal power, the tax system, and the diffusion of governing responsibilities to nonprofit entities.[8] A similar research project has been underway in work on the welfare state, as scholars have shown that the United States relies heavily on employers for social provision,[9] uses the tax code as a form of hidden welfare state,[10] and more generally relies on an opaque set of tools to achieve social welfare goals.[11] Our book continues and furthers this project of mapping the contours of the American state, seeking to understand both the causes and consequences of the distinctive ways in which public and private authority is enmeshed. We conclude that scholars need to move away from thinking about the American state as "strong" or "weak" and focus instead on concrete questions about how the administrative apparatus works, including the efficiency and effectiveness of state action, its political consequences, and its effects on redistribution and accountability.

In sum, although delegated governance has been a politically expedient way to expand social programs in a hostile political environment, this mode of administration has often undercut the effectiveness of public programs and has generated a self-fulfilling prophecy of bureaucratic incapacity and permeability to organized interests. Delegation to non-state actors is perhaps the most feasible way to navigate the shoals of public opinion, but it leaves Americans chronically unsatisfied with government. And although delegation has been championed as a way to reduce the size of government, it has tended in practice to result in a government that is different rather than smaller.

The Case Study of Medicare

The *Delegated Welfare State* explores these questions through a case study of the 2003 MMA that places this reform within two larger contexts: the creation of the Medicare program in 1965 and its evolution since then; and, more generally, the nature and structure of the American welfare state. The focus on Medicare is beneficial to our study yet poses some limitations. On the one hand, Medicare is one of the most important social programs in the United States, as it provides health insurance to 47 million people and is the second-largest social program in the federal budget, after Social Security. It is one of the most important social programs ever created, when measured in terms of size and impact on both the population and the greater health care system. Moreover, Medicare was the first large-scale federal program in which much administrative power was delegated to private authorities, and in the succeeding decades policy-makers added more marketized versions of delegated governance to it. A longitudinal analysis of one program can therefore tell us a lot about the politics of delegated governance, its evolution through different forms, and how these practices have affected the workings of the program and its consequences for beneficiaries.

At the same time, however, it might be difficult to generalize from a study of one policy area, particularly given that the health care arena may have some distinctive qualities. For instance, perhaps no other social policy arena encompasses such a densely populated interest group landscape, as Medicare is a vital, if not predominant, source of revenue for hospitals, physicians, insurance companies, pharmaceutical firms, medical suppliers, and other health-related industries. In addition, as a purely federal program, it may not be representative of the dynamics that shape state-level programs, where much of the administration of social policies takes place. Given these possibilities, we repeatedly place Medicare in a cross-policy context, comparing it to Social Security, public assistance and welfare-related social services, Medicaid, and the Veterans Administration health care system, where applicable. We use these and other shadow cases as a way to test our suppositions and probe the limitations of our argument for other policy areas.

From its inception, much of the responsibility for the Medicare program was delegated to private authorities, and the program has experienced all three types of delegated governance. When Medicare was created in 1965, payment administration was given to nonprofit Blue Cross/Blue Shield entities (and some other commercial insurers), and as a result, just 5,000 new federal employees were brought in to run the program (compared to the 60,000 people managing the more straightforward Social Security program). Over time, Medicare adopted other forms of delegated governance by shifting program responsibilities to risk-bearing, profit-making firms. In the mid-1980s, Medicare policy changed such that HMOs contracting with the federal government to provide benefits moved from being paid on a cost basis to receiving a fixed, monthly, capitated payment per beneficiary. This means that they bear some risk for providing Medicare coverage, but also can make profits on the program if they successfully restrain or channel beneficiaries' utilization of care. Subsequently, the 1997 Balanced Budget Act aimed to increase reliance upon managed care firms, although unintended features of the bill had the opposite effect and reduced the use of private plans.

In response, the 2003 MMA again increased subsidies to managed care firms, created a PPO option more likely to take root in rural areas, and increased payments to Private Fee-For-Service Plans (PFFS)—private plans that are exempt from the requirements placed on managed care plans to develop provider networks and employ utilization management techniques. The MMA also introduced a prescription drug benefit, enrolling 60 percent of Medicare beneficiaries by 2010—a consumer choice variant of delegated governance because it delivers the new benefit entirely through private, risk-bearing firms and requires beneficiaries to choose among a large number of competing private plans for their drug benefits.[12] As of 2010, 24 percent of beneficiaries had left traditional fee-for-service Medicare for private plans—now called Medicare Advantage—up from around 13 percent in 2003. Hence within this government program we can examine delegated governance in all its forms.

To explain Medicare's trajectory through these iterations of program design, we contrast the origins of Medicare's administrative arrangements with those of Social Security—a rare federal program that is directly administered by civil servants. Social Security was created at a time of private market collapse that enhanced the legitimacy of direct federal intervention in the economy. Just as important was the fact that the program was hatched with a minimum of Congressional involvement, being created behind the closed doors of the Committee on Economic Security. It also benefited from the lack of private competitors, given the inadequacy of private pension arrangements at that time.[13] By contrast, the decision to exclude health care from the New Deal and instead furnish markets with generous subsidies through the tax code and hospital-building programs after World War II, spurred the expansion of a large and dynamic private market of health providers and insurance products. By the 1950s, the health care marketplace was taking off, with the expansion of nonprofit and commercial insurers, the explosion of the hospital sector, and the emergence of an internationally competitive pharmaceutical industry.

Medicare was thus forged in a context that was much more hostile to direct federal intervention into the market sphere than had been the case with Social Security. The private health care market had generated powerful interests that worked to block government constraints on their activities. Medicare also had to overcome the opposition of conservatives who were well aware of just how effective bureaucrats in the Social Security Administration had been in both running the program and promoting the expansion of social insurance. With strong public support for providing old-age health insurance, and a large majority in Congress after the 1964 elections, Democrats perhaps could have overcome these diverse objections and created a system of direct governance. Indeed, some government officials favored just such an arrangement, fearing that an unchecked flow of dollars into the health care arena would fuel medical inflation. However, officials chose delegated governance to promote peaceful relations with health care providers, build a larger political coalition in Congress, and preempt the mobilization of public sentiment against a "big government" program.[14] Policy-makers thus intentionally chose to tie the hands of the federal government in its relationship with private providers, constructing a system of deliberate administrative weakness.

Although politically expedient at the time of passage, Medicare's delegated design and resultant bureaucratic limitations have often hampered officials in their efforts to manage the Medicare program in the succeeding decades. Initially, program costs escalated rapidly, and although costs have since been better controlled, fraud has frequently gone unchecked and Congress has meddled in the minutiae of the program, often to protect provider interests in their states or districts. Although truncated bureaucratic capacity had been part of Medicare's design from the beginning, the program's failings seemed to confirm the claims of conservative critics that the federal government could not effectively run social programs. One lesson for some was that the federal government, and Congress especially, was incapable of standing up to powerful, organized interests. At the same time, the health care marketplace continued to expand and change, generating a new insurance product—managed care—that promised nirvana: the prospect of delivering higher quality care while also keeping down costs. For the growing numbers of market-oriented advocates in think tanks, the executive branch, and Congress, marketizing public programs was the best way forward—particularly given the obstacles to enacting direct cuts in popular benefits and services.

It was in this climate—that of a seemingly inept and easily co-opted federal government juxtaposed with dynamic private markets—that some policy-makers

embraced marketized forms of delegated governance. At first, Medicare beneficiaries were given the option to have all benefits provided by managed care companies, but when an insufficient number took up this option, advocates pushed to
make this possibility more attractive. At the same time, Medicare's bureaucratic
power was seemingly strengthened through the adoption of a prospective payment system, in which payments were made on a predetermined, fixed basis using
a procedure classification system, rather than simply reimbursing provider bills.
Despite evidence that this measure had some success in containing costs, it only
fueled the discontent of some conservatives who viewed this as a system of
administered prices. Many also were not convinced that federal policy-makers
had sufficient spine to stand up against physicians and other providers, and
believed instead that the answer lay in shifting more power to private insurers
whose profits are at stake.

After years of rancorous debate over the program, conservatives had their
chance to reshape Medicare in 2003, when Republicans controlled both branches
of government. Popular demand for a prescription drug benefit had been building
since the late 1990s, but this put Republicans in a bind. They could hardly ignore
the clamor for a universal drug benefit but were against expanding the Medicare
program in its current form. Contrary to many accounts of the MMA that see the
Bush administration as having directed the reform, the Congressional Republican
leadership was the dominant force in crafting legislation to reconcile these competing goals. A different form of delegated governance—a system that maximized
consumer choice—offered these Republicans a handy "out," as they could provide
a politically popular benefit but do so in a way that conformed to conservative
principles (although not all conservatives were convinced) and drew in insurance
and pharmaceutical industry allies to help bolster support for the measure. Some
also hoped that, by implanting market principles in the workings of the program,
the law would lay the foundations for a larger transformation of the Medicare
program in the years to come.

The Medicare case study provides a powerful lens through which to examine
the politics and development of the delegated welfare state in the United States.
Important in its own right as the second-largest line item in the federal domestic
budget, Medicare has served as a testing ground for each wave of delegated governance and allows us to trace both the forces behind each turn to delegation and
the consequences of these profound policy choices.

The Methodology and Organization of This Book

This study employs a mix of qualitative and quantitative methodologies. At the
heart of the book is a case study of the passage and consequences of the 2003
MMA. We perform detailed process-tracing of the entire legislative process surrounding the creation and passage of the MMA, utilizing an array of primary and

secondary sources as well as personal interviews with Congressional and executive branch staff; lobbyists and other officials from the pharmaceutical, insurance,
and other involved industries; representatives of consumer and senior citizen interest groups; think tank analysts; and other relevant participants and observers.
We also conducted a panel survey of Medicare beneficiaries that measures their
attitudes and tracks their experiences with the new benefits, interviewing the
same group of seniors three times: in December 2005, prior to the implementation of MMA provisions in January 2006; in May 2007, during the program's second year; and again in February 2009, during the program's fourth year. To
analyze the political and economic environment in which the MMA was wrought,
we also analyze patterns of campaign finance and candidate advertising.

Our larger claims about the origins and politics of delegated governance in the
welfare state are drawn mostly from secondary historical sources and additional
public opinion data (see Appendix A for a detailed description of data sources
utilized). As our analysis focuses on only one case—the United States—we make
use of within-case comparisons that look at changes in delegated governance over
time, and the adoption of a wider array of both delegated and directly administered programs. Through these comparisons, we are able to pin down the forces at
work shaping the delegation of program governance to private authorities, and
shifts in the nature of delegated governance over time.

Chapter 2 develops the notion of the delegated welfare state and discusses
why a new concept is needed to capture this phenomenon. The chapter also
places the American practice in historical, comparative, and cross-policy perspective, analyzing how the United States differs from other countries, but also how
delegated governance in the welfare state has evolved over time and differs across
policy areas.

To explain why delegated governance has long been a pervasive feature of federal policy-making, chapter 3 examines the creation of Medicare through the lens
of conflicts over state-building in the post-1945 period. We also compare its development with two directly administered programs, the Veterans Administration health care system and Social Security. In contrast to these two programs,
which were created in the 1920s and 1930s, Medicare was forged in the 1960s,
when a thick array of health care interest groups was already present. Direct federal administration of health insurance was abandoned to build consensus around
the program and counter fears of excessive state intervention in health care. We
follow the subsequent trajectory of Medicare and discuss how the consequences
of this decision for program cost and quality made Medicare a frequent site for
subsequent experiments in delegation.

Chapter 4 examines the ideational and political movements advocating market-
based forms of delegated governance, beginning in the 1980s. In part, the embrace
of marketizing reforms reflected the refinement of ideas about the inefficient and
oppressive nature of government as juxtaposed with the dynamism, efficiency,
and liberating qualities of markets and individual choice. Some conservative and

centrist policy-makers also believed the American state was inherently weak—a self-fulfilling prophecy given their long-standing resistance to building effective bureaucratic capacity at the federal level. In a context of rising health care costs, some policy-makers sought ways to make private insurers do the tough work of disciplining health care interests, delegating to these non-governmental authorities responsibility for meting out pain to medical providers. We trace this impulse through the push for allowing HMOs to administer Medicare benefits; the gathering enthusiasm for managed competition and the Clinton health care reform effort of 1993–1994; proposals that emerged in the 1990s for complete Medicare voucherization; and the movement for Health Savings Accounts.

Chapter 5 follows the path of the MMA from development to passage in a complex institutional and political environment. The account shows how the Republican Congressional leadership used delegated governance to reconcile competing electoral and free-market aims. As the party in power, Republicans faced intense pressure to address popular demands for a drug benefit, but they also sought a response that would both muster a conservative majority in the House and pass the more moderate Senate. We trace the efforts of the Republican leadership to navigate a treacherous political and institutional context and how they enlisted interest group allies like the pharmaceutical and insurance industries to help build a majority. In so doing, we show how the Republican leadership turned to administrative design as a way to reconcile the competing preferences of conservatives worried about the creation of a vast new entitlement, moderate Republicans worried about constituents in rural areas, insurers worried about bearing risk for the new benefit, pharmaceutical companies worried about government control, and health care providers worried about reimbursement rates. The result was a complex system of delegated governance, an extraordinarily complicated piece of legislation designed to meet the desires of many different factions but that left considerable uncertainty as to whether it would work.

Chapter 6 is the first chapter that explores the consequences of delegated governance through an analysis of Medicare administration in general, and of key elements of the 2003 MMA—the Medicare Advantage program and the Part D drug benefit. Although delegated governance has been politically expedient—enabling the passage and growth of government programs in an anti-government political climate—this has frequently come at the cost of good governance. Outsourcing program responsibilities to non-state actors does not appear to produce more efficient or effectively run government. Moreover, when the delegation occurs in a way that brings market forces into a program, this creates potential hazards (e.g., marketing abuses, fraud) that require oversight by a muscular political agency. Yet, the same hostility toward government that drives the decision to delegate governance in the first place also impedes the growth of an effective oversight body. As a result, various program failures arise that are frequently blamed on government officials who have never been sufficiently empowered to deal with these problems.

Chapter 7 examines political feedbacks of the MMA on both elite and mass politics. We use our own panel survey data to explore the claims of both scholars and pundits that market-based social provision can change mass attitudes about privatizing social programs. We find that the new design of Medicare, with private entities providing the Part D and Medicare Advantage benefits, has not fundamentally changed attitudes about the relative role of the state and the market in health care, nor has it undermined feelings of group consciousness and solidarity among the elderly. We also find that the Republican Party has made few gains in ownership of issues like prescription drugs, Medicare, or health care in general. However, the party did achieve "issue preemption," in that it effectively solved the prescription drug issue and pushed it off the political agenda. The legislation also effectively demobilized the public around the prescription drug issue, offering a "good enough" policy that undercut efforts to improve the benefit or institute a directly governed alternative within Medicare. The MMA also created new constituencies protective of their programs, with Democratic opponents of the Medicare Advantage program unable to eliminate it in the 2010 health care reform bill. Subsidies to MA providers were cut, although with Republican gains in Congress in the 2010 election, insurers may be successful in getting them restored if senior constituents begin to feel the effects. In sum, by demobilizing public demand for reform while also mobilizing commercial stakeholders, the MMA is generating a self-reinforcing logic that is difficult to challenge, absent unanticipated instability in the new Medicare marketplace or a fiscal emergency.

Chapter 8 explores the consequences of delegated governance and the market model for Medicare beneficiaries specifically and democratic citizens more generally. Although the MMA assumed that seniors possessed the ability to choose among large numbers of competing alternatives, exit bad plans, and contest inadequate benefits, we find that many Part D enrollees make poor initial choices and then fail to switch plans, thereby increasing costs for themselves and undermining the market logic behind the reform. And although seniors report high rates of problems with their prescription drug plans and low levels of satisfaction compared to those covered by other sources like the Veterans Administration or former employers, they profess favorability toward the prescription drug reform. Using Hirschman's classic framework, we conclude that recipients have responded to problems with their plans with loyalty (or passivity) rather than with exit or voice. More broadly, we analyze mechanisms of accountability and assess the degree to which individuals can have their voices heard when they operate as consumers facing for-profit businesses, as opposed to citizens confronting public bureaucracies and elected officials.

Finally, in our concluding chapter, we summarize the main findings of the book and probe its implications both for scholarship on the American state and contemporary entitlement politics. The delegated governance lens reveals the merit of examining what states do rather than whether they are "strong" or "weak." Our research thus not only sheds light on an important episode in

American politics, but aims to advance our thinking about the complex realities of the American state. A second set of implications has to do with the nature of redistributive policy in the United States, which some would argue has been captured by well-heeled interests and become increasingly unresponsive to mass opinion. Although interest group power is certainly part of the story we tell, we find that because the public sends fundamentally contradictory signals to American politicians about what the role of government should be in their lives, delegated arrangements often reflect the views of an ambivalent public. Moreover, because deeply rooted ideational and institutional forces have driven the recourse to these kinds of governing arrangements again and again, we expect this pattern to continue in the foreseeable future. To show this, we close this chapter with a brief examination of the 2009–2010 health care reform effort in which both the fight over the appropriate scope and power of the federal government and the solution—delegation to private health insurers and states—reflect the political forces we trace in this book.

2

Exploring the Delegated Welfare State

In recent years, scholarship on the American welfare state has increasingly focused on what some have called the "private welfare state" of employer-provided benefits and individual self-servicing that are subsidized through the tax code. This work has opened our eyes to the complex mix of public and private action that constitutes the American approach to social welfare. There is, however, another way in which public and private action is entwined. Even in seemingly public social programs, private actors often play a critical role in the delivery of benefits and services, and sometimes in the administration of programs themselves. In the case of Medicare, for instance, responsibility for administering the program has always been largely in the hands of private insurers and other nongovernmental entities, overseen by only a small number of federal civil servants. Similarly, in most states, managed care firms bear much of the responsibility for delivering Medicaid benefits.[1] And since the 1996 welfare reform, a number of localities and one state government have contracted out the administration of their welfare programs to for-profit firms.[2] By looking closely at the actual governance of the welfare state, we can see that much responsibility for social provision is delegated from federal authorities to state and local ones, and—of chief interest here—from public authorities to the private sector.

How extensive are these arrangements, and does it matter whether programs are administered by public or private agencies? This chapter develops the concept of delegated governance, maps the different forms it has taken over time and in different policy areas, and provides a comparative perspective on the phenomenon. As this chapter will show, the United States is not alone in relying on private actors in the delivery of social programs, but is distinctive in the degree to which it does so and in its enthusiasm for profit-making welfare providers—particularly in the reliance upon for-profit firms in publicly funded health insurance programs. The nature of delegated governance in the United States has varied over time: in its earliest phases the emphasis was on delegating responsibilities to nonprofit organizations and trusted professionals, both of which were viewed as public-regarding in their motives. Since the 1980s, however, there has been a policy shift toward encouraging for-profit actors, market competition in social welfare provision, and consumer choice. Along with this has come a change in the locus of decision-making and risk. Whereas previously, governments made decisions about contracting out and bore risk for cost overruns, more recent forms of delegated governance put decision-making responsibility on individuals and shift risk from government to profit-making firms and individual consumers.

The chapter also raises some of the implications of delegated governance, a topic to which we will return in depth later in the book. The way programs are actually administered is no mere technical factor, but affects the real-world functioning and effectiveness of social programs, their redistributive effects, and their political consequences (or "policy feedbacks"). In addition, for academics less concerned with the nitty-gritty of social policy regimes, delegated governance has importance for how we conceptualize the nature of the American state—an issue that has received growing attention in recent years. We argue that scholars need to get away from abstract conceptualization of "the state" and look more concretely both at *what* states actually do and *how* they do it. An examination of the delegated welfare state takes us away from a view of the state as a unified entity—and away from conceptualizations of "strong" versus "weak" states—and instead reveals the multiplicity of functions in which states engage and how power relationships vary across governing structures. Being attentive to different forms of governance and their consequences for effectiveness, redistribution, and accountability helps us to better grasp the real-world meaning of governmental action.

Conceptualizing the Delegated Welfare State

Delegated governance is the delegation of responsibility for publicly funded social welfare provision to non-state actors. Rather than set up bureaucratic agencies to directly achieve a particular set of objectives, such as distributing benefits or providing public services, collective goals are realized through private entities that may be profit-making or nonprofit organizations. The government role is one of financing, regulation, and oversight, but not direct provision. By contrast, in a situation of direct governance, government agencies directly provide benefits or services. Some examples of direct governance in the United States include Social Security, which is administered by a federal agency, the Veterans Administration (VA) health care system—a domestic example of "socialized medicine"[3]—and, at the local level, public schools.

Why do we use the term "delegated governance"? "Delegation" is employed to highlight the deliberate act that is involved in assigning responsibility for social welfare to non-state actors. This is not something that simply evolves in the private sector; rather, a decision is taken to shift the provision of a social welfare benefit or service to the private realm.[4] The term also reflects the notion that governing involves delegation from the legislative branch to the administrative authorities that implement policy, as well as the legal "non-delegation doctrine" that limits the ability of Congress to delegate its lawmaking power to other public or private entities.[5] Although often invoked around the delegation of power to executive agencies, some courts have imposed greater scrutiny on the delegation of governing authority to private actors whose self-interest may conflict with public objectives.[6] In practice, however, delegation to private actors has occurred with great frequency, leading some scholars to conclude that the non-delegation doctrine cannot be used to limit the granting of authority to private actors.[7] Regardless of where one stands on the legal question, the non-delegation doctrine embodies a similar concept to that which we are studying—the notion that when public responsibilities are shifted to non-state actors, this represents a delegation of governing authority to those entities.[8]

The term "governance" has many uses and thus also requires some explication. "Governance" has become a fashionable term in the scholarly literature on public administration, yet it has many meanings.[9] For some scholars, the word "governance" conveys the idea that governing power is not confined to public authorities but is often exercised through private firms, international organizations, and other non-state entities. Scholars writing from this perspective often emphasize the decline of hierarchical, command-and-control governing relationships and their replacement by networks and other forms of horizontal relationships.[10] Another approach is to use governance in a narrower and more traditional sense— the act of governing—and leave the site and nature of this governing to be specified, e.g., public sector governance, corporate governance, networked governance, etc. We would like to reclaim the original use of the term, which can then be qualified and made more precise. Rather than assume that governance involves diffused authority, extensive private involvement, and negotiated contracts, we assume only that governance involves governing and then examine how this governing takes place.

Why not simply describe delegated governance as other scholars frequently have, as "privatization" or "contracting out"? There are several reasons that we think delegated governance is an improvement on these two terms. Privatization has been used to describe quite distinct phenomena, ranging from the complete shedding of state responsibility for social provision, the selling-off of state-owned enterprises, or the contracting out of the provision of public services.[11] Given these disparate meanings, we find that the concept has been stretched to the point that it tends to obscure the object of study rather than clarify it. In addition, privatization connotes the withdrawal of public responsibility in a particular area, such as complete load-shedding by public authorities. This more aptly describes phenomena such as the sale of state-owned enterprises, but fails to capture that which most commonly occurs in countries such as the United States—the intertwining of public and private responsibility.[12] Moreover, administering public programs through private actors often entails substantial government involvement through financing, oversight, and regulation, contrary to what the term "privatization" implies. Finally, privatization has acquired ideological connotations related to the free-market movement that emerged in the 1970s and 1980s in many Western countries.[13] This renders the term less useful to describe the larger phenomenon of delegated governance, which predates the market reform movement and lacked that ideological orientation.

A term that is closer to that of "delegated governance" is the idea of "contracting out"—contracting with private providers to deliver public benefits or services.[14] Although this more accurately captures the phenomenon of interest to us, and we use it at times, we still believe that delegated governance adds something to the existing social policy lexicon. In the arena of social provision, the government is doing more than simply contracting out service provision, as a municipal government might do for garbage collection, or the Defense Department might do in the procurement of weaponry. When responsibility for administering social welfare programs is contracted out, this effectively shifts power and authority over the lives of program beneficiaries—some of whom are deeply dependent upon these programs—from the state to non-state actors.[15] Governance, and governing, is ultimately about power: the ability to make people do what they otherwise might not be able or inclined to do. Delegating governance is about moving this power from public to private actors.[16] Although contracting out may technically describe the practice, it fails to convey the wider implications of it in the way that delegated governance does.

We see delegated governance as a subset of a larger phenomenon in the United States—the reliance upon indirect mechanisms and private actors to provide for collective welfare. By now, this phenomenon is well-known: in the 1980s, scholars began noting that private firms bear much of the responsibility for social welfare provision in the United States through employee benefits systems.[17] This "hidden welfare state" is subsidized by features of the tax code, as is individual self-servicing in private markets for, among other things, housing (mortgage interest deduction), child care (dependent care tax credit), and health care (tax break for medical expenditures).[18] In more recent years, scholars have more fully explored the origins and evolution of the public-private divide in social welfare, focusing on employer-provided pensions and health insurance benefits.[19] More recent research has examined the system of subsidies via government-sponsored enterprises (e.g., Freddie Mac) and tax credits for the provision of higher education and housing.[20]

The result is what might be called, adapting a term developed by Elisabeth Clemens, the Rube Goldberg welfare state. In looking more broadly at the American state, Clemens argues that it functions less like the Weberian ideal-type and more like one of the complex machines dreamed up by Rube Goldberg.[21] Thus, instead of directly exerting authority through centralized, hierarchically organized public bureaucracies, the American state has frequently relied upon non-state actors to achieve its objectives. This blurs the boundaries between public and private while obfuscating lines of authority and accountability. The same is clearly true of the American welfare state, as evidenced by the above-mentioned means by which social policy goals are attained. Tax expenditures, government-sponsored enterprises, tax-subsidized employer-provided benefits—all involve indirect governmental involvement to secure social welfare aims.

We view delegated governance as one subset of this Rube Goldberg welfare state that has been neglected thus far by students of social policy. One reason for the research lacuna is that, in general, political scientists often end their analysis with the passage of policy, paying only limited attention to the way in which programs are actually implemented and administered. An important exception is the literature on policy feedback effects, which explores the ways in which public policies shape the consequent politics around an issue. As several scholars have argued, program design is of paramount importance, as it can influence the interest groups that subsequently mobilize, beneficiary self-perceptions of political efficacy or worth, and mass perceptions of the role of government.[22] Outside of this literature, however, political science generally focuses more on explaining the passage of policy than on tracing its implementation and lasting effects.

On the other hand, scholars of public administration have been highly attentive to program administration and have long been charting the development of what they have called "third party government," "government by proxy," or "the hollow state."[23] Most of these scholars have not looked specifically at social policy, however, and many have been less concerned with analyzing the political origins and dynamics of delegating governance than with probing its implications.[24]

What Does the Delegated Welfare State Look Like?

In developing the idea of delegated governance, we do not intend to establish it as a "one-size-fits-all" concept. To the contrary, the way in which delegated governance has been executed in practice varies by policy area, and also over time. For that reason, we categorize in Table 2.1 a number of social programs into a spectrum that reflects both the degree and nature of delegation in various arenas and the spread of delegated forms of governance over time. Some programs have always had delegated elements, such as Medicare, which since its inception in 1965 delegated much of its administration to the nonprofit Blue Cross/Blue Shield plans and the actual delivery of health care to private-sector doctors and hospitals (as opposed to the Veterans Health Administration, which has its own system of hospitals and salaried physicians). A second category of programs includes those to which delegated elements have been added over time: welfare benefits, social services, the JOBS program, child support enforcement, and Medicaid (specifically the use of HMOs). These are programs that began with traditional government provision (although Medicaid, like Medicare, always used private doctors and hospitals), but that increasingly have delegated administration and/or service delivery to private actors over time. The third category consists of programs that have been characterized by delegated governance from the outset: Medicare Advantage, Part D drug plans, Section 8 housing vouchers, school vouchers, and private prisons. Temporally, these programs tend to come later than the other programs as policymakers have increasingly embraced delegation as a mode of governance.

Program Administration and Service Delivery

A quick glance at the first two rows of Table 2.1 reveals how heterogeneous delegated governance is in practice. We differentiate between program administration and service delivery and find that different entities—governments, self-governing professionals, nonprofits, for-profits—do each of these functions for different programs, and that for a given program different entities may perform each function. We also find that for-profits are more common in service delivery than in program administration, and are more common for both service delivery and administration among the programs that were created later and that have always been delegated.

Hence we have mostly nonprofits administering fee-for-service Medicare, welfare, and social services—government administering housing vouchers—and a mix of government and private actors administering the small number of extant school voucher programs.[25] Even though the actual administration of social programs by market-oriented for-profits is less common, we do see it with Medicaid HMOs, Medicare Advantage, and private prisons. Service delivery is performed in some cases by a mix of government, nonprofits, and for-profits (as in social services and JOBS programs), but mostly government stays out of service delivery in the other areas, delegating responsibility either to private professionals and organizations (as with Medicare, housing, and school vouchers) or to for-profit firms (child-support services, Medicaid HMOs, Medicare Advantage, Part D plans, and private prisons).

There are two main points to take away, besides an appreciation for the complexity of these arrangements. The first is that there has been a movement toward for-profit providers over time, both because older programs, whose benefits were originally provided by government or nonprofits, are now using for-profits, and because newer programs have utilized for-profits from the outset. The second is that for-profits are particularly common in service delivery, with potential implications for the quality of provision. Profit-making entities may have incentives to meet consumer demand, but they also face incentives for cost-cutting and cream-skimming (serving only the "easiest" or "cheapest" customers). This is an empirical question, however, and some have argued that growing competition with for-profits and other voluntary organizations has spurred many nonprofits to behave more like proprietary actors.[26]

Table 2.1. **Forms of Delegated Governance**

	Programs with DG Elements	Programs with DG Added Over Time					DG Programs				
	FFS Medicare	Welfare benefits (pre- post-TANF)	Welfare services	JOBS	Child support enforcement	Medicaid (HMOs)	Medicare Advantage	Part D drug plans	Section 8 housing vouchers	School vouchers	Private prisons
Who administers program	Federal govt.; nonprofits; for-profits (esp. in Part B)	Pre-TANF: state/local governments Post-TANF: some nonprofits, for-profits	Pre-TANF: state/local governments Post-TANF: some non-profits, for-profits.	Federal government	State and local governments	State governments; for-profits	Federal govt.; for-profits	Federal govt.; for-profits	Govt.	Public, private lottery programs	For-profits
Who delivers service	Private providers—nonprofits or perceived as non-market actors	Local governments, nonprofits, for-profits.	Mostly non-profits, for-profits.	Mix of government, nonprofit, for-profit centers.	Local governments, for-profits	For-profits	For-profits	For-profits	Private landlords	Private schools (non-profits)	For-profits

24

Locus of decision making	Government contract with intermediaries; individual chooses provider.	State, local government contract	State/local government contract; individuals w/ vouchers	Government contract	Government contract	Government contract	Individual chooses provider	Individual chooses provider	Individual chooses provider	Individual chooses provider	Individual chooses provider	Government contract
Who bears risk	Government; providers.	Government	Government; individual for costs above voucher amount.	Government	Government	Provider; individual for poor choice of plan.	Individual for poor choice of plan; provider bears market risk	Individual for poor choice provider; provider bears market risk	Individual for poor choice provider; provider bears market risk	Individual for poor choice of provider; provider bears market risk	Individual for poor choice of provider; provider bears market risk	Provider bears market risk
Can services be denied?	Yes, but rare (doctors refuse Medicare patients)	Yes: sanctions imposed.	Yes: sanctions imposed.			Care is 'managed': services may be denied.	Care is 'managed': services may be denied.	Drug use is "managed": therapies denied (or more expensive)	Yes	Yes	Yes	

Locus of Decision-making

An important aspect of delegated governance is the locus of decision-making: Who makes the decision to engage a certain provider, the government or the beneficiary? Traditionally, the delegated welfare state was set up such that the government would contract with a provider. The government solicits bids, prospective providers compete to gain the contract, and government selects a contractor, with that decision in place until the next contracting period. This is the pattern we see in Medicare administration, the JOBS program, child support enforcement, Medicaid HMOs, and private prisons. This differs from programs in which individuals, typically holding vouchers for services or an entitlement to benefits, select a provider on their own. Individuals select their own Medicare Advantage and Part D plans, their own physician under Medicare, their own apartment under Section 8, their own private school under the education voucher programs, and sometimes their own social service providers. Individual choice of provider is more common among programs that come later, when the concept of delegated governance— especially the consumer choice variant—was adopted more broadly, although it was present in Medicare and the initial incarnation of state Medicaid programs from the beginning.[27]

Shifting the decision-making locus from government to individuals has consequences for the nature, quality, and comprehensiveness of the information brought to the decision-making process. On the one hand, when government chooses a service provider, clients are stuck with that provider, which may not be to their liking. But in theory the government choice is a considered one, with much data and relevant criteria brought to bear. With individual choice, beneficiaries may be pleased with their autonomy, but they also may be paralyzed by too much choice or fail to use the most salient considerations to inform their choices. For example, in selecting Part D prescription plans, many beneficiaries are overwhelmed by too much choice—studies show they are more likely to select an optimal plan when faced with ten or fewer choices rather than the 40-plus they typically encounter[28]—and they tend to use the wrong criteria, weighting monthly premiums more than overall out-of-pocket costs, or choosing plans that cover the "doughnut hole" coverage gap even though their annual drug costs are well below the doughnut threshold.[29] Unconstrained individual choice has its downsides as well as its appeal.

Risk Bearing and Service Denial

Another major issue concerns who bears risk under these various governance scenarios and who determines whether services can be denied. In most of the "older" programs, the government ultimately bears the financial risk of provision—if services cost more than projected, then the government absorbs the cost, with traditional Medicare being a chief example. Contrast that with the newer programs, in which the provider bears the brunt of market risk: if Medicaid or Medicare Advantage capitated plans fail to deliver care under the budget they are allotted for each patient, they must absorb some of the cost. Similarly, private prisons must run their facilities under the contracted budget from the state or their profit margin will suffer. Private landlords and private schools bear the risks of taking in Section 8 or education voucher holders.[30]

In the most recently developed forms of delegated governance, individual clients themselves bear some risk. These programs offer their clients choice, but they also impose upon the clients the risks of poor choices. If a prescription drug that a senior citizen needs is not covered by the Part D plan they chose, or if their plan imposes unanticipated costs, that person has to remain in the plan until the annual open enrollment period rolls around at the end of the year. Individuals must similarly bear the risks of poor choice of a Medicare Advantage plan, an apartment, or a private school.

In addition, services can be denied by private actors in some forms of delegated governance. Doctors can refuse to take Medicare patients (few do, but more threaten to every time reimbursement levels are cut), and private landlords and schools can refuse voucher holders. Under Medicaid HMOs, Medicare Advantage, and Part D drug plans, care is supposed to be "managed" and channeled in the most cost effective way for the provider, which may be experienced as service denial by patients who wish to get a test or see a specialist or get a brand name rather than a generic drug but are prevented from doing so. The constraining effects of this are somewhat limited for Medicare recipients because they can exit a Medicare Advantage plan and return to the fee-for-service government program, and can choose among a wide array of Part D plans, although in general they can do this only once a year when the open enrollment period comes around. Medicaid recipients often lack those kinds of choices, as do welfare recipients who face the prospect of service denial determinations that are made by private entities.[31]

In sum, the delegated welfare state is extremely heterogeneous in form, involving a plethora of actors and administrative arrangements that have changed over time. One key change has been the shift in the locus of decision-making and risk from government to private actors and, in some instances, to clients themselves. The nature of delegation also has changed over time, as has the array of actors to whom responsibilities are delegated, with nonprofits and self-governing professionals joined later by for-profit firms. Although we use a single term to cover these multitudinous administrative arrangements, the implications and consequences of delegation do change. In some instances, what is delegated is the processing of claims so that a non-state entity merely implements rules determined by a government agency. Altogether different is delegation of the power to determine eligibility or benefit levels—in which a non-state entity exerts decision-making power over clients' outcomes. In each case, one must think through the implications of shifting governing authority to private entities for accountability, distribution, and program effectiveness.

A Cross-National Perspective on Delegated Governance

How unique is the governance of the American welfare state when viewed in cross-national perspective? Clearly, the United States is not alone in having "Rube Goldbergesque" arrangements for the delivery of social programs. The Weberian ideal-type of bureaucratic governance is just that—an ideal-type that has been frequently violated in reality by the concrete practices of social welfare regimes across the advanced industrialized world. In many countries, we find complex mixes of public and private social provision and blurring of boundaries between these two sectors. Although in some countries this has long been the case through heavy reliance on the voluntary sector, it has become more so with the adoption of marketizing reforms since the 1980s, which have further broken down state monopolies in health, education, and welfare; increased the role of private actors in the delivery of social programs; and promoted consumer choice in social welfare markets.

At the same time, however, it is important not to lose sight of the ways in which the United States has been, and remains, distinctive. Although a number of European countries long relied on voluntary associations to deliver social programs, these entities are often highly coordinated and serve essentially as state appendages. In the United States, the voluntary sector has always been less structured and more decentralized than that in western Europe. Although marketizing reforms and other forces have challenged voluntary association monopolies in western Europe, the same tendencies have done even more to fracture the sector of social welfare providers in the United States. In addition, although scholars have noted a trend in a number of western European countries toward increased reliance on private delivery of services since the 1980s, it remains a relatively recent phenomenon. In the United States, by contrast, we argue that virtually the entire construction of the American welfare state, outside of Social Security, occurred through systems of delegated governance and that this pre-dated the marketization fervor that took hold in a number of countries in the past three decades. Delegated governance is particularly pronounced in the health care arena, where the United States is distinctive in the degree to which it has delegated governance to non-state—and particularly for-profit—actors.

A final, fundamental difference lies in the continued existence of effective, Weberian bureaucracies in western European countries, despite reliance in some upon private actors for the delivery of services or administration of public programs. Outside of the Social Security program, the federal bureaucratic infrastructure around health and welfare programs in the United States is distinctively fragmented, uncoordinated, and in some cases quite small. This is especially pronounced in the field of health.[32]

Delegated Welfare States Abroad

In the American popular press, European welfare states are often lumped to-gether and tagged as state-run socialism. In fact, direct governance of social programs—in which the state not only funds but also directly provides social benefits and services—is relatively rare and most comprehensively found in the Nordic countries, where social benefits and services are funded through general taxation and provided by public bureaucracies. For example, day care centers in Nordic countries are largely publicly run, and these countries have integrated health care systems in which government not only funds health care but also provides it.[33] A number of other countries, including the United Kingdom, New Zealand, Australia, and several southern European countries utilize direct governance in health care, having created integrated health systems—often called national health services—in which public authorities play a major role in the delivery of care.[34] In these systems many health care personnel are public-sector employees—although some may be private con-tractors receiving public funds, a practice that is particularly common in south-ern Europe[35]—and the hospital sectors are largely public.[36] Until the 1980s, the British public housing system was, in addition to being quite extensive, directly administered by local authorities.[37] Outside of these exceptions, how-ever, direct state provision of social services did not extend to most other areas of social welfare, and these responsibilities were effectively left to families and voluntary organizations.

Non-state actors have long played a vital role in the administration of health, education, and welfare programs in much of continental Europe. In countries such as Germany and the Netherlands, nonprofit welfare associations have for decades been the preeminent providers of educational and social welfare pro-grams.[38] In the Netherlands, for instance, 70 percent of primary and secondary school students are in publicly funded, privately run schools.[39] Moreover, the "Bismarckian" welfare state model, found in countries such as Austria, Belgium, France, Germany, and the Netherlands, employs non-state insurance funds to distribute benefits such as pensions, health insurance, and family allowances.[40] Usually governed by employers' associations and labor unions, these insurance funds effectively "share public space" with state actors.[41] In Germany, there are hundreds of nonprofit sickness insurance funds that are governed by representa-tives of business and labor and provide coverage to all. Similarly, in France, people receive their health coverage through private health insurance funds that collect payroll taxes and pay providers, and family allowances are distributed through non-state entities—family allowance funds.[42] The actual power of the social partners in managing social insurance funds does vary across continental Europe; in some cases, parliamentary decisions set the main policy parameters, whereas in some other countries more policy-making power has been delegated to the social partners.[43]

In these countries, as well as in Canada, the national health service model was rejected in favor of a system of publicly funded insurance coverage and privately delivered care. Thus, medical facilities are largely privately run and physicians are not salaried public employees, as they would be in a national health service, although hospitals may be publicly run. Individuals choose their own health care provider whose costs are reimbursed by the insurance fund. Each country differs in its public-private mix, however; France, for instance, has both an extensive public hospital system as well as the largest private hospital sector in Europe.[44] France also has a large sector of private, supplemental health insurance that covers gaps in public insurance plans, and in Germany, formally private insurance funds serve higher income clientele. In short, in continental Europe, the governance of social programs has long been distributed across a wide array of state and non-state actors.

Even so, the delegation of governance in the American welfare state does differ from that found in other countries. In much of continental Europe, the non-state welfare and educational sectors have been fairly centralized and have had an institutionalized function as welfare provider and partner in corporatist governing arrangements. Thus, nonprofit welfare associations in Germany have long been members of centralized peak associations that, since the 1960s, have been "functional equivalents of public sector institutions"[45] or a "branch of government"[46] that are part of a corporatist regime.[47] Similarly, Dutch nonprofit social service providers originally were independent of the state but gradually became "quasi-public" entities in the post–World War II period[48] for which, in some cases, government payments covered nearly 100 percent of staff and program costs.[49] Social insurance funds in continental Europe are semi-public entities whose actions have been increasingly subject to state constraints, such as global budget caps and greater parliamentary controls.[50] As will be discussed later in this chapter, the system of delegated governance to nonprofits in the United States is considerably more decentralized, which undercuts the coherence of policy interventions.

Perhaps a closer parallel to the United States is the adoption of market-based reforms in many Organisation for Economic Co-operation and Development (OECD) countries since the 1980s, which altered the governance of some social programs by increasing the role of non-state (and often for-profit) actors in service delivery.[51] Probably the most-publicized reforms along these lines were in the United Kingdom under both Conservative and Labour governments. For instance, starting in the 1980s, public housing was sold to tenants and the remaining system was converted from a largely state-run affair to one in which nonprofit housing associations play a growing role.[52] The long-term care sector in the United Kingdom was also transformed, with a significant increase in the role of for-profit care providers. By 2004, private institutions accounted for 88 percent of users of residential facilities, and the public provider share of home health care was just 31 percent, down from 95 percent in 1993.[53] Between 1997 and 2010, New Labour governments dedicated greater resources to social welfare programs but often did so by subsidizing consumers and non-state providers of social services, thereby moving "the center of gravity of governance away from the bureaucratic state."[54]

Similarly, the child care and old-age care sectors in many countries have been shaped by a shifting mix of government, nonprofit, and for-profit providers and a growing emphasis on consumer choice and voucher-type support. In Germany, the long-term care insurance program created in 1994 allowed for-profit providers into the system, and they now make up about half of long-term care providers—a clear departure from the past practice of directing subsidies to voluntary organizations.[55] In France, rather than continue to develop expensive, municipally run child care centers, successive governments have subsidized parents who purchase care (and other domestic services) on their own. In 2006, the Netherlands converted its child care subsidy system into one that reimburses parents through the tax code for the care they purchase in private markets.[56]

Perhaps more startling are the reforms that have taken place in Sweden, where there was always a strong commitment to direct state provision of services in order to assure equal access to high-quality programs. Since the 1980s, the role of non-state (and often for-profit) actors has grown in health care, old-age care, child care, and education.[57] The public school system has been converted to a voucher-type system that allows private schools to receive public funds and compete for pupils, and old age care has been transformed from an almost entirely state-operated sector to one in which for-profits play a significant role in running residential facilities and home care services.[58] The child care sector also has been altered somewhat since the 1990s, as private providers now account for about 20 percent of centers, most of these being parental cooperatives or other nonprofit associations. Finally, since 2003 when a major reform to the pension system was fully implemented, a portion of an individual's pension contributions goes into an individual investment account, with individuals able to choose among a large array of funds.[59]

How significant are these kinds of changes? Although there have been some clear shifts in the governance of welfare programs in a number of countries, in most places they come nowhere near the kinds of reforms that took place in the United Kingdom. Neo-liberal reform movements have held much less sway in continental Europe,[60] and thus have only minimally altered the governance of welfare regimes in Austria, Belgium, France, Germany, or Italy, for instance. In many countries, the nature and role of the voluntary sector has changed, but this is not necessarily due to a drive toward marketization rooted in neo-liberalism. In France, for example, a leftist critique of bureaucracy spurred the drive to decentralize governance from Paris to regional and local governments, and to augment the role of the nonprofit sector.[61] In Germany, there also have been changes in the nature of the German voluntary sector, but not due to marketizing reforms. Instead, new organizations have successfully challenged the privileged status of the traditional voluntary groups, thus opening up equal funding opportunities for these challengers and rendering the voluntary sector more pluralistic.[62]

In addition, those countries that have adopted marketizing reforms have done so in the past three decades, with some initial reforms in the 1980s and an accelerated marketizing trend in the 1990s or 2000s. In other words, these are relatively recent phenomena for welfare states that scholars long characterized as having hierarchical, bureaucratic, and centralized forms of governance. By contrast, the U.S. welfare state has always relied heavily upon delegated governance as its mode of administration and service delivery, and this way of structuring social programs predated the marketization movement. Explaining the governance of the American welfare state thus requires one to dig deeper than the international privatization movement that began to take hold in the 1980s.

Finally, a basic difference between the United States and western European welfare states concerns the role of bureaucratic authority in structuring public-private relationships. In France, for instance, where many elements of the "old" American health care system—including fee-for-service medicine and independent physicians—have been maintained, and health insurance is paid through para-public funds, the central state weighs heavily upon the entire medical sector. From the state's control over medical schools to its role in setting reimbursement rates for pharmaceuticals, bureaucrats in France play a vital role in shaping the organization of the medical field and the prices charged.[63] In the Netherlands, despite reliance upon private organizations to deliver many social and educational services, the expansion of the welfare state post-1945 spurred the growth of administrative authority, producing a "strongly centralized Dutch state" that intervened considerably in how non-state actors delivered these programs.[64] We can find this across western Europe—the presence of welfare state bureaucracies that, while one should not exaggerate their power, have considerably greater authority in managing social programs in their societies than is, by the large, the case in the United States (with the exception of the Social Security Administration).

In sum, there have been changes in how government programs are actually delivered, but in many countries these changes have been limited, at least so far.[65] Although the importance of marketizing and privatizing reforms in recent years should not be downplayed, in most cases these developments have not altered the basic architecture of social welfare systems along American lines of not just delegated, but highly decentralized, governance that is often ineffectively overseen by bureaucratic authority.

The Limits on Market-Based Reforms in Health Care

Another notable observation that emerges from a comparative perspective on governance is the limits of marketizing or privatizing reforms in the health care arena, the area where marketization has been pursued the most in the U.S. context. Instead, the rhetoric surrounding privatization and marketization of health care generally exceeds the realities of what has taken place, as few countries have enacted (and stuck with) reforms that significantly increase the role of private actors in this arena.[66] In some countries with national health services, such as New Zealand, Sweden, the United Kingdom, and much of southern Europe, governments created an internal market by dividing purchasers from providers, so that the governmental entities that previously were responsible for both are now choosing services from an array of competing providers. Although this introduces some degree of competition into these systems, it has not led to the empowerment of private actors in the delivery or purchasing of health care; instead, most actors in these health care systems remain public. Even in countries that are said to have enacted major reforms to their public sectors (Czech Republic, Netherlands, New Zealand, Sweden, UK), the public sector remains, by far, the largest payer of health care.

In the Bismarckian systems, in which health insurance funds have always been non-state actors, a number of countries have required those funds to compete for beneficiaries' business. In general, this did not spur the growth in for-profit insurance entities or generate strong competitive pressures that fundamentally changed the architecture of these systems. In Germany, the insurance funds increasingly offer special benefits in order to compete for beneficiaries and have gained some power as health care purchasers. At the same time, however, state intervention has steadily increased in what was once a self-governing insurance system, with the state setting sectoral budgets and mandating a fixed contribution rate for insurance coverage.[67] In Belgium, reforms sought to change the incentives facing the insurance funds toward more cost control but also limited the degree of competitive pressures on the funds.[68] Sidestepping the pro-competition movement altogether, France has experienced a steady *étatisation* of its health care system that has diminished the power of the para-public insurance funds and the social partners in managing the system.[69]

Moreover, resistance against market-oriented reforms in health care has impeded the drive to delegate governance to private actors. In New Zealand, for instance, policy-makers in the early 1990s sought to transform their integrated health care system such that public and private purchasers (insurers) would compete for business—not unlike some of the market-based reforms that have been proposed for Medicare. After strong opposition was voiced, including fears that the "Americanization" of the health care system would result (by which was meant a system based in markets that is both wasteful and exclusionary), the plan was dropped.[70] Thus, after all the hoopla surrounding the reform proposals, the New Zealand health care system ended up being only "marginally more private" than it was before the reforms.[71] In the United Kingdom, resistance to turning more of the health care sector over to private forces actually came from the Conservative government in power, which ultimately prioritized fiscal austerity over market-based reforms. Allowing consumers more choice and/or decentralizing decision-making to non-state actors threatened to *increase* costs, not reduce them, in the immediate term. Alan Jacobs sums up the UK experience well, concluding, "Consumers would have a voice in the new NHS. But it was to be a faint whisper, muffled by the thunderous engine of public administration."[72] As Doorslaer and Schut conclude more generally about the drive to shift more authority to non-state purchasers of health care:

> Are the respective governments willing to hand over some of their tradi-tional supply-side regulatory tools (contracting, fee setting, quality con-trol) to individual insurers? In the logic of the managed competition model, the answer self-evidently has to be "yes," but in practice there appears to be substantial reluctance on the part of governments and reg-ulatory agencies to give up these [regulatory] instruments and "jump in[to] the competitive dark." This reluctance seems to be fueled primarily by the fear that insurers individually may be less successful in resisting new demands by patients and providers for more resources, and that such a weaker negotiation position may result in cost increases.[73]

Ultimately, cost control would be the driving force shaping health care reforms, which often produced *more* government intervention through regulatory and spending controls, not less.[74]

Two countries outside the United States that have promoted consumer choice in health insurance markets are the Netherlands and Switzerland.[75] Both systems require individuals to buy insurance from an array of private plans. These plans are heavily regulated to prevent cream-skimming: companies must offer a basic plan of benefits; cannot turn any applicants away; must charge community-rated premiums; and cannot make a profit on the basic plan (in both countries, insurers can make profits from supplementary benefits they offer to consumers). Both countries also have a risk equalization scheme to compensate funds that end up with a sicker patient load. Finally, individuals with incomes below a certain level receive income-adjusted subsidies to help them cover the cost of health insur-ance—an arrangement that is considerably more generous in the Netherlands, where more than 50 percent of households received such a subsidy in 2008, than in Switzerland.[76] In short, the Dutch and Swiss health insurance models resemble the premium-support model advocated in the United States for Medicare, in which beneficiaries would receive subsidies to purchase care from a regulated, private insurance market of plans.

Despite these apparent resonances with the American health care system, the insurance markets in the Netherlands and Switzerland are still tightly regulated and the state plays a large role in controlling costs. Okma argues that the Dutch health care system is less a model of market competition with only modest state interference than a system with a "modest amount of competition, with a large dose of government regulation."[77] The Dutch Health Ministry not only heavily regulates insurers but uses global budgets and price controls to keep down health care costs.[78] Similarly, according to Reinhardt, there is "pervasive government regulation that guides the Swiss health care system,"[79] including federal setting of formularies and maximum prices for pharmaceuticals, federal determinations over which lab tests and medical devices are covered by the mandatory insurance plan, and canton-level planning of hospital and nursing home capacity. Although insurance companies negotiate with health care providers over the cost of care, they do so "under the watchful eye and heavy hand of government."[80]

Thus, even in countries that have sought to introduce more competition into their health care systems, public bureaucracies still weigh heavily upon these systems, regulating insurance plan competition and shaping the price of health care services and technologies. Non-state actors may play important roles in the provision of health and welfare services and/or the administration of benefits programs, but the influence of the state remains significant.

Why Did the Delegated Welfare State Emerge in the United States?

Why has the United States developed a "Rube Goldberg welfare state" of delegated and diffused authority? We argue that the interplay of public opinion, political institutions, and organized interests shaped choices about the way social programs would be delivered. Delegation has proven a way for policy-makers to address a basic dilemma at the heart of American public opinion: that Americans simultaneously want small government but also social protections from life's risks and perils. Delegating social welfare functions to non-state actors has been a way to satisfy the public's desire for an apparently small governmental sector while also securing a broad array of social welfare programs that might have been blocked if administered directly through public bureaucracies. In addition, decentralized administration of programs emerged as a way to appease Congressional moderates and conservatives—such as Southern Democrats—who opposed the growth of the federal government, and to secure the support of powerful interests, especially in the health care sector. Such groups were often opposed to and successful in blocking direct governance but were quite happy to provide the same services themselves with government paying much of the bill. Delegation has thus been a way to build coalitions and negotiate the shoals of a veto-ridden, status-quo oriented set of policy-making institutions. Over time, the rationale for delegated governance changed, as market advocates pushed for delegating authority to risk-bearing, profit-making actors in the hope of improving government efficiency and performance. However, beneath these new rationales lay the same political calculus: delegated authority as a way for anti-statists to respond to public demands for social support without increasing the size of government or antagonizing private interests.

Less Persuasive Reasons for Delegated Governance

The large body of research on both the welfare state and administration of government programs offers some potential explanations for delegated governance. Perhaps the first explanation that might jump to mind is simply that delegated governance makes sense for technical-administrative reasons: it may be an efficient and effective way to administer programs or deliver services. For instance, in contrast to a relatively straightforward program like Social Security, Medicare may be too large and complicated to directly administer. Thus, delegating those administrative responsibilities to private insurers and accreditation organizations, and delivery of care to private providers, could have been a logical choice on the part of policy-makers. Moreover, in more recent decades, some have argued for administrative and delivery arrangements that stimulate market competition in the belief that this will improve the cost-effectiveness and quality of public programs. For these and other reasons, it could be that policy-makers have been choosing the best possible means of administering public programs.

It is less than obvious, however, that delegated governance in any of its forms has been the more effective or efficient way to administer programs and deliver services. As chapter 6 discusses, there is a large body of research questioning whether contracting out improves program delivery, and local governments have been moving away from such arrangements after promised savings and efficiency gains did not materialize. Beyond the fact that the merits of this approach are contested, such an explanation is functionalist and apolitical, positing that when a policy is needed or makes sense, it is adopted. Yet much decision-making in the political sphere fails to follow an efficiency-maximizing logic.[81] As political processes determine what kinds of programs are adopted and how they are administered, we must look carefully at those processes to uncover the forces driving policy change.

Research comparing the welfare states of rich democracies offers another potential explanation—the weakness of left-wing political power in the United States. Not only have left-wing political parties often been strong advocates of income redistribution but they have typically favored centralized and direct state administration of programs and delivery of services so as to prevent inequalities in access to programs of equal quality.[82] Certainly, the relative weakness of labor unions in the United States, and the long-time fracture within the Democratic Party between Southern conservatives and Northern liberals, impaired the growth of the welfare state.[83] Instead, business groups have been highly influential in American politics, and while they have not always been antipathetic toward the growth of social welfare provision, they have had distinct visions of what the welfare state should look like.[84]

We view these political factors as a crucial backdrop for thinking about the politics of the welfare state in the United States. Yet they beg many questions about why, given ample public support for social programs, a more unified Left did not emerge to represent these views. Attention to the institutional structures of American politics, as well as to the power of organized interests in the policy-making process, certainly offers some answers (treated below). Moreover, as Christopher Howard has persuasively shown, the welfare state has often significantly *expanded* under Republican political control, or otherwise been vitally shaped by powerful Southern Democrats.[85] These works suggest that we should not view conservatives or centrists solely as a blocking force against the welfare state, but rather one that favored particular *forms* of social provision. Why then were conservatives sometimes willing to countenance, or even actively pursue, the growth of social programs? The answer to that question lies, in part, in the structure of American public opinion.

The Basic Dilemma at the Heart of American Public Opinion

Observers of public opinion in the United States have long noted a fundamental ambiguity: that many members of the public hold anti-government views in the abstract but also very much like what government does when it comes to specific instances and programs. They are, to use the terminology of the first researchers to describe this phenomenon, "ideological conservatives" and "operational liberals."[86] Large majorities hew to an anti-government line when considering the role of government in general. However, when asked to consider specific government functions or programs, the very same individuals who described themselves as conservatives or who distrust government respond with much enthusiasm when asked whether government spending should be increased in various concrete areas.

Public opinion pioneers Lloyd Free and Hadley Cantril first reported this phenomenon during the 1960s. Their survey data showed that large proportions of Americans described themselves as conservative or said government has too much power or that "we should rely more on individual initiative and not so much on governmental welfare programs." But what they also discovered was that similarly large proportions of respondents—from two-thirds to three-quarters—also said that spending by the federal government on a number of programs should be kept at the present level or increased: Head Start, job retraining, federal aid to education, Medicare, grants to build low-rent public housing, unemployment reduction, and so on.[87] Subsequent researchers demonstrated that these two sides of public opinion were not merely a phenomenon arising from a particular epoch in American politics. Analyzing survey data collected 40 years later, Benjamin Page and Lawrence Jacobs uncover the very same patterns: skepticism about government and an ideological commitment to free enterprise remain widespread, but so too does considerable support for government help in areas from nursery schools to health insurance to retirement.[88] Analysis of survey respondents' reasoning about their beliefs shows that these seemingly contradictory viewpoints arise from the diverse values embedded in American political culture, values that are themselves contradictory: individualism, liberty, and opposition to big government on the one hand, but humanitarianism, equality, and a recognition that some need help, on the other.[89]

Analysis of the 2008 American National Election Study (ANES) illustrates these points and shows that it is the very same individuals who often profess these seemingly contradictory preferences. Significant proportions of Americans identify as conservatives in questions that tap either their ideological self-identification or their general orientations toward government. In the 2008 ANES study, 32 percent of respondents identified themselves as conservative, compared to just 21 percent who identified as liberal (the plurality of respondents, 47 percent, either identified as "middle of the road" or said that they had not thought much about it). Thirty-seven percent said they were Republicans or were independents who leaned toward the GOP. Even larger proportions professed skepticism about government in other ways: 70 percent said they trusted the government to do the right thing only some of the time or not at all (up from 54 percent just four years earlier), 73 percent said the government wastes "a lot" of the money they pay in taxes, and 70 percent said that they thought the government in Washington was too strong.[90]

However, although many Americans profess to being conservatives in the abstract, when we examine preferences about specific government aims and programs, Americans turn out to be operational liberals. Means-tested programs are an exception: in recent ANES surveys, just 17 percent of all respondents wanted spending on food stamps increased and 27 percent favored higher spending on welfare (Table 2.2, column 1). But when asked about spending on vulnerable groups rather than reviled welfare programs, support is much higher—61 percent want increased spending on the poor and 58 percent want more spending on the homeless. Programs that would benefit middle class Americans garner even higher levels of support, with 53 percent desiring increased spending on financial aid for college students, 58 percent for child care, 66 percent for Social Security, and 75 percent for public schools.[91]

Where ambiguity in American public opinion becomes most apparent is in the programmatic spending preferences of those who say they are conservative, who identify with the Republican Party, or who otherwise hold negative views of government (Table 2.2, columns 2 through 6). Not only do Americans overall want increased spending on many social welfare programs, so do self-described conservatives and government skeptics. Two-fifths of conservatives and Republicans support increased spending on the poor, the homeless, child care, and financial aid for college, and one-half to three-fifths want increased spending on Social Security and public schools. The proportions desiring increased spending in these areas are the same or even greater among those who trust government none or only some of the time, think government wastes a lot of the money it collects in taxes, and believe the government in Washington is too strong—majorities of respondents who are skeptical about government by these measures nonetheless want increased government spending in nearly all of these areas (Table 2.2, columns 4 through 6). Contradictory strands in American public opinion thus appear not just at the aggregate level but are characteristics of individual-level preferences.

Indeed, this attitudinal ambivalence is widespread among the public. Figures 2.1 and 2.2 take two of the issue areas discussed above, Social Security and spending on the poor, and analyze spending preferences among different population subgroups. These figures show the percentage of the total sample and of each subgroup that falls into one of five categories (arrayed from left to right in the figures): liberals; moderates who support increased spending in that area; conservatives who support increased spending in that area; moderates who want spending kept the same or decreased; and conservatives who want spending kept the same or decreased. The second and third groups—moderates and conservatives who want spending increased—are shaded gray

Table 2.2. **Desire for Increased Government Spending among All Respondents, Conservatives, Republicans, and Government Skeptics, 2008**

	(1) All Respondents	*(2) Conservatives*	*(3) Republicans*	*(4) Trust Government None/Some of Time*	*(5) Government Wastes a Lot of Tax Dollars*	*(6) Government in Wash. too Strong*
Food stamps	17%[c]	9%[c]	8% [c]	17%[c]	16%[c]	12%[c]
Welfare	27	15	13	26	25	12 [c]
The poor	61	43	43	57	59	42[c]
The homeless	58[b]	42[b]	43 [b]	56[b]	53[b]	66[a]
Financial aid for college	53[b]	43[b]	43 [b]	51[b]	50[b]	55[a]
Child care	58	39	39	58	56	52[c]
Social Security	66	56	55	66	65	55[c]
Public schools	75	61	62	73	73	66[c]

Note: Cells show percentage of respondents of each description who want program spending increased (as opposed to decreased or kept the same). Data from 2008 except [a]1992; [b]1996; [c]2000.

Source: American National Election Study cumulative file.

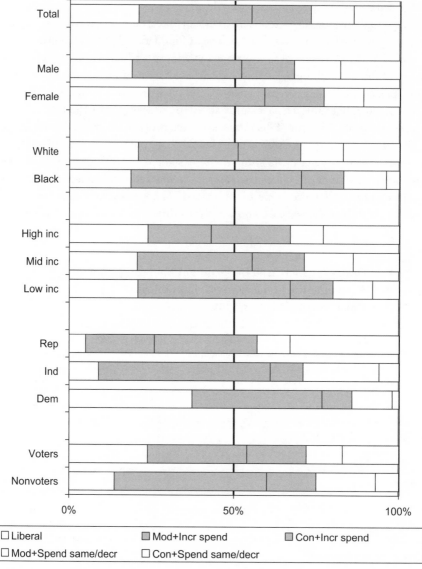

Figure 2.1 Ideological and Operational Ambivalence: Social Security. Source: American National Election study cumulative file. Note: Figure shows, from left to right, the proportion of respondents overall and of each demographic/political category who are liberals, ideological moderates who want federal government spending on Social Security increased (ambivalent group, in gray), ideological conservatives who want spending on Social Security increased (ambivalent group, in gray), ideological moderates who want spending on Social Security kept the same or decreased, and ideological conservatives who want spending on Social Security kept the same or decreased. Income is in terciles. The Republican and Democratic categories include leaners. Data are from 2008.

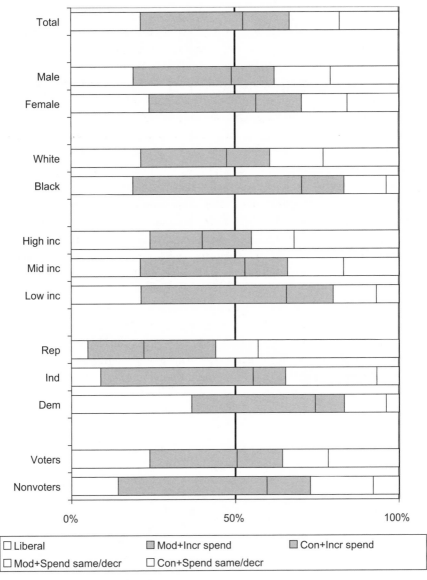

Figure 2.2 Ideological and Operational Ambivalence: The Poor. Source: American National Election study cumulative file. Note: Figure shows, from left to right, the proportion of respondents overall and of each demographic/political category who are liberals, ideological moderates who want federal government spending on the poor increased (ambivalent group, in gray), ideological conservatives who want spending on the poor increased (ambivalent group, in gray), ideological moderates who want spending on the poor kept the same or decreased, and ideological conservatives who want spending on the poor kept the same or decreased. Income is in terciles. The Republican and Democratic categories include leaners. Data are from 2008.

and represent the most Janus-faced members of the public: ideologically they state that they are moderate or conservative, but operationally they are liberal, desiring increased federal government spending on Social Security or on the poor (a very small proportion of liberals are ambivalent in the opposite direction, desiring a decrease in spending; we do not break them out separately). Note that ideological and operational ambivalence is widespread and not confined to certain demographic or political subgroups: we see large proportions of individuals by gender, race, income, party identification, and turnout—often majorities—holding ambivalent views. Also note that the rightmost two groups—moderates and conservatives who want spending in these areas kept the same or decreased—that is, those who are consistent in both ideologically and operationally embracing small government—are in the minority, both overall and within every subpopulation (the one exception being that a small majority of Republicans are both ideological and operational conservatives when it comes to spending for the poor). Far more common overall and among most subgroups is ambivalence rather than ideological and operational consistency.

Moreover, the findings from Free and Cantril and Page and Jacobs across the decades suggest that not only is this ambiguity in American public opinion long-standing, but also it has not changed much over time. To be sure, the proportion of Americans holding conservative, anti-government stances has varied over time: Figure 2.3 shows that while the proportion of self-identified conser-

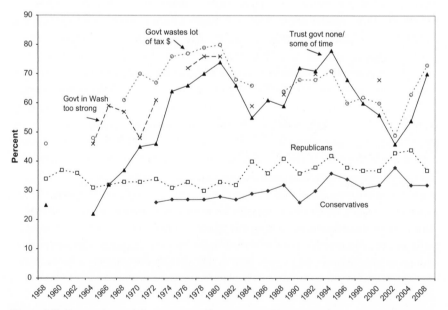

Figure 2.3 Proportions of Government Skeptics over Time. Source: American National Election study cumulative file.

vatives increased modestly, from 26 percent in 1972 to 32 percent in 2008, and the proportion of Republicans increased from 34 to 37 percent over the same period, the percentage of ANES respondents with low trust in government, who say the government wastes a lot of tax money, and who say the government in Washington is too strong has varied over time, with government skepticism peaking in 1980, 1994, and 2008, and diminishing in 1984 and 2002, after the 9/11 terrorist attacks. However, the relationships revealed in Table 2.2—the strong support of government skeptics for government spending outside of food stamps and welfare—are very similar whether we examine a high-trust or a low-trust year. Table 2.3 shows that in both 1994 (low trust) and in 2002 (high trust), large proportions of conservatives, Republicans, those trusting government to do the right thing only some or none of the time, and those saying government wastes a lot of tax money, also desire increased spending on the poor, child care, Social Security, and public schools. The proportion of respondents desiring increased spending is a little higher in 2002, the high-trust year, and openness to increased spending even on welfare is higher in the high-trust year, but overall the same relationships hold. Americans embrace small government but strongly support government programs—even those Americans who are the most skeptical about government, and even in years when overall trust in government is the lowest.

The abstract conservative-operational liberal dichotomy is also seen in public opinion surrounding the Obama health care reform. Support for the reform overall was lukewarm, hovering between 35 and 47 percent in the major polls in the months before passage,[92] likely reflective of Americans' antipathy to large government efforts. However, when asked about specific features of the legislation, support was far higher. Just as Americans embrace individual programs or spending areas, as shown above, so too did they support particular pieces of the health care law: tax breaks for small businesses to make coverage more affordable (90 percent in favor); new health exchanges (81 percent); requiring insurers to cover those with preexisting conditions (80 percent); filling in the Medicare prescription drug doughnut hole (79 percent); the employer mandate to offer health insurance (69 percent), federal and state government review of insurance premium increases (66 percent); increased taxes on high-income households (64 percent); and preventing insurers from dropping coverage for those who are sick (62 percent).[93] The micro-level data from these surveys were not available as of this writing to allow us to examine how many individuals who objected to the health care reform overall nonetheless supported these specific features. However, given the large proportions that supported many of the individual provisions, there was certainly considerable overlap, squaring with the patterns observed in other social policy areas.

In short, American public opinion about government is fundamentally ambiguous. Americans—often the very same individuals—hold contradictory views,

Table 2.3. **Government Spending Preferences among Government Skeptics in Low and High Government Trust Years**

	(1) All Respondents	*(2) Conservatives*	*(3) Republicans*	*(4) Trust Govt None/Some of Time*	*(5) Govt Wastes a Lot of Tax Dollars*
a. Low Trust Year: 1994					
Food stamps	10%	8%	4%	9%	9%
Welfare	14	10	8	13	12
The poor	—	—	—	—	—
Child care	58	44	44	55	54
Social Security	54	41	42	53	52
Public schools	70	59	62	68	68
b. High Trust Year: 2002					
Food stamps	—	—	—	—	—
Welfare	23%	13%	14%	24%	21%
The poor	57	45	46	55	53
Child care	58	48	48	59	54
Social Security	63	52	54	62	63
Public schools	75	66	69	71	70

Note: Cells show percentage of respondents of each description who want program spending increased (as opposed to decreased or kept the same). The item on the poor was not asked in 1994; the food stamp item was not included in the 2002 survey.

Source: American National Election Study cumulative file.

professing an abstract preference for small government but also robust support for increased spending on many specific government programs. Survey questions asking people whether they are conservative or liberal, how much they trust government, and whether they think the government wastes tax dollars seem to prime one set of values that constitute what has been called the "American ethos"[94]—the aspect of Americans' underlying beliefs that are skeptical about government. But questions about specific programs seem to invoke the other side of American beliefs—and people express support because the program names prime positive experiences with those programs, or thoughts of friends and family who have been helped by them, or the equality of opportunity they may provide.[95]

How is it that people can hold these contradictory views simultaneously? In the course of everyday life we are seldom called upon to reconcile such contradictions.[96] Instead, we profess on the spot the particular attitude triggered by our proximate environment at that moment, due to the previous question on the survey, recent events in one's own life, or the nature of political discourse at that time. The crucial point is that because people hold competing considerations simultaneously, public opinion becomes a resource that can be tapped by political actors seeking either to expand or to contract the government role.[97] Either set of attitudes—skepticism of government in the abstract, or support for specific programs and government action—can be primed; both kinds of attitudes are pervasive among the public, waiting to be brought to the fore.

Precisely because the public is antipathetic toward a large federal government staffed by armies of bureaucrats, but *also* supports the development of redistributive programs, this Janus-faced nature of public sentiment affects the parameters of social policy. Contracting out to private actors responds to public demand for help with their economic needs but does not appear to increase the government's reach. Delegated governance thus poses a convenient solution to the inherent ambivalence in American public opinion.

Interest Group Influence

A second factor in the rise of the delegated welfare state is the role of interest groups, although sorting out the nature and degree of their influence is more complicated than one might think. Journalistic and other popular accounts of policy-making often assume that these groups dominate the policy-making process, using their financial and lobbying power to muscle their way into congressional offices and dictate the kinds of programs they want to see or prevent.[98] Yet the political science literature on organized interests has yielded conflicting findings. On the one hand, some have persuasively shown how the rising influence of business groups since the 1970s shifted the terrain upon which political battles are fought, in part by injecting new ideas into the political system through think tanks and other intellectual venues.[99] Yet political scientists have struggled to find consistent evidence that, when controlling for ideology and other factors, campaign donations translate into votes in Congress or that lobbyists systematically impact decision-making.[100] Part of the problem stems from the difficulty of decisively showing influence. Another is the complicated nature of the relationship between interest groups and politicians. It could be that politicians are employing these groups for their own purposes, and not the reverse. In the case of delegated governance, for instance, using private agents to deliver programs may help build allies in the private sector, creating dependencies that can then be exploited by politicians seeking reelection or bureaucrats seeking political support for the programs they oversee.

We use a method of detailed process-tracing to try to uncover the power dynamic between advocates of public programs and organized interests. We find that the great degree of delegation in the health care sector is in part due to the particularly dense thicket of preexisting interest groups and their access in the political system. Medical interest groups, such as those representing physicians, hospitals, insurers, and the pharmaceutical industry, have long fought expansions of the federal role in health care and, when faced with the political inevitability of such expansions, worked to undercut any accompanying growth of federal bureaucratic capacity in this area. They have wielded power through alliances with like-minded legislators, shaping bills that provide the social protections the public wants but that use publicly subsidized private actors to provide the services. Doing so meets the goals both of interest groups, who wish to expand their businesses and are glad to do so on the government nickel, and of lawmakers who wish to satisfy public demands without seeming to increase the reach of government.

Institutional Fragmentation, Congress, and Social Policy

A third factor contributing to delegated governance are the institutional arrangements of American government. A number of scholars have emphasized how the fractured, veto-ridden structure of American politics turns the policy-making process into an obstacle course that is extremely difficult to navigate.[101] Fewer have explored the full implications of that which is particularly distinctive about American government: the preeminent role of Congress in making social policy.[102] Nowhere in the world of advanced industrialized states is there a legislative branch that is so powerful, so independent of the executive, yet so fragmented in its organizational structure. Added to this are other peculiar features of the Congress that have worked against the growth of a conventional welfare state—the way in which it empowered Southern Democrats, for instance, through a seniority system that rewards those who are consistently reelected.[103] With their lock hold over local and state-level politics, Southern Democratic Congressmen and Senators secured control over the levers of institutional power for decades and exerted tremendous influence over redistributive policy.[104] While political realignments and institutional reforms since the 1970s eroded the power of Southern Democrats, opponents of policy change have made growing use of the institution's various veto points—the Senate filibuster, for instance—to block new initiatives.

There are several ways in which the power of Congress over public policy has shaped the use of delegated governance. First, given the strong status quo bias that results from institutional fragmentation, the passage of social programs often requires the assembly of large political coalitions in support. One way to do so has been to draw in supportive interests, cutting them into the deal, for instance, by allowing them to govern publicly funded programs or to otherwise shape program administration in ways to their liking. This, in turn, enables political leaders to create Congressional coalitions in support of new policies, as potential opponents retract or muffle their opposition to legislative initiatives. In addition, members of the coalition may have different policy visions, with some viewing delegated governance as a way to achieve marketizing reforms, while others are simply leery of governmental growth and its accompanying fiscal burdens. Still others may embrace delegated governance as a second-best option—a compromise that enables a particular bill to pass. By agglomerating these diverse views, delegated governance has made possible the growth of federal responsibilities but also produced "jerry-built" systems of social policy administration that often sacrifice managerial efficiency to the demands of well-organized groups.[105]

A second important aspect of congressional decision-making is the aversion of its members to doling out pain to constituents or organized groups.[106] Although social programs offer many opportunities for credit-claiming, they also require tough decisions, either now or down the road. Thus, although adding a prescription drug benefit to Medicare might seem to create a win-win situation for its architects, it also requires determinations about how the benefit should be structured, how it will be paid for, and how its use should be limited for reasons of fiscal sustainability. Delegating those responsibilities to private insurers, who in turn engage in contentious negotiations with drug companies over prices and decide what drugs are available to beneficiaries, enables policy-makers to avoid having to make these politically fraught decisions. As Crenson and Rourke sum it up: "A system that allowed national policy to be administered in different ways in different places could also reduce the necessity of achieving agreement in Washington about just what the policy was in the first place."[107]

In the case of health care policy, delegating authority to private managed care firms, who are supposed to make tough decisions about cost and coverage, holds particular allure, as it offers politicians a way out of difficult dilemmas while enabling them to reward interest groups knocking on their doors. As Robinson has remarked,

> The interest among private insurers in serving public programs is reciprocated by the interest among public programs in outsourcing the management of their coverage benefits, provider networks, and enrollee expectations to private health plans. State and federal coverage sponsors increasingly lack the will to navigate the conflicting claims for resources between beneficiaries, taxpayers, and other stakeholders. They seek someone else to perform that inevitably thankless task.[108]

In sum, the delegated welfare state results from the confluence of public opinion, political institutions, and interest group power—with the latter an especially important factor in the health care sector, compared to other social policy areas. American political institutions make it particularly difficult to pass redistributive programs, as they have given weight to anti-statist political forces and have provided access to organized interests threatened by the expansion of federal authority and power. The mixed and ambiguous character of public opinion matters in that it provides resources to political actors and interest groups seeking to exploit either the support for public programs or the opposition to federal expansion.

Hence liberals have often been constrained in their ability to develop publicly provided programs, but centrists and conservatives have also been unable to entirely ignore the public clamor for new social programs. Attempting to square the circle—to navigate the institutional and political obstacles to new social programs—policy-makers repeatedly have turned to delegated governance as a way to buy off interest group support, tamp down claims that a new program expands oppressive federal authority, and yet respond to public demands for assistance with life's risks and costs. The result has often been policy arrangements that are Rube Goldbergesque in their structure—think about the complex legislation that is Medicare Part D—in order to satisfy these conflicting demands.

Does It Matter How Social Programs Are Administered?

The question of how social programs are delivered has important real-world and theoretical implications. The administration of social programs impacts the effectiveness of public policies, the form of redistribution that follows, and the extent to which the providers of services are accountable to the mass public. All of these questions are hotly contested and are at the crux of debates about state versus non-state social provision. We do not aim to definitively settle these debates for all policy areas, but in the succeeding section will lay out some of the competing arguments that we test in the case of Medicare in several later chapters. The nature of program administration also has important implications for academic debates in the social sciences, particularly those concerning the nature of the American state. Political scientists have paid insufficient attention to what public policies actually look like, on the ground, as most analyses tend to stop with a policy's passage. By looking concretely at the implementation and effects of policies, we can gain insight into the nature and functioning of the American state.

Real-World Consequences of Delegating Governance for Social Provision

Does it matter how social programs are administered? One could argue that whether one administers programs through local governments, private actors, or federal bureaucracies is less important than the existence of a program, its eligibility parameters, and its generosity. Perhaps social policy ends justify whatever administrative means are necessary to make a program work. Yet, for many programs, the devil lies in the details: how programs are actually administered and experienced on the ground by stakeholders and beneficiaries can be tremendously consequential for program effectiveness, equity, and democratic accountability. Given the importance of these questions, much of the political heat generated around particular social policy reforms concerns modes of governance.

One major question about program design and implementation concerns effectiveness: Are program goals met in a relatively efficient and effective manner? Or do governing arrangements impede the effective delivery of promised benefits and services? This issue has featured prominently in debates about privatization, with advocates arguing that government is an intrinsically poor provider of most benefits and services. Some argue that significant delegation problems arise between legislators and the bureaucrats who administer public programs, as the latter have incentives to expand spending on their agencies and possess the information needed to outmaneuver legislative efforts at control.[109] Moreover, government employees receive salaries that are not tied to their performance in delivering services to the public, and bureaucratic organizations are funded through budgetary appropriations instead of having to prove their worth in a competitive environment. As a result, some argue that there are few organizational incentives for good performance when government has a monopoly over the provision of services.[110] Moreover, in many areas, civil servants tend to be paid more than people working in the private sector, in part due to their high degree of unionization. This may make it more expensive to directly administer government programs than to contract them out to private agencies.

Government bureaucracies are also said to be rule-bound and rigid, focused more on meeting legal requirements than innovating in their service provision. Or, they may become *too* independent of the legislative branch, generating bureaucratic drift as agency officials pursue their own agendas. Either way, directly administered programs may fail to be accountable to public needs. By contrast, advocates of market- or community-based organizations argue that these organizations are more likely to deliver high-quality services in a low-cost manner, thereby reducing public spending and enhancing popular accountability.[111] In the case of market actors, as long as the contracting relationship is structured such that their profits are at stake and there is sufficient competition among providers, they should work to survive in a competitive marketplace and thus deliver quality services while holding down costs.[112] In the case of community-based actors, some argue that because they are closer to the people they serve, they are better able to respond to the needs of particular communities.[113] Voucher programs should generate a similar dynamic, creating competition between suppliers for the business of beneficiaries and thus promoting innovation.[114] Finally, contracting with private actors may also enable greater governmental flexibility because contracts can quickly be arranged or terminated as needs wax and wane.

An opposing view challenges whether private sector actors are generally more effective in providing social welfare benefits and services than government agencies. First, some argue that contracted government services rarely represent a real market.[115] Especially in many social welfare areas, there are only a small number of potential service providers—and sometimes only one in a given area—which limits the degree of competition.[116] Providers who successfully procure contracts also tend to have them renewed, perhaps because they gain political influence over the contracting agency, or simply because they are trusted or develop expertise that is valued and cannot immediately be acquired by new providers.[117] These realities may vitiate the theoretical effects of market competition on the quality and cost-efficiency of service delivery. In addition, many have noted that relying on private agencies for the delivery of programs and services rarely leads to the elimination of any role for government in this area. To the contrary, there may be the need for a more *muscular* set of government agencies that can establish, regulate, and monitor the social welfare marketplace.[118] The effect may be to multiply the number of people working in a particular social welfare field in both the public and private sector, leading to *less* efficient production than if there were simply one set of actors involved. Finally, some critics of contracting find that it tends to produce less flexibility, and not more, as agencies get locked into relationships with particular contractors.[119]

A second question concerns the effect of program administration on democratic accountability.[120] This is a concern for any system of bureaucratic administration: civil servants are unelected and only indirectly accountable to the public through the oversight of democratically elected officials. Moreover, their actions can never be perfectly supervised: program execution requires some degree of bureaucratic discretion that cannot be fully overseen by elected politicians, although legislators do have an array of control mechanisms at their grasp.[121] In the course of using their discretion, agency officials may not only make inefficient choices about program delivery, but also may prove indifferent to the population they should be serving. In light of these problems, advocates of community- or market-based provision argue that such arrangements improve democratic accountability.[122] Community organizations are not elected bodies but may nonetheless contain members of the community who can hold them accountable to the public. In the case of for-profit firms, because their survival is tied to their ability to attract clients, they should scramble to respond to the diverse needs and preferences of their users. Thus, even though the chain of accountability from elected officials to service providers is obscured in a system of delegated governance, this may improve democratic accountability, not weaken it.[123]

Critics of these arrangements worry about lodging administrative discretion in the hands of non-public institutions. One consequence could be to create an administrative void, a situation in which ". . . responsibility is broadly shared, but no one is fully in charge."[124] Additional problems may arise in the case of publicly traded firms, whose fiduciary responsibility is to shareholders and not to program beneficiaries. A more general issue concerns whether or not social welfare markets actually work to make firms accountable to their customers. For instance, when beneficiaries have a choice between competing service providers, are they able to effectively navigate between options, making optimal (or at least not ruinous) decision? Some argue that consumers are notoriously bad at decision-making in commercial markets, with paradoxically more choices leading to paralysis and decisions based on the wrong criteria (e.g., glossiness of marketing materials). Perhaps even more important is whether or not people leave bad service providers, forcing the kind of market accountability that advocates theorize should exist. If people fail to "exit" bad providers, or use "voice" to contest poor service provision, then markets will fail to convey the right information to firms, thus weakening the accountability mechanisms in private welfare markets.[125]

The governance of social programs also has important redistributive consequences. The Left has often championed the ideal of direct governance in the belief that when benefits and services are highly heterogeneous, inequalities of access will develop. Particularly when markets deliver services, people of a higher socioeconomic status will likely benefit by having their preferences catered to, while less educated and lower income people will have inferior services. On the other hand, defenders of markets might point to failures in government-provided services to the poor—inner-city school systems in the United States, for instance—and argue that markets can do a better job of responding to these disempowered citizens.[126]

Yet another question concerns how the administration of public programs affects the politics of social provision. Some critics of contracting out public services argue that it gives power to private organizations, which then use this power to further enrich themselves. One consequence may be corruption, as public officials develop cozy relationships with private firms whose campaign contributions, or outright bribes, ensure their continued access to valued public contracts. A softer version of this dynamic may simply be to increase the voice of private provider groups in the political process. Consumers are a notoriously difficult group to organize, and while consumer groups may work hard to insert the perspective of program beneficiaries into policy debates, they may be outgunned by well-financed private groups who have a strong stake in protecting their interests. How the relative power of these groups plays out in the political process is an empirical question, likely to vary in different social policy arenas. It may be that giving private actors a stake in public programs promotes the *expansion* of spending on these programs, contrary to what market reformers might desire.[127] Such was the case with the 2003 Medicare Modernization Act, which was supported by both insurance companies—who would profit from delivering the benefit—and pharmaceutical companies, who benefited from the increased volumes and promise of no government involvement in determining prices. Thus, delegated governance may be the distinctive way that welfare states grow in societies and polities marked by antipathy toward public officials and "direct" forms of government.

One final question is more clearly normative and concerns the suitability of giving private actors power over the lives of individuals. This is part of what makes the social welfare sphere distinctive from other areas of government contracting.

There is a difference between employing private firms to provide routine office services or deliver products to federal agencies, and delegating responsibility for programs that affect people's health, welfare, and livelihood. When firms have the ability to determine eligibility for welfare programs and to mete out sanctions for failure to meet certain requirements, these firms are exerting power over these individuals.[128] Similarly, when a private drug plan uses its formulary to "manage" a beneficiary's use of prescription drugs, this is again a form of power being exerted over that beneficiary's life. Of course, we all live in a world of public and private institutions that exert power over us, and over which we do not have full control. This fact should not prevent us from probing the differential consequences of public and private power, however. As Grant McConnell argued over four decades ago, ". . . the persistence and growth of private power have posed an embarrassing problem for all who are involved in exercising it. What justifies the existence of power; by what principle is it rightful?"[129]

In public provision there is a principle of democratic accountability that exists at least theoretically if not empirically: governing arrangements are structured so that bureaucrats are accountable to elected officials in some way, and elected officials are periodically accountable to the public. Unless markets can be shown to offer improved accountability through their responsiveness to consumers, accountability is diminished in a system of delegated governance to private actors.

Theoretical Implications

This study also has implications for how we should conceptualize the nature of the American state, which has long been a source of scholarly puzzlement. When measured in terms of public sector employees or public spending, the federal government in the United States is smaller than the national states of many other western European countries, and this has been true since the founding of the American Republic. This fact has long inspired claims about the relative "statelessness" of the United States.[130] By most objective measures, the nineteenth-century federal administration was miniscule in size, and the dominant actors in the American polity were courts and parties, not federal bureaucrats.[131] Although the twentieth century brought the rise of "bureaucratic autonomy" in key domains, the overall size of the federal government remains fairly truncated,[132] particularly when compared to other advanced industrialized countries. For instance, measured in terms of total tax receipts, including taxes collected at all levels of government, U.S. tax revenue as a proportion of GDP is nearly eight percentage points lower than the OECD average—28.0 percent compared to 35.9 percent—and is notably lower than countries we tend to think of as similarly market-oriented, such as the United Kingdom (37.1 percent) or Canada (33.3 percent).[133]

At the same time, however, the twentieth-century American state has been one of the most powerful actors in the world. Even in the nineteenth century it would be misleading to focus excessively on bureaucratic incapacity: the federal government created the public land system, propelled the settlement of a vast territory (which involved the forced removal of native peoples), engaged in internal improvements to develop the nation's public infrastructure, and upheld the institution of slavery.[134] In the social policy sphere, the federal government did not develop the social insurance programs that were emerging in Britain and Bismarckian Germany at the time, yet did institute a large-scale system of veterans' pensions and created a progressive income tax—a tax that the federal government did a far better job collecting during and after World War I than did the allegedly "strong" French state at the time.[135] In the twentieth century, the United States fought and won two world wars and a cold war, and is now the dominant superpower in the international arena—hardly what we might expect from a "weak" state.[136]

How can we reconcile these two images of the American state? Part of the problem lies in the difficulty scholars have in getting away from a dichotomous, "strong versus weak" understanding of states.[137] Thus, in the laudable effort to combat images of perennial state weakness, scholars have sought to prove that the American state was in fact *stronger* than we might think by pointing to pockets of bureaucratic development or effectiveness. Yet this hardly helps us make sense of the many other instances or indicators we can find of bureaucratic failure. The social policy arena offers numerous examples of both strength and weakness. To take the example of health care, analysts from across the political divide agree that the Centers for Medicare and Medicaid Services, which oversees Medicare, Medicaid, and other health policy, is undermanned, under-resourced, and frequently outmatched by powerful organized interests in the health care sector. Yet the same organization has been able to implement a complex system of price-setting in the health care sphere, and somehow, despite its lack of resources, manages to oversee the processing of around one billion health care claims a year.

Instead of asking whether the American state is strong or weak, we need a vocabulary that better captures how the American state actually works in practice. Here, we take inspiration from William Novak's view that scholars should reclaim the tradition of American pragmatism that developed over a century ago but has been displaced in the social sciences by abstract European theory. Rather than start with an ideal type and see how the phenomenon of interest measures up, we should instead seek to understand how the object of study actually functions, letting the concrete realities that we can observe and describe inform our categories and drive our conclusions about it. In the words of Theodore Lowi, we are interested in the "almost forgotten [issues] of what kind of government, what ends of government, what forms of government, and what consequences of government. . . ."[138]

Such an approach has often been lacking in political science analyses of public policy, which tend to stop with passage of the law rather than examining how programs and policies are actually implemented on the ground. Yet a lot of the conflict around public policy concerns precisely how services or benefits are going to be delivered. Thus, debates over universal health coverage have not only been over philosophical questions of economic redistribution, but have been centrally concerned with who is going to deliver this insurance, who will provide health care services, and precisely how all of these actors will be paid. The answers to these questions, in turn, determine the structure of governing institutions—the nature of the state and how it actually functions. When we are attentive to how, in actuality, abstract programs are turned into concrete realities, we gain a better understanding of the political stakes around many redistributive programs, but also can see more clearly how it is that American governing institutions actually work.

What does such an approach yield in looking at the American state? The American state is better described not as institutionally strong or weak, but as a system of delegated and diffused authority.[139] Contrary to the Weberian ideal-type of the centralized, hierarchically organized bureaucratic structure characterized by clear lines of authority and accountability, the contemporary American state is, as Elisabeth Clemens says quite bluntly, "a mess." This was true in the first decades of the twentieth century when, at a time of expanding governmental responsibility, program administration was achieved through heavy reliance upon private actors for the delivery of social services and the use of intergovernmental grants.[140] The tremendous expansion of federal responsibilities in the post–World War II era created ever greater dependence upon non-federal actors for the implementation of federal programs.[141] Federally funded programs would be delivered by state and local governments through intergovernmental arrangements, such as grants-in-aid. Many functions are contracted out to private actors: in 2005, the number of contract employees working for the federal government has been estimated to be four times the number of civilian employees, rendering the "true size of government" significantly larger than we might think when looking only at government employees.[142] There also are hybrid governing institutions that defy simple categorizations as public or private, including government-sponsored enterprises, such as Fannie Mae and Freddie Mac. As Frederick Mosher once put it:

> The use and the extent of all of these tools have grown enormously in recent years—even as federally performed operations virtually stood still. Few new policies and programs failed to rely upon other governments or institutions in the private sector for a major part or all of their execution. The extension of federal interest and intervention into the nooks and crannies of our economic, social, cultural, and even personal lives seems almost unlimited. And most of this is being done through others, not strictly a part of the federal government itself. The growth of federal influence defies precise quantitative measurement, but there can be no question that it has been pervasive. . . .[143]

Do these governing arrangements produce a "strong" or "weak" state? A better way to frame the question is to explore the implications of delegated governance along the lines we described above: the cost-effectiveness of state action; its political consequences; and its effects on redistribution and accountability. The answers to these questions are empirical and hinge on the nature of the governing arrangements developed in different sectors of public policy. Were we able to cumulate studies of a large number of different areas, we could paint a general picture of the American state, how it functions, and the political forces that have shaped its development. We can only do this in one domain—the welfare state, which we winnow down even further to the area of Medicare—but we hope to demonstrate the merits of analyzing how programs are governed, why they are governed that way, and what consequences this has for societies and polities.

Conclusion

The American welfare state intertwines public and private authority in pervasive ways. We develop the concept of delegated governance—the delegation of administrative authority for publicly funded programs to private actors—to describe some of these arrangements. Although the United States is not alone in the world in relying on private actors for the implementation of public programs, it does so to a great extent and in some unusual ways. Historically, the United States often turned to nonprofit organizations to deliver social welfare benefits and services. In more recent decades, however, the emphasis has shifted to building social welfare marketplaces comprised of competing, for-profit actors in the social welfare field. Along with this change has come a shift in the locus of decision-making and risk. Hitherto, the government made decisions about who would provide services and who bore risk for these decisions (often, the government itself). Increasingly, individuals are expected to choose from a menu of competing providers, and both for-profit providers bear risk (their profits are at stake), and individuals bear risk (for their choice of welfare provider). Moreover, the extent of delegation, the embrace of the market form, the relative lack of governmental supervision, and the spread of delegation to health care set the United States apart from peer nations.

The ways in which programs are administered are hardly technical details deserving only of attention in public administration textbooks. Yet political scientists have generally ignored these arrangements, ending their analyses with the passage of policy. This is unfortunate, given that much of the political conflict generated by public policy concerns how programs will actually be put in place, such as who will provide them and how providers will be paid. Can we really understand the political stakes around public policies if we do not explore the implications of policy design and implementation for government bureaucrats, interest group stakeholders, and beneficiaries? We believe that one cannot, and thus argue that scholars of the welfare state should give attention to its governance, which has profound implications for effectiveness, redistribution, and accountability.

3

Medicare and the Delegated Welfare State in the Postwar Era

As the previous chapter showed, one distinctive feature of the American welfare state is its administration. Centralized authority is frequently limited, with state and local governments administering many federally funded programs. Even in federal programs, the actual administration of programs and delivery of services are often done by private actors of various stripes and motivations—nonprofit organizations, professionals, and profit-making firms. Indeed, much of the expansion of the federal government post-1945 relied heavily on diffusing and delegating authority to non-state entities.[1] What explains this heavy reliance upon private and other non-federal entities to achieve public aims?

We address this question by examining the growth of American social programs since the New Deal through the lens of conflicts over state-building. Although today many think of the contracting out of social provision as a product of neo-liberal influences, public administration scholars attentive to the actual administration of government programs have identified this as a phenomenon that predated the free market movement.[2] Starting in the 1930s with the programs of the New Deal, but continuing during World War II and in the decades following it, the United States underwent a tremendous expansion in federal responsibilities. This growth of federal capacity would not go unchallenged, however, particularly by conservative members of Congress, who used their control over institutional levers of power to slow the growth of federal bureaucratic capacity. At times aided by interest groups similarly opposed to increased federal authority, conservatives also were able to tap ambivalence in American public opinion toward the federal government. Yet even conservative legislators could not deny growing public pressures for programs that would meet basic social needs. In response to the basic dilemma at the root of American public policy— that the public desires both social protections and small government—policymakers compromised on governance: rather than build federal governing capacity, that capacity was farmed out to private actors.

Medicare was born of these same influences, and the delegation of Medicare administration to private insurers allowed the program's framers to achieve a number of goals: circumventing the public's chronic unease about big government; allaying organized interests' concerns about state interference with their business; and satisfying the preferences of powerful conservatives in Congress for a circumscribed government role in health care and private-sector "buffer" between providers and the state.[3] Other social welfare programs were shaped by a similar environment, although interest group influence was often less important, at least in the beginning. In the case of social assistance programs, for instance, the decision to contract out service provision reflected a calculation on the part of bureaucrats that their programs would fare better in an unfriendly political environment if they created a constituency of service providers. Over time, contracting out for services became an accepted mode of public administration—one strongly favored by a large community of service providers—and later spread to the actual administration of some programs.

In this period, the delegation of program governance was *not* the product of a cohesive set of philosophical principles. Certainly, principled arguments were made on the Right, and at times on the Left, about the need to limit the direct role of the federal government and keep social welfare responsibilities at lower levels of society. But there was no equivalent to the free market beliefs that would take hold later in the twentieth century to justify delegated governance. Instead, the practice often emerged as a pragmatic response to a political landscape rife with forces hostile to direct governance and barriers to the passage of social welfare legislation.

The Emergence of the Delegated Welfare State

The earliest form of delegated governance in the United States was that which assigned responsibility for the provision of publicly funded health, education, and welfare services to nonprofit organizations and professional groups, such as physicians and other health care providers. Today, it may seem entirely natural that such arrangements would emerge: Why would the state usurp the responsibility of physicians for the delivery of care? Why not leave social service provision to existing nonprofit organizations, which are often rooted in communities and thus better able to gauge citizens' needs than can distant government bureaucrats? In fact, the idea of voluntary associations receiving public funding had been fiercely resisted by many within that sector for decades, and while physicians mounted successful opposition to the socialization of their profession from the 1920s on, the federal government did create a system of socialized medicine for military veterans—the Veterans Administration (VA) health system of publicly employed health care providers and state-run facilities. There was nothing inevitable about the governance of the American welfare state; rather, it emerged out of ongoing political struggles over the drive to expand the reach of the national state.

Resistance to the Emerging National State

Since the founding of the American Republic, one of the deep divisions in American politics has concerned the size and power of the federal government.[4] Many Americans have hewed to a "belief in small units of social and political organization," and periods of major political turmoil—such as the founding of the nation's governing institutions and the Civil War—often have revolved around questions about where governing power should lie.[5] Constitutional limits on the role of the federal government, as well as institutional barriers to its growth, ensured that "every effort to expand the role of the national government would have to fight its way through hedgerows of judicial as well as legislative resistance."[6] As a consequence, for most of the nineteenth century, the national state was underdeveloped by any measure or sense of the term—it had limited powers, there were a small number of governing agencies at the federal level, and federal budgets were limited. Instead, much authority lay in courts, in the patronage-based parties that dominated local politics, and in state and local governments.[7]

This situation began to change by the turn of the century, as the dislocating effects of industrial capitalism gave rise to demands for national regulation of the economy. With the emergence of large corporate, labor, and other professional organizations, there was rising political demand for public sector bureaucracies that could exert some control over private ones.[8] Reacting against the pervasiveness of patronage politics, Progressive reformers enthusiastically sought the development of a merit-based civil service at all levels of government. Still, many Progressives felt ambivalent toward the expansion of federal authority, preferring instead to focus their efforts on modernizing the apparatuses of state and local government.[9] Given these conflicting sentiments and pressures, the federal government grew in fits and starts, with bureaucratic development more advanced in some areas than in others.[10]

Yet, the expansion of federal authority in the late nineteenth and first half of the twentieth centuries frequently met with resistance, most powerfully from Southern politicians who feared federal challenges to the racial and economic hierarchies on which their political power was based. Many Republicans also opposed federal expansion and economic intervention as a threat to the manufacturing interests they represented. More generally, many American thinkers and politicians struggled with a fundamental question of how to reconcile the need for greater centralization of political authority with a desire to protect individual freedoms and the constitutionally prescribed prerogatives of states and local governments.[11] Even a major national emergency such as the mobilization to fight in World War I failed to create enduring, centralized power in

Washington, D.C., as war-related offices were staffed with volunteers from private industry, and the apparatus was quickly disassembled after the war was over. As Karl wryly notes:

> The speed with which Congress dismantled the machine at the war's end, to the point of leaving Washington office workers to find money for their passage home when federal funds were abruptly cut off, suggests that national management was basically viewed as something temporary, even dangerous.[12]

In the 1920s, Commerce Secretary Herbert Hoover's vision of an "associative state" took shape, as he sought to address a host of social and economic problems without expanding the federal bureaucracy. Instead, he promoted a "private government" of trade, professional, labor, and farm organizations that federal authorities could nudge and guide toward the achievement of various goals.[13]

Until the 1930s, the federal government also had only minimal responsibility over social welfare, which was left largely to state and local governments. These lower levels of government often relied heavily upon charitable associations to address problems of indigence, ill health, child welfare, and old age. Clemens, for instance, finds that one-quarter of all state government spending in the early twentieth century went to charities.[14] Reliance on voluntary organizations was particularly heavy in the care of abandoned or orphaned children, as state and local governments often turned to religious charities to house these children[15] as a way to "borrow capacity" rather than hire the staff and build the facilities necessary to care for such children directly.[16] Still, some leaders of the charitable sector denounced this intermingling of public and private power, viewing government as a corrupting influence over voluntary organizations, particularly given the predominance of patronage politics at the time.[17]

A brighter line between public and private started to emerge during the Depression and adoption of New Deal programs—some of the first federally funded, and federally administered, social welfare programs. The way in which this drawing of boundaries came about was less deliberate than one might think, as there was no overarching vision of federal administration underpinning the early programs of the welfare state. Indeed, reflecting the assumed weakness of the federal government at this time, and their own experiences working in state governments, many of the reformers serving on the Committee on Economic Security (CES) who crafted these programs envisioned administering them at the state rather than at the federal level, including the new program of old-age insurance. There were also more pragmatic fears, expressed by Roosevelt and others, that expanding federal responsibility would antagonize Southern Democrats.[18] After much internal debate, federal administration was accepted for the old age insurance program, apparently because an advisory group of labor and business leaders agreed that this was the most sensible way to administer a pension system in a national labor market.[19] Later, planners working within the Social Security Administration (SSA) advocated direct federal governance of a host of social welfare programs, but this model was not adopted for most. Public assistance and unemployment insurance, for example, have been federal-state hybrids that are largely administered at the state level.

How then did the Social Security Administration come to be one of the few examples of direct federal governance—staffed by civil servants free of political patronage who administered a federal program with uniform national standards? One reason is that the program provided a pension benefit that hardly existed in the private marketplace. Prior to the New Deal, private pensions reached only a limited number of people, and they were widely judged to be inadequate in assuring retirement security.[20] Private pensions were viewed as a supplement to Social Security, but attempts to allow them as a substitute for old-age insurance—for instance, by allowing employers to opt out of Social Security and buy coverage from private insurance plans, as they had with workmen's compensation—were repeatedly defeated.[21] A number of influential business leaders also did not favor reliance on private corporate welfare arrangements, preferring instead to level the playing field between firms that provided private pensions and those that did not.[22] Moreover, debates over the new program took place at a time when the economy was in deep crisis, which further undermined confidence that private markets could be relied upon to deliver economic security to workers and retirees.

The crisis also temporarily undercut the power of Congressional conservatives to block the growth of the federal government. At a time of severe economic turmoil, power shifted from the Congress to the executive branch, which played the preeminent role in drafting the Social Security Act of 1935.[23] The bill was then largely accepted by both chambers of Congress, although there was heated debate around it and changes made to the original CES proposals.[24] Certainly, administration officials avoided controversial areas (such as health insurance) to avoid stirring up opposition in Congress, but maintained considerable power over the design of the new program. They also structured the program in a way that sidestepped potentially anti-statist currents in American public opinion that could have been tapped by conservative opponents. On the one hand, a compulsory payroll tax might have excited the anti-government strain of American attitudes—the long arm of government reaching into people's wallets at precisely a time when it was hard to make ends meet. However, vigorous salesmanship by Social Security's framers sought to resonate with the "social protections" current of public opinion instead, while the emphasis on individual entitlement and "contributions" rather than "taxes" helped skirt the big government charge.

Although direct federal administration proved relatively rare, executive branch officials did sharpen the line between public and private power in federally funded state and local programs through a requirement that public dollars be spent only through public agencies. Harry Hopkins, the head of the Federal Emergency Relief Administration (FERA), instituted this requirement almost immediately after he took the helm of the new organization in 1933. As one who had spent much of his professional life working in the voluntary sector, Hopkins believed that public funding often led to politicization of these organizations, and in this, he was not alone. For decades, many involved in charitable welfare activities viewed public dollars as a vice that voluntary groups ought best avoid.[25] Hopkins and others in the voluntary sector also believed that these organizations were incapable of responding to the magnitude of the need. Instead, many in this community believed that social welfare should be transformed into a public service that was not only funded through government dollars, but staffed by government employees.[26] In fact, many worried that allowing private organizations to receive public subsidies would undercut the growth of the public sector.[27]

The FERA rule spurred a transformation in local governments around the country, in some cases converting voluntary sector employees into new public sector equivalents.[28] The principle of public administration was later applied to other areas, such as federal child welfare and public assistance programs.[29] In the case of public assistance, despite the fact that the federal government was in essence contracting with state governments to deliver the program—a situation that enabled the development of inter-state differences in eligibility requirements and benefit levels—federal statutes also imposed standards of public administration on the state and local bureaucracies that administered the program.[30] A larger consequence of the New Deal was thus to draw a fairly strict boundary between public and private sectors that helped spur the professionalization and bureaucratization of social welfare provision. Moreover, despite the fact that federal administration was not necessarily the intent of the New Dealers, and that program administration in the welfare sector often involved state or local governments, the many initiatives of the New Deal did produce a significant expansion in federal bureaucratic capacity.

The expansion of federal authority in this and other areas crystallized opposition to the FDR administration. Although many New Dealers interpreted his landslide victory in 1936 as a mandate for the further expansion of government programs, in fact many people personally supported Roosevelt while maintaining suspicion about the ever-growing size of the state.[31] As Brinkley has argued,

> As on other occasions both before and after the Great Depression, much of the American electorate welcomed (even expected) assistance from government in solving their own problems but remained skeptical of state power and particularly of efforts to expand and concentrate it.[32]

Conservative Republicans and conservative Southern Democrats were well aware of public sentiment and sought ways to block the further extension of the New Deal agenda. Their opposition intensified after the court-packing episode in which

Roosevelt tried to add sympathetic justices who would outnumber opponents to the New Deal. Even though his efforts failed formally, the Court afterward essentially blessed the expansion of federal programs and agencies, removing a barrier to the growth of federal responsibilities. With the loss of their judicial allies, a conservative coalition of Republicans and Southern Democrats in Congress mobilized against the continuation of the New Deal agenda and efforts to centralize power in the White House through administrative reorganization.[33] One unintended legacy of the New Deal, then, was a conservative coalition that would regularly appear to slow down or block social welfare, civil rights, and other legislation that threatened to expand federal power.[34] Another mixed legacy was the growth of constitutionally sanctioned federal and bureaucratic authority, coupled with continued uncertainty about how government would actually function. "The administrative state came into being, but the question of who would administer it remained unresolved."[35]

The imperatives of fighting a huge and costly war enabled the Roosevelt administration to enhance the power and scope of the federal government but also fueled a backlash as "(w)hat was tolerable in an emergency (became) repellent in its wake."[36] At the end of the war, conservatives were eager to shrink the size of the national government, yet as the nation became embroiled in both a cold war and a hot one—the Korean War—many feared they could no longer contain the growth of the federal government. A counter-mobilization in Congress, led by Mississippi Democrat Jamie L. Whitten, took legislative shape in the adoption of hard limits on the total number of federal civilian employees. The 1951 Whitten Amendment imposed a ceiling on federal civilian employment and barred the creation of any new, permanent positions. The 1953 amendment went further, limiting the number of permanent federal civilian employees to the total number as of September 1, 1950.[37] The Whitten Amendment remained in place for decades, putting tight limits on the number of government employees. As Light notes, this was in part due to the fact that Whitten was in office for 53 years and wielded significant political power from the House Appropriations committee. But the political popularity of capping federal employment also helped keep these limits in place.[38]

The Whitten Amendment was decisive in spurring the contracting out of federal programs and the rise of the "shadow government" of private sector workers heavily (or entirely) dependent on public funds.[39] Although members of Congress were happy to constrict the growth of the federal government, they could hardly ignore the many new demands being placed upon them. The cold war, the space race, public support for medical care, education, and income support—how to meet these demands with a stagnant federal workforce? Contracting out was the answer, enabling politicians to "indulge in the fiction that Big Government does not grow if the civil service does not."[40] The technique was embraced by administrators of federal agencies; not only did contracting out enable programs to exist, it created private groups, such as "government-oriented corporations" with a strong stake in the continuation of these programs.[41] Soon, these various forms of delegation became the norm, spreading across agencies and programs and leading to a progressive "hollowing out" of the federal government.[42]

Delegating Social Welfare Delivery to the Nonprofit Sector

The squeeze on federal employment shaped the development of social welfare programs as well, as the New Deal's commitment to the public provision of social programs steadily eroded over the 1950s and was largely abandoned by the mid- to late 1960s. For advocates for redistributive programs, political realities dictated the turn to delegated governance. These advocates faced an implacable wall of opposition in Congress and, during much of the 1950s, the White House. At the same time, however, there was clear public and political support for many social programs, which opponents of these programs grudgingly had to admit. As President Dwight D. Eisenhower remarked in a 1954 letter,

> . . . this country is following a dangerous trend when it permits too great a degree of centralization of governmental functions. I oppose this . . . (but) it is quite clear that the Federal government cannot avoid or escape responsibilities which the mass of the people firmly *believe* should be undertaken by it . . . Should any political party attempt to abolish social security, unemployment insurance, and eliminate labor laws and farm programs, you would not hear of that party again in our political history.[43]

Seeking to tap public support for action on the nation's social problems, the Kennedy administration sought in particular to tackle the problem of entrenched poverty, and Lyndon B. Johnson's landslide victory over Barry Goldwater in 1964 opened the door to an expanded federal role in the social arena. Even the drive by conservatives in Congress to reduce welfare dependency often implied an *expanded* government role in the form of work-promoting social services.

As in other domains of public policy, delegating governance became a way to engage in "antibureaucratic state-building" that created new social programs without visibly enlarging the size of government.[44] One way to achieve this was through grants-in-aid to state and local governments, which put the onus on them to figure out how to administer programs.[45] The size of state and local governments thus grew markedly in this period even as federal civilian employment remained flat. In the 1960s, for instance, the federal government added about 400,000 workers, while state and local governments hired almost 4 million—a 40 percent increase.[46] Many state and local governments also contracted out the delivery of services to private sector groups, such as charities, although this was done on an ad hoc basis. Such a practice accelerated in the 1970s and 1980s, often encouraged by federal policy.

Given the difficult climate for redistributive programs at the federal level, some reformers and government administrators began to discover that contracting out program delivery could help forge private sector allies. One pioneer of this practice in the area of welfare services was Mary Switzer of the Vocational Rehabilitation Agency, who believed that purchasing services from non-state entities would help build a supportive constituency for her programs.[47] Gradually, others came over to her point of view, and Switzer moved into a more prominent position in the Department of Health, Education, and Welfare (HEW) that enabled her to shape social services policy. In the lead-up to the 1962 Public Welfare Amendments—a law that brought about a significant expansion in publicly supported social services—the idea of contracting out service provision to voluntary organizations was considered but put aside. At the time, voluntary organizations were generally leery of such a practice, given long-standing views within the charitable sector that public funds could taint private organizations.[48] Yet, because state and local government agencies were allowed to contract with other public agencies, some of which then contracted with nonprofits for service delivery, the 1962 amendments indirectly furthered the practice.

Contracting out was then enabled in the 1967 amendments to the Social Security Act that further expanded the range of social services available for public assistance recipients. The law allowed states to contract with nonprofits, proprietary agencies, individuals, or other state agencies to deliver these services. One of the driving forces behind this measure was the belief held by a number of government officials that work-promoting services could help combat welfare dependency.[49] These officials, rather than the voluntary organizations themselves, were the impetus behind the move. Although voluntary organizations did not have much influence over this shift, they did abandon their past reluctance to accept public funds, in part owing to growing competition between organizations for scarce charitable dollars.[50] Henceforth, they would become strong advocates of the practice.[51]

These groups also faced competition from organizations that received federal funds as part of the War on Poverty launched by the Johnson administration. Not only did the War on Poverty spur other groups to also seek out federal dollars, but it further eroded the boundaries that had been established between government and nonprofits in the welfare sector. The ideological impetus for delegating the administration of these new services to voluntary organizations now came from a *leftist* critique of unresponsive welfare bureaucracies and racist state and local government.[52] Thus, rather than spend anti-poverty funds through these traditional entities—either public or private—the federal government channeled them to Community Action Agencies, many of them nonprofit organizations, which then directed the funds to community-based groups. The express purpose was to circumvent perceived problematic governmental structures and outmoded voluntary organizations, forging a direct relationship between the federal government and local community organizations that promoted the "maximum feasible participation" of the poor.[53] Another goal was to shift conflicts over contested issues from the national to the local level.[54] Even though the amount of money spent was relatively limited, the episode was "an important landmark in the privatization of public social provision."[55] As one observer noted in 1966, "Gone are the days when most people in Washington would agree with the once widely held view that public money should be spent only by public agencies."[56]

By the late 1960s, the Community Action Agencies were being reined in, but the drive to contract out social services provision in other areas had intensified. In 1969, restrictive language on the purchase of welfare and other services was dropped, and the Code of Federal Regulations asserted that states should "assure progressive development of arrangements with a number and variety of agencies . . . with the aim of providing opportunities to exercise choice with regard to the source of purchased service."[57] Voluntary organizations now mobilized to get state and local governments to purchase services from charitable groups, which helped fuel a boom in social spending as states sought to scoop up unlimited federal matching dollars promised by the 1967 Social Security Amendments.[58] A 1972 law put an end to the gold rush by capping the total amount to be spent on social services, but the addition of Title XX to the Social Security Act in 1974 expanded eligibility for social services and thus contributed to a tremendous growth in the purchase of services from non-state actors at the state level, with voluntary organizations now eager advocates of this practice.[59] The result was what Gilbert and Smith have called "private federalism" in which public funds flowed through a variety of intergovernmental mechanisms into nongovernmental organizations.[60] Many of these organizations were new and included a growing number of proprietary entities that emerged with the realization that "there's money in poverty."[61]

Although a form of privatization, the drive to contract out social service provision was driven by motives that were quite distinct from those that would motivate the practice in the 1980s and 1990s. In the 1960s, contracting out was not viewed as a way to save money, and often did not involve competitive bidding processes to assure that the most cost-effective service providers would get contracts. In addition, nonprofit organizations were often the main recipients of contracts because there generally were few for-profits working in the area of welfare services, although proprietary outfits were becoming more prevalent by the 1970s.[62] Instead, the turn to purchase of service reflected the constrained political environment of the period: on the one hand, many sought to use government programs in the fight against poverty, racism, and welfare dependency, yet they did so at a time of strong criticisms—largely from the Right, but also from the Left—condemning the ineffectiveness of government. Sending public dollars to private agencies was a way to engage in governmental action seemingly without government.

It also should be noted that, in general, service provision was delegated, not the actual administration of programs. In the emerging health care programs of the 1960s, by contrast, both would be delegated to non-state actors.

Delegating the Governance of Medicare

Advocates for Medicare also labored within a constrained political environment. A coalition of Republicans and Southern Democrats in Congress strongly opposed government-sponsored health insurance for any but the indigent, and their dominance of key Congressional committees, such as the House Ways and Means Committee, assured that they would be gatekeepers for any health-related reform.[63] Yet, even they could not deny the rising public clamor for a new health insurance program for senior citizens or the landslide victory of Lyndon Johnson in 1964, who was a strong Medicare advocate. What then made the crafting of Medicare so complex was that the reform threatened a densely populated landscape of private actors. Unlike the social welfare sector, there was a well-developed private health care arena filled with increasingly powerful interests—prosperous physicians, a fast-growing hospital sector, and a nonprofit and commercial health insurance sector that had exploded in size since the 1930s—that hotly opposed a public health insurance program. These medical interest groups took advantage of an institutional and political context that was already conducive to their objectives. By forging a tight alliance with Republicans and conservative Democrats opposed to the growth of the federal government—and making highly publicized claims about the threat of government-run, socialized medicine that had potential resonance with mass opinion—these groups were able to exert considerable influence on the reform.

In seeking to overcome both political and interest group opposition, advocates made many compromises, which included how the program would be administered. Creating a national health service was entirely out of the question, given the very large private health care sector that had developed by this point, but reformers also conceded that even as these providers would start to receive public funding through Medicare (and Medicaid), they would remain largely self-governing. Moreover, rather than directly pay physicians, hospitals, and other providers for their services, the federal government would utilize private, often nonprofit insurance entities as "intermediaries" between the state and the health care sector. More generally, policy-makers constructed a permissive payment and regulatory environment that limited the federal government's role in the health care system. In a classic example of anti-bureaucratic state-building, policy-makers constructed a program in which government would pay hefty subsidies to private actors but leave substantial responsibilities for the governance of the program to the private sector.

The Growth of Private Medical Interests

A foregone conclusion in the debate over Medicare was that the new program would rely upon private providers to deliver health care services. Indeed, the idea of creating a national health service (NHS) had gained virtually no traction in the political arena; proposals in the 1930s, 1940s, and early 1950s had been only for a system of national health *insurance* (NHI)—one that would reimburse private physicians, hospitals, and other health care providers for the cost of care—and these proposals had resoundingly failed. As one of the architects of the Medicare program, Robert Ball, noted in retrospect, "There was overwhelming political agreement that Medicare did not have a mission to reform delivery of, or payment for, medical care."[64]

A key reason for this overwhelming political agreement was the power of organized medicine in combating *any* effort in the public or private sector to exert control over the way they practiced medicine and how they were remunerated for it. State-level attempts since the 1910s to create broad-based health insurance coverage repeatedly collapsed in the face of opposition by physicians, business associations, and labor unions.[65] Proposals for a federal program developed most seriously during the 1930s, but President Roosevelt jettisoned health insurance from the social welfare legislation he submitted to Congress in 1934, fearing that controversies around it would jeopardize the entire package of reforms.[66] Even the sentence in the proposal that said the new Social Security Board should study health insurance generated a flood of telegrams to members of Congress, leading the Ways and Means Committee to eliminate it from the final legislation.[67] Efforts by individual members of Congress and President Truman to pass a program of NHI also foundered due to stiff opposition in Congress. The election of Dwight D. Eisenhower to the presidency in 1952—who expressly opposed government-sponsored health insurance as "socialized medicine" during the campaign—pounded one more nail in the coffin of NHI and prevented serious discussion of a British-style NHS.[68]

There is, however, a puzzling exception to this narrative of failed initiatives, and that is how the VA system of "socialized medicine" came into being in this same period. The VA medical system is a striking example of direct governance in a country that otherwise leaves responsibility for medical care and insurance in private hands. Physicians are government employees, hospitals and other medical care facilities are publicly run, and the program is directly administered by a federal bureaucracy. For opponents of NHI in the medical field, such as the American Medical Association (AMA), this made the VA system an object of great concern—a "Trojan horse of ominous dimensions."[69] This was particularly true in the period after World War II, when the federal government devoted considerable resources to modernizing and expanding the VA medical system. By the early 1950s, the system included 136 hospitals, 95 outpatient clinics, and employed over 80,000 people full-time, including physicians, dentists, and nurses, and was slated for further expansion.[70] Why then were powerful medical interests, said to be so influential in blocking other public interventions in health care, so ineffective against the VA?

Both the unquestioned worthiness of veterans and the relative ease with which they could be cordoned off from the rest of the population defanged medical interest groups opposed to the VA system. The foundations of the system were laid in the 1920s, when the quality of many medical facilities was low and there were limited numbers of public facilities. Leaving war veterans to poor quality care was widely viewed as unacceptable, given the tremendous sacrifices they had made for the nation.[71] Rather than contract with existing private institutions, the federal government began building its own medical facilities, and the medical profession was unable to stop this. Certainly, the AMA tried, both in the 1920s and again after World War II, but with patriotism on the side of war veterans, they "were one lobby even the medical profession could not overcome."[72] It also helped that the veteran population could be fairly easily delimited, although the decision to extend coverage to wives and dependents, and the practice of allowing non-service-related ailments be treated through the VA system, stirred concern among NHI opponents. Still, by providing medical care to a distinct and deserving group, some conservatives who might otherwise be opposed to such a program of direct governance believed they were stymieing the drive for NHI, eliminating one particularly valued constituency from the coalition for compulsory, national coverage.[73]

Once in place, the VA system would also benefit from the pork-barrel characteristics of Congressional politics. With hospitals spread across states and congressional districts, the VA system became a "Congressional fiefdom" that few politicians dared to challenge.[74] Even physicians would benefit because the system offered them advantages through the affiliation between many VA hospitals and academic medical centers. Medical school committees were allowed to vote on appointments to VA facilities, and the schools also benefited from residency training and research programs conducted in these institutions.[75] In other words, the very institutional features of American government that make it difficult to pass large-scale redistributive programs can actually serve to foster and protect distributive, pork-barrel programs, and this has worked to the advantage of the VA system.

Outside of the VA, the private health care arena continued to expand, in part because of public policies that fueled the growth of health care sectors that then worked to block greater government control over their activities. First was the vast growth in the private insurance industry, typically supported by government action.[76] From early on, Blue Cross and Blue Shield plans, viewed as community oriented because they would accept all applicants and charged everyone in a community a single insurance rate regardless of individual risk profile, received favorable government treatment in order to promote their expansion.[77] State governments exempted them from insurance regulations that would have required these plans to maintain large reserves, and as nonprofit plans they enjoyed tax-exempt status. Private health insurance also grew during World War II as another government policy, wage and price controls, drove employers to search for other means to compensate employees, such as health insurance. For their part, commercial insurers were attracted to this employer market because it minimized their exposure to the worst risks, such as retirees or people too sick to work. Favorable tax treatment for employer contributions to employee health benefits, introduced in the 1940s and codified in the 1954 Internal Revenue Code, cemented this system in place.[78] The resulting expansion in private coverage was dramatic—the proportion of the population with private health insurance rose from 9 percent in 1940 to nearly 63 percent by the early 1950s and almost 76 percent in 1957—and weakened the mass constituency for NHI.[79]

Additional government policies fueled the growth of a high-cost medical industry. The Hospital Construction Act of 1946 (known as Hill-Burton) directed federal support to the construction and modernization of hospitals across the country. With its emphasis on the wide geographic distribution of hospitals and the construction of acute care facilities (as opposed to primary care clinics or general medical centers), Hill-Burton encouraged the expansion of high-tech hospitals and acute care personnel and thus contributed to the growth of an expensive medical system.[80] The federal government also made massive investments in medical research and the development of medical schools. In an example of delegated governance, these investments into the medical sector were done in a way that minimized federal government oversight and control.[81] Thus, in contrast to the European research model of spending government research funds on government-run laboratories—a model the United States also adhered to until the 1930s—U.S. federal dollars flowed into universities, research institutes, hospitals, and other nongovernmental institutions.[82] The Hill-Burton act also expressly prohibited federal interference in hospital policy, outside of mandating that segregated facilities in the South provide "separate but equal access" to care (until that was ruled unconstitutional by the Supreme Court in 1963) and requiring the hospitals to provide care to all, including indigent and uninsured patients (although many did not).[83]

One result of federal policies that promoted the growth of a private insurance sector and a high-tech, high-cost medical industry was to inadvertently reinforce the power of groups opposed to the extension of governmental influence into their domain.[84] In their battles with liberals over the creation of government-sponsored health insurance, medical interests often prevailed, in part because of institutional features of the American political system that offer access to groups that are nationally organized with a broad geographic presence.[85] With hospitals an important job-creating industry in states and Congressional districts across the country, and physicians being important figures in many local communities, the concerns of these groups would be heard not only through elite-level lobbying groups but would also filter up into the offices of individual members of Congress. The influence of medical interests was further buttressed through their alliance with Republicans and Southern Democrats already opposed to government-sponsored health insurance as a worrisome expansion of federal power. Moreover, physicians were especially effective in deploying anti-statist rhetoric that resonated with conservatives and some of the mass public, and they spent huge sums on lobbying and publicity campaigns to mobilize public opinion.[86] The American

Medical Association (AMA) thus played a critical role in defeating the drive for NHI and slowing the march toward Medicare.[87]

Private insurers also gained influence because they offered conservatives an "out" in dealing with rising public demand for help with the cost of medical care. Within a short space of time, insurance products had developed that offered an alternative to government-sponsored care. Opponents of NHI expressly promoted these private insurance products in an effort to undercut the push for a public program.[88] Throughout the 1950s, conservatives held up the idea of publicly subsidizing private plans to provide health insurance for senior citizens, and groups such as Blue Cross hastened to show that they could deliver, particularly if they received public subsidies.[89]

At the same time, a number of other policy developments seemed to show the potential of working with private intermediaries or providers to administer federal programs. In the 1950 Social Security Amendments, states were allowed to make direct payments to medical providers, including physicians, hospitals, and nursing homes, who provided care for the indigent.[90] At the behest of Social Security Administration planners, these payments expanded continuously during the 1950s, rising from $52 million in 1949–1950 to $493 million in 1959–1960.[91] In 1956, the Eisenhower administration reluctantly agreed to a new disability insurance program that would be fully funded by the federal government (through Social Security taxes), but with state agencies making determinations of disability. Although some government planners initially opposed this as a loss of federal control over the program, they ultimately embraced state administration as a way to mollify physicians and conservative Southerners in the Senate.[92]

Finally, the Federal Employees Health Benefits Program (FEHBP), created in 1959, contracted with private insurance plans to provide health insurance to federal government employees, rather than have the government directly provide coverage. Although the FEHBP did not attract a lot of attention at the time, it would later be held up by some centrists and conservatives as a model for market-oriented reform of Medicare.[93] The law also revealed the ability of the Blue Cross Association to influence government legislation—the law was heavily shaped by the Association for its benefit—and showed policy-makers what role Blue Cross and other insurers could play in dealing with the diverse technical questions that arise in administering a health insurance program.[94]

In sum, both government action and inaction had spurred the growth of a health care industry that profited handsomely from the growing use of medical care and spread of third-party coverage. While benefiting in many ways from government policy, this industry fiercely resisted a more direct federal role in providing or paying for health care. Thus, as NHI advocates shifted their focus from universal insurance coverage to covering discreet, needy groups, they confronted an array of private interests with both close allies in Congress and an anti-government message that could potentially resonate with the mass public.

The Construction of Medicare

The decision by NHI advocates to focus on providing public health insurance to senior citizens reflected a calculated assessment of the political obstacles facing large-scale reform. Clearly, this was a group in need: the retiree population was growing markedly with improvements in life expectancy and the lowering of the retirement age in the 1950s, and older people were more likely to use the health technologies and facilities that were becoming available. This created problems of care for families but also burdened employer-sponsored health plans with high cost beneficiaries, many of whom were dropped from these plans upon retirement.[95] These factors helped slacken, but did not eliminate, the strength of interest group opposition to a senior-citizen-only proposal for government health insurance.[96] Although seniors were clearly an undesirable risk group for insurers, and a growing burden on hospitals and physicians who often provided charitable care, medical interest groups feared opening the door to government influence over their sector. Conservatives in Congress shared their concerns and used control over the levers of policy-making power to stymie the drive for Medicare that began gathering steam in the late 1950s and early 1960s.

Yet, opponents of a new program of health insurance for senior citizens could not deny that there was strong public support for such a reform. In the 1960 presidential campaign, Kennedy's advisers were aware of this issue's political potential, guided by internal polling that showed the public concerned about the well-being of seniors and in favor of assuring medical coverage for this deserving group.[97] By deciding to highlight this issue, Kennedy put Medicare on the political agenda, forcing Republicans and other conservative opponents to come up with their own solutions to the problem.[98] In the succeeding years, Kennedy, supportive members of Congress, and interest group advocates such as organized labor worked to publicize the problems seniors faced in getting access to medical care, and public support for Medicare would remain firm.[99] Public polling between 1961 and 1965 revealed that large proportions of respondents—60 to 67 percent—favored public health insurance for the elderly, support far greater than that obtained for national health insurance in the 1950s.[100] Opponents increasingly realized that blocking Medicare held political risks, particularly as the issue seemed to contribute to the defeat of a number of anti-Medicare representatives and senators.[101]

Despite growing public support, however, Medicare advocates worried about the other face of public opinion—that which feared an expanded federal government as an intrusion into one's personal affairs.[102] Although trust in the federal government was far higher in the early 1960s than it would be later—three-quarters of respondents in the 1964 American National Election Study said they trusted the government in Washington to do the right thing "most of the time" or "always"—suspicion of government activity was apparent in other survey findings. Almost half of respondents in the same survey said the government "wastes a lot of the money we pay in taxes,"[103] and more people told the Gallup organization in 1965 that "big government" was the "biggest threat to the country in the future" than singled out "big labor" or "big business."[104] In the past, the AMA had proven particularly skillful in exploiting these fears, leveling charges of socialism and un-Americanism at NHI proposals.[105] Given the permeability of Congress to such groups, and the strength of anti-Medicare forces in key committees such as the House Ways and Means Committee, reformers sought ways to inoculate their proposals from accusations of a federal government takeover of the practice of medicine.

One crucial area of compromise was in how the new Medicare program would be administered, as policy-makers promised physicians, hospitals, and other providers that the government would interfere minimally with the existing system of medical care.[106] Government would be Medicare's payer, but when it came to program administration, policy-makers constructed a system of truncated bureaucratic capacity. Thus, rather than use federal dollars to promote improvements in the quality of care delivered by the nation's hospitals, Medicare would allow payments to go to any hospital approved by the existing professional accreditation organization.[107] Rather than institute utilization review to ensure that providers were not offering excessive care to Medicare beneficiaries, physicians and hospitals were to set up their own systems of peer review. And rather than assume direct responsibility for receiving, auditing, and paying medical bills, Medicare would employ "fiscal intermediaries"—private nonprofit and for-profit companies that would form a mediating layer between the federal government and the nation's medical providers. Other responsibilities, such as policing provider fraud, would be assigned to other federal departments. With so much of its administrative responsibilities farmed out to public and private entities, the Medicare administration was a classic manifestation of the "hollow state" that was emerging in the postwar period.[108] As Berkowitz and McQuaid have written, Medicare would be "the American version of national health insurance: federal money and private control."[109]

The decision to use private entities to process claims and pay providers is worth exploring in detail, as this was the first time that the contracting out of social welfare administration had been done on such a scale.[110] One could argue that the use of intermediaries and other private organizations to administer much of Medicare was done because it would have been difficult for the federal government to directly run such a large-scale health insurance program. Although the Social Security Administration was much admired for its efficient, centralized bureaucracy, figuring out how to reimburse medical care is far more complicated: the costs of care vary tremendously across the country, and determining what those costs should be is more complicated that calculating a beneficiary's Social Security check. With their many years of experience working with medical providers and determining reimbursement rates, perhaps private insurers had the expertise that the federal government would never have been able to acquire.[111] The same could be said of determining whether hospitals met quality standards or making sure providers did not provide excessive care in order to generate more reimbursements. Certainly, this was the argument that many insurers made at the time to justify allowing them to administer the program.

However, many government officials at the time believed that they could play a more muscular role in Medicare administration. In early discussions about the program, HEW and Bureau of the Budget (BOB) officials not only believed that a strong government role in running the program was essential to control spending, but that administering such a program was eminently feasible. These officials thought the government could set minimum standards of care, negotiate contracts with providers, and directly make payments to them, creating a governmental machinery to achieve these and other administrative functions in a relatively efficient manner.[112] Moreover, although the implementation of Medicare in 1966 went fairly smoothly, federal officials were frequently stunned at the poor performance of the contractors in managing the program. As former SSA official Arthur Hess would later recall with regard to the Part B carriers, "They didn't know from beans about how to pay certain kinds of claims, or they didn't have an automated set up at all that could handle them."[113] Private insurers ultimately developed the capacity to administer the program only after SSA officials had spent considerable time on-site showing many of them how to do so. In short, private contractors did not have the capabilities to implement the program as quickly and efficiently as they claimed—they had to build up the capacity to do so, just as the federal government would have had to have done.

Instead of technocratic factors driving the choices around Medicare administration, political dynamics shaped these decisions. The idea of private contractor administration emerged in the minds of reformers as a way to deal with implacable political opposition to an expanded government role in providing health insurance. By the early 1960s, HEW Assistant Secretary Wilbur Cohen and other reform advocates began to view contracting out Medicare administration as a way to fragment provider opposition.[114] In contrast to many physicians, hospitals were less fierce in their resistance, given the burden on their books of the uncompensated charitable care they provided to many senior citizens. In 1962, they began indicating that they might support (or less determinedly oppose) a government program for seniors as long as it was administered by Blue Cross plans. Moreover, although many physicians opposed the Medicare legislation to the end, Cohen and other advocates used the delegation of program governance to private actors as a way to undercut assertions by the AMA that the federal government was usurping physician control over the delivery of medical care.[115]

Although private insurers were against virtually any government role in health care, some began maneuvering to grab a piece of any such program in the event they were unable to stop it. As the discussions of old-age health insurance intensified in the early 1960s, the Blue Cross Association began promoting the idea that it should serve as the provider of health insurance to seniors but receive government subsidies to do so. As the Blue Cross Association (BCA) president Walter J. McNerney claimed at a 1962 meeting of the BCA and American Hospital Association, ". . . it is traditional for government in the United States to purchase services from private institutions where such services are available on a sound basis, or to help purchase them."[116] Still, the Blues and commercial insurers continued to oppose Medicare until its passage, with the Blue Cross Association muting its opposition but still preferring a system that would allow government subsidies to enable them to provide a Blue Cross card for all. Advocates of using private insurers as intermediaries thus had to try to convince these groups that Medicare was in their interest, and not the other way around.[117]

Just as important, contracting with private insurance companies helped overcome political opposition in Congress to a federally administered program. A core sticking point for many conservatives had been the idea of federal administration of any health insurance program. A representative from the AMA captured the concerns well in testimony before a congressional hearing:

> The government would control the disbursement of funds; the government would determine the benefits to be provided; the government would set the rates of compensation of hospitals, nursing homes, and patients; and the government would promulgate and enforce the standards of hospital and medical care. . . . The professional relationship between the doctor and his patient would be hampered. Government regulations would be imposed on patient and physician alike.[118]

Medicare opponents thus cast about for alternatives, including a state-administered program and a system of subsidized private plans.[119]

In search of compromise, the reformers working within the Department of Health, Education, and Welfare (HEW) studied the idea of using Blue Cross as a program administrator in 1962, and saw many advantages of doing this, even though some worried that the government would be giving control over the program to nongovernmental entities that had close ties with the hospital industry.[120] As Arthur Hess wrote in a memo to Cohen in 1962:

> A considerable price would be paid in order to get the initial public relations advantages with professional groups that might come from using Blue Cross, e.g. loss of direct contact with providers so that the Federal Government would not have detailed knowledge of problems and because of this, the loss of ability to react quickly to problems of administration, budget, program, etc.[121]

Yet, negotiations with the House Ways and Means Committee produced an understanding that the Medicare program would use private insurance intermediaries who would deal directly with medical providers. One crucial change made from Republican proposals was to have Blue Cross and other insurers simply doing reimbursements on behalf of the federal government, and not underwriting risk.[122] This turned insurers into contractors working within more delimited federal guidelines that would prevent them from making profits on the program and ensure that risk for the new program would be borne by the federal government.[123] Future iterations of the Medicare bill included non-state "fiscal intermediaries" who would administer payments.[124] Despite these measures, the strength of the anti-Medicare coalition in Congress continued to frustrate efforts to pass the legislation.

With the electoral landslide in 1964, which brought a large Democratic majority into the House and Senate, one might have thought the door was open to a Medicare program directly administered by the federal government, as had initially been advocated by some HEW and BOB officials.[125] Instead, executive branch officials deferred to the powerful chairman of the Ways and Means Committee, Wilbur Mills (D-AR), who had long been a major obstacle to the passage of Medicare.[126] Mills made clear to Medicare advocates that he wanted a layer of intermediaries between the federal government and health care providers—such as nonprofit organizations like Blue Cross.[127] In the 1965 hearings leading up to passage of the bill, Mills went out of his way to highlight the fact that the federal government would be only minimally involved in administering the new program, and brought in several witnesses to support this view. There also was much discussion about how utilization review would be left to hospitals themselves without much government interference, and that existing accreditation standards would be used for hospitals.[128] Thus, Mills used the hearings to demonstrate that relying on intermediaries would prevent the development of an extensive bureaucratic apparatus to run Medicare. In the words of one Southern member of the Ways and Means, John C. Watts (D-KY), using insurance carriers as intermediaries would prevent "burdening the HEW with the necessity of having a whole tribe of people running all over the country inspecting hospitals and checking on claims, and one thing and another."[129]

Interestingly, the initial proposals were to delegate responsibilities for claims-processing and payment to nonprofit entities—the Blue Cross plans—and not to allow commercial insurers to gain a foothold in the program. Labor union officials strongly opposed allowing the commercials into the program, but there was also a belief that for-profit insurers violated the spirit of a government program. Mills captured that sentiment in the 1965 Ways and Means hearings, when he stated:

> We could come nearer getting by as a matter of public policy in the use of a nonprofit organization to perform the function than we can the Secretary entering into an agreement with an organization that is based on profit because of the inference, always, when you are dealing with a profit-making organization, that it is there to make a profit. If people are going to pay a tax to support this program and then conclude, in the final

analysis, that part of that which they are paying in the form of a tax is going to some private intermediary's profits. I don't know how they would take it. But if the intermediary is a nonprofit setup, then I would think you would have less criticism from those who are paying the bill in the form of a tax.[130]

Certainly, the Blues had been holding themselves up as community-oriented, public-spirited organizations for decades, contrasting themselves with both profit-seeking private insurers and inflexible government bureaucracies.[131] They were ideal for the delegation of administrative authority, although some labor union officials were concerned about the close ties between the Blues and the hospitals and thus whether the Blues would effectively scrutinize reimbursement claims.[132]

Commercial plans found their way into Medicare through unexpected circumstances rather than through any concerted effort to rely upon them for program administration. In an attempt to circumvent physician opposition, the initial Medicare proposals covered only hospital costs, and the plan to do this was hashed out over several years and repeatedly refined through discussions with the Blue Cross Association. The role of intermediaries was thus reasonably well thought out and the program was structured in a way that would encourage the use of Blue Cross plans—namely, by allowing hospitals to nominate their own intermediary. Given the historically close ties between hospitals and Blue Cross, it was not surprising then that more than 90 percent of them chose Blue Cross plans as intermediaries. Part B, however, was hatched only several months before the final legislation passed. Faced with criticism that Medicare covered only hospital costs, and concerned that this would create inexorable pressure for expansion of the program, Mills decided to add an additional system of coverage for physician bills in which beneficiaries could voluntarily enroll. Adding this change at a late date meant there was less time for interest groups to influence Part B's administrative details. Legislators decided that the government would select Part B's "carriers," which were so labeled to signify their lesser independence when compared to the Part A intermediaries. The result was greater competition among insurers to deliver part B benefits, with Blue Shield covering about 60 percent of beneficiaries, and commercial and other independent insurers covering the remaining 40 percent.[133] As an article in Time magazine reported in late 1965, "Many insurance companies now realize that Medicare, far from being the disaster they once predicted, may prove to be a welcome pep pill for their industry."[134]

Given all the concern about federal intervention in the practice of medicine, the first section of Title XVIII of the Social Security Act creating the Medicare program was entitled "Prohibition Against Any Federal Interference" and stated:

Nothing in this title shall be construed to authorize any Federal officer or employee to exercise any supervision or control over the practice of medicine or the manner in which medical services are provided, or over the selection, tenure, or compensation of any officer or employee of any institution, agency, or person providing health services; or to exercise any supervision or control over the administration or operation of any such institution, agency, or person.

Of course, there was a more fundamental delegation of authority taking place in Medicare that reflected the way nearly the entire American system of medical care was developing. This was the delegation of responsibility for the provision of medical care to private actors and institutions—physicians, nurses, hospitals, nursing homes, and other providers—creating, in essence, a partnership between public authority and self-governing professionals.[135] This was hardly something anyone questioned by this time: it was difficult enough to create a national health insurance program and so there was virtually no discussion about a national health service along the lines of the British model. As Payton notes, such a partnership between the state and professionals is "ideal where there is a demand for government services but no constituency for growth in the apparent size of government."[136]

Conclusion

How did the hollow welfare state come into being? Contrary to the belief that the contracting out of social programs is a neo-liberal phenomenon, we locate the origins of this practice in a much earlier historical period. With the exception of Social Security and the VA health care system, the growth of the welfare state since the 1930s came about through a series of delegations—delegation to state and local governments and delegation to an array of private actors, professional organizations, and firms for service provision and program administration. Medicare is a quintessential example of delegated and diffused authority, as from its inception the program relied upon private providers to deliver care, professional organizations to supervise quality, and private intermediary organizations to scrutinize and pay bills. These types of administrative arrangements extended throughout much of the welfare state, turning federal agencies into a set of "holding companies" for the organizations that would actually run publicly funded programs.[137]

We explain these developments by reexamining the rise of the welfare state through the lens of pervasive conflicts over state-building in the twentieth century. Industrialization, economic crisis, modern warfare, and the emergence of the United States as a global superpower created a host of new burdens, demands, and desires that only government could meet. The core dilemma facing federal policy-makers was how to respond to these many demands without building up a large administrative apparatus, one that might threaten individual freedom and private enterprise. Although desirous of assistance in dealing with life's vagaries and costs, mass opinion also lent support to those who would curb the growth of the state. Politically, these views were championed by a powerful conservative coalition of Republicans and Southern Democrats who made effective use of their control over the levers of Congressional power to stymie the growth of the federal administration. The solution for policy-makers was to direct public funds toward private actors, as well as state and local governments, in the hope of sating the public's appetite while keeping the federal government small.

Although these dynamics were at work in the creation of an array of social welfare programs, health care politics were more subject to interest group pressures than were other social policy areas. Supported by favorable government regulations and subsidies, private health care providers, facilities, and insurers rapidly expanded in the post-1945 period and became a powerful force against expansion of federal authority over medical care and insurance. Providers, in particular, exploited public ambivalence about the federal government and took advantage of their location in congressional districts across the country. And providers found a sympathetic ear with the Southern Democrats in Congress who shaped Medicare and who were deeply opposed to any hint of socialized medicine. Not only did the power of these groups ensure the continuation of the fee-for-service payment system in which individuals choose their provider and third party actors unquestionably pay the bills, but they received generous payment terms from the new program and inserted their own creation, Blue Cross/Blue Shield, into its administration. Delegation proved a successful way to provide publicly funded social protections with minimal apparent growth of government.

4

The Rise of the Market Reform Movement

Starting in the mid-to-late 1970s, the nature of delegated governance changed. Whereas previous forms of delegated social policy were largely to nonprofit organizations and professionals, now there would be a growing reliance upon proprietary firms and the construction of social welfare marketplaces. And whereas previously the goal of delegated governance was to contain the size of the federal government or better link communities to service providers, now the aim was to harness the power of market forces in the hope of improving the cost-efficiency and quality of public programs. In chapter 5, we address the politics driving the new variants of delegated authority—marketized governance and consumer-choice reforms—through a detailed case study of the 2003 Medicare Modernization Act. Here, we lay the foundations for that analysis by examining the origins of the market reform movement, the new theory of governance that it promoted, and how the movement shaped debates over health care.

There is now extensive scholarship on the origins, emergence, and influence of the free market movement in American politics. Still puzzling, however, is the seemingly limited policy impact of the "drive to privatize" on the size of the American welfare state. Outside of abolishing AFDC and replacing it with TANF (which would have important implications for program governance, discussed below), efforts to wholly cut programs have largely failed. Instead, Howard argues that there has been an *expanded* government role in social welfare since the 1970s, one often championed or acceded to by Republicans.[1] Thus, in the early 2000s, when Republicans had control over the executive branch and both Houses of Congresses (albeit by slim margins), they did not substantially diminish the role of government in providing for social welfare; instead, they crafted and passed the 2003 Medicare reform that, at the time, represented the largest expansion of a social spending program since the Great Society programs of the 1960s.

How can we make sense of this surprising turn of events? One explanation lies in a shift from the initial focus of conservatives on cutting social spending to contracting out and voucherizing the American welfare state—which can result in *more* government, not less. Faced with the political popularity of most social programs, some conservatives and centrists in both parties embraced delegated governance as a way to show they had a positive governing program that could meet public needs and demands. Marketized versions of this—which relied increasingly upon for-profit actors, introduced more competition into the contracting process, and promoted more consumer choice—enabled politicians to maintain or expand social programs while adhering to the market-reform ideas that had such weight within the party and resonated with some of their voters. Such proposals created their own political hazards, however, as they often shifted risk onto individuals and, in the case of vouchers, put a ceiling on the government's contribution and thus froze or cut an individual's benefits. In addition, this approach to governing would come at the expense of fiscal conservative goals of cutting spending and reducing the size of government. Instead, this new approach often produced a different kind of government rather than a smaller one.

The Complex Politics of Welfare State Reform

The drive to slash the federal government, privatize its many functions, and introduce competitive principles into its remaining operations grew out of the confluence of favorable ideational, economic, and political circumstances. The intellectual foundations of this movement were laid by a small number of economists, journalists, and conservative activists who had been laboring in the political wilderness since the 1950s.[2] By the 1970s, there were a growing number of think tanks that were dedicated to nurturing and promoting free market ideas in the policy sphere.[3] Economic stagnation and social turbulence in the 1970s opened up a political window for their ideas, as public dissatisfaction with and declining trust in government fueled anti-tax initiatives at the state level and an anti-welfare backlash at the federal one.[4] Political conditions were also ripe, with the civil rights movement, legal rulings, and policies spurring a realignment of electoral coalitions. Southern Democrats moved into the Republican party, and moderate Republicans dwindled in numbers, making the Republican Party's constituency increasingly white, rural, and affluent, while that of the Democratic Party became more ethnically diverse, urban, and lower-income.[5] This sharpened the divide between the two parties on socioeconomic issues, leading Republicans to embrace a more strident free market orientation and many Democrats (particularly in Congress) to adopt a similarly strident liberal agenda on redistributive issues.[6] The election of Ronald Reagan to the presidency in 1980 seemed to signal a watershed in American politics, as these streams of ideas and political opportunities converged.[7]

Yet, once in power, free market conservatives faced numerous barriers to achieving their reform agenda. Certainly, they had success in cutting taxes, which put government in a fiscal straightjacket throughout the 1980s and first half of the 1990s.[8] They also successfully promoted deregulation in a number of

industries, although this succeeded in part because it had some bipartisan support.[9] Yet, when it came to cutting the welfare state, free marketeers repeatedly
ran into trouble. An attempt to cut Social Security spending in the early 1980s
blew up in the face of public opposition.[10] Similar attempts to slash Medicare and
Medicaid in the mid-1990s not only failed but damaged the political fortunes of
Republicans in Congress, especially of the champion of these reforms, House
Speaker Newt Gingrich. If the many veto points in American government had
served conservatives well in enabling them to block the growth of government,
these same veto points stymied their own attempts at major reform.

Ambiguities in public attitudes toward both the role of government and private
enterprise lie at the heart of the problem for pro-market reformers, as Americans
are fundamentally ambivalent about both government and the free market. As
chapter 2 noted, there is much public support for redistributive programs, particularly the major universal entitlements for senior citizens. From its earliest days,
Social Security has been enormously popular with the public, with majorities as
large as 90 percent supporting the program in the late 1930s and early 1940s.[11]
Polling data in subsequent decades continued to show support; even when confidence was low during the trust fund turmoil of the late 1970s and early 1980s,
support for the system remained high.[12] From the 1980s through the 2000s, solid
majorities both supported spending more on the program (61 percent in 2002)
and wanted the president and Congress to make its financial stability a "top priority."[13] Medicare obtained similar levels of support, with 71 percent of Americans
saying in 2001 that Medicare's financial stability should be a top priority for the
president and Congress and 63 percent in 2002 wanting to increase Medicare
spending.[14] Means-tested programs are generally less popular—particularly the
despised public assistance or "welfare" program—but other social assistance programs that give in-kind aid rather than cash assistance, such as Medicaid and food
stamps, occupy a middle ground between Social Security and Medicare on one end
of the spectrum and welfare on the other.[15]

Especially for the retirement programs, many Americans are well aware of how
little they have saved for their own old age and how importantly those programs
will figure in their futures. Fully 88 percent of respondents in a July 2009 survey
for the Rockefeller Foundation and National Academy of Social Insurance agreed
that "with the economy and the stock market as bad as it is right now, Social
Security benefits are more important than ever to ensure that retirees have
a dependable income when they retire."[16] A similarly large percentage said it
was "important"—and two-thirds said "very important"—for "Congress to make
adjustments in the next two years to keep Social Security financially solvent."[17]
Thus, even after several decades of conservative efforts to reduce support for
redistributive programs, public regard remains high.[18]

On the other hand, suspicion about government is a steady current in American public opinion that can be tapped by those aiming to curtail the state role.
As noted in chapter 2, trust in government has plummeted over time, with the

percentage of National Election Study (NES) respondents saying they "trust the government in Washington to do what is right" just about always or most of the time declining from 73 percent in 1958 to a low of 31 percent in 2008. Similarly, the percentage of NES respondents who say that the "people in government waste a lot of money we pay in taxes" increased from 43 percent in 1958 to 78 percent in 1980, 70 percent in 1994, and 73 percent in 2008 (see Figure 2.1 in chapter 2). Between 1987 and 2007, Pew Research Center polls revealed that 53 to 70 percent of respondents agreed that "when something is run by the government it is usually wasteful and inefficient."[19] Two-thirds of respondents in a 2006 *CBS News/New York Times* poll said that "in general, the federal government creates more problems than it solves," a level that has stayed about the same since the question was first asked in 1981.[20]

Other longitudinal data supports an overall upward trend in anti-government sentiment. In a series of polls conducted by various organizations since 1959, respondents were asked whether big business, big labor, or big government "will be the biggest threat to the country in the future." The proportion citing big government and big business have grown over time, as the relevance of big labor has diminished, but big government has grown more, with 61 percent in 2006 saying it was the biggest threat (see Figure 4.1). And there is skepticism about government regulation of business as well, with answers to poll questions fluctuating quite a bit over time. In general, Americans have split fairly evenly on questions such as whether "government regulation of business [is] necessary to protect the public interest" or whether "government regulation of business usually does more harm than good." During the 1990s, responses moved slightly to the "harm" side; during the 2000s more to the "public interest" side. But even in December 2008, during the height of the economic crisis, the "public interest" side prevailed by only 47 to 43 percent.[21]

This anti-government strain in public opinion would seem a great boon to those who wish to enact market-oriented reforms and wrest program control away from government and grant it to non-state, particularly for-profit, actors. However, there are risks associated with trying to harness this strand, as suspicions of big business and profit-making actors run deep as well. In a June 2008 Gallup Poll, only 7 percent of respondents said they had a "great deal of confidence" in big business, which ranked the third lowest out of 16 institutions, above only HMOs and Congress.[22] Skepticism about large corporations predates the financial crisis of 2008–2009, however: when a NBC/*Wall Street Journal* poll asked respondents how much confidence they had in various institutions in 2000, only 9 percent said they had a "great deal" of confidence in large corporations, and 11 percent in the financial industry—only slightly more than in 2009 (Bowman and Foster 2009, 2). The percentage of respondents to Harris polls saying they had a "great deal of confidence" in the "people in charge of running major companies" fell from 55 percent in 1966 to 11 percent in 1992, rising a bit during the prosperous 1990s, but then falling again to 11 percent in 2009.[23] The percentage

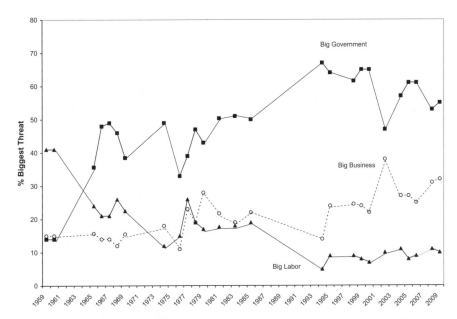

Figure 4.1 Biggest Threat to the Country in the Future. Sources: For 1959 through 2006, Gallup, Harris, Opinion Research Corporation, and Look polls as compiled in Bowman 2008, pp. 7–8. For 2008 and 2009, Gallup polls from iPoll database of the Roper Center at the University of Connecticut. Responses averaged in years in which there were multiple polls.

of Americans saying that they do not think "most corporate CEOs are honest and ethical" rose from 54 percent in 2002 to 73 percent in 2009.[24] Eighty-five percent of Americans think big companies have too much influence in Washington, and 65 percent agree that they make too much profit.[25] Skepticism of large corporations and profit-making enterprises extends to the health care arena as well. Americans' hatred of health maintenance organizations is well documented.[26] As *The Economist* magazine put it in 1999:

> The good news for medical managed care companies is that they are not as unpopular as racists. A recent poll in *Business Week* revealed that 32 percent of Americans thought they would not be able to deliver an impartial verdict in court cases involving white supremacists. The percentage saying the same thing about HMOs was a mere 12 percent.[27]

Health insurance companies in general are not rated much higher.[28] Nor have Americans tended to embrace market-based reforms in health care. During the 1990s, polls showed that just 32 percent of Americans embraced a voucher system for Medicare; twice as many—64 percent—wanted the program to "remain as it is today, with a defined set of benefits for people over 65 and the government providing them with a single insurance card."[29] While the new prescription drug plan for Medicare was being debated, Americans rejected private insurance plans and wanted Medicare to pay directly for part of prescription costs, by a 36 to 57 percent margin, according to a 2000 Kaiser/*Washington Post* poll. This dislike of market-oriented reforms extends to the public pension program as well; seniors have roundly rejected individual accounts for Social Security, including in 2005, when George W. Bush made privatization the centerpiece of his domestic agenda.[30]

These complexities in public opinion have created quandaries for Republicans trying to figure out how an anti-government party governs once in power. Certainly, they can cut taxes and offer plenty of tax breaks to try to address various social needs.[31] Ultimately, however, they have needed to devise a positive governing agenda that shows they can not only keep down the size of people's tax bills, but have solutions to the real problems that people face. In 1995, Gingrich and the House Republicans failed in their goals—having erred too far on the side of draconian budget cuts—and the GOP faced pressure in subsequent years to devise a positive governing agenda. As chapter 5 will show in detail, these pressures led Republicans to develop a Medicare prescription drug proposal in the late 1990s that would be an expensive new universal entitlement, contrary to many of the small government principles they had been articulating for years. This in turn generated intra-party conflicts about how to proceed on entitlement reform: How could Republicans satisfy both the advocates of free markets and fiscal responsibility while also protecting and even expanding a popular social program?

A new form of delegated governance—one that explicitly employs the techniques and rhetoric of competitive market forces but does not require major cuts in social programs—has offered one way out of these quandaries. Administering programs through private actors promises to limit the role of government, maximize the influence of competitive market forces, and return as much decision-making as possible to program beneficiaries, now redubbed "consumers." As with earlier forms of delegated governance, this technique can build allies among private sector providers of health-and welfare-related services, who could not only be campaign contributors but could help foster political dynamics that may one day reverse the entrenchment of public programs. Some have hoped that fostering private sector allies who benefit from privatization can develop a constituency in favor of continued market-based reform.[32] In addition, delegated governance can be more than "a painless alternative to the budget cutter's knife,"[33] as it offers conservatives a positive governing agenda that puts liberals on the defensive.[34] As Stuart Butler of the Heritage Foundation argued in a 1993 lecture, "Why Conservatives Need a National Health Plan":

> For us to simply deny that people do clamor for certain basic goods or services is to ignore the tide of history, and we will be overwhelmed by that tide. Conservatives should in most instances try to convince individuals that they are wrong to expect these things. . . . But if an overwhelming

majority of citizens are emphatic that all citizens—not just themselves, but all citizens—should have a legal right to a basic supply of a good or service, then conservatives must take a different tack. They must explore ways of allowing people to be provided with these things in accordance with certain principles. One is that the basic level should be provided in an efficient manner. And another is that there should be the least probability of government intervening extensively in people's lives.[35]

There was no better statement of this approach than that made by Speaker of the House Newt Gingrich in October 1995 before a Blue Cross/Blue Shield conference. Rather than directly cut Medicare and go after its administering agency— the Health Care Financing Administration (HCFA, now CMS)—Gingrich argued for a variety of market-based reforms that could draw beneficiaries out of traditional fee-for service Medicare:

> So what we're trying to do, first of all, is say, okay, here is a government monopoly plan. We're designing a free-market plan. Now, they're very different models. You know, we tell Boris Yeltsin, "Get rid of centralized command bureaucracies. Go to the marketplace." Okay, what do you think the Health Care Financing Administration is? It's a centralized command bureaucracy. It's everything we're telling Boris Yeltsin to get rid of. Now, we don't get rid of it in round one because we don't think that that's politically smart and we don't think that's the right way to go through a transition. But we believe it's going to wither on the vine because we think people are voluntarily going to leave it—voluntarily.[36]

Democrats seized upon this surprisingly frank statement of Gingrich's strategy, alleging that Gingrich wanted the entire Medicare program to "wither on the vine" when in fact he was referring to HCFA's role in overseeing traditional fee-for-service Medicare. What is more important, and was lost in the controversy, was the underlying strategy of reform that Gingrich articulated: that of creating a competitive alternative to traditional Medicare that would draw in beneficiaries without forcing any abrupt change in existing program. As Gingrich went on to say in the speech about the Republican approach:

> . . . first is you get to stay in HCFA if you want to. Nobody has to move. The second is that there's a Medicare Plus system of choices because seniors should have the right to choose . . . we maintain the mandatory core Medicare benefits. This is a very cautious transition. It's a very bold architectural change, but a very cautious transition.

The quest for a positive governing agenda and a political coalition to support it has thus led some conservative thinkers and politicians to abandon pure privatization and instead embrace delegated governance in a new, marketized form. The ideational support for this approach emerged in the late 1960s and 1970s, an early statement of which can be found in Peter Drucker's widely read 1968 essay, "The Sickness of Government." According to Drucker, the problem with government is not necessarily that it is big but that it is badly run. As Drucker wrote, "[w]e do not face a 'withering away of the state.' On the contrary, we need a vigorous, a strong, and a very active government."[37] He proposed to separate "governing" from "doing," so that policy-makers concentrate on drawing attention to issues, mobilizing public support, and making decisions, but then let nonstate actors actually do the work of administering programs.[38] A. E. Savas, an influential proponent of privatization who served in the Reagan administration, favored outright load-shedding of government functions, but given the frequent political obstacles to doing this, he saw contracting out and voucher programs as second-best alternatives. Some centrists also embraced these ideas. In an influential book, *The Public Use of Private Interest*, Brookings economist Charles Schultze made a strong case for government using private actors as much as possible to achieve its goals. Assailing the "command-and-control" government that he believed increasingly dominated American life, Schultze favored structuring incentives for market actors to help meet collective goals.

Were these intellectuals unaware that, contrary to their image of the federal government as a command-and-control bureaucracy, so much of the government's business had already been farmed out to private agents that the ratio of civilian employees to the population had steadily declined since the 1950s?[39] As a number of public administration scholars observed at the time, for all the claims of the "newness" of privatization, the United States had been engaging in a form of privatization for decades.[40] One explanation is that these advocates were reacting to other aspects of governmental decision-making that they perceived as oppressive. As Monica Prasad has argued, since the postwar period the federal government levied significant taxes on high incomes, business, and capital investment, and possessed a regulatory regime that was in many ways more aggressive and punitive than that found in many other Western countries. By the early 1970s, it seemed that this regulatory apparatus would grow even stronger in reaction to the consumer rights, environmental, and other social movements gaining steam and influence in that period.[41] In fact, much conservative criticism of "Big Government" concerned the way in which regulation altered the functioning of markets, distorting incentives or protecting private interests.

In addition, the criticism was not only of government per se, but was more broadly about the way in which American society was being governed. The neoliberal economic vision was not simply about changing specific policies or practices; it sought to re-envision much of American society and government through the lens of public choice. Few were spared this re-envisioning. Government was assailed as a "monopoly" peopled by bureaucrats who constantly sought to expand their responsibilities and budgetary resources. Physicians, long viewed as trusted professionals acting in the interests of patients, now were seen as market rationalists who worked to guard entry into their profession and maximize their revenue stream. Nonprofits lost their hallowed status as public-serving organizations, now being described as driven by the goals of monetary maximization and a desire to fiercely protect their turf. Wherever these monopolies existed, reformers argued that they needed to be broken down, enabling real markets to emerge.

Finally, the aim of reformers was not just to hold down the size of government, but to introduce competitive market forces into public contracting and other programs. The key element here was *risk*: unless firms' profits are at risk, advocates argued, they are unlikely to make good decisions. Thus, contracting with entities that have guaranteed government contracts but do not put their profits at stake will not produce the efficiencies and quality improvements that true market forces provide. As Drucker wrote, "Of all our institutions, *business is the only one that society will permit to disappear*."[42] Faced with the threat of extinction, businesses work to maximize their own profits and survivability and, in the process, raise the overall level of welfare. The same is true for individuals, it was argued: when people spend "someone else's money," as they do when they are covered by health insurance, then they do it profligately and irrationally. By contrast, when people have their own money at stake, they make better decisions. In the end, the welfare of society is maximized through the many individual decisions made according to a calculus of profit and loss.

This vision of efficient, smoothly functioning public programs was alluring not only to many Republicans but won centrist and conservative Democratic adherents as well. Located disproportionately in Southern congressional districts or states in which voters viewed government with considerable suspicion, these Democrats grappled with many of the same political dilemmas facing Republicans: how to put forth a positive governing agenda without igniting animosity against the federal government.[43] Faced in the 1980s with repeated electoral drubbings by Republicans from what seemed to be "the party of ideas, the party with a sense of mission . . ." centrists and conservatives worked to move the party away from the "liberal fundamentalism" that they believed associated the party with welfare dependency, big government, and moral values out of tune with those of ordinary Americans.[44] These moderates created or participated in the Democratic Leadership Council, which was founded in 1985 and became a crucial vehicle for the development of Third Way ideas, including the need to "reinvent government" along the lines envisioned by the New Public Management approach to governance. One way that this reinvention could take place was though "public-private partnerships" in which the government would steer the actions of private actors rather than row the ship of state itself.[45] The New Democrat movement made its influence felt not only through the election of former DLC chairman Bill Clinton in 1992 but also with the formation of the New Democrat Coalition and Blue Dog Coalition in the House, which continue to this day.[46]

The Free Market Movement in Health Care

Market reform ideas became well developed in the health care field, where the public choice school shaped influential figures in the emerging discipline of health economics. Initial thinking in the health economics field had been strongly influenced by Kenneth Arrow's 1963 essay, "Uncertainty and the Welfare Economics of Medical Care," which argued that the medical care system lacked key attributes of a competitive market. "Informational inequality" between doctors and patients over medical needs and treatments, adverse selection and moral hazard in insurance markets—Arrow believed that these types of problems were intrinsic to the delivery and insurance of medical care and undermined the functioning of market forces. Arrow especially emphasized the difficulty that individuals have in making decisions about medical care, given the specialized knowledge required. They therefore relied upon trusted agents—physicians—who were in the unique position of both determining demand for services and being the suppliers of them. This delegation of power to physicians was acceptable only because they were "collectivity-oriented" agents who should have their patient's best interests at heart, rather than their own.[47]

By the 1970s, however, a number of economists began challenging this view.[48] At the heart of this critique was an attack on the expertise and alleged public-mindedness of medical providers.[49] Medical care did not only reflect the straightforward application of scientific knowledge to medical problems; instead, it sometimes was shaped by the pecuniary interest of physicians and other providers in prescribing more services, and the fact that third-party payers (insurance plans, government) shielded consumers from the true costs of this care. Not only did these providers form monopolies and bar entry into their field, but they also influenced other payers, such as the federal government and the Blue Cross and Blue Shield plans that were dominated by provider interests.[50] These analysts argued that much medical care is closer to a conventional consumption good than Arrow believed, and that patients could reasonably differ on how much care they wished to consume.[51] This meant that if competitive forces were unleashed in the medical care market—particularly by empowering consumers to make their own decisions about medical care and insurance coverage—then costs would come under control, the quality of care would likely improve, and people's individual preferences for medical care would be respected.

Free-market approaches to health care came in two general approaches.[52] One approach aimed to make consumers face the true costs of care by removing the shield provided by employer-sponsored coverage, insurance plans, and physician claims to professional expertise and authority. Instead, cost-sharing (e.g., deductibles, co-payments) and vouchers could give people a stake in how much they were spending on medical care, which would then induce them to shop around for the best care and scrutinize its cost.[53] One early proposal, put forth by Martin

Feldstein, would have provided every family with health insurance that had a large deductible to ensure that they would be more discerning of the cost of care, supplemented by government-guaranteed post-payment loans so that people could spread their medical costs over the year.[54] Feldstein's claim that employer-sponsored health insurance obscures the true cost of medical care helped build the case for scaling back or eliminating the tax subsidy for employer-provided insurance—a theme that steadily gained prominence in conservative critiques.[55]

A second approach shifted the choice point from the doctor's office to the purchase of an insurance plan.[56] Impressed by the ability of health maintenance organizations (HMOs) to squeeze savings out of providers, these advocates sought to transform the entire health care delivery system along the lines of managed care. Rather than simply take the prices that physicians and hospitals are offering, HMOs either directly provide care or else contract with providers with whom they have negotiated payments. They also manage individuals' care by limiting the use of unnecessary services. Competitive forces work at two levels in such a system: first, individuals choose from an array of competing insurance plans based on price and quality; and second, HMOs receive capitated payments per enrollee that create incentives for them to limit the cost of care. Among other beneficial effects, advocates believed a health system organized along the lines of managed care would break down the professional monopoly held by providers, would empower consumers as they chose between insurance plans, and would hold down health care costs. They also believed that HMOs would have incentives to not only keep costs down but also to keep their beneficiaries healthy by providing preventive health services.

These market reform visions thus challenged the belief that the best way to rationalize the medical system, ensure quality care, and control costs was to expand government planning, subsidies, and regulation.[57] To the contrary, managed care represented a way to harness private interests to achieve public aims, just as Brookings economist Schultze had advocated.[58] Reflecting Schultze's pessimistic view of the effectiveness of much government action, the debate between "competition" and "regulation" that began in the 1970s expressed diverging perspectives about the effectiveness of public administration in the health care field. Advocates of regulation believed that, if so empowered, government could manage health care costs. Competition advocates rejected these views, in part because of the widely held belief among economists that government price controls generate distortions and inefficiencies in private markets.[59] They also argued that government agencies were simply incapable of managing large, complex programs, and thus would inevitably make poor decisions. Liberals had already ceded some of these points in the system of Medicare administration. After all, one of the justifications for delegating so much administrative responsibility to private actors had been that government simply could not handle the large number of complex decisions involved in managing a public health insurance program. The difficulties that the program faced in controlling costs then only seemed to confirm the claims of critics that government-run health insurance would necessarily be badly run insurance.[60]

Many competition proponents were also influenced by a public choice perspective on government bureaucracy, which held that government agencies tend to be "captured" by the interests that they are supposed to regulate. Producer groups, such as physicians, are precisely the kind of narrow interest that has strong incentives for political mobilization. By contrast, the consumers who favor lower cost goods and services are a huge and diffuse group that, owing to free rider problems, is unlikely to organize.[61] The problem of how to resist the power of organized medical interests is an important theme in the writings of Enthoven and other managed care backers. Public programs such as Medicare are believed to be hopelessly compromised by the unequal power relations between providers and patients.[62] As Enthoven wrote with regard to the Medicare program's attempt to limit daily hospital costs:

> They cause delegations of hospitals administrators and trustees to descend on their representatives in Congress. And they inspire the development of ingenious accounting strategies to shift costs to other categories. Limits on physician fees are met by numerous strategies by which physicians maintain their incomes. The efforts to change or to evade the regulations force regulators to deal with many individual cases. They subject regulators to continuing pressures to grant exceptions. This makes for even more complex regulations. . . .[63]

Market forces, by contrast, are believed capable of disciplining powerful provider groups and making tough choices about health care in a way that bureaucrats and politicians cannot. If markets render a product obsolete, the producer simply goes out of business, being unable to appeal to a higher power. Thus, if a hospital is not needed in a particular area, better for market forces to determine that rather than government planners or politicians, who would cave against the pressures of hospitals administrators and employees who will lose their jobs. Leaving such decisions in the hands of markets would not only bring about greater overall efficiency, but was seen as a way to empower consumers against powerful supplier groups. As Enthoven put it, ". . . the choice between a regulated and a competitive market system of health care services is a choice between service that responds mainly to the interests of providers or to those of consumers."[64] This fit with a more general theme among privatization advocates, who argued that markets were more democratic than government agencies because they were more responsive to individual preferences and needs.[65] According to Havighurst:

> . . . consumer choice, under cost constraints, is an ethically attractive way to deal with the difficult value questions that pervade the provision of health services. . . . Privatization of these hard choices—that is, rationing

care through market choices rather than through governmental mechanisms—has always seemed to me to be preferable, on balance, to bringing
them out into the open for emotion-laden public debate and decision.[66]

The best way to achieve these democratic goals was to remove politics from the
decision-making process, allowing market actors to make the tough allocative
decisions that would result in superior overall results.[67]

These ideas gained steam because of changes in the health care system that
seemed to confirm claims that, with the right reforms, it could be a competitive
marketplace. One important development was the growing prevalence of proprietary health care providers. Previously, nonprofits had dominated the provision
of medical services, and Arrow had even pointed to this fact as evidence that the
medical care system operated differently from other markets.[68] In the 1970s and
1980s, however, there was a significant increase in the number of for-profit hospitals and other providers of medical services.[69] Competitive pressures, as well as
the squeeze on costs by third-party payers, also spurred nonprofits to change
their structure and behavior to become more like proprietary entities.[70] It was as
Paul Starr had predicted: because the government did not intervene to rationalize
the delivery of care, the private sector tried to do so instead.[71]

Also important were changes in the insurance industry. As with medical care
providers, the field of health insurance initially was dominated by nonprofit organizations, such as Blue Cross and Blue Shield. In the postwar years, with the rapid
growth in employer-sponsored coverage, for-profit insurance companies moved
in and began out-competing the nonprofits for clients, which in turn induced
changes in the behavior of the nonprofits. The Blues, for instance, first raised
their premiums and then abandoned the practice of community rating altogether
as private insurance companies lured away healthier individuals with lower premiums.[72] There was a similar transformation in another form of insurance—the
prepaid group practice, later known as an HMO—which first emerged in the
1930s as a largely nonprofit entity.[73] During the 1980s, there was a dramatic shift
in the nature of the HMO, which went from being locally controlled, nonprofit
organizations to for-profits affiliated with national firms.[74]

In addition, as employers sought to tamp down the rising cost of health care,
they turned to managed care plans in the hope that they could control utilization
and negotiate lower fees from providers.[75] Various forms of managed care spread
rapidly in the 1980s and 1990s: in 1987, only 27 percent of people with employer-
sponsored coverage were in managed care plans, but this figure reached 74 percent by 1996.[76] The "managed care revolution" was viewed by a number of analysts
as responsible for the slowdown in the pace of health care spending in the 1990s.[77]

These and other developments made it seem like price competition was a
growing force in the health care sector.[78] As one insurance industry representative
and advocate of market-based reforms to Medicare declared:

. . . there is a fullscale revolution under way. The health care industry is becoming a truly price-competitive sector of the economy for the first time. . . . In my view, as a result of price competition, total costs are in fact coming under control. Quality is rising. Some companies, some hospitals, and some individual practitioners are going under; they are exiting the industry. Most individual consumers and group buyers are and will be better off, but some will get hurt. Consolidated and integrated delivery systems are becoming the order of the day. A cottage industry is collapsing. Traditional indemnity insurance is dying. In short, the health care sector is beginning to operate like the housing sector operates, or like the food, clothing, or transportation sectors operate.[79]

It also began to appear that Medicare was lagging behind an innovative private sector, where managed care plans were not only controlling costs but developing integrated approaches to the management of chronic conditions. By the 1990s, it became increasingly clear that Medicare was the last bastion of fee-for-service medicine. Reform advocates thus argued that Medicare needed to be "modernized" or brought in line with these latest developments in private health insurance.

These perspectives shaped proposals for free-market reform of Medicare. Some called for giving senior citizens a subsidy that they could use to choose among competing health plans, much as federal employees do in the Federal Employee Health Benefits Program (FEHBP).[80] In the words of two proponents, this would essentially change Medicare from a "defined-benefit" to a "defined-contribution" system,[81] in which beneficiaries receive a fixed amount and then choose the package of health insurance coverage they desire. Such proposals actually predated the creation of Medicare in 1965: in the late 1950s and early 1960s, some Republicans advocated an FEHBP-type model to provide health insurance for senior citizens, but the idea failed to gain traction at the time.[82] Only later would the FEHBP be held up as a model for health care reform.[83]

The idea also gained support among centrist thinkers, such as Brookings Institution economist Henry Aaron and Robert Reischauer, a former chief of the Congressional Budget Office who went on to head the Urban Institute. Together, they developed the concept of a "premium support" model for Medicare in which the federal government subsidizes the premiums paid by senior citizens for their own health insurance coverage.[84] A more limited variant of this approach is simply to promote greater choice for Medicare beneficiaries by allowing HMOs to provide benefits to them. This idea was never one that conservative intellectuals really cared for, and in fact some actively opposed it.[85] For these critics, the basic problem with the health care system was its domination by third-party payers of any stripe, be they public, nonprofit, or proprietary agencies. As John Goodman put it, "The problem with the existing system is it's totally dominated by bureaucracies. . . . About 95% of all money that goes to hospitals comes from insurance companies, employers or government."[86]

Thus, the aim of "consumer-directed health care," as it came to be known, was to shift the locus of decision-making to individuals through the creation of Health IRAs—savings accounts into which workers make tax-subsidized deposits, and from which they later draw funds to directly pay their health care costs and/or purchase an insurance policy that would do so.[87] These ideas have been associated most closely with Goodman of the National Center for Policy Analysis, but also have been central to the health care reform agenda of analysts at the Cato Institute and have featured prominently in the opinion pages of the *Wall Street Journal*. Although initially put forth as a solution to Medicare's financial difficulties, the idea gained steam as a general health care reform alternative. All workers would be able to make use of "Medical Savings Accounts" by taking their employers' current contributions to a low-deductible insurance policy and redirecting them into both a health savings account and a high-deductible insurance policy. Individuals would then use the funds in these tax-privileged accounts to pay their medical costs up to the point at which their high-deductible policy stepped in. Any money left over at the end of the year would accrue interest, creating incentives for the individual to spend wisely on his or her medical costs.[88]

A common element of these various reform ideas was their reliance upon risk-bearing agents to make decisions about the cost and use of medical care. For instance, the locus of risk distinguished proposals to increase the role of HMOs in the delivery of Medicare from the existing system, which also relied upon private insurance companies to administer the program. In the original system, the federal government, not the insurance intermediaries and carriers, bore risk for the program. The administrative contractors received cost-based contracts to administer Medicare and had few or no incentives to act efficiently, because any savings they generated would go to the government, and not to them.[89] Introducing capitated payments to HMOs, by contrast, would shift risk onto the health plans that would then negotiate with hospitals, physicians, and other providers over the kinds of care they provided and how much they would be reimbursed. Plans that did not do this effectively would bear the cost and be forced to exit the program. Because Medicare beneficiaries would be choosing between competing plans, they would move away from lower-quality, higher-cost plans.

These various reform ideas also shifted risk onto Medicare beneficiaries and other health care consumers. As Butler and Moffit note about their proposal to turn Medicare into a defined contribution system, ". . . Medicare beneficiaries would be exposed to future differences between the budgeted voucher and their total cost of coverage."[90] First, they would be choosing between competing health plans, and if they selected a bad plan from the standpoint of quality or cost, they would bear the consequences for that poor choice. On the other hand, those who made good choices would reap the rewards in terms of more and better health care services and/or lower premiums or cost-sharing. Consumer-directed health care would put even more of the onus of decision-making on individuals: beyond having to choose a good health insurance policy, they would also be responsible for making sound decisions about the kind of care they received and how much was charged for it. Again, good choices would be rewarded, while people making bad decisions would face the consequences.

The Politics of Market Reform

It took some time for the market reform ideas that emerged in the 1970s to affect the governance of social programs. Advocates had to fight many battles, and they were least successful in marketizing programs that had strong, well-organized defenders of the status quo, such as Social Security and public schools. By contrast, where clients were disempowered and there were either few defenders of the status quo or groups that would benefit from marketizing the governance of a program, reforms were more likely at both the state and federal level. Thus, many state governments moved toward using private firms to run their Medicaid programs: beneficiaries hardly had the influence to complain, and private firms stood to gain from the opening up of a new market for them. Similarly, the 1996 law abolishing the federal entitlement to public assistance spurred the increasing use of for-profit firms in running welfare programs—again, an example of disempowered beneficiaries and empowered private interests.[91]

Medicare posed particular challenges for market-oriented reformers, and efforts to significantly cut the program showed the political perils of attacking Medicare. Senior citizens liked the program as it was, and Democrats were quick to exploit this. Slowly, however, centrists and conservatives laid the seeds for the 2003 Medicare Modernization Act by nurturing a set of reform ideas and incrementally developing a private insurance plan alternative within the program. At the same time, however, they also had to accept the adoption of more traditional government mechanisms to control program costs—de facto price controls—as the only way to garner immediate budgetary savings.

Vouchers and For-Profit Contracting in Social Welfare Programs

The first changes came at the state and local level, as the use of private contractors, service providers, and franchises accelerated in the 1970s. As Henig notes, state and local government officials were often pragmatic when it came to the structuring of public programs, which meant that some localities had long used private actors to provide public services.[92] By the 1980s, federal policy accelerated the use of this practice in two ways. First, faced with big budget deficits and the anti-tax political climate, federal policy-makers increasingly shifted burdens onto state and local governments. These often unfunded, or inadequately funded, mandates were a way for national politicians to "(e)xperienc(e) the joy of creating new benefits while passing down the pain of paying for them."[93] As many state and local governments were also being buffeted by anti-tax movements, this intergovernmental dumping of burdens led to fiscal crises that, in turn, spurred efforts to shed as many public responsibilities as possible.[94] Second, federal laws were altered to remove restrictions on state contracting out of social programs and to encourage the embrace of this and similar market-based reforms.

Not all program areas have been equally subject to these kinds of reforms, however, and it is precisely in these differences that we can understand some of the political forces shaping these phenomena. We might predict that voucherization and contracting-out to for-profit providers would be most likely for programs with diffuse, politically weak constituencies and/or that lack other defenders. Strong, well-organized constituencies and those programs with allies favoring the status quo should be better able to resist being contracted out or voucherized. This is certainly what we see in two programs benefiting weak clienteles, Medicaid and welfare.

In Medicaid, states faced costly federal mandates to cover certain groups, such as pregnant women and children, at the same time that other program costs like nursing homes were increasing. With anti-tax political movements restricting their ability to raise revenues, and limits on the amount of borrowing they could do, many state governments found themselves in desperate fiscal straits in trying to meet these requirements. Many policy-makers also were critical of the effectiveness of Medicaid in reaching those in need and ensuring that good care was provided. Hoping to improve the quality of care while limiting costs, many state governments began shifting more responsibility for delivering Medicaid benefits to private, managed care organizations (MCOs) by the mid-1990s. The 1997 Balanced Budget Act then eliminated a previous requirement that states seek a waiver before they could mandate managed care enrollment, opening the door to the wholesale transformation of Medicaid programs across the country. Some states turned to a particular form of managed care—the primary care case management model, in which primary care physicians receive a case management fee to provide and coordinate care for Medicaid recipients. However, what has become increasingly common is the risk-based capitation model that pays MCOs a capitated, monthly fee per enrollee. The latter model more strongly embodies the principles of competitive market reform because it shifts financial risk onto MCOs to deliver services to the beneficiary population. Plans also compete for enrollees, and states use cost-effectiveness criteria to determine the plans with which they will contract.[95]

Whether or not the reliance of Medicaid on managed care has improved the functioning of the program is debated, with some researchers finding cost savings for state governments and improvements in the quality of care delivered,[96] while others find little evidence of budgetary savings or improved health outcomes.[97] What one can say about managed care, however, is that it shifts control over the care that one receives to a private organization. Rather than reimbursing providers for the care that one has sought out and may be entitled to through a public program, managed care organizations have considerable discretion to determine what that care will be.[98] It is for that reason that the public revolted against the spread of managed care organizations and techniques in private insurance markets in the late 1990s and early 2000s, leading MCOs to drop a lot of their more restrictive practices.[99] Despite this, enrollment in Medicaid managed care has steadily climbed: by 2008, over 70 percent of Medicaid beneficiaries were enrolled in managed care plans.[100] According to Grogan, the growing use of managed care (and specifically the risk-based variety) to deliver care for welfare populations reflects broader assumptions by policy-makers about this group—namely, that behavioral modification is justified in the name of improving and empowering them.[101] Moreover, the mandating of managed care enrollment is telling about the lack of political power of the recipient population: Medicare recipients continue to have discretion over whether or not they enroll in managed care, but a politically vulnerable group—the poor—does not have that ability.[102]

Similarly, in welfare policy, federal policy-makers removed restrictions on contracting out and encouraged states to embrace this practice and other market-oriented reforms. The welfare reform of 1996, which replaced the entitlement to Aid to Families with Dependent Children benefits with block grants to states, devolved authority over the program to state governments, allowed states to further devolve their responsibilities to local governments and private entities, and opened up contracting to large for-profit firms and religious organizations. Although state welfare programs had long paid private organizations to deliver specific services, such as child care or job training, now they could contract out program administration, giving greater discretion to local governments and allowing private entities, including for-profit firms, to administer much or all of the program. Wisconsin did just that, contracting out the administration of the Wisconsin Works welfare program to nonprofit, for-profit, and county agencies.[103]

Thus, non-state actors can now determine eligibility and impose sanctions on welfare recipients—a major change in the standards of public administration that had guided the program since the 1930s. Previously, the law required that the program be run uniformly across the state and that one state agency run the program or supervise the subunits that were doing so. Now, those standards have been removed at a time when the discretion assigned to front-line welfare administrators has increased.[104] Researchers studying program administration in Florida found wide variability in the imposition of sanctions, with sanctions more likely to be imposed in politically conservative regions, on African-American and Hispanic longer-term recipients, and in local programs run by for-profit firms.[105]

In contrast to Medicaid and public assistance, where beneficiaries—or their allies—are vocal and well-organized, these marketized versions of provision have made considerably less headway. School voucher programs, despite their popularity with conservative and religious movements, are limited to just a handful of locations, never having grown beyond the few publicly funded voucher experiments studied by academics and several private programs funded by conservative foundations.[106] Teachers' unions—well-organized and located in every Congressional district—recognized that their jobs were at stake and have successfully blocked such programs. Social Security privatization, despite a couple of decades of conservative policy development, and a committed push by President George W. Bush upon reelection in 2005, failed as well.[107] With both AARP (formerly the American Association of Retired Persons) and the majority of senior citizens opposing individual accounts, this reform proposal was a non-starter.[108]

Medicare: The Perilous Politics of Market Reform

Conservatives also faced considerable difficulties promoting market-oriented reform of Medicare, given its status as a highly popular social program for a constituency widely viewed as deserving. Convincing senior citizens that there should be changes in a program they generally liked was a formidable task, and ultimately the only way to achieve such reforms was to make sure that seniors got *more* benefits. Paying for these kinds of reforms, and for the burgeoning fee-for-service Medicare program more generally, also put limits what could be achieved. Ultimately, although conservatives would "talk Right," they would "legislate Left," implicitly accepting the regulatory approach championed by liberals as the most reliable, short-term way to wring savings out of the program.[109] Even so, they attempted to implant market principles and practices in the program, hoping that in the long run these might show the way toward a full-scale transformation of Medicare along competitive lines.

Throughout the 1970s, the question of cost control dominated debates over health care in general, and Medicare in particular.[110] Between 1970 and 1980, total Medicare spending went from $7 billion to over $35 billion, while the proportion of GDP devoted to health care went from 7.0 percent to 8.8 percent.[111] This did not, however, lead to a shoring up of the federal government's power over the program, as "[e]xpanded bureaucratic discretion and a stronger central administrative capacity to bargain with providers would not do."[112] Instead, the initial policy response was to continue delegating responsibilities for utilization review and cost control to private agents. Thus, the Social Security Amendments of 1972 created Professional Standards Review Organizations (PSROs)—local organizations dominated by physicians that would conduct utilization reviews for Medicare.[113] Another part of the law turned to a different private sector actor— the prepaid group practice, or HMO—as a potential agent of cost control. The 1972 Amendments changed the terms by which HMOs could participate in the program, as they had been doing in a very limited way since 1966.[114] This was followed by the 1973 HMO Act, which offered HMOs federal subsidies, created a federal certification process, and required that all firms with more than 25 employees already providing health insurance offer an HMO option, if one were available in the area.[115] Neither of these measures made much of an impact on the

Medicare program. PSROs were declared a failure by the end of the 1970s, as Medicare costs continued to escalate and the proportion of Medicare beneficiaries in HMOs remained miniscule.

The failure to contain medical inflation—or indeed, inflation more generally—helped erode confidence in the capacity of the federal government to effectively manage social and economic problems. Ironically, these failures in the Medicare program were often held up as proof of the incompetence of government, even though federal agencies had never been given any real capabilities for the effective management of the program, beyond making sure that claims were processed relatively quickly (which they generally were). Claims of government failure in the field of health care were self-fulfilling prophecies: because few believed that federal agencies would be capable of managing a complex social program, they were never given the power to do so. When programs such as Medicare then failed to live up to expectations or produced perverse results, its government managers were lambasted for their incompetence and were held up as examples of precisely what future attempts at health care reform should avoid.

Pro-competitive ideas offered, to a growing number of observers and politicians, a way out of the health care morass that was enveloping the American economy. The sweeping Reagan presidential victory of 1980 and Republican takeover of the Senate seemed to open the door to their influence. Reagan's director of OMB was David Stockman, a Republican congressman from Michigan who championed market-based reform of health care and Medicare,[116] and there were many others in Congress—including some Democrats who later played an important role in the centrist Democratic Leadership Council—who held similar views.[117] By the early 1980s, there were a number of legislative proposals for market-oriented health care reform, and the administration voiced support for converting Medicare into a system of vouchers that beneficiaries would use to purchase their own health insurance.[118] The Tax Equity and Fiscal Responsibility Act of 1982 represented one step toward introducing greater competition in Medicare, as it created "risk contracts"—a way of reimbursing HMOs for serving Medicare beneficiaries that put their profits at stake. Previously, HMOs had mostly been paid on a cost basis, which created few incentives for cost-savings or to even enter the program at all. Henceforth, HMOs could receive a fixed, monthly, capitated payment per beneficiary and then would have to bear risk for the provision of all required Medicare services, but could also make profits on the program.[119] This change, fully implemented in 1985, began drawing more HMOs into the program.

However, the Reagan administration disappointed advocates of pro-competitive health care reform for several reasons. First, at a time of large budget deficits in the mid-1980s, administration officials proposed an *expansion* of Medicare by extending the program to cover catastrophic costs. The legislation that ultimately passed in 1988—the Medicare Catastrophic Coverage Act—was considerably larger than that which the administration originally envisioned, but Reagan signed the law nonetheless. Following a backlash by senior citizens against funding the new coverage through higher taxes and premiums on them, the law was repealed.[120] Nonetheless, the episode revealed how willing a Republican administration could be to expand an already very large entitlement program for a well-regarded constituency.

Second, except for the HMO provision in Medicare, none of the legislative proposals for market-based reform of the health care system succeeded. Instead, Congress adopted, with the consent and even active participation of some in the Reagan administration, a system of de facto price controls in Medicare: the Prospective Payment System (PPS). The PPS abandoned the retrospective payment system in Medicare that had essentially said to providers, "Send us your bills, we'll pay them." Henceforth, the federal government would specify payment rates for hospital services in advance. The Bush Administration then not only accepted the extension of a similar method of payment to physicians in 1989—the resource-based relative value scale—but also called for a global cap on Medicare spending, which was enacted as the Volume Performance Standard. As economist Uwe Reinhardt wryly remarked, "It is no small irony that these ostensibly market-oriented administrations, when challenged by our entrepreneurial health system, so quickly and so willingly lapsed into pricing policies resembling the centrally administered price systems favored in the former Soviet bloc."[121]

It is clear why market-oriented reform of Medicare not only failed, but was not seriously attempted in the first place. The most pressing domestic issue facing policy-makers in the 1980s was how to contain the size of the deficit, and given the enormity of the Medicare program, controlling program costs was essential. Yet, pro-competitive reforms offered virtually no short-term savings. Faced with large and growing federal budget deficits in the 1980s, the administration and Congress set aside market-based reform ideas and instead tried to find ways of immediately tamping down Medicare spending, which is why they turned to the PPS.[122] In addition, although Reagan seemed to usher in a mandate for sweeping change in federal programs, there was little support for concrete reforms that would challenge cherished entitlements. The administration and some of its Republican allies in Congress discovered this fact to their dismay when they attempted to enact cuts in Social Security in the early 1980s.[123] Senior citizens liked Medicare, and the most that could be done along the lines of free market reform was to give them the *option* to join an HMO, if they so desired. Not very many did: the growth rate in HMO offerings and enrollment by the early 1990s was certainly rapid, but by 1995, only 9 percent of beneficiaries were in HMOs.[124]

Republicans were not the only ones looking for market-based solutions to the nation's rising health care costs. Many Democrats also began embracing delegated governance as a way of promoting social policy reform without significantly expanding the size of government. This was the essence of the Clinton health care initiative—the rise and fall of which has been amply discussed, so such an analysis will not be repeated here.[125] Of interest from the standpoint of delegated

governance is how the Clintons turned to these kinds of administrative arrangements as a way to square the circle—to achieve universal coverage and a broad-
based restructuring of the health care system *without* expanding the role of
government or raising taxes. This, they hoped, would enable them to respond to
the evident public support for health care reform, while also preserving Clinton's
image as a "New Democrat" who favored market solutions over traditional government ones.[126] That Americans appeared to favor reform but were also deeply
skeptical and distrustful of government at this time enhanced the arguments for
delegated governance as well. The decision to go this route reflected the culmina-
tion of a longer ideational and political trajectory in which liberal thinkers and
Democratic politicians increasingly turned to various forms of managed competition to reform the health care system. In this way, they hoped to achieve universal
coverage and cost control, while shielding themselves from attacks by conservatives and medical interest groups that they were expanding the role of government bureaucrats in the health care system.[127]

Thus, rather than embrace direct, federal governance of the program, the
Health Security Act proposed by the administration in the fall of 1993 largely
relied on private entities and state governments for administration. Private insurers—mainly HMOs—would do the work of negotiating with providers and
managing the utilization of medical care. New, nonprofit regional health alliances
would serve as group purchasers of insurance that would be involved in tasks such
as collecting premiums, supervising the marketing of insurance plans, and providing information to consumers about quality. State governments were charged
with creating and overseeing these alliances, determining how to risk-adjust premiums, and regulating the insurance plans. Finally, one new federal entity would
be created—the seven-member National Health Board—to oversee the entire
system and make sure that a global health spending cap was obeyed.

With this complex and interwoven array of public and private actors, the
Health Security Act had many characteristic features of the Rube Goldberg welfare
state. Many agreed that the plan was unwieldy and unduly complicated, making it
difficult for even the administration to explain to the public how the new system
would work. Moreover, the proposed administrative architecture appeared to a
number of critics to be seriously underdeveloped.[128] Much authority was delegated to actors whose actual capabilities in the health care field were suspect or
unknown. State governments, for instance, were given a host of new functions,
yet many of them had shown minimal aptitude for complex administrative tasks
in the past.[129] The Clinton administration also seemed to have given limited
thought to how the new regional health alliances would be run, leaving open questions of who would serve in these alliances, how they would make decisions, and
what would assure their accountability to the public.[130] Once again, policy-makers
had adopted the vending machine model of governance—the belief that if one
inserts money, a program simply pops out of the machine without one having to
give thought to how the program would actually be run.[131]

Ironically, however, one of the most damaging charges leveled against the plan was that it represented a massive expansion of "Big Government." Critics assailed the Health Security Act as a monumental increase in federal authority and power. As Representative Richard K. Armey (R-TX) wrote in the *Wall Street Journal* in 1993:

> . . . the Clinton health plan would create 59 new federal programs or bureaucracies, expand 20 others, impose 79 new federal mandates and make major changes in the tax code. . . . [T]he Clinton plan is a bureaucratic nightmare that will ultimately result in higher taxes, reduced efficiency, restricted choice, longer lines, and a much, much bigger federal government.[132]

These kinds of claims were mainstays of the attacks against the proposal. For instance, the famous Harry and Louise advertising campaign sponsored by the Health Insurance Association of America raised the specter of "Big Government," using terms in its ads such as "another billion dollar bureaucracy," "government monopoly," and "run by tens of thousands of bureaucrats" to highlight the negative consequences of government involvement in health care.[133]

Were these conservative and interest group critics ignorant about the hollow administrative nature of the proposal? Certainly, there were "Big Government" features of the plan, most notably the limit on national health spending that would have to be administered by government officials. The prospect of a global spending cap was particularly alarming to many free market thinkers who feared it would open the door to government-imposed rationing of care. In general, however, claims that the Clinton proposal represented the extension of "Big Government" into health care were overblown and reflected political calculations about how best to defeat the reform. Although polls showed that much of the public favored the general goal of reforming the health care system, many of these same individuals also nurtured a deep distrust of government.[134] In 1993, for instance, only 23 percent of the public expressed trust in government, and 65 percent agreed with the statement, "The federal government controls too much of our daily lives."[135] Painting the Health Security Act as a bureaucratic monstrosity could tap this rich vein of anti-government sentiment. Although these attacks were clearly not the only reason that the reform failed, they helped erode public confidence in the Clintons' reform proposal, and in the Clintons themselves. By the start of 1994, the Clinton health care reform was clearly in trouble, and was declared moribund by the fall of that year.

The GOP Tries Market-Based Reform

After the GOP successfully defeated the Clinton initiative and scored big in the mid-term elections of 1994, the ball was now in their court. Perhaps the public was responsive to the portrayal of the Clinton plan as unduly bureaucratic, but problems in the health care system remained there for Republicans to try to solve. They also faced large budget deficits, which meant that they had to deal with the big and rapidly growing health care programs, Medicare and Medicaid. In addition, in 1995, the Medicare Trustees announced in their annual report that in seven years, the Hospital Insurance trust fund would fall into deficit, creating a sense of urgency that something needed to be done about Medicare spending. How then to proceed?

Initially, the GOP believed it had a much bigger mandate than it in fact did for government-cutting reform. The 1994 mid-term election was interpreted by many Republicans as a referendum on the Clinton health care reform, one that they believed showed that the public was responsive to their message of small government and market-based reform of health care. The GOP leadership thus set out to enact this vision in 1995 by eliminating the entitlement to Medicaid and turning the program into a block grant, transforming Medicare along competitive lines, and significantly cutting spending on both programs.[136] The Medicare reform involved elements that had been swirling around conservative think tanks and opinion pages for some years, but that had also been embraced by a number of centrist thinkers and politicians. In "MedicarePlus" (called Medicare Choice in the Senate), a larger array of private plans would be allowed to participate in Medicare, and would compete with the fee-for-service program for beneficiaries. This was not unlike the "managed competition" idea that underlay the Clinton proposal of the previous year, and the administration's proposed Balanced Budget Act of 1995 expanded the choice of private plans but did not pit private plans against fee-for-service Medicare in a competition for beneficiaries.[137] After much lobbying by advocates, the House-crafted law also included Medical Savings Accounts as one option for beneficiaries— a tax-favored savings account that a beneficiary would use to pay many medical expenses, combined with a high-deductible MedicarePlus insurance plan.[138]

Why did the Republicans adopt a risky strategy of tackling a popular entitlement head-on? Much as the Clinton administration inaccurately gauged the size of their electoral mandate for reform, the Republicans similarly misread public opinion and the lessons of the 1994 mid-term elections. Although the public was responsive to criticism of the Clinton health reform as "Big Government in Your Health Care," this did not mean that the majority of the public favored significant cuts in, or changes to, Medicare. Once again, the two sides of public opinion sent conflicting signals about what the public wanted—a better health care system but a limited government role in managing it—yet Republicans read only one side of the coin. In addition, both Clinton and the Republicans failed to grasp public skepticism about health maintenance organizations—skepticism that would erupt in a full-blown revolt by the end of the 1990s, with the percentage of Americans saying HMOs do a "good job" the lowest of any industry asked about, save tobacco companies.[139]

The deeper cause of the disjuncture between elite behavior and mass belief was the steady process of political polarization that had driven the two political parties further apart, leading to an "incredible shrinking middle" in Congress.[140] This would precede, not follow, a similar polarization in mass opinion, although the public has not become as divided as the elite level political discourse might lead one to believe.[141] Many of the people most active in politics, however—campaign workers, party members, and politicians themselves—were moving further apart on the political spectrum. One consequence was more unvarnished ideological conflict over entitlement programs—breaking with the tacit bipartisan consensus on cost control that had dominated Medicare politics since at least the 1980s, for instance.[142] Sacred cows were attacked, third rails were touched, all in the belief that there was a supportive public out there that just needed to be led on these issues. As Gingrich confidently stated in 1995:

> Medicare transcends everything. . . . If we solve Medicare, I think we'll govern for a generation. If we don't solve Medicare, we're going to have a big fight next year. It's just that straightforward. We are really putting a lot of time in Medicare, but I think we're winning on it. . . . We said that it is legitimate to tell senior citizens that (the) Medicare trust fund is going broke, and that in fact we need to improve Medicare and preserve it—and we can do that by offering choices. That's beginning to be increasingly accepted, although people argue on the margins.[143]

Gingrich was wrong. Clinton's veto of the Balanced Budget Act of 1995 led to a government shutdown in which both sides hurled blame at the other, but the GOP was most damaged by the episode. The Republicans might have been able to see this coming earlier in 1995 when Democrats successfully affixed the "Grinch" label onto the GOP for its attempt to cut spending on the school lunch program.[144] Yet, Gingrich marched confidently into the fray around Medicare, becoming inextricably associated with the proposed reform. With an eye on polls showing seniors fearful of changes to Medicare, Democrats such as House Minority Leader Richard Gephardt declared that "the Republicans' massive mugging of Medicare means that seniors will have to pay more for health care out of their own pockets, eating into their Social Security checks and endangering their basic health and security."[145] Their cause was helped by various missteps on the part of Republicans, such as Senator Bob Dole announcing in a public forum that he had opposed Medicare from its inception in 1965, and Gingrich's remark that traditional Medicare, or at least the federal agency running it, should "wither on the vine."[146] Such statements provided easy fodder for Democrats. After President Clinton's veto of the 1995 BBA led to a government shutdown, Democrats repeatedly outmaneuvered Republicans.[147] By the start of 1996, the GOP's unified front had crumbled as they abandoned the BBA and instead acceded to a set of continuing resolutions that enabled the federal government to operate once again.

In the recriminations that followed, enthusiasm for the Republican Revolution waned and Gingrich ultimately lost control of the speakership in late 1998. Yet, this by no means signaled a complete failure of the GOP's attempt to institute market-based reform of Medicare. Instead, there were a number of ways in which the failed 1995 initiative laid the foundations for later changes in the program. First, through his skillful cultivation, or co-optation, of organized interests, Gingrich developed a political method for furthering free market reform that would be repeated later on. For all his public bluff and bluster, Gingrich could often be a savvy backroom operator who carefully plotted strategy about how best to achieve his goals. This was evident in his courting of organized interests—precisely the kind of allies the Republicans needed if they were going to build a coalition in support of major market-promoting reform.[148] Particularly important here were insurers, some of which stood to gain a lot of new business through a system of Medicare vouchers.[149] The Speaker cultivated other groups, such as physicians, who favored Medical Savings Accounts, malpractice reform, and other elements of the GOP health care reform agenda.[150] Gingrich even worked quietly to try to defang a potentially powerful opponent—the American Association of Retired Persons (AARP)—through repeated meetings with officials from the group and promises that the reform would allow trade associations like the AARP to create their own provider networks for their members. Such a provision could generate millions in profits for the organization.[151] For whatever reason, the AARP was fairly quiet about the 1995 BBA. As chapter 5 will show, these techniques for managing interest groups were later used to build a coalition for the 2003 Medicare Modernization Act.

A second legacy of the BBA was that many of its pieces were enacted in later legislation, reflecting both the supportive interest group environment for some of these reforms, and the fact that many Democrats supported them as long as some of the more radical elements were toned down. In the 1996 Health Insurance Portability and Accountability Act, Republicans successfully added a pilot program of Medical Savings Accounts. Then Congress passed, and Clinton signed, the Balanced Budget Act of 1997—a bill that had bipartisan support yet contained pieces of the 1995 Act, shorn of their more controversial elements. By now, Republicans had learned something about how difficult it would be to reform a large and complex program such as Medicare, and so they tread more cautiously.[152] They abandoned the idea of converting Medicare into a defined contribution program and instead sought to shore up the ability of seniors to voluntarily choose to enroll in a private insurance plan through a newly named Medicare+Choice option. The law allowed a larger array of plans to participate in the program, attempted to make private plans available to a wider geographic area, and made changes in the payment formula to these plans. Given the need for more immediate budgetary savings, the law also extended the prospective payment system to skilled nursing facilities and home health care. Thus, although the legislation did advance the goal of market-based reform in some ways, it also extended some of the "command-and-control" aspects of the program that many conservatives strongly opposed.[153]

The 1997 BBA also created the Bipartisan Commission on the Future of Medi-care—a third, important legacy of this entire period. The Commission failed to attain the two-thirds vote required to submit a reform proposal to Congress, but it did enable the Commission's co-chairs—House Republican Bill Thomas and Senate Democrat John Breaux—to develop and publicize the idea of converting Medicare along the lines of the premium support model. It is worth noting that a Kaiser Family Foundation survey in 1998 found that only 26 percent of respon-dents favored turning Medicare into defined-contribution program.[154] Nonethe-less, this formed the basis of many future GOP proposals for Medicare. A number of Democrats also embraced the model as a way to cope with the rising cost of Medicare in a market-friendly way.[155] Perhaps just as important, the deliberations over the future of Medicare were influenced by unexpected manna from heaven—budget surpluses and improved forecasts from the Trustees about the financial health of the program. This enabled a shift from austerity politics to expansionary politics, with the Clinton administration and other Democrats proposing to add a prescription drug benefit to Medicare.[156] As the next chapter will show, Clinton's action set off a competitive spiral, with both sides jockeying to show that they would do more for seniors through the Medicare program. That spiral actually started within the Medicare Commission, when Clinton administration appoin-tees raised the idea of a prescription drug benefit as a condition for them to sup-port large-scale change to the program.

The 1990s closed with intensified competition over entitlement programs such as Medicare. The Democrats had discovered that "Mediscare" politics could be good politics for them—enabling them to portray Republican policies as taking a cherished social program away from deserving grandparents.[157] Democrats instead proposed expanding the generosity of the program—adding a prescription drug benefit, for instance—and they then assailed the Republican majority in Congress for failing to address this important issue. Republicans and some centrist Demo-crats remained determined to enact market reforms to the program, yet were aware of the political obstacles to doing so. They had succeeded in shoring up the role of private plans in Medicare in the 1997 Balanced Budget Act—or so they thought. But as the new Medicare+Choice program failed to bring the changes they hoped, a number of Republicans began pondering new ways to further their reform objective. As chapter 5 will show, this pondering ultimately culminated in the 2003 Medicare Modernization Act.

Conclusion

As the free market movement became a major source of governing ideas for con-servative Republicans, they faced a quandary: How does an anti-government party actually govern once in power, given strong public support for much of the welfare state? Outright privatization was not an option and so contracting out or voucherizing programs allowed Republicans, and some "new Democrats," to address citizen demands for social protection without appearing to increase the size of government. And yet, delegation and marketization had an unsteady course. Vouchers and contracting were achieved most fully for programs with weak clienteles, such as Medicaid and public assistance. Attempts by Republicans in the mid-1990s to turn Medicare into a defined contribution program were rebuffed, although they succeeded in rejuvenating private insurance options outside traditional Medicare with the Medicare+Choice program. Some Democrats were attracted to delegated governance as well and for some of the same reasons. Wanting to distance themselves from the negative connotations associated with government bureaucracy, some Democrats also turned to vouchers and public-private partnerships as a way to respond to public needs.

Both parties thus sought to navigate the conflicting signals sent by public opinion through delegated governance, yet as the fiascos of the Clinton health care reform and government shutdown showed, politicians were treading upon treacherous political ground. Social policy reform could neither go too far down the path of budget cuts and privatization, nor could it threaten too direct a role for government in people's lives. This threading of the needle would become an acute challenge for Republicans when they found themselves in the next administration with unified control of government and a promise of prescription drug coverage for the elderly on their hands.

5

Crafting the Medicare Modernization
Act of 2003

On December 8, 2003, President George W. Bush signed into law the Medicare
Prescription Drug, Improvement, and Modernization Act of 2003 (MMA), creating a new prescription drug benefit for Medicare and enacting other important
changes in the program. He did so despite strong criticism of the measure by his
party's conservative base, fierce Democratic opposition, and a lack of enthusiasm
among the general public for the law as written. That Republicans would enact the
largest Medicare expansion in the history of the program is puzzling. Although a
few extensions of the American welfare state took place under Republican presi-
dents, such as the Social Security disability program and the Americans with Disability Act,[1] most major developments occurred during periods of Democratic
political control. Moreover, as chapter 4 detailed, since the 1990s many Republicans had favored fundamental reform of Medicare that would turn it into a system
of competing private plans. The MMA certainly augmented the influence of private actors in the program, but it failed to achieve the main objective of many
Republicans: the transformation of Medicare into a premium-support program in
which beneficiaries receive subsidies to choose their own insurance provider. The
MMA also flatly contradicted much of what Republicans had been saying for
decades about the need to pare back domestic spending programs. The last thing
one might have expected them to do was to add a new, universal entitlement for
senior citizens on the eve of the baby boomer generation's retirement.

Why did a Republican-dominated Congress pass the MMA, and why did the
legislation take the form it did? Republicans felt intense electoral pressure to address a widely perceived social problem—the lack of prescription drug coverage
in the Medicare program. The pressure was in part a consequence of the decision
by Republican leaders in the 1990s to abandon the party's tacit acceptance of the
basic principles underpinning federal entitlement policy. Instead, House Speaker
Newt Gingrich and others chose to tackle federal entitlements head-on, spurring
a fierce response by Democrats who espied a political opportunity to defend a
popular social program. *Expanding* Medicare to cover prescription drugs was

one answer to the program's problems, Democrats said—a more appealing message than one of cuts and privatization—and as the pressure on Republicans ratcheted up around this issue during elections, Republicans realized that they needed some kind of affirmative response. As the party in control of Congress and, after the 2000 election, the White House, many within the Republican Party felt they needed to show the electorate that they could address public concerns.

But how to do so without violating deeply held tenets about the need to cut the size of government and promote market-based solutions to social problems? Delegated governance offered the answer, enabling Republicans to expand a universal entitlement in a way that relied heavily on private market actors. By using insurance companies and other private firms to deliver the drug benefit in a competitive market environment, Republicans could put forth a market-based vision of how social entitlements should be governed that helped justify the expansion of government spending (although not all conservatives were convinced by these claims). Just as important, delegating governance enabled the Republicans to draw in the support of interest groups that helped them pass the legislation—insurance companies that stood to profit from providing drug benefits to seniors; pharmaceutical companies that preferred the dispersion of negotiating authority over drug prices across a wide array of private actors; and the AARP (formerly the American Association of Retired Persons), which saw in the Republican proposals an opportunity to lock in a new entitlement for senior citizens. Although none of these groups was the definitive force behind the legislation, they were all influential through their ability to help Republicans build a legislative coalition around the bill. Ultimately, the legislation resulted from a favorable confluence of programmatic, political, and interest group objectives, all of which pushed in the same direction—toward a system that delegated responsibility to private, risk-bearing agents competing in a social welfare marketplace.

A final, crucial point about the MMA is that it was largely a product of Congress. Certainly, President Bush's support for the new entitlement was vital, and the administration at times provided useful technical and political assistance. But the bill was fundamentally shaped by legislative politics, which meant that it had to satisfy a host of geographic, constituent, and interest group pressures, as well as ideological and electoral imperatives of the Congressional party leadership. The result was a set of programs that were Rube Goldbergesque in their structure and administration, adding further complexities to Medicare's already opaque administrative system and further blurring the boundaries between public and private authority in the American welfare state.

Delegated Governance in the MMA

The 2003 MMA is a large, complex piece of legislation that made the most significant changes to Medicare since its creation in 1965. The centerpiece of the law is Part D—a voluntary benefit that, effective since 2006, covers a portion of seniors' prescription drug costs. The benefit is provided entirely by private entities—insurance companies and pharmacy benefit managers (PBMs)—that receive subsidies from the federal government and monthly premiums from beneficiaries. These prescription drug plans (PDPs) must provide a basic package of benefits set by the federal government or the actuarial equivalent, and they must hew to federally defined formulary guidelines. Otherwise, they are free to define their benefits package and drug formulary as they wish. Seniors choose among these plans during a limited enrollment period, with the opportunity to change plans once a year. To help lower-income people cover the cost of the benefit, there are subsidies for people with incomes below a certain level or who are dually eligible for Medicaid and Medicare.[2] As of 2009, some 12.5 million beneficiaries were eligible for these low-income subsidies, with 9.6 million people actually receiving them.[3]

The MMA also shored up the role of private insurance companies in providing all Medicare benefits—Parts A, B, and now Part D. As chapter 4 discussed, since the 1980s the role of private companies—often HMOs—in delivering Medicare benefits had steadily increased. Following complaints that these plans were paid more than the cost of covering beneficiaries in the fee-for-service program, the 1997 Balanced Budget Act altered the reimbursement formula in a way that cut payments to many plans. This led to a precipitous drop in private-plan participation in the program. The 2003 MMA sought to reverse this trend and included measures to augment the number and range of private plans participating in the program. The law changed the reimbursement system in a way that effectively increased the subsidies that private plans—now renamed Medicare Advantage—receive. It also created a regional Preferred Payment Organization (PPO) option for beneficiaries—plans that covered beneficiary costs both within and outside approved networks of physicians. Finally, the MMA created a $10 billion stabilization fund that, if needed, could be used to assure adequate development of Medicare Advantage in the program.

With its heavy reliance on private insurers to deliver Medicare benefits, the MMA is a paradigmatic example of marketized, delegated governance. As chapter 3 showed, private entities had always been deeply involved in administering Medicare benefits, but they had done so as non-risk-bearing government contractors. These contractors were barred from making a profit on the program, and if spending on benefits exceeded expectations, the federal government would pay the price. Only in the HMO risk contracts, which paid plans on a capitated basis, were plans at risk for the cost of the care they covered. In the new prescription drug benefit, the private entities delivering the benefits bear risk. For instance, PDPs have no guaranteed place in the program but have to compete with other PDPs for the business of beneficiaries. If a PDP puts together an alluring package that does not cost too much money, it stands to profit, while less successful plans could lose money and decide to exit the program entirely.

Certainly, there are plenty of cushions in the government subsidies assured these plans: PDPs receive a subsidy worth, on average, 74.5 percent of the cost of providing standard coverage. The subsidy consists of both a direct, capitated payment and a reinsurance payment equal to 80 percent of plan spending above the catastrophic threshold. PDPs also live within a set of "risk corridors" that limit both plan losses and profits, but that widened in 2008 so that plans would bear more risk. In 2012, the Secretary of Health and Human Services (HHS) is authorized to further widen these corridors if desired.[4] Medicare Advantage plans also have a cushion against risk, as they receive government payments that exceed that which is spent on similar beneficiaries in traditional Medicare. As of 2009, per enrollee payments were estimated to be 114 percent of spending on beneficiaries in fee-for-service Medicare (the 2010 health care reform reduces those outsized subsidies over time, although insurers can earn bonuses for quality, and they still share risk in receiving capitated payments).[5] Because of these mechanisms, it is more accurate to say that the private plans *share* risk with the federal government rather than entirely bearing it themselves. Still, a central idea shaping the design of the legislation was that PDPs and MA plans should have something at stake so that they would have incentives to keep costs down and offer good coverage.

Following the ideas of the consumer choice model discussed in chapter 4, the new system also shifts risk onto beneficiaries. In the fee-for-service Medicare program (Parts A and B), benefits are essentially uniform across the country, although there are some regional variations in coverage due to differences in the coverage policy of individual contractors. Beneficiaries have long been able to choose an alternative—Part C plans in which the package of benefits varied—but this is optional and the majority of beneficiaries have not participated in it. Now, for the first time, beneficiaries must choose among competing private entities in order to receive some of their benefits. The MMA also included another favorite of consumer choice advocates, Health Savings Accounts (HSAs), tax-favored savings accounts, which, coupled with a high-deductible insurance plan, are used to pay medical expenses (see chapter four). The 1996 Health Insurance Portability and Accountability Act (HIPAA) had created a precursor to the HSA, Medical Savings Accounts, but limited who could enroll in them and the total number available (750,000). The 1997 BBA then created the possibility of Medicare+Choice MSAs as a private plan option available to beneficiaries, but again limited the number available and allowed this only as a demonstration project. The 2003 law created HSAs, which are now a permanent feature of the tax code and do not have restrictions on enrollment.[6]

In short, the MMA shifted the locus of decision-making and risk from the government to private firms and individuals, and this was one reason that the reform was controversial. Democratic proposals often relied on PBMs to be the main agents delivering the benefit, for reasons that will be discussed in more detail below, but opposed their bearing risk. PBMs were to act much like the existing government contractors did: delivering a benefit that was defined by federal officials and for which the government bore risk. The various Republican proposals instead aimed to create a social welfare marketplace of competing drug insurance and Medicare Advantage plans.

There were other components of the MMA that aroused controversy. One was the "doughnut hole"—the gap in coverage during which beneficiaries have to pay all of their drug costs. The law specified a standard drug benefit in which a beneficiary's prescription drug costs are covered up to a certain threshold—$2,250 in 2006—beyond which an individual has to pay his or her costs until a maximum ($5,100) is reached. That means a person is liable for up to $3,600 in out-of-pocket spending before catastrophic coverage kicks in (the 2010 health care reform reduces what beneficiaries have to pay out of pocket in the coverage gap from 100 percent to 25 percent by 2020). Because PDPs and Medicare Advantage plans design their own benefit package, the exact size and nature of the doughnut hole varies, and some offer a degree of "gap" coverage. However, as of 2010, 80 percent of stand-alone prescription drug plans offered no gap coverage and the remainder offered some coverage of generics. Forty-eight percent of Medicare Advantage plans had no gap coverage.[7]

Another controversial feature of the law was its "non-interference" clause, which barred the federal government from negotiating with pharmaceutical companies over the price of drugs. Much like the original Medicare program, which used private insurers as intermediaries between the federal government and providers, the 2003 MMA created a mediating layer of PDPs and MA plans between the government and the pharmaceutical industry. And, in another parallel with the 1965 Medicare law, which included in its first section a "Prohibition Against Any Federal Interference" in the practice of medicine, the 2003 law stated that:

> . . . the Secretary—(1) may not interfere with the negotiations between drug manufacturers and pharmacies and PDP sponsors; and (2) may not require a particular formulary or institute a price structure for the reimbursement of covered Part D drugs.

This provision generated much political acrimony, with Democrats arguing that the non-interference clause prevented the federal government from using its bargaining leverage to wrest lower prices out of the pharmaceutical industry, savings that could be used to provide a more generous benefit.

A third, controversial aspect of the 2003 MMA was that it instituted a number of income-tested features in Medicare. As noted above, low-income people were subsidized in the new benefit. In part, this was done because people dually eligible for both Medicaid and Medicare who often had drug coverage through Medicaid would now have their prescription drug costs covered through Medicare, itself a controversial decision because it subjected dual eligibles to the cost-sharing requirement of the benefit (e.g., premiums, co-pays, and the doughnut hole). As some critics argued, these low-income subsidies eroded the principle of universalism that underpinned the Medicare program. Even more contested was the fact that, for the first time, the Part B premium would be income tested. Effective in 2007, individuals with a modified adjusted gross income of $80,000 ($160,000 for couples) pay a higher monthly Part B premium, with the amount rising on a sliding scale as income increases above that threshold. This affects only a small number of people—5 percent, according to CMS[8]—but impacts their premiums quite significantly. In 2010, the monthly premium for Medicare Part B is $96.40 for most, but can be as high as $353.60 for those in the highest income category.[9] Critics worried that this would erode cross-class solidarity in the program, inducing higher income people to exit the voluntary Part B program and find other forms of coverage.[10]

Finally, there were some other important changes brought by the MMA that aroused less commentary. Of interest from the standpoint of delegated governance was a major reform in the way that CMS contracts with fiscal intermediaries and carriers in Parts A and B. These entities had had an unusual relationship with the federal government, one that was marked by a lack of competition—given that contracts generally were automatically renewed—and often informal relations with HCFA/CMS. The reform sought to institute greater competition between plans for contracts and required that they be subject to the formal rules governing relationships with other contractors (e.g., the Federal Acquisition Regulation). The division between intermediaries and carriers was abolished and a new entity was created—the Medicare Administrative Contractor (MAC) that processes both Part A and Part B claims. Non-insurance organizations are now allowed to compete for contracts and CMS has greater authority to terminate contracts with poor performers. Overall, the goal was to modernize the contracting relationship, moving away from the special relationship that had been created between federal administrators and private intermediaries in the original Medicare legislation.

The Political Context: Polarization, Electoral Competition, and Partisan Conflict

Making sense of the 2003 Medicare Modernization Act requires an understanding of the political and institutional context within which it was forged. As chapter 4 noted, by the 1990s American politics was highly polarized, with an ever-widening gap between the political parties and an "incredible shrinking middle" of moderate Democrats and Republicans in Congress.[11] The phenomenon reflected deeper forces at work in American politics. Since at least the 1970s, the two political parties had become steadily more socioeconomically homogeneous, as the constituency supporting the Republican Party generally became affluent, and voters for the Democratic Party less so.[12] This sharpened the stances that politicians take on redistributive questions, generating increased political conflict on issues such as taxation, social entitlements, and the size of government.[13] These trends were fueled by growing socioeconomic inequality in American society since the 1970s.[14]

Polarization also changed the way in which Congress operated. With less common ground over legislation, and more to be gained by scoring political points against one's opponents, gridlock became more common as political polarization intensified.[15] At the same time, however, polarization contributed to a strengthening of the political parties in Congress, empowering them to become, at times, more capable agents of change.[16] This came about as the political parties became more ideologically uniform and the stakes of electoral conflict increased.[17] Members of Congress not only needed to bring home the bacon to their districts, but increasingly they wanted to hold up a coherent legislative agenda that they were working to enact. To achieve this, they needed leadership, which led the members to delegate more authority and power to the leadership of the Congressional parties.[18] Whereas the Congressional parties were once viewed as fairly toothless organizations, now they became fighting machines, with aggressive, strategically minded leaders who sought legislative results. This climate contributed to the decline in bipartisan cooperation but could also mean more unified partisan action on legislation that offered opportunities for credit claiming.[19] Even so, the degree of party discipline still remained lower than what one commonly sees in European parliamentary systems, and the margins of party control were slim. Forging a legislative majority was still challenging, as the tortuous path of the MMA would show.

The MMA and its prescription drug benefit emerged in the late 1990s out of this context of partisan polarization, which generated fierce electoral competition around old-age entitlements. Prior to the mid-1990s, Medicare politics had been characterized by relative agreement between Democrats and Republicans about the basic contours of the program. Certainly, there had long been proposals for either an expansion of program benefits or market-based reform, but neither was possible in a climate of budgetary austerity. Fiscal constraints thus created a broad consensus about the need to restrain Medicare costs, preventing much partisan jousting over the program.[20] No Democrat made improving the coverage of Medicare a major campaign priority,[21] and Medicare decision-making largely took place behind closed doors—well away from the electoral limelight.[22] Within this negative consensus on fiscal restraint, policy change took place at a fairly incremental pace.[23]

All of this changed in the mid-1990s when, as was discussed in chapter 4, Republicans broke with the tacit bipartisan consensus on the basic principles underlying the Medicare program.[24] Instead, under the leadership of Speaker Newt Gingrich, the GOP took on Medicare, attempting to transform the program along market-based lines while making major spending cuts. To achieve their goals, Congressional Republicans adopted a strategy of full political mobilization. Rejecting the incrementalism and consensus-building style of Medicare politics in the past, Republican leaders treated reform of the Medicare program like a military campaign, one that required the marshalling of both public opinion and interest group support.[25]

What conservative leaders failed to anticipate was that re-injecting partisan politics into the Medicare program would provoke a fierce Democratic response, unleashing competition over who could best assure the future of Medicare and gain one of the biggest electoral prizes—senior citizen voters. In response to Republican calls for spending cuts and more market competition in Medicare, Democrats countered with a politically appealing message about the need to shore up the program and expand its benefits. Moreover, the emergence of the first federal budget surplus since 1969 meant that policy-makers could promise seniors new benefits without having to find ways to pay for them. President Clinton and Congressional Democrats began proposing new program spending, but it was the idea of adding a prescription drug benefit that took off like wildfire.

There were a number of reasons that a new drug benefit resonated with both political elites and mass opinion. When Medicare was created in 1965, prescription drugs were a relatively marginal expense that policy-makers believed did not need to be included in the program. By the 1990s, many agreed that Medicare's lack of prescription drug coverage was an illogical gap in coverage that deprived some people of needed drugs or threatened their financial well-being. Particularly in the 1990s, there were significant increases in prescription drug spending as both the number of prescriptions rose and drug prices increased.[26] The average number of prescriptions and refills per elderly person climbed from 19.6 in 1992 to 28.5 per year in 2000, according to Families USA.[27] A June 2000 study by a pharmacy benefit manager, Express Scripts, found that prescription drug spending increased 17 percent in 1999, with the elderly facing the largest increases. As of 1999, 80 percent of Medicare beneficiaries regularly took prescription drugs, but a third had no coverage to help pay the costs of their drugs.[28]

Adding to the intensity of perceived need was the development of direct-to-consumer (DTC) advertising following a loosening of FDA restrictions on this practice in 1997. Previously, DTC was allowed only if a medical condition was discussed without a brand name or if a brand was mentioned without the medical condition and the ad urged consumers to see their doctors regarding the brand. Once the rules changed in 1997, the amount of money that pharmaceutical companies spent on these ads exploded and intensified the demand for many of the blockbuster drugs coming onto the market. One study found that DTC advertising was responsible for 12 percent of the increase in prescription drug spending between 1999 and 2000,[29] while other research, reported by the General Accounting Office (GAO), found that in a sample of 64 drugs, there was an average increase in sales of $2.20 for every $1 spent on DTC ads.[30] With the public's appetite whetted for these elixirs of health and well-being, attention then turned to the cost of these much-marketed products.

Many seniors had some kind of drug coverage: about 12 million Medicare beneficiaries were covered through former employers, 4 million through Medicaid, and just over half a million through privately purchased Medigap plans.[31] Yet, the proportion of large employers (200 or more employees) offering retiree health benefits fell throughout this period, from 66 percent in 1988 to 36 percent in 2004.[32] Among the dwindling number that still offered retiree health benefits, many were cutting back on drug benefits or increasing co-payments. The price of Medigap premiums also was rising, and Medigap plans with drug coverage were so expensive that only a small proportion of beneficiaries purchased these plans. In 1995, only 9 percent of seniors who had some coverage for their pharmaceutical costs got it through privately purchased Medigap policies.[33]

Efforts to get senior citizens to join Medicare HMOs with prescription drug coverage also had largely failed. Although the 1997 Balanced Budget Act (BBA) aimed to encourage seniors to join HMOs, by 1998, many insurance plans were pulling out of many markets or cutting back on benefits for elderly retirees, especially drug coverage.[34] Indeed, 1999 was the peak year for Medicare beneficiary enrollment in HMOs, at 6.7 million, a figure that dropped each year through 2003. The plans complained that their federal payments, set by the BBA at 95 percent of the average amount spent for traditional Medicare beneficiaries, were too low to sustain benefits at the current levels.[35] By 2000, no HMOs were offering free drug coverage.[36]

In these problems, Democrats spied an opportunity to put forth their vision of Medicare, yet a triggering event was needed to transform these objective conditions into a problem requiring, in the public's eyes, government action.[37] The spark came from President Clinton's January 1999 State of the Union speech, in which he proposed using part of the projected budget surpluses over the next 10 years to bolster the Medicare program's trust fund and add a new drug benefit. As chapter 4 noted, Clinton apparently chose this moment to unveil these ideas in an effort to preempt the report of the Bipartisan Commission on the Future of Medicare. As Congress was supposed to vote on whatever proposal they put forth, Clinton sought to influence the course of these debates in a Democratic direction. Later, in June, Clinton unveiled the specifics of his plan, which aimed to offer first dollar coverage to all seniors and then some assistance with catastrophic drug costs, but not full coverage for them.[38] The goal of the plan was to provide drug coverage for less than what comparable Medigap policies cost and to make the coverage as attractive as possible since it would be voluntary.[39]

This agenda-setting moment had two crucial effects. First, there was increased media attention to declining employer-sponsored and Medicare HMO coverage of prescription drugs, which gave credence to Clinton administration claims that while two-thirds of seniors might have drug coverage of some sort, it was imperiled.[40] Second, public attention was now focused on the issue. Before Clinton's announcement, there was no apparent groundswell of public opinion in favor of expanding coverage. In Kaiser Family Foundation surveys asking Americans what they thought was the "most important problem in health or health care for the government to address," concerns about the costs of health care and insurance and the lack of coverage for the uninsured dominated the polls in 1997 and 1998; neither the price of prescriptions in general nor need for prescription coverage

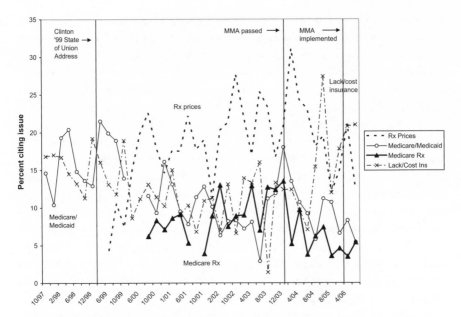

Figure 5.1 Most Important Health Problem 1997–2006, 65+. Source: Author calculations from Kaiser Family Foundation Health Poll Report Surveys.

for the elderly appeared in these polls at all. Indeed, other Kaiser Family Foundation polls showed that, when prompted, seniors favored adding a prescription
drug benefit to Medicare, but few volunteered prescription drug coverage as a
priority when asked about major policy issues. After Clinton's speech, concerns
about the prices of prescription drugs and the need for senior coverage began
appearing in the most-important-health-problem surveys, as Figure 5.1 shows
for senior citizens.[41]

Once the possibility of a prescription drug benefit for seniors was raised, lawmakers could not stuff the cat back into the bag. While drug coverage had been
mentioned before—most recently in the Clinton health care reform effort of
1993–1994—many Democratic lawmakers were "stunned at the power of the
issue."[42] Moreover, desire for drug coverage spread well beyond the target population. A September 2000 *New York Times/CBS News* Poll found that 65 percent of
respondents overall—and 71 percent of women—said that lowering the costs of
prescription drugs for the elderly mattered to them "a lot."[43]

Program Design: The Turn to Delegated Governance

In 2000, Congressional Republicans made consequential decisions about how to
structure the new drug benefit, and so exploring those decisions helps get at a core
question: Why have policy-makers repeatedly turned to delegated governance as a

way to administer social programs? As in the creation of Medicare in 1965, delegating program administration to private actors was a way to create a popular social program without seeming to expand the size of the federal government. This was vital if Republicans—now in control of government—were to reconcile two conflicting goals: first, their electoral objectives—to satisfy public demand for a new program and thus undercut bruising Democratic attacks; and second, their programmatic aims—to advance the role of consumer choice and competing, private firms in the Medicare program. It also was essential given the Congressional context within which the reform was hatched and would have to be passed. The Republican leadership needed to hold together a fragile coalition as they guided the legislation through the treacherous legislative process in both chambers. As key industries stood to benefit from the delegated structure of the benefit, the Congressional leadership could call upon these interest group allies to help persuade Republicans skeptical about creating a new Medicare entitlement. This enabled these groups to have influence over the reform, ensuring that it was done on terms largely favorable to the pharmaceutical and insurance industries, in particular.

The Political Momentum for a Drug Benefit

The growing political momentum behind the prescription drug issue created dilemmas for the Republican Party. Electoral pressures pushed in the direction of a popular new entitlement, as senior citizens are an important voting bloc that is in play for both parties. Because an older cohort of senior citizens—socialized to politics during the New Deal—was increasingly replaced by a younger group socialized under Eisenhower and in the work force during the Reagan era, traditional Democratic dominance of the senior vote was replaced by party competition.[44] This shift is apparent in Congressional elections, with exit polls showing the 60+ vote shifting from Democratic in 1980 through 1992 (except 1984) to Republican in the House races of 1994, 1996, and 1998.[45] House members, in particular, are often attentive to the demands of senior citizens because they face elections every two years. By 2000, the Republican leadership was hearing reports from their members that they were getting beat up by Democrats on the prescription drug issue.

Yet, adding an expensive new entitlement to an already burgeoning social program ran counter to the beliefs of many within the party. Some strongly opposed creating a new universal entitlement, particularly because many seniors already had some form of drug coverage through their former employers and other sources. A generous public benefit could crowd out these existing sources of coverage, replacing private insurance with public insurance. In this view, the government should focus its energies on low-income beneficiaries, perhaps through block grants to state governments for their means-tested pharmacy assistance programs. Others thought that a universal drug benefit could be a sweetener for a wider reform of the program along the lines recommended by the National

Bipartisan Commission on the Future of Medicare (discussed in chapter 4).[46] The Commission favored a premium support model for Medicare so that rather than have the government serve as the health insurance agent of senior citizens, beneficiaries would henceforth choose between competing private plans and have their premiums subsidized by the federal government. The prescription drug benefit would help overcome what some seniors might perceive as threatening—tinkering with the popular Medicare program. Yet, the prospects for turning Medicare into a system of competing HMOs faded with the growing popular backlash against managed care in the late 1990s, and market-based reform of Medicare was unlikely to rally much support. As one Congressional staffer put it, there was a political realization that seniors were unlikely to respond to the message that "we're going to give you more competition."[47] What they really wanted was an additional benefit, but keeping that harnessed to a major transformation of the program would likely doom them both.

Faced with these conflicting imperatives, the initial response of Congressional Republicans toward the prescription drug issue was ambivalence and hedging. Republicans reacted cautiously to Clinton's initial proposal for a drug benefit and when the Congressional Budget Office declared that the Clinton plan would cost 42 percent more than first estimated—$168 billion over ten years rather than $118 billion—Republicans seized the opportunity to promote a more limited Medicare drug benefit.[48] Legislative efforts largely stalled in 1999, and in his 2000 State of the Union address, Clinton reiterated his call for a new prescription drug benefit, albeit one that would now cost $160 billion over ten years. Republicans continued to criticize the president's plan, especially its universal coverage, which they thought unnecessarily expensive and inefficient.

However, the GOP's tardiness in coming up with an alternative became increasingly problematic during the 2000 election season. Many Democrats were starting to make the drug benefit a central issue in House and Senate campaigns, with some taking busloads of senior citizens to Mexico and Canada to highlight the fact that prescription drugs could be purchased far more cheaply across the border. These actions garnered much media attention and were reinforced by political ads making the same claims.[49] In fact, Medicare became the third most prominent theme in Congressional campaign ads (Figure 5.2), and Democrats outnumbered Republicans significantly in these mentions: nearly 60 percent of Congressional ads that mentioned Medicare were run by Democrats, compared to just under 40 percent run by Republicans.[50] Clearly, Democrats were on the attack, taking advantage of both the popularity of Medicare and the public's antipathy toward the pharmaceutical industry.

Republicans did not fail to observe these developments. As Senator Bill Frist said in early 2000, "The prescription drug issue is so hot politically. That's all you're going to hear about in the Congressional elections."[51] This led many to argue that the Republicans had to act to "take a huge entitlement program off the table" so that Democrats could no longer use it against them.[52] "They've put us in

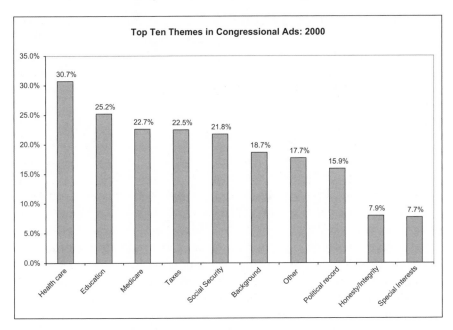

Figure 5.2 Top Ten Themes in Congressional Ads, 2000. Source: Wisconsin Advertising Project. The data are the percent of House and Senate campaign ads mentioning these issues.

the corner of defending large prescription drug companies at the expense of granny," said Scott Reed, a GOP strategist who headed up the Republican Leadership Coalition.[53] Republican pollster Glen Bolger, who advised the Congressional leadership on health care and other issues, similarly said that the GOP needed to pass some kind of legislation on health despite a likely Clinton veto.[54] In a June 2000 meeting with the House Republican Conference, Bolger showed Republicans poll results that only 20 percent of Americans thought Republicans would do a better job "helping elderly Americans get access to affordable prescription drugs," whereas 53 percent believed Democrats would do a better job. Focus groups done by the RNC showed similarly grim results, as people said, "Republicans aren't doing anything for seniors."[55] As Deborah Steelman, a health care lobbyist and strategist for the GOP warned, "We can win if we have a voice, if we visit the seniors [sic] centers, if we 'do' this issue. . . . But you cannot be a majority party unless you talk about issues that the majority of people care about."[56]

Faced with the need to reconcile electoral imperatives with the programmatic beliefs of many in the party, Republican House Speaker Dennis Hastert took the initiative in forging a prescription drug plan that could pass the House in time for the 2000 election campaign. This meant devising a plan that sufficiently satisfied conservative demands for more fundamental reform of Medicare—and thus could muster enough Republican votes in the House—but that also promised a good enough drug benefit to inoculate Republican candidates against Democratic attacks during the election. Hastert appointed a working group to develop a Republican plan that included the leaders of the two committees with jurisdiction over Medicare: Ways and Means (Chairman Bill Thomas of California) and Energy and Commerce (Chairman Thomas Bliley of Virginia).

In the spring of 2000, they set forth the main lines of the GOP policy approach that would ultimately be enacted as the MMA. A crucial decision was to create a universal benefit, rejecting the idea of block grants to state pharmacy-assistance programs or some other kind of means-tested relief to low-income seniors. Instead, the new benefit would be available to all, although it was voluntary. Notable about the proposed benefit was that it provided both catastrophic coverage of high costs but also "first dollar coverage" (after a $250 deductible) in order to provide immediate benefits to the largest number of people. Yet, because Republicans were only willing to spend so much on a benefit—spending too much risked antagonizing fiscal conservatives—the benefit had to have some kind of coverage gap. In this initial iteration of the legislation, the benefit would cover 50 percent of drug costs up to $2,100, followed by what some wryly called a "coverage holiday" until total drug costs reached $7,050 (with $6,000 having been paid out of pocket by the beneficiary). Catastrophic coverage would then kick in. In these self-imposed fiscal constraints, then, the doughnut hole was born.

The proposal also did not require people to join an HMO or other Part C plan to receive their drug benefits, as some Republicans and centrist Democrats favored, and abandoned the stance of many Republicans that a new universal entitlement had to be tied to a larger, structural reform of Medicare. Instead, the proposal injected market forces into Medicare through its reliance upon private firms to deliver the new benefit. Plans had to offer either the legislatively defined benefits package or its actuarial equivalent, and they received subsidies to help cover high-cost beneficiaries. In short, Republicans delegated the governance of the drug benefit to competing private firms, subsidizing their efforts and regulating their activities but relying upon them to provide the new benefit.

The plans put forth by the Clinton administration and most Congressional Democrats also depended upon proprietary firms but assigned responsibility for administering the new benefit to PBMs—private entities such as Medco or Express Scripts that often administer prescription drug benefits for employers and other insurance carriers. The government would contract with one or two PBMs in each region of the country that would in turn determine the structure of their formularies and pay beneficiaries' costs. The reason for delegating the administration of the benefit to private firms was that, much like the liberal planners who developed Medicare in the 1960s, Democrats were leery of provoking a powerful medical interest group—in this case, the pharmaceutical industry. By creating an intermediary layer of private organizations, indeed a set of organizations with which pharmaceutical companies already worked, they sought to fend off assertions that the government would be directly involved in negotiations over the price of drugs or structure of formularies. In addition, as with the fiscal intermediaries and carriers created in 1965 to administer Medicare benefits, the PBMs would not be risk-bearing entities. After successfully winning a bid to be the provider in a region, they would be paid a regular sum from the government to provide the benefit and would have few incentives to aggressively manage drug utilization (e.g. encouraging use of generics) or to push for big discounts from drug companies, because this would add little to their bottom line. If a beneficiary's drug costs went up dramatically, that would be a risk the government would bear, not the PBM. However, the hope was that, by pooling seniors' bargaining power into one or two regional PBMs, these entities would be able to negotiate bigger price discounts from pharmaceutical companies.

This is where the Republican approach was different, as Republicans wanted to do more than contract with private actors to deliver the benefit. They wanted to harness market forces because they believed this would promote efficiency and better performance. Although the Republican approach also used private entities to deliver the benefit, they allowed an indefinite number of them to come into the market and compete for beneficiary business. And Republicans wanted these firms to bear risk: if beneficiary drug costs spiked, they risked losing money, but they would also gain if they found ways to successfully limit drug utilization or prices. Advocates of this approach believed that these risk-bearing insurance entities—which would include PBMs but also health insurance companies that were more accustomed to bearing risk—would have incentives to bargain down prices with pharmaceutical companies and encourage substitution of cheaper drugs.[57] The resulting efficiencies would lower overall costs and potentially reduce premiums for beneficiaries. The role of the government was to make sure that these plans stayed within certain regulatory boundaries (which would be more loosely drawn than what many Democrats envisioned) and subsidize coverage for high-cost beneficiaries. Publicly subsidizing these high-cost people would, it was hoped, make it profitable for firms to offer affordable coverage available to a larger number of beneficiaries.

The intellectual foundations of this approach had been developed by market-reform advocates who argued that only entities with their profits at stake could discipline powerful health care interests. As chapter 4 discussed, this was an important part of the conservative case against government-sponsored health insurance. Believing government agencies to be frequently inept and captured by the private interests they are supposed to regulate, conservatives argued for market competition that put a firm's survival and profitability at stake. These actors would then make the hard decisions about the allocation of scarce health care resources, all while avoiding politicized fights in Congress. Thus, in the case of the drug benefit, advocates argued that HCFA/CMS lacked the capability to negotiate effectively over formularies and reimbursements, would set prices badly, and would be constantly under the gun from members of Congress acting at the whim of pharmaceutical lobbyists.[58] Many assailed what they believed were the failings of Medicare's prospective payment systems for providers, arguing that the system was unduly complex, ineffective in dealing with changes in technology and medical practice, and thus often set prices at the wrong level, creating distortions and inefficiencies. Allowing the federal government to determine how to pay for prescription drugs would only replicate this flawed system.[59]

These views took shape in earlier attempts at Medicare reform. The risk-bearing, private drug plan was a direct intellectual offshoot of a long-standing idea among conservatives and centrist Democrats to convert Medicare into a system of competing private plans. The outlines of this approach can be found in the 1995 Balanced Budget Act, which created a new MedicarePlus program that aimed to increase private plan choices for beneficiaries and augment the degree of competition between them. The 1995 BBA gave these plans greater flexibility in the kinds of benefits they offered and what they could charge beneficiaries for them. It also instituted a system of competitive bidding that delinked payments for private plans from the FFS program (which had always been used as the basis for determining private plan payments).[60] After the law was vetoed by President Clinton, some of these ideas resurfaced in modified form in the 1997 Balanced Budget Act, which aimed to shore up the Part C program of private plans.

However, declining Medicare HMO enrollment following the 1997 BBA, and public backlash against managed care, made it increasingly unlikely that Medicare could be transformed into a system of competing private plans. Instead, these ideas were re-channeled into the concept of the stand-alone prescription drug plan that would compete for beneficiaries. The single most influential bearer of this idea during the prescription drug debates was Ways and Means Chairman Bill Thomas (R-CA), one of the main architects of the MMA, who had chaired the Bipartisan Commission on the Future of Medicare and was a strong advocate of the premium support model. In 1999, he weighed two different approaches—that of providing assistance only to low-income seniors versus a universal but privately delivered benefit—and finally came out in favor of the latter if done through risk-bearing plans.

Beliefs about the greater efficacy of market-based provision of health insurance also shaped the development of the Medicare Modernization Act in other ways. One especially consequential moment in the life of the legislation was the determination by the Congressional Budget Office that the use of risk-bearing plans would save more money than would having the government bear risk, either through direct administration of the program or by employing one PBM per region.[61] The logic that underpinned this determination was outlined in a 2002 CBO publication and is based upon no studies or quantitative evidence—probably there were none, given the novelty of the issue—but instead appears to reflect a set of judgments about the ability of the federal government, or a single PBM, to negotiate lower drug prices when compared to risk-bearing insurance plans. The latter have their profits at stake and thus are more likely to be aggressive in their negotiations. Leaving these negotiations up to a single, non-risk-bearing PBM, by contrast, was seen as unlikely to produce the same kinds of savings, both because of the lack of profit incentives, but also because of the likelihood of political inference by government officials to protect the interests of the pharmaceutical industry. As the CBO document states:

> Having a single PBM administer the Medicare drug benefit in each region, as some proposals envision, could pose problems for the use of formularies. If each PBM established its own formulary, enrollees in the Medicare drug program would have to pay different prices for the same drug solely on the basis of where they live. Those differences might not prove acceptable politically. Conversely, if Medicare adopted a nationwide formulary, that formulary would probably not be very restrictive, because nationwide exclusion from the Medicare market could threaten the profitability—and even the survival—of some drug manufacturers.[62]

Tough bargaining—which involved threatening to exclude certain drugs from the formulary or reimbursing them at less favorable rates—could thus be better achieved by private entities competing for beneficiaries on the basis of premiums.

This determination proved important because it shaped the CBO's unfavorable scoring of various Democratic proposals. While the House GOP's plan was assigned a "cost-management factor" of 30 percent—meaning that it was expected to reduce spending on drugs 30 percent below that which it would be in a non-managed setting—the Clinton administration proposal's cost management factor was only 10 percent. This meant that, given the limited budgetary resources available, a program designed around competing, risk-bearing plans would come out ahead, leaving more resources to be spent on making the benefit more generous or providing side payments to other health care interests.[63]

From a political standpoint, structuring the new drug benefit around competing private plans was a way for an anti-government party to show that it could govern, meeting public demands for a universal program in a way that was congruent with deeply held beliefs in the merits of market competition. The design of this reform enabled Republicans, on the one hand, to champion their commitment to a universal social program, but on the other hand to reassure skeptical conservatives that they were laying the foundation for a larger transformation of Medicare through market-based reform. This became a vitally important claim that the Congressional GOP leadership and White House officials made to conservatives in an effort to bring them on board with this major expansion of an entitlement.

The Role of Organized Interests

What role did interest groups play in the crafting of the prescription drug benefit? Many have asserted that the 2003 MMA was essentially written by lobbyists for health care interests, and it is true that these groups often have had considerable influence over health care policy due their deep pockets, well-placed lobbyists, and skilled use of political advertising. Yet, these claims about the MMA presume a degree of uniformity and influence that was in general lacking among the two key industries involved in debates about program design—pharmaceuticals and insurers. Instead, both had to be persuaded that it was in their interest to support (or at least not actively oppose) the Republican private plan approach. This was obviously vital in the case of the insurers and PBMs that were supposed to deliver the drug benefit, but that initially balked at the idea. For Republicans, it was also important to get pharmaceutical companies on their side to help build a legislative coalition in support of the measure. Thus, in both cases, the influence of these groups stemmed not from their ability to direct the marionette show like master puppeteers, but because the Republican architects of the reform sought out these groups as key coalition partners and, in the case of insurers, essential participants in delivering the new benefit.

Just as Medicare administration was delegated to private actors in 1965 to alleviate provider fears about government intervention in the practice of medicine, so too did delegated governance in the late 1990s and early 2000s seek to mollify a pharmaceutical industry that had long opposed adding a prescription drug benefit to the program. Much like physicians in the 1960s, who wanted the freedom to charge what they wished for their services, the pharmaceutical industry wanted to set its own prices and was chafing at the growing role of third-party payers—especially managed care firms—in setting formularies and reimbursement rates. Now, they faced the prospect of government involvement, which not only meant a third-party payer with greatly consolidated bargaining power, but also a bully pulpit that could be used to browbeat the industry to lower its prices. Of particular concern was government control over the benefit formulary—the list of what drugs are covered and how they are covered, such as what co-payments are charged, whether generics are favored, etc. Threatening to exclude a drug from a formulary or place it in a less-favored tier could give the government powerful leverage over the industry.

Even though pharmaceutical firms were unified in their concerns about a Medicare prescription drug benefit, their response to the various proposals of the late 1990s was not. Some firms, such as Pfizer, favored outright opposition to any universal benefit, and instead advocated some form of means-tested assistance, such as block grants to state pharmacy-assistance programs.[64] This was certainly a view championed by a number of Republicans in Congress, and could very well have become the dominant GOP response to the issue. Others embraced the premium support approach, arguing that any new drug benefit should accompany a complete structural overhaul of Medicare into a system of competing private plans. Yet, early on, there were a few within the industry who recognized both the political infeasibility of such a reform and the political power of the issue. By the late 1990s, pharmaceutical companies faced rising populist discontent about the price of drugs and the industry's high profits. In what they perceived to be a "new war on drugs," there were calls for limits on direct-to-consumer advertising; demands for the reimportation of cheaper prescription drugs from abroad; and increasing state government action to impose limits on drug reimbursements in Medicaid and their pharmacy-assistance programs.[65] The drug industry also was a convenient political punching bag as the Democrats, and even some Republicans, particularly those from border states, began to support legalizing drug reimportation.[66]

Initially, the Clinton administration reached out to the industry and tried to persuade it of the merits of its own reform approach. This was one reason that the administration had embraced the PBM mechanism to deliver the new benefit, hoping it would alleviate industry fears of government intrusion in pricing and formulary decisions. Some early Democratic proposals also included non-interference clauses banning government involvement in price determinations, not unlike the one in the final MMA. These attempts to placate the industry came to naught: a drug plan using only one PBM per region still concentrated a good deal of power in the hands of one actor, giving that actor considerable bargaining leverage. Moreover, during the 1990s, PBMs had become increasingly successful in cutting the cost of brand name drugs—and therefore the profits earned by the industry.[67] The pharmaceutical industry thus vigorously opposed the Clinton proposal and in 1999 they funded an advertising campaign that featured Flo, an arthritic bowler who asserted darkly, "The White House plan puts bureaucrats in charge of our medicines."[68] A pharma-funded organization, Citizens for Better Medicare, began running a $20–$30 million advertising campaign that claimed the Clinton plan threatened 75 percent of seniors with employer-sponsored coverage (the CBO put that figure at 25 percent).[69] In response, the administration stepped on to the bully pulpit with zeal, calling for a study of the negative impact of rising prescription drug prices on seniors and warning the industry that it would face price controls if it continued to fight a Medicare prescription drug benefit.[70]

With the heat rising between the Clinton administration and the industry, some executives began to realize that a Medicare prescription drug benefit was coming, like it or not, and that it was better to get involved early in shaping the reform in a pharma-friendly direction. Early in 2000, before the GOP had begun crafting its reform strategy, Merck CEO Raymond V. Gilmartin articulated what would ultimately be the Republican approach: a system of competing stand-alone drug plans. As he said in a January 2000 interview about the Clinton proposal, "The Administration's plan is competition among health plans or PBMs to win a bid for the government. And if they modified that so that *the PBMs or health plans were competing for beneficiaries*, then they would be closer to the model that we are talking about" (emphasis added).[71] Merck then played an important role in pushing this vision of reform, both through its Washington-based officials and through Gilmartin's lobbying of other pharmaceutical CEOs to at least lessen their hostility to a government-sponsored benefit.[72]

At one point, Gilmartin reached out to the Clinton administration. On January 20, Gilmartin, the CEOs of Amgen and Johnson & Johnson, and the president of

PhRMA met with high-level Clinton officials. This followed a similar meeting with Senator Edward M. Kennedy (D-MA). As reported at the time, the CEOs and the administration reached a tentative agreement on basic principles, with industry officials dropping their insistence that a drug benefit be accompanied by structural reform of Medicare into a system of premium support; agreeing that the new benefit should be universal rather than targeted; and conceding that the federal government could seek ways to purchase drugs in bulk and get volume discounts. In a potentially significant change from its earlier proposal, Clinton officials allowed that competing private plans would provide the benefit. The agreement also stated that the new benefit would cover all drugs, instead of favoring certain drugs over others.[73]

Republicans were furious at the apparent détente between the pharmaceutical industry—which was perceived to be a close ally of the GOP—and the Clinton administration.[74] The two parties are always protective of their interest group allies, but since the 1990s, Republicans had pursued the "K Street Project"—an attempt to cultivate stronger ties between the party and lobbying interests. This involved making sure that lobbying firms hired Republicans loyalists, often former Congressional staffers or members of Congress, and then demanding loyalty from the various interests they represented. In this case, Senate leadership aides warned Merck and Amgen that they were undercutting Republican efforts to prevent a new government-dominated drug benefit, and some GOP officials refused to meet with anyone from the industry for months following the meeting.[75] Republicans were also unhappy with the ineffectiveness of the industry's ads against the Clinton proposal, with one Republican leadership aide in the House calling Flo "a wretched old hag."[76] Combined with the pressure that Republicans were facing back home on the issue, this threatened shift in the industry's position intensified discussions among GOP officials about the need to put forth a proposal. Pharmaceutical industry officials, in the meantime, backtracked and claimed that their opposition to the Clinton proposal was unchanged.[77]

By the spring of 2000, the House GOP leadership embraced precisely the vision that Gilmartin had put forth—a system that not only delegated responsibility for delivering the benefit to private insurance companies and PBMs, but also had these entities competing for beneficiaries' business, thereby diffusing their negotiating power vis-à-vis the drug companies. Formally, the industry got behind this idea, although some continued to nurse reservations in private. Companies such as Pfizer continued to be skeptical about allowing PBMs to deliver the drug benefit, as they were concerned that PBMs would use aggressive formulary management techniques to limit access to certain drugs.[78]

For the GOP, having the industry's stamp of approval helped support claims they made to skeptical conservatives that the legislation was not just another big entitlement, but was market-friendly. The industry could also be counted upon for campaign support to Republican members up for reelection, although during the first half of 2000, GOP officials were angry at the industry for what they perceived to be insufficient support of Republican candidates.[79] As the year went on, Citizens for Better Medicare ramped up its efforts, spending over $1 million per week on issue ads—more campaign spending than any other organization outside of the political parties.[80] The Chamber of Commerce also devoted $20 million to Republican candidates on health care issues, with most of this money coming from the pharmaceutical industry but distributed through local Chambers of Commerce that were seen as having local credibility.[81] By the end of the election season, the industry spent some $80 million in total, with $50 million from CBM for issue ads, $10 million to the Chamber of Commerce, and $19 million in direct donations to candidates.[82]

The industry also could be called upon as lobbyists working on behalf of the leadership to persuade recalcitrant members. Long an important presence in Washington, pharmaceuticals had by this time become a formidable lobbying force, hiring more than 600 lobbyists over the 1990s, including many former legislators.[83] According to the Center for Responsive Politics, the Pharmaceutical/ Health Products Industry spent the most of any industry (over $900 million) on lobbying Congress and federal agencies between 1998–2005.[84] From 1997 to 2000, lobbying expenses by pharmaceutical/health products companies grew by 27 percent.[85] Moreover, pharmaceutical companies have headquarters and facilities in most states, giving them some leverage with lawmakers worried about antagonizing firms in their districts.

The support of the pharmaceutical industry also proved useful in the legislative jockeying around the GOP proposal. In the spring of 2000, many insurers balked at the idea of providing stand-alone, risk-bearing drug plans, creating an ugly rift between two supposedly "Republican" allies—pharmaceutical and insurance companies—and providing endless talking points for Democrats who lambasted the GOP plan as unworkable. The issue reinforced doubts among some conservative Republicans about the proposal as well. To counteract these doubts and undercut the Democrats, Representative Bill Thomas suddenly held up a letter during a contentious Ways and Means hearing from Merck's partner in the PBM world, Merck-Medco, which said they were willing to provide a stand-alone drug plan in a competitive marketplace.[86] "It says, we're ready to go," announced Mr. Thomas, while, in the words of one reporter, Democrats "sat stone-faced."[87] The chair of the Ways and Means subcommittee on Health, Bill Thomas, was thus able to proclaim this as proof that the Republican proposal could work.[88]

Why then were the other important industry players—PBMs and insurers—so skeptical of the GOP proposal? PBMs were particularly leery of what they were being asked to do in the new benefit. Traditionally, PBMs administered drug benefits on behalf of employers, unions, and insurance companies but did not bear risk for their clients' pharmacy costs (which are borne by third-party payers), or have to be directly responsible to beneficiaries. Most PBMs therefore preferred the Clinton approach, which replicated these existing relationships. Although they did not come out against the Republican legislation and provided technical assistance during the drafting of bills, most PBMs remained skeptical to the end.[89] The one exception was Medco, which was tied to the pharmaceutical giant Merck until August 2003 and which became a major supporter of the GOP approach.

Among private insurers also, there was uneasiness about the role being proposed for them by the Republicans. Charles N. ("Chip") Kahn III, president of the Health Insurance Association of America, was especially vocal in his opposition, arguing that because this was a voluntary benefit for only one type of spending—pharmaceutical costs—firms offering stand-alone drug insurance would be overwhelmed by adverse selection, as only people who knew they needed drug coverage would buy insurance.[90] "It would be like providing insurance for haircuts," said Kahn.[91] Healthier people would stay out of the market, and as the drug plans failed to be profitable and left the program, insurers could face another public backlash like the attacks on managed care. "Private drug-insurance policies are doomed from the start," declared Kahn.[92] The HIAA instead favored block grants to state governments for their pharmacy-assistance programs coupled with tax breaks for other seniors.[93] During the spring of 2000, when the GOP was first developing and voting on its proposal, the HIAA's dogged opposition to the plan was a nettlesome problem for the Republican leadership. Democrats seized upon Kahn's statements to argue that the Republican plan would not work.

Another insurance industry group—the American Association of Health Plans, led by Karen Ignagni—did endorse the Republican approach.[94] The organization represents managed care companies, and it both pushed for increased Medicare+Choice payments and lauded the merits of private plans in Medicare. Over time, HIAA also adopted a more moderate stance as the subsidies available for private insurers were increased.[95] Officials in some big insurance companies continued to believe that it did not make sense to provide stand-along drug insurance, but they generally kept these views to themselves for fear of antagonizing lawmakers.[96] In the fall of 2003, HIAA merged with AAHP to become America's Health Insurance Plans (AHIP), putting the full insurance industry formally behind the MMA. AHIP has a grassroots arm, the Coalition for Medicare Choices, which claimed several hundred thousand members at the time and held rallies in Washington, D.C., and around the country in support of the Medicare+Choice program. The organization also sunk millions into lobbying and campaign contributions.

In April 2000, House Republicans finally put forth their plan to provide drug coverage through competing private plans. They did so after months of internal debate that finally led them to jettison the idea of requiring a structural overhaul of Medicare in return for a new drug benefit, or of providing only means-tested assistance to beneficiaries. Instead, they embraced the idea of stand-alone, risk-bearing drug insurance plans that, in the words of Merck CEO Gilmartin, "would compete for Medicare beneficiaries, not for a contract with the federal government."[97] As this account has shown, the role of organized interests in the development of this idea was complex: a few within the pharmaceutical industry were among the first to voice the idea of competing private plans, but they faced resistance from other industry officials. Still, the stance taken by Merck and others in favor of this approach, and tentative courting of the industry by the Clinton administration, spurred the House Republican leadership to forge a deal that would keep the pharmaceutical industry allied with the GOP. The insurance industry, by contrast, was the spoiler at the party that only later got on board.

Political Competition Keeps the Prescription Drug Issue Alive

The political fight over a Medicare prescription drug benefit continued for the next three years, fueled by tight electoral races, the mobilization of senior citizens and their advocates, and the perception that this battle was decisive for the future of Medicare. By spring 2000, the basic parameters of the Republican proposal had been defined. Now, the question for the Republican leadership was whether they could maneuver a bill through an obstacle-ridden legislative process and show the public that they could solve a pressing social problem. Until 2003, the GOP lacked enough votes in both chambers to see the legislation through, but there was powerful political momentum that kept the prescription drug issue alive. Throughout the battles over the bill, Congress remained the center of the action, whereas the White House played more of a supporting role in the drama.[98]

The GOP-controlled House first passed a prescription drug bill in June 2000, largely along party lines (217–214). The bill had little chance of passing the Senate, where Republicans lacked the 60 votes to circumvent a filibuster or a budget point of order,[99] and Clinton would veto it anyway. But at least House Republicans now had a positive proposal that they could show to their constituents and use in electoral fights back home. As one Republican put it, "Our guys couldn't go home empty-handed."[100] By mid-summer the presidential candidates became involved as well, with Gore proposing a generous $253 billion plan over 10 years,[101] and the Bush team finally announcing a $158 billion plan in September, after months of attacks by the Gore campaign on this issue and the growing competitiveness of Florida, where seniors were anxious about rising prescription drug costs.[102] The Bush plan proposed to subsidize seniors' purchase of private insurance for all their health care needs, including prescription drugs, or else allow them to remain in traditional Medicare and have the option of buying a subsidized plan for prescriptions.[103]

At first, it appeared that the Republican victories in the November 2000 election—which gave the party unified control of the House, Senate, and executive branch—raised the prospects for concrete legislative action. Republicans knew that the intensity around this issue was not going to dissipate now that the election was over, and that Democrats would not let them forget it. As Urban Institute director Robert Reischauer remarked at the time about the Republicans: "They have a gun to their heads. They have to do something. If they don't, they will give Democrats a club to beat them over the head with."[104] Some Republicans also thought that it would only be a matter of time before this benefit was created, and that if Republicans did not do it their way, then eventually "Hillary is going to do it" in a way more amenable to Democrats.[105]

However, the window of opportunity for the GOP closed without action in 2001. Many Congressional conservatives were leery of expanding an already expensive, and rapidly growing, federal entitlement. Reflecting these concerns, the Bush administration instead proposed to give block grants to states to provide drug coverage for low-income seniors, but the idea was immediately shot down by Republicans in the House and Senate who knew that only a universal benefit would be politically acceptable to senior citizens.[106] To justify providing such an entitlement, Republicans needed to convince their own members that the legislation did enough market-based reform, but they could not go too far in this direction because the GOP needed the support of all Senate Republicans *and* a small number of Democrats in the evenly divided Senate in order to overcome procedural challenges to the bill.

However, other developments rendered moot the question of how to balance these conflicting imperatives. Party control of the Senate switched to the Democrats in May 2001 when Jim Jeffords of Vermont declared himself an independent. Some Democrats were still willing to work with Republicans to craft a drug benefit, including Ted Kennedy and the chairman of the Senate Finance Committee, Max Baucus. However, the June 2000 House bill would be the basis for the reform, and the Democratic leadership had few incentives to cooperate. Passing a bill would allow Republicans to claim credit while removing from Democrats a potent political weapon. In the Senate, several proposals failed in 2001 as the Democratic leadership supported legislation more generous than what Republicans would agree to. Then the terrorist attacks of September 11 intervened, pushing domestic policy matters aside.

Attention soon returned to the prescription drug issue, especially since the leadership of both parties was aware that mid-term elections usually turn on domestic policy issues, and that seniors become an even more important slice of the electorate in these elections because more non-senior voters stay home. In addition, Republican strategists such as pollster Bill McInturff argued that passage of the prescription drug benefit in 2000 had been crucial for the GOP's ability to hang onto the House in that election. Many Republicans believed that they would be vulnerable to Democratic attacks on this issue again.[107] Finally, although President Bush's approval ratings shot up in the months following the attacks, many recalled how quickly the first President Bush's wartime advantage dissipated after the successful conclusion of the Gulf War.[108] Domestic issues could not be ignored.

In June 2002, House Republicans again succeeded in passing a prescription drug bill, this time a more generous one—$350 billion over 10 years, utilizing private insurance firms to provide the drug benefit. The bill also increased subsidies to these firms and to Medicare providers and secured the endorsement of the HIAA, now that Kahn had left the organization, as well as that of the American

Medical Association, the American Hospital Association, and the Federation of American Hospitals.[109] Even with a growing number of interest group backers, the House GOP leadership had to work hard to round up enough Republican votes, with some conservatives still doubtful about creating a broad-based new entitlement. The White House made phone calls and personal appeals to the hold-outs. An array of health care interest groups also were engaged to lobby Republican members. Finally, on June 28, the measure passed 221–208, at 2:30 A.M., driven by the aim of passing a drug benefit in time for the July 4 recess.[110] As Representative Clay Shaw (R-FL) remarked: "This wasn't an easy vote. The leadership really had to work for it . . . [drug coverage] is a new entitlement, and Republicans basically are against starting entitlements."[111]

However, in the Senate, where the Democrats still had control, efforts to pull together bipartisan support for a drug bill came to naught. Some Democrats, such as Baucus and Kennedy, seemed open to a compromise that would use the Republican delivery mechanism for the benefit (competing private plans) but shore up other elements of the benefit along Democratic lines. But there were tensions between Baucus and Senate Majority Leader Daschle that made it difficult to advance a bill (Daschle, unhappy with Baucus's support for the Bush tax cuts, tried to bypass Baucus's Senate Finance Committee and introduce a drug benefit on the Senate floor, which failed). Other proposals failed to gain the 60 votes necessary to circumvent a budget point of order. It appeared that many Democrats and Republicans were uninterested in compromise because it might advantage the other side in an election year.[112]

As in 2000, the prescription drug benefit became a hot issue in the mid-term elections. This time, House Republicans felt more confident about their positioning on this issue, as they had passed a prescription drug benefit twice and could blame the "do-nothing," Democratically controlled Senate as the obstacle. They also had strong support from the pharmaceutical industry, which bankrolled issue ads supportive of the Republican proposal and lambasting that of the Democrats, giving Republicans a three-to-one advantage on issue ad spending (in 2000 spending on issue ads had been equal across the parties).[113] In contrast to the 2000 election, Republicans now ran as many ads as Democrats did that mentioned the Medicare prescription drug issue (see chapter 7). After the election, many Republicans concluded that their strategy had worked: the GOP held onto the House and regained control of the Senate, and Republicans beat Democrats by 12 percentage-points among the elderly, winning half of those saying in exit polls that the Medicare prescription drug benefit was the most important issue to them. At the very least, if Republicans did not win on this issue, they did not lose because of it. As Frist remarked at the time, "I advised all of our candidates to go on television early and put down a marker on where you stand before someone else does it to you . . . It's the one issue besides Social Security that people say they are traditionally most comfortable having Democrats deal with. We neutralized that." Or, as Kahn said of the Republicans: "Health is not their central issue, but it's an issue that, if they engage on it, can clearly help them against the Democrats . . . Republicans, after two election cycles, have learned to talk about health."[114]

But could they deliver on their promises? That was the question for 2003.

Passing the MMA in 2003

In 2003, Republicans controlled both chambers of Congress and there was a Republican in the White House who supported the addition of a drug benefit to Medicare. The time for the legislation had come, but the same difficulties remained about how to maneuver the bill through the legislative process. Enough moderates needed to be kept on board in the Senate to keep the bill from falling victim to procedural hurdles. Yet, some conservatives in both chambers were still uncomfortable with the measure and thus suspicious of legislation that garnered too much approval from Democrats. The task for the Republican leadership in the House and Senate was to thread this delicate needle, and they pursued a strategy of passing the bill on almost entirely party lines in the House and picking up a small number of moderate Democrats in the Senate. In so doing, they had the support of the Bush administration, but most of the heavy lifting was done by the Congressional party leadership as they struggled to muster the votes for the bill.

It did not start out well, as the Bush administration initially proposed requiring seniors to join an HMO or other subsidized private plan, through which they would receive all of their Medicare benefits, in order to receive drug coverage. This ran contrary to a basic principle on which the Republican Congressional leadership had agreed: for reasons of political acceptability, they needed to offer a universal benefit, available to people regardless of whether or not they were in a Medicare HMO. Of requiring senior citizens to join an HMO in order to get a drug benefit, Hastert said: "I don't think you can do it humanely. I don't think you can do it politically. I don't think it's practical . . . you can't ask a 75-year-old woman to leave the [Medicare] system" in order to get a drug benefit,[115] while Energy and Commerce Chair Tauzin put it more pungently: "You couldn't move my mother out of Medicare with a bulldozer. She trusts it, believes in it. It's served her well."[116] House Republicans had already developed and repeatedly voted on their own approach to the drug benefit, and they were going to stick with that in 2003, regardless of what the White House said.

The more constructive proposal offered by the administration was to reserve $400 billion in new spending for Medicare reform and a drug benefit for fiscal years 2004–2013. This figure became the ceiling for the drug benefit plus anything else (e.g., provider subsidies) that would be added in, and had significant consequences for the shape of the benefit. For that amount it was impossible to have a universal benefit, catastrophic coverage, low-income subsidies, and coverage of most drug costs.[117] Carving out a zero-coverage doughnut hole in the middle of the benefit was the solution, enabling the inclusion of both first-dollar coverage—seen as essential for providing seniors immediate cost savings and an incentive to sign up for this voluntary benefit—and catastrophic coverage, needed for political acceptability and for relief for those with very high drug costs. Given these budgetary and political realities, then, the doughnut hole would remain, although the precise shape of it shifted over the course of the year.

Many lamented that a greater sum of money enabling a more generous benefit was not put aside. However, the budget surplus in place at the beginning of the Bush presidency had rapidly disappeared, following hundreds of billions in tax cuts and spending on the wars in Iraq and Afghanistan. Still, some Democrats did put forth alternatives that offered more comprehensive coverage, but such proposals, such as an $800 billion plan developed by liberal Democrats Charlie Rangel (NY), John Dingell (MI), and Pete Stark (CA), would have cost far more than the MMA,[118] money that simply was not there in the rapidly deteriorating budgetary picture.

Other aspects of the House legislation essentially conformed to the bills passed in earlier years: competing private plans; low-income subsidies; and a prohibition on government negotiation over prices or setting of formularies. Once again, the legislation also included new spending on provider payments—money that had been promised in the 2002 legislation that failed to pass. But this time, rural members of Congress took advantage of the close nature of votes on the bill to push for increased payments to rural providers, one of many side payments that would become necessary for the MMA to achieve passage in both chambers.

One of the biggest challenges facing the GOP leadership in the House was including enough market-based reform measures in the bill to win over conservatives leery of creating a new entitlement. One such measure was a watered-down version of premium support, requiring the regular Medicare program to compete with private plans (HMOs, etc.) beginning in 2010. HMO premiums would be allowed to vary so that, if these plans were more efficient, they could offer lower premiums and draw more people out of the regular Medicare program into private plans. Another measure was added on the House floor: tax-preferred personal savings accounts that could be used to pay for medical expenses, a measure estimated to cost $174 billion over the next decade. Finally, the leadership argued to conservatives that a privately delivered benefit was different from simply adding a government-run entitlement.

Debate over the measure was sharply partisan as Democrats assailed the GOP-designed bill as "a radical effort to dismantle Medicare."[119] Minority Leader Nancy Pelosi and the other Democratic leaders successfully kept their caucus together. With almost no votes forthcoming from House Democrats, Republicans had to scramble to prevent too many conservative defectors. The White House deployed Dick Cheney, HHS secretary Tommy Thompson, and others to try to persuade recalcitrant Republicans, and President Bush met with House conservatives as well. The GOP leadership had to increase the time for the floor vote from the usual 15 minutes to nearly 50, as they persuaded (or strong-armed, some would allege) some members to switch their votes. Finally, the bill passed, 216–215, with 19 Republicans voting against, and only 9 Democrats voting in favor. As Hastert told reporters the next day, "We got it done. Sometimes it's pretty. Sometimes it ain't."[120]

Passage was easier in the Senate, where shifting political dynamics proved crucial to the ability of this legislation to advance. Control of the Senate reverted back to the Republicans in 2003, but their margin of control was small and not filibuster-proof. Their failure to add a drug benefit to Medicare had proven politically useful for the Democrats, and some sought to block legislation yet again so as to deny the Republicans a signing ceremony and successful co-optation of an issue that Democrats traditionally "owned." What broke the political logjam was the decision by Max Baucus, minority leader of the Senate Finance Committee, to negotiate with the Republican chairman of the committee, Chuck Grassley, over a Senate bill similar in its basic structure to the House legislation. In April 2003, Majority Leader Frist pushed the two to negotiate, but this was kept under wraps.[121] Then, Ted Kennedy embraced their bill, enraging some Democrats but providing political cover for others. Kennedy had long been interested in a compromise bill and he had accepted the idea of allowing competing private plans to deliver the benefit well before Baucus came around to the idea. Some charged that this was because Kennedy was close to pharmaceutical interests, given the important presence of biotechnology firms in Massachusetts, while others believed he simply saw an opportunity to lock in $400 billion for a new benefit that might not come around again for some time. As he said at the time, "We can always work to improve it in the future, and we will."[122] Once the bill had his stamp of approval, many other Democrats were more willing to support it as well.

Baucus and Grassley's compromise bill had the same basic structure as the House bill, but was more moderate in several ways: no provision that required that Medicare and private plans compete for beneficiaries' business; more generous low-income subsidies; no health savings accounts; and a requirement that the government offer a fallback drug plan in areas where a sufficient number of private plans did not emerge—long a fear of rural lawmakers. Such a fallback provision—which would involve direct government provision of the benefit—was lacking in the House bill. The bill passed in June with a large majority, 76–21, which included 35 Democrats voting in favor.

Now, the Republican leadership had to resolve the differences between these two pieces of legislation and address the larger challenge that had faced them all along: how to show that the GOP could address a pressing political issue in a way congruent with deeply held beliefs about the need for market-based reform of entitlements. If the final bill looked too much like the Senate bill, it risked losing support among conservatives. Already, many House conservatives were skeptical about voting for anything that Ted Kennedy had supported. Both inside and outside of Congress, some conservatives were mobilizing against the Senate bill, with Robert Goldberg of the Manhattan Institute labeling it a "socialist time bomb of Medicare," and the Heritage Foundation declaring the drug bill to be "an Impending Disaster for all Americans."[123] Yet, if the final bill were too conservative, it risked losing critical bipartisan support in the Senate, and even if it had a bare majority to pass, would not exceed the Senate's supermajority requirements should Democrats decide to mount a filibuster.

Given this delicate situation, conference negotiations were protracted and contentious, with conflicts erupting both between the parties and within them. After some of the "underbrush" of relatively easy issues had been cleared in August, nearly all of the Democrats appointed to the conference committee were excluded from future meetings, with only centrist Democratic Senators Max Baucus and John Breaux allowed to remain. This enraged many Democrats, who were furious at the Republicans for excluding them, but also angry at Baucus and Breaux for their willingness to continue negotiating with the Republicans. Conflicts also erupted between Republicans Grassley and Thomas over aspects of the bill, and within the Republican caucus over how much conservatives should give in order to get a bill through the Senate. The GOP leadership was determined to try to keep Baucus on board in the hope that he could bring along with him enough moderate Democratic votes in the Senate, but this meant jettisoning some of the more controversial aspects of the House bill. It also meant infuriating the right wing of their own party, some of whom complained bitterly that Baucus had become the crucial dealmaker in the conference committee.

One contentious issue was whether people dually eligible for Medicare and Medicaid, most of whom previously had drug coverage through state Medicaid programs, should be moved into the new Medicare drug benefit. The House bill did this but the Senate bill did not, as some believed that the state programs were more generous than the proposed Medicare benefit. Nor did the White House want to move dual eligibles into Medicare, perhaps because the administration wanted to keep the fiscal pressure on state governments to force more fundamental reform of their Medicaid programs.[124] In the final bill, the dual eligibles were moved, but the administration's intransigence delayed action on this issue during the conference committee, with the result that insufficient thought went into how the movement of millions of low-income beneficiaries from Medicaid programs into the new Medicare benefit would be managed. As will be discussed in chapter 6, this would become one of the biggest transitional problems for the new program.

To help keep conservatives on board, other things were added to the bill during the conference committee. One was the inclusion of Health Savings Accounts, now a $6 billion measure, scaled back from the $174 billion measure passed in the House. Another was the creation of a Medicare spending trigger: Medicare Trustees must issue a "funding warning" if the proportion of Medicare financed by general revenues exceeds 45 percent of total spending (compared to the amount funded by payroll taxes and premiums); and if this is projected to occur two times in the coming seven years, the president must submit legislation to

Congress that reduces this proportion back to 45 percent or less through new revenues or spending cuts. A third measure increased part B premiums for upper-income people. These measures were inserted expressly to try to convince conservative Republicans to support the legislation, but angered some moderate Democrats. Some conservatives could not be placated by these measures, however, and passionately opposed the bill to the end.

In September and October it looked like the MMA would fail yet again as the conference deadlocked on the terms by which competition would be introduced into the Medicare program. Here, conservatives were intransigent, announcing several times during conference negotiations that they would not support a bill that did not require Medicare to compete with private plans for the business of beneficiaries. As Stephen Moore of the influential Club for Growth asserted, "We don't see any room for negotiations on that, because that's the key reform. I don't see how anybody in good fiscal conscience could vote for something without it."[125] House Ways and Means Committee Chairman Thomas was determined to preserve competition in the program as well.[126] Yet Baucus signaled that this provision would doom Senate passage. The determination of both sides on this issue led to a standstill.

At this point, the Republican leadership made an unusual move, stepping outside of the conference committee and turning to AARP for support. AARP had been playing its own delicate game since the start of 2003. On the one hand, the group publicly supported more liberal legislation and stood by the Democrats in their criticisms of the GOP bills. Yet, since early in 2003, top AARP officials had been secretly meeting with the Republican leadership in an attempt to find common ground on a prescription drug benefit.[127] Early on, AARP's CEO, Bill Novelli, let it be known that he was willing to compromise in order to achieve a benefit.[128] In fall 2003, with the conference committee on the verge of breaking down over whether to require Medicare and private plans to compete, Hastert and Frist negotiated an agreement with AARP officials that turned this measure into a demonstration project slated for 2010, rendering it essentially toothless. The GOP leadership then brought this deal to Baucus and Breaux, which they agreed to as well, although Baucus was angry that the AARP had engaged in these kinds of negotiations without consulting any Democrats.[129] The deal broke the conference logjam, enabling a package of measures that could conceivably gain the support of enough Democrats in the Senate to pass, but not alienate too many conservatives in the House. Thomas was furious to find that he, chairman of the conference committee, had been outmaneuvered by the GOP leadership, but he ultimately swallowed his anger and agreed to vote for the bill.[130]

Once the final bill had been fashioned in the conference committee, the fight was on to get the agreement passed in the House and Senate. Here is where the various interest group backers—an estimated 400 different groups—would prove important.[131] One crucial development was that on November 17 the AARP decided to endorse the legislation and launch a $7 million television and print advertising campaign to promote the bill.[132] Leaders of the organization argued that, even though the bill was not ideal, they believed this might be the last opportunity to lock in $400 billion in improvements to the Medicare program. Objectionable elements could be removed later, they claimed.[133] Many Democrats were livid because once the AARP supported the legislation, it was hard for Democrats to oppose it. Many did not vote for the final bill in the Senate, yet mounting a filibuster in the Senate was seen as considerably more difficult now that the bill had the AARP's "good housekeeping seal of approval."[134]

The bill also included subsidies for a wide range of organized interests in an effort to improve the chances of passage, including over $14 billion in subsidies to employers who continue to offer drug benefits to retirees, $25 billion for hospitals, physicians, home health agencies, and rural providers, and subsidies for private health plans at higher levels than traditional Medicare.[135] As Judith Feder, dean of the Georgetown School of Public Policy, remarked:

> There's a tremendous amount of money floating in this bill. While we think it's about prescription drugs, the promoters of this bill put money into every interest group—physicians, hospitals, rural providers, cancer doctors . . . the pharmaceutical and insurance industries, and it's tough to fight all those bucks.[136]

Hundreds of lobbyists mobilized on behalf of the bill, focusing mostly on recalcitrant conservatives. Pharmaceutical and insurance industry lobbyists were also active, but so was their money. As Figures 5.3 and 5.4 show, House legislators of both parties who voted in support of the MMA conference bill had been receiving significantly more in campaign contributions from these industries for years. There is a similar relationship among Senate votes, although it is less straightforward: there were a number of Republican Senators who voted against the MMA despite receiving hefty contributions from these industries (see Figures 5.5 and 5.6). To organize the energies of their K Street allies, House Majority Whip Roy Blunt (R-MO) set up a war room in his Capitol Hill office. Coordinated by Susan Hirschmann, a lobbyist and former chief of staff to Tom DeLay (R-TX), the operation turned not only to groups with a direct interest in the legislation, but also to long-standing friends in the business community who had little at stake in the bill.[137] According to reports at the time, some of the active participants in the group included the Securities Industry Association, Ernst & Young, the U.S. Chamber of Commerce, Caterpillar Inc., CIGNA, PhRMA, and the American Association of Health Plans.[138] Overall, hundreds of lobbyists were involved in the mobilization on behalf of the bill, focusing their energies mainly on recalcitrant conservatives.

Others worked behind the scenes to rally skeptical conservative opinion-shapers and members of Congress as well, including former House Speaker

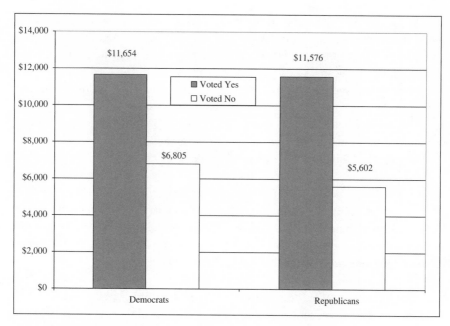

Figure 5.3 MMA Final Vote and Average Health Service/HMO Contributions to House Members, 1999–2003. Source: www.opensecrets.org.

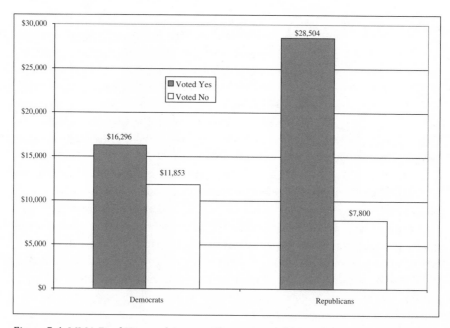

Figure 5.4 MMA Final Vote and Average Pharmaceutical Manufacturer Contributions to House Members, 1999–2003. Source: www.opensecrets.org.

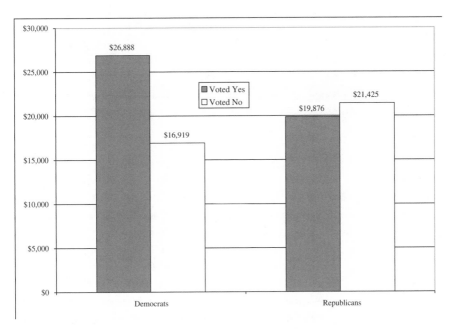

Figure 5.5 MMA Final Vote and Average Health Service/HMO Contributions to Senators, 1999–2003. Source: www.opensecrets.org.

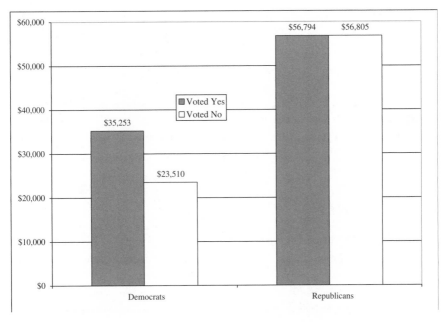

Figure 5.6 MMA Final Vote and Average Pharmaceutical Manufacturer Contributions to Senators, 1999–2003. Source: www.opensecrets.org.

Newt Gingrich, who argued that even if true privatization—converting Medicare into a system of premium support—had failed, the reform still represented a down payment on that kind of transformation.[139] If nothing else, the Health Savings Account measure was important enough to merit passage of the bill. However, conservative activists in think tanks such as the Heritage Foundation, AEI, Cato, and American Conservative Union were not convinced, nor was a small group of hard-liners in the House and Senate.[140] Many simply did not believe that there was much market-based reform in the law, and that $400 billion was a high price to pay for Health Savings Accounts. As a November 20, 2003, editorial in the *Wall Street Journal* opposing the legislation declared: "Entitlements are forever."

Conservative opposition made the final vote on the bill grueling, particularly in the House, where Minority Leader Pelosi largely succeeded in maintaining Democratic party-line discipline. This meant that the GOP leadership had to hold on to as many Republicans as they could. At one point, Democrats had an absolute majority of votes against the bill and began savoring their victory, but the House leadership kept the vote open for several more hours while they tried to persuade enough Republicans to switch their nay vote to a yea. This was the longest electronic vote tally—two hours and 53 minutes—since the use of electronic voting began, and Republican leaders almost literally had to twist arms to get enough Republicans to support the bill.[141] One Republican Congresswoman hid behind a banister on the Democratic side of the House, hoping not to be found, while others turned off their cell phones or stood in a large group that could fend off attempts by the leadership to pick off vulnerable individuals.[142] President Bush had already made a number of phone calls to conservatives from Air Force One, on his way back from Britain, but made more calls at five in the morning. At 5:51 A.M. on November 22, the MMA passed, 220–215, with 25 Republicans voting against, and 16 Democrats voting in favor.

In the Senate, many Democrats changed their mind and opposed the final law, particularly after Ted Kennedy came out against it. Kennedy had been moving away from the legislation as it took on a more conservative flavor during the conference committee, but the last straw appears to have been the premium support demonstration that was included in the final legislation. As he declared on the floor of the Senate, the proposed bill was "a right wing Republican assault on Medicare in the guise of a prescription drug program . . . a fat deal for HMOs and pharmaceutical companies—and a raw deal for the elderly."[143] Still, 11 Democrats voted for the legislation, and it passed on November 25 by a margin of 55 to 44. A number of these Democratic supporters were from rural states that stood to benefit from the additional payments to rural providers in the bill.[144] Others saw an opportunity to lock in $400 billion in new Medicare spending. Critically, Minority Leader Daschle decided not to mount a filibuster against the legislation. Given the support among some Democrats, and the AARP endorsement, he did not think he had the votes to make a filibuster succeed.[145]

The Politics of Delegated Governance

As in the creation of Medicare in 1965, delegated governance in the Medicare Modernization Act was a way to achieve a popular political objective without seeming to directly expand the size of government. Or at least that was the claim put forth by the champions of the reform. By relying on private, competing plans to provide the drug benefit, Republicans tried to square the circle within their own camp: to both offer a universal entitlement estimated to cost $400 billion over 10 years, and to further long-term objectives of Medicare privatization and market-oriented solutions to social problems. Delegated governance also helped appease powerful health care interests, in this case the pharmaceutical and insurance industries who were initially skeptical about the various ideas being bandied about for a Medicare drug benefit. The insurance industry came to see profit-making potential in the new benefit, once assured of sufficient government subsidies, while many pharmaceutical companies liked the dispersion of negotiating authority among a larger number of competing private entities. Once satisfied that their interests were sufficiently protected, these industries helped the Republican architects of the MMA build a majority in Congress in support of the law.

Building that majority was extremely difficult, given the fragmented structure of authority in Congress. Moreover, even as party discipline has increased in recent decades, legislators still have incentives to go their own way, which puts conflicting burdens on the Congressional party leadership. On the one hand, legislators expect the leadership to deliver policies for which credit can be claimed during elections, but leaders also have to be attentive to their members' diversity in ideological preferences and electoral needs. The difficulty of the balancing act is revealed by the razor-thin margins by which versions of the law often passed and the compromises that were made along the way. In 2003, the GOP leadership had to hold open the vote for considerably longer than the conventional 15 minutes to get both the initial bill and the final conference report passed. In both cases, considerable arm-twisting was required to round up enough Republican votes in support of the bill. In part, the close margins are reflective of the polarized political environment on Capitol Hill, particularly in the House, where the vast majority of Democrats stood resolutely opposed to the legislation. Yet, it also was revealing of the difficult sell the Republicans had within their own caucus: many conservatives grumbled each time about the legislation, and although many ultimately came on board, a smaller group remained intransigent and angry about what they viewed as a costly, unnecessary new entitlement.

The intra-party rancor aroused by the legislation also is telling about an important aspect of delegated governance: it often obfuscates and confuses more than it reveals. Was the MMA an expansion of a government entitlement, or a form of welfare state retrenchment? People from across the political spectrum held competing views on this, and the congruencies of opinion were often surprising. Some liberals deeply opposed the MMA as a form of "stealth privatization" (in the words of columnist Paul Krugman), and they were joined in opposition by conservatives angry that the MMA did not go far enough in privatizing the program. As Don Devine of the American Conservative Union declared, "Bush supporting and now signing this new $7 trillion unfunded entitlement, it is official. The GOP has now become the nation's new welfare state party."[146] Other conservatives and moderate Republicans favored the bill, arguing that it in fact *did* contain significant reform elements that could ultimately transform Medicare politics down the road. Yet, at the same time, the few Democrats who supported the MMA argued that it did *not* have that kind of long-term, reformist potential. How can we reconcile these diverse viewpoints? We cannot; instead, ambiguities over the larger significance of the law help explain why the bill passed at all, and what political function delegated governance has in a political system in which there is little agreement about the appropriate role of the federal government in addressing social problems.

This episode also reveals the need to understand aspects of policy design—such as how the program would actually be administered—for making sense of the politics of social provision. Even many informed observers might not see much difference between delivering a drug benefit through risk-bearing or non-risk-bearing entities. Yet, this was a source of tremendous controversy and debate—an example of a nitty-gritty decision about program administration that would have major consequences for the experiences of beneficiaries, the profit-making potential for organized interests, and the programmatic aims of the architects of competing bills. The degree to which private plans would bear risk also was critical to building support for the bill, as it was believed by powerful groups such as pharmaceutical firms to have tremendous implications for the future of their industry.

Finally, delegating governance of the drug benefit to private insurance companies is, once again, a way to pass the responsibility for making tough choices onto private firms. Republicans favored this because they lacked faith in the ability of government to face up to powerful health care interests. Looking at the experience of Medicare with containing hospital and physician costs, they saw failure, not success, arguing that government price-setting failed on the grounds of market efficiency but also because of endless Congressional meddling in reimbursement policy that distorted decision-making. Republicans were determined not to repeat this model of policy-making toward pharmaceuticals. Although many liberals and some Democrats have defended the Medicare program's ability to contain costs, some Democrats in Congress also have shown little willingness to stand up to the pharmaceutical industry. Certainly, there would later be proposals to eliminate the non-interference clause banning government negotiation with pharmaceutical companies over drug prices, but those laws have thus far never allowed the government to get involved in setting formularies—a *sine qua non* for effective negotiations with the industry because the government needs to be able to *threaten* that it will remove a company's drug from the reimbursed formulary in order to extract a better price. Democrats thus seem no more willing to tell senior citizens which drugs they can take and how much they have to pay for them. Delegating governance for such decisions to private insurers guarantees that these companies will be the bad guys, doing the dirty work for the federal government of bargaining with drug companies and intervening in the choices seniors make about health care.

6

Administering the Delegated Welfare State

The Cases of Medicare and the 2003 Medicare Modernization Act

How well does the delegated welfare state actually work? Is it an efficient and effective way to administer government programs? Or do such practices add layers of private bureaucracy to the public ones, diffuse governing authority to the point of incoherence, and undermine the effectiveness of public programs? Answering these questions is complicated by the fact that delegation has taken varying forms. For instance, as the previous chapters showed, Medicare now contains within it different models of delegated governance—the contracting-out of administrative functions to non-state actors in the original Medicare program and the growing reliance on a publicly subsidized and regulated marketplace of private plans that provide benefits. In other policy fields, such as Medicaid, public assistance, and college education financing, we can find an array of hybrid public-private arrangements in which governing authority is shared with private actors but the relationship is structured in particular ways. Given this complexity, it would be an impossible task to evaluate the effectiveness of this delegated welfare state as a whole, and we would risk making some of the facile generalizations that have often surrounded the debates around privatization and contracting out.

Instead, we advance a more modest set of claims based on an in-depth analysis of the functioning of Medicare, using this case study as a way to address some larger questions about both conventional contracting out and consumer-choice forms of delegated governance. Has the contracting out of program administration been a cost-effective way to run Medicare, one that not only saves the government money but facilitates the effective administration of the program? How well-functioning is the publicly subsidized marketplace of private plans? Has Part D, for instance, achieved its goal of improving access to prescription drugs, saved the government money, and resulted in a good quality "product" for Medicare beneficiaries? The latter questions are especially important, given ongoing debates over how best to reform federal entitlement programs and extend health care coverage to the uninsured. In the 2009–2010 debates over health care reform, some explicitly held up Medicare Part D as a model, arguing that it had saved the government money, provided a high-quality benefit to seniors, yet avoided the need for intrusive government intervention in the health care sphere. Does the experience of Part D since 2006 support these claims?

Looking first at the contracting out of much of the administration of traditional Medicare since 1965, we argue that while this setup may have helped achieve various political objectives, this has often come at the cost of effective administration. Although many lauded the successful launch of Medicare in 1965, problems soon became apparent in the administration of the program. Diffusing so much responsibility to a decentralized field of private agents hampered the government's ability to contain program costs or assure the quality of care. Over time, the performance of private contractors improved, but only federal price-setting effectively reined in Medicare spending. Other problems in the management of the program continued, such as difficulties controlling fraud and abuse. These problems stem less from inherent governmental incompetence than from political antipathy to the expansion of federal administrative capabilities over health care. A small, hollow agency is charged with the task of overseeing a vast terrain of decentralized, largely self-governing agents, and thus it is hardly surprising that this agency has frequently been outgunned.

The experience of private plans in Medicare also has been mixed. After the chaotic and flawed implementation of the new prescription drug benefit early in 2006, the program began improving access to prescription medications and lightening the cost burden on beneficiaries, particularly of low-income and/or chronically ill individuals. Moreover, the total cost of the program to the federal government has been lower than expected, as have average premiums. However, the available evidence casts doubt on the extent to which market forces should be credited with these achievements. These markets are underpinned by generous public subsidies, without which both the Medicare Advantage and Part D markets would hardly exist. Moreover, Medicare Advantage plans have been overpaid relative to traditional fee-for-service Medicare, and the lower-than-expected costs of the prescription drug benefit result largely from overall declines in pharmaceutical costs, greater use of generic drugs, and the initially slower-than-projected pace of enrollment. While private plans have lifted administrative burdens from the federal government, some also have engaged in manipulative or fraudulent marketing practices and failed to provide good customer service to beneficiaries. As in conventional Medicare, the small number of federal employees charged with overseeing this vast new marketplace have struggled to restrain these practices.

In sum, the same forces driving the creation of the delegated welfare state—namely, ambivalence or outright political hostility to the growth of state power—have also hollowed out the administrative apparatus needed to ensure the efficient and effective functioning of these programs. Delegated governance is not doomed to fail, but the political conditions that make such arrangements more likely also work against the development of state capacity that could help such a complex system function.

Delegated Governance in Traditional Medicare:
A Mixed Picture

The travails of Medicare administration over the years provide some insights into the costs and benefits of delegating administrative authority to private actors. Although the diffusion of authority in Medicare has probably been important to the program's political viability, this frequently has come at the cost of good governance. Delegating the governance of the original Medicare program may have made political sense, but is problematic from the standpoint of effective government administration.

As chapter 2 discussed, there are two layers of delegation in the original Medicare program. One is the delegation of responsibility for the delivery of publicly funded medical care to professionals, such as physicians, nurses, hospitals, and other health care facilities. As Sallyanne Payton notes, such an arrangement creates a "governance partnership" between the federal government and professionals in which the latter are largely self-governing.[1] Thus, in the system of fee-for-service medicine embraced by Medicare in 1965, medical providers determined what care to provide and how much to charge for it, relatively free of third-party constraint. The commitment to preserving clinical and financial autonomy of providers was then reflected in the second form of delegation—the contracting out of authority over program administration to intermediating entities, many of which were products of the medical community's existing system of self-governance. Determination of the fitness of providers to participate in Medicare was delegated to existing, private accreditation organizations. Claims administration similarly was delegated largely to Blue Cross and Blue Shield plans that had been created by the provider community as a preferable alternative to either commercial insurers or government payers. And a "non-interference" clause in the original Medicare statute reinforced the point that the federal government would not interfere in the practice of medicine, but would simply be a third-party payer along the lines of existing indemnity insurers.

This diffusion of authority has probably been essential to Medicare's political success. For instance, given the fierce opposition of medical providers to an expanded federal role in medical care, it was difficult to do anything but embrace the existing system of fee-for-service medicine and promise minimal government interference in it.[2] Similarly, creating a buffer zone of intermediary actors to conduct reimbursements and determine that basic quality standards were met was a way to minimize political tensions between federal authorities and practitioners.[3] Such arrangements were particularly important in the early days of the program because provider participation is voluntary and some physicians threatened to refuse Medicare. Although an attempted boycott quickly flared out, government officials were extremely preoccupied with maximizing provider participation so as to make sure that seniors could immediately gain access to the new benefit while using the physicians of their choice.[4] Government officials also found it useful to shift responsibility for problems away from the federal government. As Robert Ball later recalled, using intermediaries "helped to 'spread the heat'. Some of the criticisms were directed at them."[5] Finally, one can wonder whether the political will ever would have been there to hire the large number of civil servants that would have been necessary to administer the program directly.[6]

Delegating governance has had some advantages from a technical-administrative standpoint as well. As Payton notes, in governance partnerships the government essentially borrows existing private capacity and thus the expertise, skills, and knowledge that already exist in the private sphere. This may be especially useful in managing a health insurance program, given the vast and greatly decentralized nature of the American health care system and the complex nature of the services being delivered. Whereas a program such as Social Security distributes benefits that are calculated according to statutorily defined and relatively straightforward criteria, Medicare pays for services provided by a heterogeneous provider community that differs in the way that it practices medicine and in the fees that its members charge.[7] Determining that services were necessary or that the fees charged were appropriate is thus no easy task and is an argument for localized administrative arrangements.

Similarly, assessing the quality of the medical facilities whose costs would be reimbursed by the new program posed some daunting challenges. A federal initiative to directly certify that hospitals and other medical facilities met basic quality standards would have required a significant buildup of bureaucratic capabilities, and delegating these responsibilities to states also was not an option, given their limited staffs and capabilities in the area of hospital licensing.[8] Moreover, existing accreditation organizations already were believed to have expertise in this area, and it has not been uncommon for Congress and public agencies to delegate authority to these entities rather than try to build up their own independent capabilities.[9] Thus, Medicare officials ceded responsibility for these determinations to the Joint Commission on Accreditation of Hospitals (or JCAH, later renamed the Joint Commission on Accreditation of Healthcare Organizations [JCAHO], and more recently rebaptized The Joint Commission [JC])—a nonprofit organization created in 1951 by medical provider associations to provide voluntary accreditation of hospitals.[10] In the 1965 statute, Medicare accepted any hospital with JCAH accreditation as meeting Medicare standards for participation in the program, and barred the federal government from imposing additional requirements on hospitals. Government officials were not even allowed to read the JCAH's accreditation reports.[11]

Over the years, program officials acquired greater authority over the process of ensuring that basic quality standards are met—gaining access to Joint Commission reports, for instance, and contracting with state agencies to determine whether facilities that are accredited also meet Medicare's standards of participation.[12] HCFA/CMS has embarked on other initiatives with regard to improving quality, such as contracting with Quality Improvement Organizations (previously known as Professional Standards Review Organizations and later Peer Review Organizations) that review the quality of care. At the federal level, rather than continuing to accept what these decentralized organizations claimed were standards of practice, new resources flowed into health services research that sought to establish medical practice guidelines.[13] The National Center for Health Services Research was revamped and twice renamed (since 1999 it has been called the Agency for Healthcare Research and Quality), although its mission is limited to advice and guidance. Moreover, the QIOs are also private (mostly nonprofit) associations composed of health care professionals, and CMS still relies heavily on the JC and other accreditation bodies rather than developing independent capabilities for assuring minimum quality standards. Assuring quality in the Medicare program has been, and remains, largely contracted out, although the 2010 Patient Protection and Affordable Care Act mandates the creation of a new Center for Medicare and Medicaid Innovation in 2011 within CMS to test and promote modes of payment and service delivery that improve the quality of care.

How well has such a system worked? Some have argued that the Joint Commission (and its predecessors) have been reasonably effective at upholding minimum standards, or at least that the federal government is unlikely to have done a better job.[14] The latter claim is based on an untested counterfactual: because the federal government never was allowed to build up the bureaucratic capabilities to directly regulate health care quality, we do not know whether delegating this function to private actors is superior to a system of direct governance. In fact, the Joint Commission and other private accreditation organizations have faced sharp criticism over the years, with concerns about whether the Commission's standards are actually enforced, the seemingly political nature of the accreditation process, the failure of the JCAHO to identify many hospitals that are "seriously deficient" with regard to Medicare requirements, and, quite fundamentally, the fact that the medical industry has largely been allowed to regulate itself.[15] Critics also have noted the rarity with which hospitals or other health care institutions have been denied accreditation, as well as the evidence of substandard care being provided at many facilities across the country, as proof that the Commission has been relatively toothless. Some of that evidence has come from investigative journalists highlighting the poor quality of care,[16] but more damning has been the work of John Wennberg and colleagues at Dartmouth University showing tremendous variations in the quality of care across the country that are not explained by levels of Medicare spending.[17] Others offer a more positive view, pointing out that health care institutions themselves hardly view the JC as one of their own, but instead find JC visits to be quite burdensome.[18] Yet, there is little evidence to show that accreditation or the rate of JC-identified problems correlate with other quality measures.[19] Lacking clear positive evidence about these organizations, it appears that reliance upon private accreditation organizations has been largely driven by political concerns—keeping federal bureaucracies out of the business of regulating health care quality—rather than about finding the best way to assure that quality care is being regularly delivered.

The experience of contracting out Medicare's payment administration also has been mixed, due in part to limitations of the contractors themselves and the difficulties that Medicare administrators have had supervising contractor behavior. Examining the early implementation of Medicare, for instance, shows that the private actors in whom much governing authority had been vested had no apparent advantages over government bureaucrats in performing their tasks. In the case of the fiscal intermediaries and carriers for Parts A and B, for instance, both the commercial firms and Blue Cross plans initially were ill-adept at administering the program, as chapter 3 discussed. A Senate Finance Committee study of Medicare administration in 1970 was especially critical of the quality of both intermediaries and carriers. As the Committee report stated about the Part B carriers, "Carrier performance under medicare [*sic*] has in the majority of instances between erratic, inefficient, costly and inconsistent with congressional intent. . . . Unquestionably many millions of dollars of public funds have gone to subsidize carrier inefficiency."[20]

The intermediating entities also failed to be effective agents of cost control, and thus contributed to rapidly growing spending in the early years of the program. The Medicare statute and accompanying regulations stated that hospitals would be reimbursed for the "reasonable cost" of providing services, while physicians would be paid based upon "customary and prevailing fees," but there was no agreement on what either of these concepts meant. One argument for using private insurers as claims processors was that they were supposed to have experience with provider claims and would know a "customary and prevailing charge" for a medical service when they saw it. Yet, it quickly became apparent that many intermediaries and carriers were neither willing nor prepared to challenge hospitals and physicians, which gave providers an opening to ramp up the prices they charged for medical services. Indeed, after program passage, doctors' fees rose between 5 and 8 percent annually, and their incomes increased 11 percent each year, while hospital costs rose 10 percent annually,[21] significant increases over pre-Medicare growth rates.[22] Medicare thus inadvertently contributed to the rapidly rising cost of medical care in this period, although it was not the only cause.[23]

The root of the problem lay in the power dynamic between medical providers and many of the intermediaries. Because the Blue Cross and Blue Shield plans were largely offshoots of the provider community, they had few incentives to rigorously scrutinize claims. This problem was exacerbated in Part A by the fact that providers selected the intermediary of their choice and could drop it and pick another one after a year. According to former SSA and HCFA official Hale Champion,

> If the providers didn't like the intermediary, they wouldn't nominate them. So that every time an intermediary started cooperating with us, started helping the federal government watch its backs, the first thing

they knew, they were no longer the intermediary. That was being controlled by the people they were supposed to watch over.[24]

The Senate Finance Committee turned up evidence that some insurers promised providers that they would not provide rigorous oversight in order to secure a nomination, and some intermediaries also sold other insurance products to the same providers they were supposed to be supervising. In theory, governmental control over Part B carriers should have been greater, as federal officials directly contracted with these plans and were supposed to deny renewal to poor-quality plans. In reality, carriers' contracts were renewed almost automatically, despite evidence that many were inefficient and ineffective.[25]

In short, although we cannot know whether the federal government would have performed these tasks any better—the government never really had the chance to do so (with the exception of the small number that SSA would process)– it is clear that at the outset the private intermediary bodies lacked the bureaucratic capacity and autonomy to administer the program. Rather, they had to build up that capacity by adding large numbers of new employees and developing the ability to process claims[26]—precisely as the federal government would have done had it directly administered the program.

Over time, the intermediaries and carriers became more adept at processing claims. For instance, a 1975 General Accounting Office report found that intermediaries processed Medicare claims more cost-effectively than did the Social Security Administration, in part because of the lower salaries they paid to their employees.[27] Medicare administrative costs have been low—shockingly low to those who argue that this is less reflective of the great efficiency of the program than the fact that it is starved for resources and has had to make do with very little (discussed below).[28] Despite this, Medicare processes a huge number of claims in a relatively speedy fashion.

Beyond the efficient processing of claims, however, outside observers have frequently been critical of the performance of the Medicare contractors. Starting in the 1990s, the HHS Office of Inspector General (OIG) began measuring the error rate in Medicare payments, including payments for medically unnecessary services, services with insufficiently documented medical records, and services that Medicare does not cover, as well as overpayments due to coding errors. The rates were at times in the double-digits—over 14 percent in 1996—and while HCFA/CMS successfully brought down error rates by the end of the 1990s, they continued to fluctuate and doubled between 2008 and 2009.[29] One reason for the more recently higher number, it seems, is a change in how CMS calculates the error rate, which the OIG pointed out had systematically been understating the degree of the problem.[30]

In addition, numerous GAO studies over the years have found that the contractors are ill-equipped to protect the program against fraudulent behavior by providers,[31] and that many carriers failed to make effective use of claims data and pre-or post-payment reviews to identify suspicious practices—such as breaking up medical procedures into individual claims so as to increase Medicare reimbursements.[32] Even worse, perhaps, is a damning set of GAO reports in the 1990s which reported that one-quarter of all claims administration contracts allegedly had integrity problems, 7 out of 58 contractors were actively under investigation, and 6 had agreed to civil or criminal settlements for fraudulent activities that had, according to investigators and former contract employees, "become a way of life" for the contractors.[33] Despite efforts since then to reduce problems of waste, fraud, and abuse in the program, in 2009, CMS estimated that improper payments for the Medicare fee-for-service program exceeded $24 billion in that year alone—a figure that likely underestimates the problem.[34]

These and other shortcomings of the contractor system do not prove the inherent fallibility of contracting out, but instead reveal how the antipathy toward government that drives the move to contract out in the first place often leads to ill-conceived systems of delegated governance that then perform poorly. Many of the problems with Medicare contractors are the result of poor oversight by the agencies charged with supervising them—the Bureau of Health Insurance (1966–1977), Health Care Financing Agency (HCFA, 1977–2001), and now the Centers for Medicare and Medicaid Services (CMS 2001–present).[35] These problems, in turn, stem from the unwillingness of policy-makers to shore up these agencies' administrative capacity. In essence, the antipathy of policy-makers toward bureaucratic power not only led to the delegation of program governance to private actors, but also hollowed out the agency charged with overseeing these private actors.

The problem is evident in the lack of resources devoted to program administration. In 1980, there were fewer than 5,000 full-time equivalent employees working for HCFA, and that number would actually decline over time, falling to 4,497 in 2002[36] and 4,483 in 2008, after the MMA added a complex new benefit to Medicare.[37] This small agency administers a budget that, according to former CMS administrator Kerry Weems, is "more than the economies of all but twelve nations."[38] By comparison, the Social Security Administration has over 60,000 employees to administer a far simpler program.[39] Not only has HCFA/CMS had to administer the Medicare program, but also has had to oversee state Medicaid and Children's Health Insurance Programs and implement many other health-related laws (such as ensuring that the insurance plans comply with the 1996 Health Insurance Portability and Accountability Act).[40]

HFCA/CMS also has been chronically underfunded, a fact that program administrators and outside observers from across the ideological spectrum periodically decry.[41] A 1999 open letter signed by individuals from the Heritage Foundation, Urban Institute, American Enterprise Institute, and Health Insurance Association of America, among others, stated that:

> . . . many of the difficulties that threaten to cripple the Health Care Financing Administration stem from an unwillingness of both Congress

and the Clinton administration to provide the agency the resources and administrative flexibility necessary to carry out its mammoth assignment . . . no private health insurer, after subtracting its marketing costs and profit, would ever attempt to manage such large and complex insurance programs with so small an administrative budget.[42]

The crunch affected intermediaries, carriers, and other contractors, contributing to deteriorations in the quality of the services they provide.[43] Ultimately, many decided to get out of the business of Medicare administration altogether. Fiscal constraints also have prevented the agency from acquiring the staff expertise needed to run a large and complex program.[44] Yet, year after year, Congressional appropriations for the agency remained below that which many believed was needed for its successful functioning, while, at the same time, Congress has regularly imposed new responsibilities on the organization.[45]

Some argue the source of the problem lies in the fact that, although Medicare is a mandatory entitlement and thus under the tax writing and House Energy and Commerce Committees, its administrative costs are determined annually by the House and Senate Appropriations committees. This means that money for Medicare and Medicaid program administration has to compete with funds for the National Institutes of Health or the Centers for Disease Control and Prevention—entities that are often more popular in Congress and with executive officials who put together annual appropriations requests. As former CMS administrator Weems has remarked, "Frankly, bureaucrats don't compete well in this environment."[46] Some also see ideological motives at work, with those hostile to national health insurance against enabling the agency overseeing existing federal health care programs to work too well.[47] According to former HCFA administrator Bruce Vladeck, "This has been a political decision: making Medicare look good would embarrass the ideologues who believe government should function poorly."[48] Or, as Payton has put it:

> Actions affecting Medicare tend to be evaluated politically, therefore, for their potential to advance or retard the cause of national health insurance, for their effect in creating or tending to block the creation of an administrative infrastructure sufficient to allow the government to make a credible claim that it can administer a national health insurance system, and for their potential to push future development toward one model or another of government-sponsored health coverage.[49]

Whatever the precise motivations, the result has been a hollow agency that has often struggled to assure the effective administration of the Medicare program by its many contractors.[50]

Additional problems in program administration reflected the lack of a competitive market of contractors serving the program prior to 2003, when a major contractor reform was enacted as part of the Medicare Modernization Act (MMA).

The 1965 law creating Medicare exempted contractors from the Federal Acquisition Regulations (FAR) that normally governed contractor relationships, allowing, for example, no open competition for intermediary contracts: provider groups such as the American Hospital Association simply chose them. There also was little accountability for contractors due to minimal written contracts with few clear performance standards, and the fact that the 1965 Medicare law required that contractors have a public hearing before their contracts could be terminated and forbade the government from ending a contract without cause. Contractors, by contrast, could end involvement in the program by giving only 180 days notice.[51] With contracts that were nearly always renewed, there also was no competition among them on performance, even though there was tremendous variation in the cost-effectiveness of these contractors.[52] In addition, the law creating Medicare called for the use of cost-based contracts, in which intermediaries and carriers are reimbursed for the costs they incur but cannot make a profit on administering the program. This meant that the contractors had few incentives to hold down costs.[53] Instead, they functioned essentially as an arm of the government that had a guaranteed role in administering a public program.

Again, these arrangements are not inherent in a contracted-out system, but they reflect both power dynamics specific to the Medicare program and practices that are not uncommon in other contracted-out social welfare programs. Given the resistance of insurers and providers to the creation of Medicare in the first place, the law was written in a way that catered to both—allowing providers to select the intermediaries in Part A, for instance, and bringing both intermediaries and carriers into the program on terms that were highly favorable. The lack of turnover or competitive bidding processes that resulted had some advantages for program administrators, however. Particularly in the early years of the program, contractor staff and agency officials forged a fairly close relationship. With the carriers and intermediaries, Medicare contracting was a distinct part of the business, and people often stayed for a long time, becoming civil servants, in essence, with vast knowledge of the program.[54] As in other social welfare programs, there are advantages to allowing bonds to form between an agency and its contractors, rather than throwing the whole sector open to regular competitive bidding. This is especially the case when, as has been the case with Medicare, the contractors know far more about the operational side of the program than does the agency itself. Frequent turnover in contractors thus could produce a loss of knowledge and operational capacity that would be hard to replace.

In short, the lack of competitive bidding therefore did have some positive aspects. Yet, these cozy relationships with contractors could also lead HCFA officials to overlook abuses occurring as well. For instance, a GAO report in the late 1990s found that HCFA officials tended to trust whatever documentation contractors supplied the agency as accurate without independently verifying it, and would sometimes notify contractors in advance about when it would conduct reviews of contractor performance and what documents would be analyzed.[55] And because it was difficult to end a contract, agency officials lacked leverage to demand better performance.[56]

These and other complaints fueled efforts to bring the contractor system more in line with that used for other federal programs—efforts that were repeatedly blocked because the contractors had allies in Congress that protected them against efforts to consolidate the number involved in the program or to create a competitive bidding system.[57] A major reform of the contractor system finally was achieved in the 2003 MMA and is to be fully implemented by the end of 2011. The law empowered CMS to eliminate the distinction between Part A intermediaries and Part B carriers, create a competitive bidding process in which CMS (and not hospitals) decides who receives a contract, and move from cost-based to fixed-price contracts, and required that contractors comply with the Federal Acquisition Regulation.[58] Thus far, the changes have produced a significant reduction in the number of claims-processing contractors, which fell from 45 for Part A and B prior to the reform to 15.[59] CMS decided not to adopt fixed-cost contracts, however, and all of the contractors selected had previously been program intermediaries and carriers. It is too early to say whether the reform will meet its stated objectives, which include improving customer service to providers and beneficiaries as well as budgetary savings. What has not changed is the lack of federal resources for the agency, something that both Republican- and Democratic-appointed administrators of the program have condemned.[60]

In sum, the contracting out of Medicare administration has had mixed results. We can easily see the appeal of such an arrangement in a political context hostile to government expansion and involvement in health care. Decentralizing payment responsibilities also has advantages from the standpoint of public administration, given geographic variations in medical practices and costs, and Medicare annually pays a huge number of claims and deals with a vast and diverse array of medical providers. At the same time, however, the same political forces conducive to delegated governance also tend to produce under-resourced, administratively weak agencies with limited supervisory capabilities and chronic under-funding of contractor budgets.

Creating a Social Welfare Marketplace: The 2003 MMA

The 2003 MMA contains marketized forms of delegated governance, in which social welfare responsibilities are delegated to agents that are supposed to bear some risk, as well as to beneficiaries who become consumers choosing their benefits from a competitive marketplace. Much as the original Medicare program represented the largest foray into social welfare contracting at the time, the MMA is the largest experiment with market-based reform of a federal entitlement program, and it has been held up by both advocates and opponents as an example of just what such reforms are likely to bring. For that reason alone, it is important to examine how effective the program has been at meeting its goals. The MMA has added significance as a potential model for reform of the American health care system. Can a system of competing private plans, in which individuals receive subsidies and then are free to choose a plan of their liking, succeed in delivering quality benefits at a reasonable cost? And can the government administer the program, protecting consumers from fraudulent practices and ensuring that individuals have enough information to serve as effective consumers in the benefits marketplace?

Early Implementation of the MMA

Implementation of the new prescription drug benefit posed some significant challenges. Medicare Part D was unlike anything the federal government had ever done before, as it intertwines federal subsidies, regulations, and requirements with an entirely new market of prescription drug plans. Beyond the usual challenges of educating the public about a new, voluntary benefit and convincing them to sign up for it, government officials had to figure out how to link up the federal program with a diverse and dynamic market of private plans and ensure that beneficiaries could access their medications at pharmacies across the nation. All of this had to be done in fairly short order: open enrollment for the new benefit began November 15, 2005, and closed in mid-May of 2006, but the "dual eligibles"—around 6.3 million low-income people on Medicaid whose coverage shifted from Medicaid to Medicare—would be abruptly transitioned to their new drug plans on January 1, 2006, when their Medicaid drug coverage ended. The dual eligible population includes some of the most vulnerable members of society, including people who are disproportionately poor and in ill health and who therefore rely more heavily on prescription medications than do other Medicare beneficiaries. Over one-third of this population is cognitively or mentally impaired.[61] Because of the nature of the population, dual eligibles who do not select a plan were, and continue to be, randomly assigned to plans that meet certain criteria.

The stakes around the new program were high, as the MMA provided a critical test of market-based reform of health care and federal entitlements. Would competitive forces generate a satisfying array of choices for senior citizens while holding down costs for both beneficiaries and the federal government? This was the proposition that the Republican leadership had endorsed and convinced enough of their Congressional members to vote for, but from the start many wondered whether the reform would actually work. First, many worried that insurance companies and pharmacy benefit managers (PBMs), some of which had voiced skepticism about the bill during its crafting, would decide not to enter the PDP market. Moreover, if senior citizens could not figure out the new benefit, or concluded it would not help them, many could choose not to enroll in the voluntary program. With only the sickest beneficiaries signing up for the new benefit, private plans were at risk of an adverse selection death spiral that could undercut the entire structure of the reform. Politically, the pressure was especially high, given that 2006 was an election year. Large-scale failure of the new benefit was sure to boomerang across the political scene, putting Republican defenders of the reform at particular risk.

The first few months of the Part D benefit were marred by well-publicized failures, some of which were due to rocky implementation, while others—like unexpectedly high out-of-pocket costs for some beneficiaries—were due to the way the law was written. As some had predicted, the biggest problems affected the Medicare-Medicaid dual eligibles at the start of 2006 when some suddenly discovered that they had not been properly moved into a new PDP or else that their new plan charged them more for their prescriptions than had Medicaid.[62] Some of the problems stemmed from inadequate national computer systems that were supposed to verify entitlement to coverage, and then were exacerbated by long waiting times when pharmacists tried to contact private plans and the Medicare program. The media coverage was rife with stories about poor, ailing beneficiaries being told they owed hefty co-payments for medications they had previously paid little or nothing for, or that they were not in the system at all and thus had no apparent form of coverage.[63] Some non-dual eligibles who signed up for the new benefit in December also did not show up in computer systems yet as being enrolled in a drug plan. While government officials blamed ill-trained pharmacists for some of the mistakes, pharmacists recounted the hours they had spent on hold on behalf of desperate beneficiaries. As the stories accumulated about people leaving pharmacies without critical medications, many state governments stepped in to cover these costs in the interim, while members of Congress lambasted the Bush administration for the failures.[64]

Added to these problems was the widespread confusion experienced by many Medicare beneficiaries as they waded through a large number of drug plan options and attempted to choose a plan before the enrollment deadline of May 15, 2006. By the time enrollment for Part D began in late 2005, there were a total of 1,429 plans across the country, with at least 40 different plans to choose from in most states, and as many as 52 in two states (Pennsylvania and West Virginia).[65] These plans presented beneficiaries with a dizzying array of options, as each plan offered a distinct matrix of premiums, deductibles, and co-payment tiers, not to mention differing drug formularies.[66] Moreover, to figure out what plan was best, beneficiaries needed to calculate not only their current prescription drug costs and needs, but also project into the future their likely requirements. Plans could change their formularies during the year with 60 days notice, but once beneficiaries signed up for a plan they could not switch to another one until the annual open enrollment period (with the exception of dual eligibles and people who move during the year). Although CMS had a web site that tried to help people select the best plan, less than one-tenth of beneficiaries visited it[67] and a 2006 GAO study found that it was often difficult for people to use.[68] The same study found that call center representatives at the toll-free helpline, 1-800-MEDICARE, correctly answered questions about the drug benefit two-thirds of the time and that only 41 percent of responses were accurate when it came to counseling a beneficiary on which drug plan would cost the least.

The complexity of the decision and pressure to choose a plan by a set deadline led to a loud chorus of complaints by Medicare beneficiaries and consumer advocates. Many Democrats seized upon the discontent surrounding the new benefit. As Senator Hillary Clinton (D-NY) stated at a Senate subcommittee hearing on the problems, ". . . it is an absolute embarrassment, outrage, deep heartbreaking disappointment to be in the presence of people who are so distraught, confused, upset and feeling abandoned,"[69] while Senator Edward M. Kennedy (D-MA) declared that "the Medicare drug programs has been a nightmare for America's seniors and is clear evidence of the Bush administration's shocking incompetence."[70] Some predicted that Democrats could capitalize on the discontent in the 2006 mid-term elections. Democratic advisers Stan Greenberg and James Carville put out an alert in February 2006 stating that the drug benefit could stir a senior citizen revolt and that "Democrats now have the opportunity to raise opposition to the drug benefit to new heights and use the plan as a powerful symbol of Republican corruption and irresponsibility."[71]

By the time of the enrollment deadline, however, many of the immediate problems facing the dual eligibles had been ironed out, most beneficiaries without existing coverage had chosen a drug plan, and the media began to offer a more positive assessment of the drug benefit.[72] Already by May 2006, public opinion polls revealed that a majority of enrollees were satisfied with Part D and felt that it was saving them money, and later surveys and focus groups showed that most seniors were happy enough with their plan to stick with it.[73] For instance, according to an April 11, 2006, *Washington Post-ABC News* Poll, 65 percent of seniors enrolled in the new benefit approved of it, and 63 percent felt they were saving either some (32 percent) or a lot (31 percent) of money compared to what they were paying for prescription drugs before. Other polls by the Kaiser Family Foundation and Tarrance Group similarly found that three-quarters of enrollees said they were somewhat or very satisfied with the new benefit, and majorities in both polls thought the program saved them money.[74]

In the succeeding years, a growing number of economists and policy analysts also started offering more favorable evaluations of the new program.[75] After keeping a low profile about the reform—President Bush failed to even mention the prescription drug benefit in his January 2006 State of the Union speech to Congress—some Republicans and other backers of the legislation also began to speak up about its merits. Some have pointed to the MMA as a model for contemporary efforts to reform the health care system.[76] As Benjamin E. Sasse, a former assistant secretary of HHS under Bush, declared, "Medicare Part D is (or should be) a policymaker's dream: a government program that efficiently delivers high-quality services, and does so under budget."[77]

How accurate are such claims about this hybrid public-private program? Although the program has improved seniors' access to prescription drugs and reduced monthly costs for many, it is less clear that market competition should be credited with some of the program's successes.

Successes of Part D

One of most important successes of the new benefit is bringing senior drug coverage near universality. As a voluntary benefit, one concern was that many eligible seniors would not sign up for it, and/or that adverse selection—in which the sickest beneficiaries are more likely to enroll in drug plans—would undermine the fledgling market for drug plans. Instead, the vast majority of beneficiaries without coverage enrolled in a Part D or Medicare Advantage plan. As of October 2010, 90 percent of beneficiaries had some form of drug coverage, with 59 percent enrolled in either a stand-alone prescription drug plan (38 percent) or Medicare Advantage plan that offered drug coverage (21 percent). The rest had employer-sponsored coverage subsidized by Medicare (18 percent) or other coverage (13 percent), while around 10 percent had no coverage.[78] This was a significant improvement over the pre-MMA situation, when about 25 percent of beneficiaries lacked insurance to cover drug costs and, when including those lacking coverage for part of the year, the proportion without coverage was nearly half of all beneficiaries.[79] Although there does appear to be some adverse selection into plans—with healthier people more disinclined to enroll in Part D plans than those who are sicker and already rely on more prescriptions[80]—this has not yet proven ruinous to this nascent market.

The benefit also has brought down drug costs for many people and increased access to medications. Several studies showed an increase in prescription drug use by between 5.9–12.8 percent for all beneficiaries and a drop in out-of-pocket spending ranging from 13.1–18.4 percent.[81] In research that looks specifically at people who previously lacked coverage, Schneeweiss and colleagues find substantially larger effects on both utilization and beneficiary spending.[82] Moreover, utilization declines when people hit the doughnut hole, revealing the importance of the new coverage for many people. Hoadley and colleagues reported that in 2007, 26 percent of Part D enrollees who filled one or more prescriptions and were not eligible for low-income subsidies hit the doughnut hole in 2007, and that among those hitting the coverage gap, 15 percent stopped taking their medication, 5 percent changed to a different drug within the same class, and one percent reduced use of the medication.[83] Another study of people without coverage in the doughnut hole found that they reduced their drug use by 14 percent.[84] Part D produced an overall decrease in cost-related non-adherence—a reduction in skipping doses, reducing doses, or failing to fill prescriptions among seniors due to cost concerns (although such non-adherence tended to reemerge in the doughnut hole, and Part D failed to reduce non-adherence among the sickest enrollees).[85]

Another indicator of success is that a market of stand-alone drug plans came into being at all. As chapter 5 detailed, some analysts and policy-makers were skeptical that such a market could sustain itself, and it was for that reason that the 2003 law included a fallback provision so that a government plan would be available in any region with fewer than two stand-alone plans. Instead, the opposite phenomenon occurred, as insurance companies and PBMs jumped in to try to scoop up market share. The coverage offered by these plans is generally comparable to that offered by other private and public plans.[86] Even with some declines in the extent to which the government cushions risk for these plans (discussed more below), there are still a large number of plans available, giving seniors a wide array of options for drug coverage. In addition, the higher subsidies directed to Medicare Advantage plans jump-started what had been a stagnating managed care market. In 2010, the average beneficiary could pick from 33 Medicare Advantage plans, and the proportion of seniors enrolled in these plans rose to 24 percent, from 13 percent in 2003.[87]

Finally, some have pointed to lower-than-expected federal spending on the program as evidence that market competition is at work. The Congressional Budget Office originally forecast that the MMA would cost $395 billion over 10 years. In 2004, the CMS actuary came out with a different estimate, which forecast the MMA costing over $550 billion over ten years. In fact, the new drug benefit has regularly cost less than expected.

While many of these successful aspects of the program are widely acknowledged and documented, the crucial question is the extent to which the competitive design of the benefit explains these successes.

The Mixed Effects of Market Competition in Part D

The first important qualification concerns the major role played by public funds in sustaining this new marketplace. The development of a large and varied market of Part D plans resulted largely from the combination of generous government subsidies and extensive risk-sharing. For each beneficiary, the federal government pays a subsidy worth around 74.5 percent of the cost of standard coverage, and plans receive additional subsidies for enrolling high-risk and low-income beneficiaries. In addition, government-defined risk corridors have limited the extent to which firms can profit—with margins projected by many to be only about 3–4 percent—but also ensure that there is little downside risk. Between 2006 and 2007, if spending exceeded 2.5 percent of expected plan costs, the federal government covered 75 percent of the amount falling between 2.5 and 5 percent of excessive costs, and 80 percent of costs over 5 percent. If plan costs came in lower than expected, they paid these sums back to the federal government. Since 2008, the risk corridor thresholds have doubled, and CMS has the power to further widen or even eliminate risk corridors after 2011.[88] The risk corridors and other subsidies helped pique the interest of private insurers in the drug benefit, once they realized, in the words of John Gorman, that "it's almost impossible to lose money in the first two years."[89]

Still, entering the Part D marketplace did require some significant start-up costs that were weighed against what some firms perceived as an opportunity to capture market share and establish themselves with a growing population of Medicare beneficiaries. For many, the calculus was clear: Medicare offered a huge opportunity that would never come around again. As the CFO of one managed care provider declared in 2005, "Frankly, I've never seen anything like this in my business career . . . a large, new market [has been] created with the swipe of a pen and put in the private sector—a $400 billion to $500 billion program over the next 8–10 years."[90] Many firms did not want to be left out on what some would call a "land grab," particularly given declining opportunities in the employer-sponsored insurance market.[91] Increasingly, administering public sector health insurance programs, such as Medicaid and Medicare, are viewed by insurance companies and Wall Street analysts as critical sources of future revenues,[92] and for firms such as Humana, over half of their business is for publicly funded programs such as Medicaid, Medicare, and TRICARE.[93]

High federal subsidies to Medicare Advantage were also important both in stimulating plan participation in Medicare Advantage and in stand-alone PDPs. Given the declining interest of private insurance plans in participating in Medicare, the MMA increased subsidies to these plans in the hope of luring them back into the market. These subsidies proved to be considerably higher than that which the program pays for beneficiaries in traditional fee-for-service Medicare. According to MedPAC, an independent agency that analyzes Medicare payment policy, private plans were paid 114 percent that of payments for FFS beneficiaries in 2009. This meant that Medicare spent around $14 billion more for MA plans in 2009 that it would have had those beneficiaries remained in fee-for-service Medicare.[94] These subsidies enable private plans to offer enhanced benefits, such as coverage for services not included in traditional Medicare (e.g., routine vision or dental care) or reduced cost-sharing. Yet, the result is higher costs for the Medicare program as a whole and higher Part B premiums for all Medicare beneficiaries (estimated by MedPac to be $3.35 higher per month in 2009 than if all Medicare beneficiaries were enrolled in traditional Medicare), who in essence subsidize the extra benefits enjoyed by those in private MA plans.[95]

Not only did these subsidies spur a renewal of the Medicare Advantage market, which covered nearly one-quarter of all beneficiaries as of 2010. The generous payments also created incentives for private plans to put forth stand-alone drug plans in the hope that they could then migrate seniors over to more lucrative MA plans. The latter offered potential profit margins that were at least double that of stand-alone plans.[96] One influential Citigroup health care analyst, Charles Boorady, estimated that the Medicare subsidies could nearly double the revenue of the managed care industry.[97] Humana was particularly open about its "enroll-and-migrate" strategy, in which it initially offered some of the cheapest Part D plans available and doubled what it paid sales representatives who signed people up for MA plans as opposed to stand-alone drug plans.[98] Other firms put their eggs in the MA basket as well. During the open enrollment period in late 2007, insurers put out three times more ads for Medicare Advantage plans than for stand-alone drug plans, and spent more than twice as much on these MA ads than they did for stand-alone plans.[99]

The law also fostered the expansion of "private fee-for-service" (PFFS) plans that differ from the managed care plans that constitute the majority of the MA program. PFFS plans are reimbursed on a fee-for-service basis and do not rely on provider networks. These private plans were first authorized by the 1997 Balanced Budget Act with the aim of increasing choices for seniors, particularly in rural areas, where it is harder to form provider networks. Their creation also reflected the influence of right-to-life groups worried that a shift to Medicare managed care would move beneficiaries into plans that they feared might deny them life-sustaining care. The 2003 MMA offered additional subsidies to these plans and spurred a rapid increase in their availability and enrollment.[100] PFFS plans have been much criticized, however, both for the hefty overpayments that have sustained their expansion and the absence of any of the averred benefits of Medicare managed care, such as care coordination, utilization management, and negotiated savings with provider networks. For that reason, legislative efforts in 2008 attempted to pare them back (see chapter 7).

In sum, generous federal government subsidies and risk-sharing underpinned the emergence of a thriving market of Medicare Advantage and stand-alone drug plans. Without this support, such a market would not exist, and the subsidies are essential to achieve a host of policy goals. For instance, generous subsidies for beneficiaries who are poor, in ill health, or both, are needed to prevent cream-skimming by plans looking to avoid paying for these high-cost beneficiaries. Indeed, computer simulations suggest that subsidies may have to be even higher to prevent the further exit of plans offering "enhanced" coverage that eliminates the deductible and covers part of the doughnut hole; the most generous plans with complete gap coverage have already disappeared due to the adverse selection.[101] And high Medicare Advantage payments have enabled the development of plans across the United States; previously, private plans would only enter certain markets, but the more lucrative opportunities that became available to them prompted much wider geographic coverage. Thus, although some have concluded from the MMA experience that private insurance markets can help solve the nation's health care woes, the lesson of the MMA is that such a market needs to be *heavily subsidized*. Or, as former health insurance lobbyist Charles N. ("Chip") Kahn, III, put it—referring to his earlier statements about the impossibility of stand-alone drug insurance—you *can* sell insurance for haircuts as long as those plans are subsidized enough.[102]

The costs of sustaining such a market might not matter if market competition in the new drug benefit has generated efficiencies that reduce overall federal spending, as some politicians and analysts have argued.[103] Some believe that insurers have been successful in holding down prescription drug costs through their negotiations with pharmaceutical firms. The fact that the cost of drugs commonly taken by Medicare recipients has declined since the implementation of the MMA lends significant credence to these claims.[104] Yet, growth rates for all prescription drug spending have slowed significantly since 2003, but for reasons that have little to do with insurance company negotiating power. Instead, the trend reflects the decreasing number of blockbuster drugs on the market, the increasing penetration of cheaper generics, and consumer safety concerns about some products.[105] Medicare Part D has contributed to this development because many PDPs have tiered formularies that encourage beneficiaries to use generic substitutes. But the overall decline in prescription drug spending suggests that there are forces at work that are well beyond the Medicare program.

Not only do these prescription drug trends reduce federal spending on Part D but also they help explain much of the gap between initial estimates and actual costs. When CBO was originally drawing up estimates of how much the program would cost over ten years, they used, among other things, forecasts of future pharmaceutical spending that reflected the explosive growth of the previous years,[106] and the Office of the Actuary at CMS employed similar assumptions. Yet, already by early 2005, a private research firm named Wood Mackenzie released a study arguing that both CMS and CBO overestimated the cost of the law because they had based their projections on exaggerated assumptions of both prescription drug cost increases and the pace of enrollment in the new plans. As the research director of the firm noted, "Slowing growth in drug costs will lower the overall price of Medicare reform. Maximum enrollment is very unlikely to happen overnight-it could take years rather than months. Because of these factors, our findings indicate that the cost overruns feared by Washington are unlikely to occur."[107] This assessment proved prescient, yet CMS officials continue to assume pharmaceutical cost increases well beyond the trend lines since 2003, a move that is guaranteed to produce "surprises" each year in how much the program actually costs.[108]

One question that is difficult to answer is whether or not a directly administered federal program would in fact be cheaper, with federal authorities either using their clout to bargain down pharmaceutical prices, or the government simply setting reimbursement rates, as it does in areas of Medicare payment policy. Advocates of direct federal negotiation argue that because the Veterans Administration (VA) system pays less than Medicare for many of the drugs prescribed to seniors, direct federal negotiations could save money for both seniors and the federal government.[109] One study found that extending to Part D the federal prices for drugs covered under the VA and other government programs could save almost $22 billion a year.[110] Others assert that the generous government risk-sharing and subsidies necessary to lure insurers into the Part D market dulled their motivation to bargain hard with drug manufacturers.[111] Skeptics reply that the federal government is unlikely to be able to credibly threaten to remove drugs from the government formulary—a threat that is essential in order to induce manufacturers to lower prices. As Yale economist Fiona Scott Morton argued at a Senate Finance Committee hearing in January 2007, it would be difficult to exclude drugs from a national plan due to the diverse health needs of beneficiaries and ". . . the process of choosing which drugs would be excluded from the national Medicare formulary would become dominated by stakeholders such as manufacturers and patient advocacy groups . . ." making it impossible to threaten pharmaceutical companies with the removal of their product from a formulary.[112] Yet, this is a political assessment rather than one based on any hard economic figures. Opponents of federal price negotiations (or setting) assume that the government would lack the will to deny seniors access to their preferred prescriptions, or the power to resist the lobbying influence of the pharmaceutical industry, while advocates of federal negotiation presume that the federal government could in fact hold out against these pressures. As yet, there is little hard evidence to confirm either viewpoint.

In short, the MMA has cost less than originally projected, but this appears to result less from its competitive elements than from overarching trends in pharmaceutical costs and a slower pace of enrollment than was originally projected. Moreover, the significant overpayments to Medicare Advantage that were needed to jump-start a stagnant market of private plans undercut claims about the cost-savings that private markets can produce.

Are there other benefits that result from the competitive design of Part D and Medicare Advantage? One positive was that it lightened the burden on the federal government to educate the population about the new program. Given the voluntary nature of Part D, it has been important to enroll a wide swath of the beneficiary population so as to avoid the problems of adverse selection. If sicker beneficiaries with high drug costs disproportionately enroll, this can undercut the viability of the private market. Because of these high stakes, the federal government mounted an extensive educational campaign in 2005 to educate beneficiaries about the new benefit and encourage them to sign up for it, but they could also rely upon the aggressive marketing campaigns deployed by the private plans themselves. At the end of 2005, one *Hill* article reported that:

> Marketing and operations for the Medicare prescription-drug benefit is big business. Aetna and PacifiCare Health Systems are spending $50 million each, while CIGNA is doling out $40 million. UnitedHealth Group's budget is $75 million. Humana has already spent $80 million on marketing.[113]

Firms used television ads, pamphlets, partnerships with pharmacies, and other tactics to reach their target audience. For instance, Humana sent a 30-foot RV around the country to advertise its Part D plans, while CIGNA hired actor Hal Linden (of Barney Miller fame) to appear in ads touting their drug plans.[114] These firms also hired additional staff to help process new enrollees, which in turn limited the number of new personnel that the federal government had to hire.

The downside of this competitive push for beneficiary business has been overly aggressive or misleading marketing techniques and outright fraud, much of which has not been effectively restrained by government overseers. From the start of the new drug program, there were reports that insurance agents were using banned marketing tactics—such as door-to-door solicitations or offering meals and gifts at promotional events—and deceptive marketing practices to convince seniors to sign up for their plans.[115] Many of the problems have involved the sale of Medicare Advantage plans, and especially the private fee-for-service plans— both of which are more lucrative to firms than stand-alone PDPs. Offering high commissions, trips, or other financial incentives to agents who sign up customers for MA plans induced some to engage in unethical, if not illegal, sales practices. Cross-selling has been one technique, whereby agents "get in the door" with the promise of signing up someone for a Part D plan, but then persuade the person to enroll in a Medicare Advantage plan instead. State insurance commissioners and consumer advocates have worried that senior citizens are especially vulnerable to such pressures given the complexity of the Medicare program and the fact that some of these beneficiaries have cognitive limitations. Some who ended up in Medicare Advantage plans were unaware that they would no longer be able to see their doctor of choice (thus leaving them with higher medical bills to cover out-of-network physicians) or that the cost of some services would be higher in Medicare Advantage than in fee-for-service medicine.[116] The aggressive marketing of private fee-for-service plans has been especially confusing to many seniors, as some sales representatives have implied that the plans work exactly as traditional Medicare does, when in fact physicians often refuse to accept this form of coverage.

Government reports and other studies also have shown widespread violations in the marketing materials available to beneficiaries. For instance, one report by the HHS Office of Inspector General (OIG) found that 33 percent of PDP web sites lacked all of the federally mandated information they are supposed to include. Particularly common areas of omission included disenrollment rights of beneficiaries, the ability of a PDP to terminate a contract, and formulary information.[117] The majority (85 percent) also violated federal requirements for web site accessibility. Another OIG study found that 85 percent of PDP marketing materials failed to meet at least one of CMS's Medicare Marketing Guidelines.[118] A Kaiser Family Foundation study of Medicare and Part D advertising found that most ads did not provide basic descriptive information about the plans, including the type of plan or premium. Print ads often included such information in fine type that may go unnoticed by the reader. Moreover, none of the ads for Medicare Advantage HMO plans included language recommended by CMS detailing network restrictions.[119]

These and other reports also highlighted how the delegation of authority to private plans and the hollowness of the federal agency charged with overseeing them have made these kinds of abuses and problems more likely. As one critical study noted, CMS essentially delegated responsibility for oversight and enforcement of their marketing guidelines to the private plans, with CMS stepping in not through any kind of regular oversight process but only in response to complaints heard from beneficiaries.[120] An OIG report found that, although firms are required to submit their marketing materials to CMS for a required review process, these reviews were in fact limited and failed to uphold the guidelines established by the agency.[121] CMS officials also have struggled to rein in fraudulent sales practices, particularly in rural areas.[122] Yet, the MMA also limited the ability of state insurance commissioners—who generally oversee insurance practices within their states—to regulate the companies that sell private plans.[123] This has created a regulatory void, as state officials receive large numbers of complaints about hard-sell and manipulative tactics yet can do little to rein them in.

Complaints about Part D and MA plans also extend to shortcomings of the services they provide to their customers. A review of federal audits in 2007 found "widespread violations of patients' rights and consumer protection standards" in Part D and MA plans, including errors in canceling beneficiary coverage, huge backlogs of unpaid claims, lengthy delays in responding to phone calls, and failures to notify beneficiaries of changes to formularies.[124] Although complaints about Part D have declined over time, CMS lacks an effective system for tracking beneficiary grievances and ensuring that they are addressed.[125]

More generally, the GAO and Office of Inspector General at HHS have argued that ". . . the size, nature, and complexity of the Part D program make it a particular risk for fraud, waste, and abuse."[126] Since 2008, Congress and CMS have taken a number of actions to crack down on such practices and strengthen the hand of CMS vis-à-vis private plans, but it remains to be seen how effective these measures will be. CMS remains a severely underfunded agency that lacks the staff and capabilities to monitor private plans. As for the plans themselves, they are supposed to be motivated by competitive pressures to provide the best service they can to beneficiaries, yet as chapter 8 will show, these pressures are largely attenuated by the tremendous "stickiness" of senior citizens when it comes to enrollment in private plans. Plans are well aware of this, which is precisely why they have been so aggressive in their efforts to attract customers and migrate them into MA plans. Once in a plan, a beneficiary is unlikely to revisit the decision, no matter how poor the service he or she receives. Without effective market-based accountability, government regulators need to step in and provide the needed oversight, but so far they have failed to do this in a systematic and effective manner.

Conclusion

One difficulty in evaluating the administrative effectiveness of delegated governance is the lack of counterfactual examples of direct governance that could be used as benchmarks for comparison. Since 1965, some have asserted that contracting out Medicare's administrative authority to private entities has been necessary because the federal government never would have been able to run such a complex program directly. However, there is no directly administered equivalent to Medicare against which to test such claims. The largest health insurance program in this country, Medicare, has always been run through a system of diffused administrative authority, with a small, under-funded agency at the top charged with overseeing a vast and complex private realm of insurers, providers, and medical suppliers. We have no idea what direct administration—under a large and well-funded agency—of such a program would look like in this country, or whether or not it would work better or worse than the status quo. The best we can do is look at the functioning of the private claims processors, quality-assurance agencies, and insurance plans that do much of the federal government's administrative work.

In the varied forms of delegated governance found within the Medicare program, we found mixed results in terms of administrative effectiveness and efficiency. At best, these arrangements have served a political function—enabling the creation and persistence of a government program in the context of strong and enduring anti-government sentiment. It may be that government claims processors could have done just as good a job as the private firms hired to do these tasks, but would there ever have been the political will to hire all of those civil servants? Perhaps the federal government could structure drug formularies in ways that tell senior citizens what prescriptions they can and cannot have, but is it not politically easier to delegate that responsibility to a private firm and direct any public resentment against them? Politically, delegated governance serves a crucial function of shifting blame and diffusing responsibility for complex, and at times controversial, decisions.

Administratively, however, the performance of these private bureaucracies has frequently been disappointing. In general, the Medicare program runs, processing a huge number of claims and ensuring coverage of the medical needs of some 47 million people. Yet, the program often does not run very well. Many private contractors have shown themselves to be competent and honorable, while others have been inefficient, ineffective, or engaged in outright fraud. Marketized forms of delegated governance implanted competitive forces in the program that have proven a double-edged sword. The lure of profits drew insurers into the Medicare marketplace, and they are providing much needed drug coverage for the majority of beneficiaries. The lure of profits also fueled an aggressive land-grab as firms scrambled to sign up beneficiaries in their most lucrative plans. Already faced with a dizzying array of choices, some beneficiaries fell victim to manipulative marketing practices and signed up for plans that did not meet their needs or minimize their costs. As chapter 8 will discuss, the stickiness of these early plan choices undermines the extent to which competition forces these firms to then be accountable to their customers.

We do not conclude that delegated governance can never work, but rather that it has not worked very well for Medicare given the weakness of the public administrative actor charged with overseeing the program. The neglect or outright contempt of government that drove decisions to outsource and marketize the Medicare program in the first place also has worked to undercut the effectiveness of these delegated arrangements. We are not the first to remark that markets work best when underpinned and overseen by effective government agents—indeed, political scientists and public administration scholars have been saying this for decades. Even strong advocates for contracting out and/or marketizing government programs admit that muscular government is needed to oversee these arrangements. Thus far, however, the architects of public programs appear unable or unwilling to confront the fact that effective public programs require effective public administrators, which in turn necessitates the growth of the governmental sector.

‖ 7 ‖

The Delegated Welfare State
and Policy Feedbacks

What impact does delegating the governance of social programs have on the politics of the welfare state? For years, scholars have argued that public policies should be viewed not merely as the consequences of political conflict, but as shapers of the political arena in their own right. Once in place, popular social programs can become potent sources of credit-claiming, generating political resources for their architects that can be exploited well into the future. They also might change the attitudes and behaviors of the mass public, encouraging political mobilization in defense of popular programs, for instance, or creating antipathy toward programs serving less favored groups (such as the "undeserving poor"). Finally, public policies are likely to alter the landscape of organized interests, empowering some groups while undercutting the influence of others. Through these and other policy feedback effects, we can expect major redistributive initiatives to leave an enduring imprint on the politics of the welfare state. One consequence should be considerable path dependency: once a set of programs are in place and begin to spawn supportive constituencies, we might expect that it is very difficult to change them.

The Medicare Modernization Act of 2003 offers a useful test of these ideas, as it was an important expansion of the American welfare state and conferred a significant new benefit on a large and politically active constituency—senior citizens. Yet, because it significantly increased the role of market forces in the Medicare program, the political consequences of the reform may differ from past policy feedback effects. In the case of Social Security, for instance, the law spawned a broad-based constituency of people that has been treated uniformly by a centralized administration agency.[1] In conventional Medicare, the program is administered by fiscal intermediaries that differ somewhat in the way they run the program, but in general seniors share a common set of experiences and have been fierce defenders of the program. In the MMA, by contrast, we might imagine that enrolling millions of senior citizens in competing managed care and stand-alone drug plans might change attitudes and behaviors because beneficiaries are split into myriad separate plans. Moreover, the government role in providing health care becomes even more obscured. Perhaps in contrast to the effects of Social Security, experiencing privatized provision diminishes feelings of group consciousness among seniors or leads them to prefer a greater role for private insurers and consumer choice in Medicare.

There are other ways that the reform could shape the political climate around health care. Traditionally, Democrats have enjoyed "issue ownership" over health care in that the public generally trusts them over Republicans to enact sound health care policies. In this case, however, it was Republicans who sought to claim credit for a major reform. Did this improve the standing of Republicans with senior citizens on an issue of great importance to them, or is issue ownership difficult to budge? Finally, the reform may have affected interest groups in a way that advantaged some and undermined the resources or political clout of others. Programs directly administered by the federal government may empower the bureaucracies that run them, giving them political resources that they can use to fight retrenchment and to promote expansion into new areas.[2] In delegated governance, however, we might suppose that private actors gain significant leverage in subsequent rounds of policy-making, given the dependence of government officials on these groups for the smooth administration of public programs. If this were the case, we would expect a lock-in of the MMA, making it difficult for Democrats to significantly change the program once they regained power.

In addressing these questions, our study holds both advantages and some limitations. One benefit is that, in contrast to most studies that are retrospective, we looked for these effects in real time during the post-2003 period. This allowed us to propose hypotheses in advance and then see whether such effects came to fruition, rather than developing causal paths that fit known sequences of events in the past. As a result, we were open to the possibility of being proven wrong by events and then reporting these negative findings, as well as the positive ones. We also conducted a panel survey of Medicare recipients that probed their attitudes toward government, markets, and politics both before and after the implementation of the MMA. Such a technique enables us to see whether attitudes have actually changed based upon people's experiences of a marketized benefit, or whether they already were predisposed toward certain views. However, the limited time span of our study also poses some limitations, as we can only uncover feedback effects that occur in the short term. Many forms of institutional change are incremental and slow-moving.[3] Some hypothesized effects that do not yet appear may materialize at some point in the future.

Another limit on assessing feedbacks with this particular reform is the degree to which it represents a significant break from the earlier policy design. If the framers of the MMA had succeeded in implementing their original vision—that the prescription drug benefit would be available only to seniors enrolled in private managed care plans—the legislation would have more fundamentally changed the structure of Medicare. Instead of "displacement," however, political pressures forced proponents to instead offer prescription drug coverage through competing private insurance plans that would be "layered" on top of the existing Medicare program.[4] Given the partial nature of the policy design change, we might imagine that effects on beneficiary attitudes are muted. On the other hand, the layering in of private insurance might become an endogenous source of change in the future, a point to which we will return.

In general, many of our starting hypotheses about the policy feedback effects of the MMA were proven wrong. There is little evidence of widespread attitudinal change among senior citizens, for instance, as they are no more favorable toward competitive reform of Medicare today than they were prior to the MMA. Experiencing a situation of market-like competition in the selection of drug plans did not make beneficiaries any more or less disposed toward this kind of market-based reform. Beneficiaries also did not become any more favorable toward the Republican Party when it comes to health care issues, and Republicans lost further credibility on the issue with those disgruntled with the new drug benefit. As for organized interests, the insurance industry at first appeared to have gained clout through their ability to block cutbacks in overpayments to Medicare Advantage plans, but this turned out to be conditioned by the partisan environment. Once power shifted definitively to the Democrats in 2008, Medicare Advantage plans became vulnerable to spending cuts as Democrats desperately sought ways to pay for large-scale health care reform. Still, even with the cutbacks, MA is not likely to disappear any time soon because of its popularity with senior citizens and with both Republican and Democratic defenders in Congress.

The most significant feedback effect of the MMA is that it undercut the drive for further reform in this area, providing a benefit that seniors are happy enough with that it largely removed the issue from the political arena. There is good evidence that "issue preemption" is what Republicans hoped to achieve from the reform, rather than believing they could more fundamentally transform public opinion. Although they were unable to gain support among the public for reforming old-age entitlements along market-based lines, Republicans did succeed in removing a politically damaging issue from the Democratic arsenal. We view this as a more general consequence of the delegated welfare state, and indeed, of the fragmented and often indirect way in which social welfare issues have been addressed in this country. By providing scattered but sufficient assistance, conservative opponents of the welfare state have often undercut political pressures for a larger and more direct role for government.

Studying Feedbacks at the Mass Level: The MMA Panel Survey

To examine policy feedbacks among beneficiaries of the MMA—whether enrollment in Part D or MA programs changed attitudes and behaviors among seniors—we conducted a panel survey of Medicare beneficiaries aged 65 and over, interviewing 1,664 respondents in December 2005 to establish a baseline prior to the implementation of the MMA. We then re-interviewed 1,255 of the original respondents in May 2007, during the second year of the MMA, when we asked the same attitudinal and behavior questions again to see whether there was any change among those enrolled in Part D or MA plans, compared to those who stayed in traditional Medicare. We also asked about their experiences with Part D in its first year and their choices for 2007, the second year of the program. In February 2009 we were able to re-contact 675 respondents for a third survey, in which we again asked the central battery of attitudinal and behavioral questions and assessed their experiences in year three of the program and their choices for year four (2008 and 2009; see Appendix A for a discussion of the survey). Most of the data reported in this chapter come from the first two waves; the third wave is small and contains a greater proportion of younger and higher income respondents than the first two waves. But results from the third wave are noted in the text, endnotes, and Appendix B as appropriate.

The MMA Panel Survey is the first survey to measure attitudes before and after a significant change in the design of a major social policy. Unlike previous researchers looking at the effects of policies on individuals, who only had cross-sectional data collected after selection into social programs, we have pre-implementation measures so that we can be more certain that any changes we see in enrollees' attitudes or behaviors can plausibly be attributed to program experiences rather than to preexisting differences among those who chose to enroll in a program and those who did not. That said, we must issue two caveats. One is that we would have liked to have established an even earlier baseline than December 2005, before the policy discussion around the MMA was widely publicized, but we did not have the funding in hand before that moment. The second is that two or four years is a short period in which to assess feedback effects. These data provide an early test, but the true attitudinal impacts of the marketization of segments of Medicare may only become apparent over time as new cohorts of senior citizens age into Medicare eligibility without having known a traditional FFS-Medicare-only world. However, as this chapter will show, some feedback effects are already evident, first in that the public, initially angry about the design of the prescription drug benefit, has been effectively demobilized, and second, that Republicans defused the prescription drug issue, preempting Democrats' ability both to use the issue for electoral gain and to push for a better benefit. Thus, while public attitudes have not experienced a deep shift, we already see feedbacks from this policy operating in the political arena. And, as will become apparent in our discussion of the Obama health care debate of 2009–2010 in chapter 9, the apparent success of the prescription drug insurance market provided one template for those who wished to expand coverage to the uninsured through private, risk-bearing insurers rather than through a public option.

The Feedbacks That Have Not Happened (Yet)

One way in which policy design changes might prove durable is through trans-forming social interpretations—fostering new understandings of "the way things are."[5] Our analysis of the MMA finds, however, no explicit changes in seniors' attitudes toward the state and the market, as might be expected from a privatizing reform, nor altered patterns of issue ownership between the two political parties. Hence basic worldviews about health policy and the political parties—such as the explicit embrace of privatization or market models or the Republican approach—do not seem to have been altered by the MMA. However, we do find significant implicit change, with considerable demobilization of the public around the MMA and a lack of pressure to change what many had previously viewed as its unattractive features. As a result, the MMA has proved durable thus far *not* because it changed beneficiaries' views about what good policy is but because they have found the benefits good enough and are not agitating for change.

No Change in Attitudes Toward the State and the Market

One possible effect of the MMA is that it might fundamentally shift attitudes and behaviors of senior citizens, including feelings of group consciousness, attitudes about government and the private sector, and patterns of political participation. In earlier decades, the development of the universal and nearly monolithic Social Security and Medicare entitlement programs forged from an otherwise disparate group a politically relevant constituency that banded together to fight off policy threats inimical to their interests, such as cuts in benefits.[6] Other studies have found that enrollment in universal welfare programs with a high degree of client empowerment is associated with greater trust in politicians, support for more state intervention and greater welfare state spending, and Left placement on the ideological spectrum. Successful encounters with government programs appeared to foster positive feelings about the possibilities for state intervention.[7]

Observers of the increasingly delegated welfare state have wondered whether privately run programs would have the reverse effect, diminishing both the actual and perceived role of government.[8] Indeed, the extensive use of tax subsidies and regulatory measures to deliver many social policies in the American context results in a "hidden" welfare state where citizens do not appear to recognize the government's role.[9] Some scholars have argued that this undercuts public support for the welfare state, as people believe that they alone are responsible for their own economic well-being, reinforcing economic individualism rather than a sense of collective solidarity in the face of life's risks.[10] A survey conducted during the Medicare+Choice period lent credence to these suspicions, finding that compared to clients of traditional Medicare, enrollees in Medicare HMOs exhibited lower levels of group consciousness and were less likely to support strategies of collective action among seniors.[11] Would the MMA's private provision of drug benefits, or the separation of some seniors into a large number of different health plans, break up the constituency, diminish feelings of group consciousness and cohesiveness, undermine support for collective action strategies, alter attitudes about the role of the government versus the market in health insurance or in other issue areas, or change patterns of senior political participation around Medicare, as some predicted?[12] Because the MMA panel study has pre-implementation measures of these attitudes and behaviors, we can look for attitude change in the aftermath of private plan enrollment.

We find, however, little evidence of fundamental attitudinal shifts. Experiencing either private drug coverage or private health plan enrollment did not undermine group consciousness and cohesiveness among MMA Panel Study respondents, nor did it alter much their views about the proper role of government versus the market, at least not during the first four years of the MMA's existence. Table 7.1 compares attitudes of seniors in the baseline survey and the first follow-up survey in May 2007, 17 months later. The first two items in Table 7.1 measure group consciousness and solidarity. If private plan participation had affected attitudes, then we would expect to see reduced group consciousness among those in Part D and MA plans relative to those who did not enroll. What we find, however, is that those who did and did not enroll in the private plans had very similar attitudes in the baseline survey, and their attitudes did not diverge much after program implementation. For example, in the baseline survey, 52 percent of those who did not enroll in Part D agreed that their "views about Medicare are based mostly on how reforms would affect me, not how they would affect other people covered by Medicare," as did 54 percent of those who went on to enroll in Part D. By May 2007, the two groups still held virtually identical attitudes, with 49 and 48 percent agreeing. In the Medicare Advantage (MA) program, we compare three groups of respondents: those who never enrolled in a private managed care health care plan (either in an HMO prior to retirement or in an MA program later); those who did enroll in an MA plan and had been in a managed care plan before, that is, during their pre-retirement years; and those who enrolled in an MA plan and who had not been in managed care before. All three groups had attitudes that were relatively similar to each other, both before and after MMA implementation.

Similar results obtain for the other items in the table that measure various attitudes toward the state and the market. Both before and after MMA implementation, Part D and MA enrollees were similar to their non-enrolling counterparts in their attitudes toward government responsibility for senior health insurance, individual responsibility for saving money for health care in retirement, government versus private health insurance, federal spending on Medicare, Social Security privatization, ideological self-identification, and trust in government. In each of these instances we might have expected those experiencing Part D or MA to become more supportive of the private market stance compared to non-enrollers, but they do not.

We also examined responses to the items in Table 7.1 for those survey respondents who remained in the survey through the third wave. Even after

Table 7.1. **Effects of Part D or Medicare Advantage Enrollment on Group Consciousness and Attitudes toward State and Market Roles, December 2005 to May 2007**

| | | Part D | | Medicare Advantage | | |
		Not in Part D	*In Part D*	*Never in private plan*	*MA now; private plan before*	*MA now; not private plan before*
Group Consciousness						
To encourage good Medicare reforms, it is impt for elders to stick together in the msgs they send Washington: % disagree	Baseline	4	4	5	4	1
	Follow-up	4	2	3	3	1
My views about Medicare are based mostly on how reforms would affect me, not how they would affect other people covered by Medicare: % agree	Baseline	52	54	53	53	53
	Follow-up	49	48	46	49	52
State vs. Market Attitudes						
The fed govt has a basic responsibility to guarantee that elderly persons have adequate health insurance: % disagree	Baseline	20	14	18	16	16
	Follow-up	17	15	17	14	19
Individuals should be responsible for setting aside enough money to pay for their health care in retirement: % agree	Baseline	32	30	30	29	36
	Follow-up	31	31	31	27	38
For health insurance rely on fed govt or private insurance: mean score on 1–7 scale, private health insurance is high	Baseline	3.7	3.6	3.62	3.93	3.67
	Follow-up	3.7	3.6	3.68	3.62	3.63

Continued

Table 7.1. (Continued)

| | | Part D | | Medicare Advantage | | |
		Not in Part D	In Part D	Never in private plan	MA now; private plan before	MA now; not private plan before
Fed spending on Medicare: % increase	Baseline	58	59	56	63	54
	Follow-up	57	61	55	65	59
Social Security privatization: % support	Baseline	28	29	29	26	25
	Follow-up	33	32	33	29	31
Ideology: % conservative	Baseline	43	46	45	40	51
	Follow-up	40	41	42	41	39
Trust in government: % only some of the time	Baseline	71	76	72	77	68
	Follow-up	76	79	75	77	80

Source: MMA Panel Study, baseline (December 2005) and first follow-up (May 2007) waves.

more than three years had elapsed between the December 2005 baseline and February 2009 third wave, attitudes did not shift in meaningful ways (most shifts were small; the few that were larger were often in the opposite of the expected direction—for example, those in MA in the third wave who had not been in a private managed care plan in the baseline became less supportive of Social Security privatization, their support falling from 34 to 20 percent, while those who had never been in a private plan shifted by 3 percent). These results appear in Appendix Table B.1.

In addition, we performed multivariate analysis, which further confirmed that those getting the private program "treatment" did not have different attitudes in the follow-up survey (results in the Appendix Table B.2).[13] After controlling for a number of demographic and political variables as well as pre-treatment attitudes, the attitudes of those enrolling in Part D did not differ from those who did not enroll. Nor did those enrolling in MA differ from those not in MA. There were just three statistically significant findings, and two are in the opposite of the hypothesized direction: those in MA plans shifted toward the government end of a 7-point scale asking if health insurance should be provided by the federal government or private entities; and those in MA (vs. those who have never been in a private plan) became less conservative. The only finding in the expected direction is that those in MA (vs. those who have never been in a private plan) became less trusting of government. Hence feelings of group consciousness and attitudes toward the state versus the market hardly changed at all among Part D and MA enrollees, suggesting that deeper attitudinal shifts have not yet taken place.

No Change in Issue Ownership

A second possible feedback effect concerns political credit-claiming. Scholars long have argued that universal programs build support for the parties that created them—such as the Left political parties that were the architects of the welfare state in the United States and Europe. For example, Gøsta Esping-Andersen finds that universalistic welfare state programs became a "power resource" for social democratic parties in Scandinavia, enabling these parties to secure their political dominance.[14] Where welfare state programs were less universal, Left parties had a harder time maintaining political power, and support for the welfare state also declined. Public policies can influence the public's belief systems so that they "accept and internalize the party's ideologies," creating a "lopsided situation" in which one party can dominate others for a sustained period.[15] William Kristol seemed to have just such an effect in mind when he wrote his famous memos urging Republican lawmakers to oppose Bill Clinton's health care reform effort in the early 1990s—its success, he feared, would create yet another generation of Democratic identifiers, as Roosevelt's New Deal had done.[16]

Thus some observers suggested that efforts to inject marketized elements into Medicare since the mid-1990s were driven by the perception among Republicans that this would undermine the political linkage between popular federal entitlements and the Democratic Party.[17] Another possible motivation could have been a belief that competitive reforms to Medicare would produce ideological and partisan feedback effects that would benefit the GOP, just as the earlier universal programs had long benefited the Democratic party. Perhaps Republicans thought they could improve ownership over this issue and gain credibility on their ability to improve social welfare provision through market-based reforms.[18]

We instead find that Republicans failed to gain much credibility on health care issues with the public after this reform was passed and are no better placed to push market-based reform of the Medicare program than they were before the law passed. Figure 7.1 shows the results of series of polls by the Winston group asking, "Which party do you have more confidence in to handle the issue of health care and prescription drugs?" Democrats maintained an advantage throughout the MMA's history, with 12–15 percent more Americans having more confidence in the Democrats on these issues in 2003, before the MMA was signed, growing to 20 points by the time MMA benefits began in January 2006. Nor did Republicans enjoy a gain in confidence as the program continued to roll out and the benefit became more familiar to people. Indeed, the gap in confidence between the parties

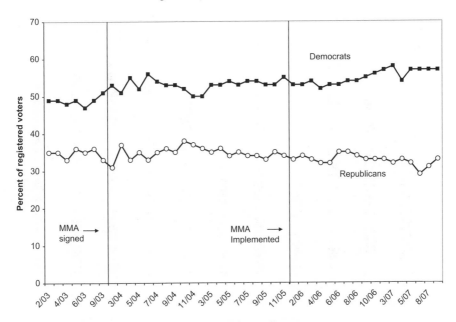

Figure 7.1 Issue Ownership: Parties on Health Care and Prescription Drugs, 2003–2007 Source: Winston Group polls, archived by the Roper Center at the University of Connecticut. Note: Figure shows responses to the question, "Which party do you have more confidence in to handle the issue of health care/prescription drugs?"

grew even greater, reaching 28 points by the summer of 2007, the second year of the program and the last year for which these data are available. The Winston group question asked about both health care and prescription drugs, and we might worry that opinions on handling of the two issues might differ but become conflated by the wording of the question. However, another set of issue ownership questions that asks about the handling of prescription drugs specifically exhibits the same pattern: a large gap between Democrats and Republicans, with no gains by Republicans over time. Figure 7.2 shows responses to a series of questions from several polling houses asking whether Republicans or Democrats would do a better job handling the issue of prescription drugs. There is some variation in question wording (sometimes the surveys asked about the Democratic Party versus Bush), but in each instance respondents were far more likely to say that Democrats would handle the issue better. Even by the last such survey in January 2007, at the beginning of the second year of the program, Republicans had not gained much ground.[19]

Data from the MMA Panel Study corroborate these findings and show that Republicans' failure to gain credit was not simply due to misunderstandings about who was responsible for the law (Table 7.2). A large majority—71 percent of respondents in the May 2007 follow-up survey—knew that the Republican Party controlled Congress when the prescription drug legislation passed, and 62 percent

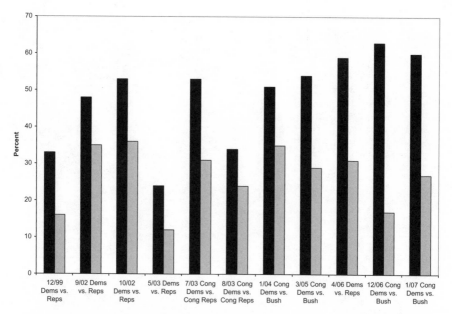

Figure 7.2 Issue Ownership: Handling the Prescription Drug Issue, 1999–2007 Source: Various polling houses, archived by the Roper Center at the University of Connecticut. Note: Figure shows responses to the question, "Who would do a better job of handling the prescription drug issue?" Black bars indicate the Democrats.

of all respondents gave the Republican Party credit for the legislation. But 62 percent said the *Democrats* were more likely to make the right decisions about Medicare, *up* from 59 percent in the baseline survey. Nor did many respondents switch their opinion; among those who did, more switched away from the Republican Party than switched to it. In the 2007 follow-up survey, 57 percent said Democrats were more likely to make the right decisions about government in general (56 percent in the baseline), and 62 percent said the Democrats would better manage the prescription drug issue in the future. It is clear then that Republicans made no gains in issue ownership by passing the MMA. Unsurprisingly, partisan identifiers are more likely to give their own party credit for the new benefit and to cite that party as making the right decisions about Medicare or government in general. However, Republicans failed to make gains between the baseline and follow-up surveys among Independents, the one group not constrained by partisan affiliation, as they became slightly less likely to say that the Republican Party would make the right decisions about Medicare or about government.

Republicans failed to make issue ownership gains by February 2009, the fourth year of MMA operations (see Table B.3 in the Appendix). The third wave of the MMA Panel Survey reveals that Democrats continued to gain credit for the reform. To the extent to which there was any movement on the

Table 7.2. **Issue Ownership, December 2005 (Baseline) and May 2007 (Follow-up)**

	Democratic Party	Republican Party
1. Which party controlled Congress when prescription drug legislation passed? (24% said not sure) (2007)	5%	71%
2. Which party deserves the most credit for the drug benefit? (2007)		
Overall	38%	62%
By Partisanship: Republicans	10	90
Independents	41	59
Democrats	60	40
3. Which party more likely to make the right decisions about Medicare?		
Baseline Overall	59%	41%
Follow-up Overall	62	38
Baseline Republicans	11	89
Independents	65	35
Democrats	94	6
Follow-up Republicans	17	83
Independents	67	33
Democrats	95	5
4. Which party more likely to make the right decisions about govt?		
Baseline Overall	56%	44%
Follow-up Overall	57	43
Baseline Republicans	7	93
Independents	58	42
Democrats	95	5
Follow-up Republicans	10	90
Independents	59	41
Democrats	94	6
5. Which party better manage prescription drug issue in the future? (2007)		

Continued

Table 7.2. (Continued)

	Democratic Party	Republican Party
Overall	62%	38%
By Partisanship: Republicans	16	84
Independents	66	34
Democrats	96	4

Note: Independent category includes independent leaners. Questions 1, 2, and 5 from May 2007 follow-up survey.

Source: MMA Panel Study, baseline (December 2005) and first follow-up (May 2007) waves.

items asking which party makes better decisions on Medicare or about government or which party will better manage the prescription drug issue in the future, the Republican Party lost some ground. For example, the proportion of wave three respondents saying the Republican Party would make the right decisions about Medicare fell slightly, from 40 percent in the 2005 baseline to 36 percent in 2009; even among Republican respondents the proportion dropped (from 89 to 82 percent). The single largest shift over time was the precipitous decline in the proportion of respondents who could remember which party controlled Congress when the prescription drug legislation passed. In 2007, 71 percent of third wave respondents still remembered that it was the Republicans; by 2009, that had fallen to 46 percent, while the "don't knows" grew from 24 to 40 percent.

We also tested whether "mid-level policy learning" had taken place, in which actual experiences with policies contributed to allocations of credit or issue ownership.[20] Perhaps enrolling in Part D or having a favorable impression of the program is associated with giving Republicans credit for the reform or enhanced issue ownership over Medicare, government in general, or prescription drugs in the future. We find, however, that policy learning does contribute to allocations of credit, but not always in ways that favor Republicans. Those enrolled in Part D are no more likely to give the Republican Party credit than other respondents (the coefficients for Part D enrollees are not positive and statistically significant in Table 7.3, columns 1 and 2), and those with favorable impressions actually give the Democratic Party more credit (the coefficients for favorability are significant and negative in columns 1 and 2, indicating more credit to the Democratic Party).[21] Some do give Republicans credit: Republicans and Independents with favorable impressions of the law (positive coefficients for the Favorable x Republican and Favorable x Independent interaction terms in column 2) and Part D enrollees who say the new drug benefit has made them feel more financially secure (positive coefficients for "more financially secure" in columns 3–5). However, respondents

Table 7.3. **Predicting Who Gives the Republican Party Credit for the New Drug Benefit, May 2007**

		All Respondents		Part D Enrollees		
		(1)	*(2)*	*(3)*	*(4)*	*(5)*
Drug Coverage	Part D	-.110	-.155			
	No coverage	-.107	-.113			
Experiences	Dual eligible	.166	.129	.346	.533	.481
	Hit doughnut			-.468	-.349	-.279
	# Problems			-.173	-.016	-.039
	Premium			-.012*	-.011*	-.010*
Demographics	# Health problems	.146*	.161*	.173	.138	.162
	Education	.166*	.145	.017	-.004	-.026
	Age	.000	-.001	.019	.011	.009
	Female	.016	.064	.402	.525	.574*
	Income	.007*	.007	.005	.007	.007
Political	Republican	2.677*	.444	2.849*	4.433*	3.191*
	Independent	.734*	-.422	1.171*	1.119*	-.047
Favorability	Favorable toward new drug benefit	-.207*	-.511*	-.261	-.316*	-.490
	Favorable x Republican		.881*			.420
	Favorable x Independent		.496*			.442
	Rx more affordable			-.201	-.204	-.228
	More financially secure			1.103*	1.153*	1.159*
Experiences x Party ID	# Problems x Republican				-.738*	-.685
	# Problems x Independent				.069	.127
	Constant	-.738	.058	-1.603	-1.242	-.664

Continued

Table 7.3. (Continued)

	All Respondents			Part D Enrollees	
	(1)	*(2)*	*(3)*	*(4)*	*(5)*
N	1055	1055	373	373	373
Cox & Snell R²	.21	.22	.29	.32	.33
% correctly predicted	72.3	73.4	75.3	74.6	75.5

Note: Cells contain logit coefficients. Reference group for drug coverage is creditable coverage. Reference group for political variables is Democrat; Independent category includes independent leaners. Favorability measures favorability toward the new drug benefit in the follow-up survey. *$p <.05$.

Source: MMA Panel Survey, first follow-up (May 2007) wave.

with negative program experiences, especially paying higher monthly premiums, are less likely to give the Republican Party credit, as are Republicans who experienced more problems (as signified by negative coefficients for those variables in columns 3–5). It appears that when people have positive experiences they credit the party of government, the Democrats, and blame the Republican Party when things go badly.

Similarly, policy learning did not uniformly benefit Republicans in issue ownership. As we might expect, Republicans and Independents said the Republican Party was more likely than the Democratic Party to better manage prescription drugs in the future, make the right decisions about Medicare, and make the right decisions about government, as revealed by positive and significant coefficients in the multivariate analysis in Table 7.4. However, the Republican Party made no gain in issue ownership from policy learning, failing to gain ownership among those enrolled in MA (Table 7.4, columns 1–3) or in Part D (columns 4–6). Moreover, negative program experiences undermined Republican ownership of the issue. We asked about six problems that individuals might have in getting their prescriptions, such as unexpected costs or lack of coverage.[22] Part D enrollees with more problems were less likely to say the Republican Party would better manage the prescription drug issue in the future, and those hitting the doughnut were less likely to say the Republican Party will make the right decisions about government (columns 7, 9).[23] On the other hand, those with a favorable impression of the MMA were more likely to cite the Republican Party as preferable on prescription drugs, Medicare, and government in general in the future (positive coefficients for favorability in columns 1–7). But those who felt that the new law makes drugs more affordable were only more likely to think Republicans would make the right decisions about government (column 9); they were not more likely to think Republicans would better manage prescription drugs in the future or make the right decisions about Medicare.

In short, people generally knew that Republicans were the architects of the new law—at least in the initial years following its passage—but this made them no more likely to think Republicans would do a better job managing entitlements or health care policy in the future. If anything, negative program experiences made people even more skeptical of the GOP's capabilities in these areas, whereas positive experiences made people think better of the ability of Democrats to conduct health care and Medicare policy. Attitudinal effects have thus generated few advantages so far to the creators of the reform.

Limited Changes in Interest Group Power

A third possibility is that the MMA altered the relative power of key interest groups. In the immediate aftermath of the reform, for instance, there were predictions that AARP's support for the bill would undercut its lobbying influence in Washington, as there were stories of AARP members tearing up their membership cards and denunciations of the organization by Congressional Democrats angered by its "collaboration" with the Republicans. We also might expect the insurance industry to gain greater political resources from the reform. With so many seniors dependent upon private plans for their benefits, the industry can threaten to exit the program if it fails to receive the subsidies that it believes it needs to provide the benefit.[24] In this, they could draw upon past experience: in the late 1990s, Congress significantly cut payments to Medicare private plans (then called Medicare+Choice), prompting many plans to exit from the marketplace and leave senior citizens without the coverage they expected. Even liberal Democrats unsympathetic to the Medicare+Choice program pushed for redress because of angry constituents.[25]

In the case of AARP, it appears to have suffered no lasting damage from the decision of its leadership to throw their lot in with the Republicans and strongly support the MMA. Indeed, the MMA was perhaps politically useful for the organization, in that backing the legislation helped the group demonstrate that it was not a "wholly owned subsidiary" of the Democratic Party, as Republican critics had alleged for years. AARP did follow up its controversial support of the MMA with a vigorous campaign against George W. Bush's 2005 push for Social Security privatization. Unlike with the MMA, AARP's membership was unified in opposing individual accounts in Social Security, and the stance proved a politically useful one for the organization in mending relations with disgruntled members—its own and members of Congress. AARP elicited controversy again in 2009 and 2010 by backing the health care reform, which many seniors opposed due to cuts in Medicare, including Medicare Advantage, and fears that an influx of newly insured persons would limit access to doctors. As with the MMA, several tens of thousands of members resigned in protest, but in an organization with over 40

Table 7.4. Predicting Pro-Republican Attitudes on Prescription Drugs and Making Right Decisions on Medicare and Government, May 2007

Republican Party more like than Democratic Party to:	All Respondents						Part D Enrollees		
	(1) Better Manage Prescription Drug Issue in Future	(2) Make Right Decisions about Medicare	(3) Make Right Decisions about Government	(4) Better Manage Prescription Drug Issue in Future	(5) Make Right Decisions about Medicare	(6) Make Right Decisions about Government	(7) Better Manage Prescription Drug Issue in Future	(8) Make Right Decisions about Medicare	(9) Make Right Decisions about Government
MA In MA	-.171	.012	-.345						
Drug Cover. Part D				.131	.123	.074			
No coverage				-.166	-.073	-.108			
Exper. Dual eligible				-.216	-.426	-.144	-.681	-.807	-.457
Hit doughnut							-.458	-.543	-1.247*
# Problems							-.227*	-.181	-.066
Premium							.005	.001	.002
Demog. # Health problems	-.005	-.123	.118	.003	-.104	.121	-.014	-.070	.052
Education	.009	-.038	-.034	.035	-.028	.000	.230	.015	.046
Age	-.012	.013	.002	-.015	.011	.001	-.011	-.014	.009

		(1)	(2)	(3)	(4)	(5)	(6)	(7)	(8)	(9)
Female		.201	.032	-.154	.156	-.076	-.202	-.549	-.325	-.612
Income		-.002	-.003	.003	-.002	-.004	.003	-.006	-.004	-.001
Political	Republican	4.775*	4.591*	4.873*	4.786*	4.611*	4.849*	5.430*	5.233*	5.405*
	Independent	2.500*	2.334*	2.322*	2.483*	2.325*	2.294*	2.114*	2.174*	2.400*
Favor.	Favorable to drug benefit	.526*	.354*	.370*	.527*	.351*	.371*	.559*	.160	.132
	Rx more afford							.581	.461	.900*
	More financially secure							-.599	-.236	-.177
Constant		-3.526	-4.426	-3.729	-3.454*	-4.243*	-3.845*	-3.384	-1.764	-3.620
N		1056	1139	1134	1047	1132	1125	363	402	398
C & S R²		.45	.42	.46	.45	.43	.46	.53	.50	.50
% predicted		84.3	83.3	83.5	84.2	83.3	83.1	89.6	88.1	85.1

Note: Cells contain logit coefficients. Reference group for drug coverage is creditable coverage. Reference group for political variables is Democrat; Independent category includes independent leaners. Favorability measures favorability toward the new drug benefit in the follow-up survey. The Make Right Decisions about Medicare and about Government items are from the follow-up survey as well. *p <.05; ⁺p <.10.

Source: MMA Panel Study, baseline (December 2005) and first follow-up (May 2007) waves.

million members, AARP officials say this amounted to about 1 percent of their membership.[26] And at the elite level, AARP's earlier championing of the MMA appeared not to be harmful politically, as the group's endorsement of the health care reform was much sought after by Democrats. In sum, AARP survived the MMA episode relatively unscathed, and in backing a new benefit that ultimately proved popular with Medicare beneficiaries, it may if anything have rehabilitated its image in Washington.

As for the insurance industry, at first it appeared that the rapid growth in Medicare Advantage enrollment was significantly augmenting its political resources. When Democrats regained control of the House and Senate in January 2007, they sought to clamp down on the rapidly growing Medicare Advantage program. Already by 2007, MA enrollment had risen from a nadir of 5.3 million in 2003 to 8.5 million—about 19 percent of all beneficiaries—and was projected to grow to 27 percent by 2016.[27] Yet, Medicare Advantage was vulnerable in a tight budgetary environment because independent analyses showed that these plans cost the government 14 percent more per person than the traditional government-provided Medicare benefits.[28] Thus, in late 2007, House Democrats tried to cut MA subsidies to help pay for expansion of the Children's Health Insurance Program (CHIP).

Initially, they bumped up against MA's growing political popularity. Insurers argued that the cuts would bring about "absolutely disastrous consequences," forcing them to increase premiums, reduce benefits, and drop coverage altogether,[29] but more problematic for Democrats was push-back by minority groups normally allied with them. Both the NAACP and the League of United Latin American Citizens argued that many minorities and low-income people get better benefits from these plans than they otherwise would.[30] The managed care industry association, America's Health Insurance Plans (AHIP), quickly formed a coalition with these groups and a few dozen community leaders across the country, and this became a prominent talking point for Republican defenders of the Medicare Advantage program.[31] Democrats responded angrily, and the NAACP ultimately reversed its stance after feeling heat from Democratic legislators.[32]

The program also had some Democratic allies. Although some House Democrats pushed on with cuts to Medicare Advantage worth $47.4 billion over five years that CBO projected would decrease program enrollment by 30 percent, behind the scenes, some House Democrats voiced concern about the destabilizing impact that these cuts would have on beneficiaries. Senate Democrats also refused to include any MA cuts in their own CHIP bill.[33] Although claims that minorities disproportionately benefit from MA plans were debunked, there are nonetheless a large number of minority and urban enrollees in Medicare Advantage, and some urban Democrats therefore have a strong interest in protecting a program used by many of their constituents. As Senator Grassley (R-IA) has remarked, "There are a lot of blue states . . . that have a lot of HMOs."[34] Legislators from rural areas are also leery of the cuts, as one reason for the higher subsidies in the first place was to lure more HMOs into rural areas.[35] In a Senate Finance Committee hearing on the MA program, Democratic Senators Ron Wyden (OR) and Maria Cantwell (WA) strongly resisted cuts to the MA program.[36] It is thus not surprising that a House-Senate conference stripped these cuts from the CHIP re-authorization bill, although President Bush vetoed it as promised.

In July 2008, Congress finally passed a bill that trimmed back certain kinds of private MA plans. The legislation garnered media attention not only because it survived a Bush veto and passed with Republican support but also because of the ailing Ted Kennedy's dramatic, last-minute appearance on the Senate floor to help get the legislation past a procedural hurdle. Behind the fanfare, however, the legislation made cuts only to a portion of the MA program, specifically the "private-fee-for-service" (PFFS) plans—private insurance plans that, unlike the managed care plans that constitute most of the MA program, reimburse medical services on a fee-for-service basis and do not form provider networks. PFFS plans fell out of favor for a number of reasons: they cost the government more than managed care plans do;[37] they are contrary to one original rationale for the MA program, which was to make use of the efficiencies and care management of HMOs; and they attracted employers seeking to shift retiree coverage onto the Medicare program, thereby crowding out private insurance dollars. An additional weakness of these plans is that they were intended to be only a temporary product that would lure private insurers into rural areas where HMOs face difficulties setting up provider networks. The 2008 bill imposed a date—2011—by which these plans need to develop a provider network, which will put some of them out of business.[38] Although CBO calculated that the bill would reduce the expected increase in MA enrollment by 2.3 million people by 2013, enrollment was still projected to grow from 9.6 million in 2008 to around 12 million people.[39]

Thus, as of the end of 2008, it appeared that Medicare Advantage had, by spawning a supportive constituency of beneficiaries, generated political resources for insurers that would make it difficult for Democrats to undo this feature of the 2003 MMA. Yet, none of these resources prevented the Affordable Care Act signed into law by President Obama in March 2010 from cutting MA payments by $132 billion over ten years, a decrease in payments to plans of, on average, 12 percent.[40] The main industry lobbyist, America's Health Insurance Plans (AHIP), ran television ads targeted to states with high percentages of Medicare Advantage beneficiaries that highlighted the proposed cuts.[41] AHIP also tried to mobilize some of the 810,000 members of the Coalition for Medicare Choices, a network of Medicare Advantage beneficiaries that is an offshoot of the association. Yet, efforts to publicize the consequences of these cuts for senior citizens gained little traction during the health care debate. Certainly, the issue became a flashpoint of heated debate, as in the Senate Finance Committee hearings in September 2009. Republicans assailed the proposed cuts to the program for taking benefits away from 10 million beneficiaries who "love the program" and betraying President Obama's claim that health care reform would not change anyone's existing coverage.[42] Yet, all versions of the health care reform passed in the House and Senate included cuts in MA payments. The Congressional Budget Office estimates that this will significantly slow the pace of MA expansion, reducing projected enrollment over the next decade by 4.8 million people.[43]

What explains this loss of political clout? Part can be attributed to party politics: once the partisan complexion of government had definitively shifted, the industry lost its political champions. Even some of the Democrats opposed to the MA cuts got behind the reform bill or did not make blocking MA cuts a key condition for their support.[44] MA also became vulnerable because of its outsized payments at a time of budgetary crunch. Here, we can find a parallel to the 1980s, when budget deficits drove the creation of the Prospective Payment System (PPS) that reined in spending on medical providers. Although Congress has been influenced by provider lobbying to minimize these cuts—with physicians proving especially effective in protecting their payments—in general, the PPS has showed that when fiscal push comes to shove, Congress can and will impose cuts on powerful medical interests.[45] Thus, in the health care reform debate of 2009–2010, the desperate need for revenues to pay for health care reform made all sources of budgetary "fat" vulnerable to trimming. As Senator Jay Rockefeller put it during Senate Finance Committee debates, Medicare Advantage "is a wasteful, inefficient program, and always has been. I recognize there are a lot of people in it, but if we are talking about the future and trying to preserve Medicare and services for seniors, you do not tend to want to preserve what does not help seniors and does not work efficiently."[46]

Still, insurers clearly do have political resources that flow from their crucial role in delivering a benefit. Democrats did not try to eliminate the MA program as a whole, but instead sought to pare it back, paying it 100 percent of the costs of beneficiaries in the existing program, 95 percent in areas with high FFS rates.[47] Cutting the program altogether would be a step too far: the Medicare Advantage program is much appreciated by millions of beneficiaries who enjoy coverage superior to that which regular beneficiaries receive, without having to pay any more for it.[48]

The program also continues to have some strong Democratic defenders, particularly in the Senate and among representatives and senators from rural areas of both parties. As Senator Bill Nelson (D-FL) stated during Senate Finance Committee hearings on the program, he had originally opposed the increased payments to the program enacted in the 2003 MMA, but now felt that policy-makers should not undermine a benefit for people who have come to depend on it.[49] Similarly, Charles Schumer (D-NY) supported the cuts in overpayments but defended the program as a whole, stating "You know, there are some of us on this side who see Medicare Advantage working in good ways. I have nonprofits who do Medicare

Advantage in parts of my State that do a very good service for seniors . . ."[50] Thus, while the program is being pared back, it is clearly here to stay. The cuts also will be phased in over a period of several years, which means that there may be opportunities to restore the higher subsidy level in the next few years, especially with the change in partisan complexion of Congress in 2010 or if there is an outcry among seniors as the effects of the cuts are felt.

What explains the failure of these various policy feedback effects to materialize? Public attitudes toward government, partisan issue ownership, and interest group power appear difficult to change, such that one new policy is unlikely to move them very significantly, especially a policy that might be viewed as "layering" rather than "displacement."[51] Attitudes toward government reflect a person's early political socialization, and as with other "symbolic" attitudes like partisanship and ideological self-identification, are durable and shift more through generational replacement than through individual-level change.[52] Issue ownership also exhibits considerable stasis—consider the work of Mark Smith and Larry Bartels on Republican issue ownership of economic stewardship, despite much objective evidence to the contrary[53]—as parties become associated with particular issue areas in ways that tend not to change over time or even in the face of actual performance. In addition, the power of interest groups ultimately often lies more in their stable alliances with particular parties than in the resources generated by policy. Certainly, we saw some constituency effects in the Medicare Advantage program in that it created backers of the status quo that made it impossible for Democratic opponents to eliminate the program. This did not stop spending cuts, however, even though this will create some disgruntled senior citizens who will be forced to change plans or experience premium hikes or cuts in benefits.

We might still imagine ways in which this legislation will have planted the seeds for greater change down the road. By layering competing private insurance plans into Medicare, Republicans may have created an endogenous source of change that over time could result in significant policy shifts. Should a financing crisis hit the Medicare program at a time when conservative politicians are in power, they might be better able to convert Medicare into a system of competing private plans by building on the system created by Part D and Medicare Advantage. There is now an insurance industry poised to take a greater role in providing health insurance to senior citizens, and because most beneficiaries make choices in a Medicare marketplace when selecting their Part D plan, this might make them comfortable with the idea of choosing all of their benefits in this way. Thus, the premium support model might resurface in the future and benefit from the foundations for it that were laid in the MMA. Indeed, the Republican's fiscal year 2012 budget, based on Representative Paul Ryan's "Roadmap for America's Future," proposed just that—a conversion of Medicare into a premium support program in which seniors would receive a voucher to purchase private health insurance. As John Breaux later remarked about the

2003 reform (which he supported), "What we did, we created a template for what, I think, will be a future health care reform that would do exactly what we did: that would combine the best of government and the best of the private sector, the best of both worlds."[54]

The Feedbacks That Did Happen: Public Demobilization and Issue Preemption

Although the 2003 Medicare reform has not yet generated some of the feedback effects we might have expected, there are other ways that the program has shaped the political and policy-making landscape. We see two interrelated phenomena: the demobilization of public opinion, as people found their needs largely met through the new benefit; and issue preemption—the elimination, by and large, of an issue on the political agenda. Both are effects that are likely to follow from major reforms that address public demands, but there are distinctive ways in which the delegated welfare state achieves these effects. In the case of the MMA, these feedback effects help explain why, despite fierce Democratic opposition to the reform, it has largely been accepted as the way Medicare will be run henceforth.

The Demobilization of Public Opinion

As chapter 5 showed, the MMA was driven in part by the mobilization of public opinion around the need for a prescription drug benefit in Medicare. Following President Clinton's promptings on this issue in the late 1990s, the public expressed its support for creating a Medicare drug benefit, with senior citizens strongly in favor. As the issue provided electoral fodder for Democrats, the mobilization of public opinion was important in pushing the Republicans to devise a broad-based benefit (rather than simply means-tested assistance, as some favored). If people were unhappy with the legislation, as seemed to be the case immediately following its implementation, we can imagine that their discontent would have kept the issue alive, enabling the Democrats to keep hammering on Republican failures.

At first, it appeared that this might be the case. During the MMA's development and early roll-out, seniors complained bitterly to pollsters about the design of Part D. They found the benefits meager, the stand-alone plans confusing, and the amount of choice overwhelming, and large majorities wanted a government option, government negotiating power over drug prices, and re-importation of cheaper prescription medicines from Canada.[55] Given these attitudes, we might expect seniors' Medicare-related political participation to increase after the passage of a law disappointing to so many. After all, senior citizens had reacted swiftly and vociferously against the Medicare Catastrophic Coverage Act of 1987, an expansion of Medicare that protected beneficiaries from catastrophic medical costs by capping annual out-of-pocket expenses and that had some additional features like a small prescription drug benefit and mammogram coverage. However, those new benefits were both mandatory and financed by seniors alone through additional monthly premiums and a surcharge on high-income seniors. Many affluent seniors already had such coverage, while many poorer seniors thought they would be hit by the new surcharges as well; both groups reacted with a surge of letter writing to lawmakers,[56] and Congress repealed the law the following year.[57] Thus, on the one hand we might expect similar dissatisfaction and a participatory surge following MMA passage.

On the other hand, the MMA's framers had learned the lessons of Medicare Catastrophic and explicitly sought to avoid the same objectionable features. They made Part D voluntary rather than mandatory and financed the new benefits mostly through general revenues rather than through higher beneficiary premiums. Moreover, the MMA created a popular new benefit for an everyday expense—prescription drugs—rather than protection from catastrophic medical expenses, an unpredictable risk that many people like to assume they will never experience. Beneficiaries therefore might be more positively disposed toward the MMA, despite its shortcomings. In addition, once the law passed, research in behavioral economics and cognitive psychology suggests that seniors would quickly become accustomed to the new policy design. Most individuals are "satisficers," to use Herbert Simon's term,[58] who adjust their internal setpoints to reflect new realities. Hence we might expect them to adjust to the new design, picking a plan that they deem "good enough" and failing thereafter to switch plans, support a government option, or participate politically on this issue.

Both our survey and other evidence show that seniors have engaged in considerable "satisficing" and that there has been a demobilization of public opinion on this issue. In the MMA Panel Survey, we asked respondents in each wave whether they had engaged in Medicare-related political participation—whether in the previous year they had voted, given a campaign contribution, or contacted a government official with Medicare in mind. The participation of Part D and MA enrollees fell somewhat between the 2005 baseline and 2007 follow-up surveys. Figure 7.3 shows the mean number of Medicare-related participatory acts (out of three) engaged in by respondents of various descriptions. Compared to their baseline participation levels, the political participation of Part D enrollees fell 11 percent, while that of MA enrollees dropped 9 percent. The participation of those facing difficulties fell less; compared to the baseline, those hitting the doughnut participated 6 percent less, while those paying above median premiums participated 4 percent less. Thus, unlike Medicare Catastrophic, the MMA did not produce a surge of senior participation. True, participation fell less among Part D and MA recipients than among those with creditable drug coverage, who were 19 percent less likely to participate around Medicare in the follow-up survey. The only

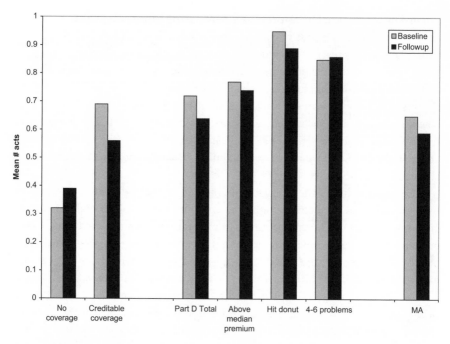

Figure 7.3 Medicare-Related Participatory Acts by Program Enrollment. Source: Medicare Modernization Act Panel Survey. Note: Figure shows average number of Medicare-related participatory acts (out of 3).

respondents whose Medicare-related political participation increased after MMA implementation were those remaining without drug coverage. The fall in participation among most of those in Part D and MA plans thus indicates some acceptance of the new policy regime. This decline in Medicare-related political participation continued among those who remained in the MMA Panel Survey through wave three (see Appendix Table B.4).

Another indication of "satisficing" concerns the attitudes of Part D beneficiaries toward a government drug option. One of the major alternatives to the MMA as structured would have been a government option that would compete with the private, stand-alone plans for enrollees. What we found in the MMA Panel Study, however, is that Part D enrollees were less enthusiastic about a government-run option than were other survey respondents, such as those with creditable coverage or no drug coverage. Respondents in the follow-up survey were asked whether they thought a Medicare option would be better than, worse than, or the same as private drug plans on several criteria: cost, coverage of drugs, ease of understanding benefits, stability of benefits, and coverage of new drugs (Table 7.5, top panel). In each instance, Part D enrollees were less likely than the other beneficiaries to say the Medicare option would be better or much better. For example, just 37 percent of those in Part D thought a Medicare option would

Table 7.5. **Medicare Option versus Private Drug Plans, May 2007**

	Cost	Coverage of Drugs	Ease of understanding benefits	Stability of benefits	Coverage of new drugs
Medicare option much better + better by type of drug coverage:					
Part D	37%	31%	34%	37%	39%
MA	43	42	45	40	45
Other creditable coverage	44	39	43	47	46
No drug coverage	57	52	56	56	52
Multivariate analysis:					
Dual eligible	-.033	.045	-.003	-.039	.011
Hit donut	.000	-.004	.012	.016	.064
# Problems	-.031	-.042	-.032	-.005	.044
Premium	-.014	.028	-.027	-.028	.038
# Health problems	-.041	-.132*	-.026	-.092	-.062
Education	-.078	-.064	-.027	-.030	-.044
Age	.119*	.137*	.142*	.138*	.020
Female	-.179*	-.195*	-.123*	-.160*	-.107*
Income	-.025	-.031	-.037	-.021	-.001
Republican	-.220*	-.289*	-.264*	-.267*	-.187*
Independent	-.132*	-.105*	-.106*	-.138*	-.134*
N	447	443	444	447	444
R^2	.09	.09	.08	.10	.06

Note: Respondents in multivariate analysis in the lower panel include Part D enrollees only. Cells contain standardized OLS coefficients from analyses where the dependent variables are 5-point scales comparing a Medicare option with private drug plans on each criterion, with higher values indicating a Medicare option being better. Reference group for political variables is Democrat; Independent category includes independent leaners. *$p <.05$.

Source: MMA Panel Survey, first follow-up (May 2007) wave.

be better or much better on cost, compared to 44 percent of those with creditable coverage and 57 percent of those with no drug coverage (indeed, those without drug coverage were most likely to think that a Medicare option would be superior across all of the criteria about which we asked). Even negative program experiences do not create much support for change: multivariate analysis (Table 7.5, bottom panel) shows that among Part D recipients, negative experiences such as hitting the doughnut, having a larger number of problems getting one's prescriptions, or paying higher premiums did not result in greater support for a possible Medicare option (that is, none of these coefficients was positive and statistically significant).

A third indicator of acquiescence to the Part D program is the increase in favorability toward the new prescription drug benefit between the baseline and follow-up surveys. In the follow-up survey, majorities of seniors both in and out of Part D reported being favorable toward the new benefit, increases of 15–17 points over the baseline (see Figure 8.1 in the next chapter). Those hitting the doughnut hole coverage gap and those having a particularly large number of problems getting their medications became less favorable toward the reform over time, but they constituted relatively small groups. Thus, even though Part D and MA drug coverage produced more problems and lower levels of satisfaction than creditable coverage, as will be detailed in the next chapter, favorability toward the new benefit increased.

In sum, whether or not people are explicitly enthusiastic about the competitive structure of Part D and Medicare Advantage, there is implicit acceptance of the new regime. The decrease in Medicare-related political participation, lesser support for a Medicare drug option among Part D recipients compared to other seniors, and an increase in favorability toward the new drug benefit over time among most beneficiaries all have diminished the force of public opinion on this issue. This demobilization is important given that in our survey we also found that Part D and MA enrollees were less satisfied with their drug coverage than were those with creditable coverage, and also experienced more problems getting their prescriptions, factors that might lead to agitation for change. Instead, many recipients regard their Part D and MA plans as good enough. Lack of agitation for a government option, muted political participation around Medicare, and increased favorability toward the law undermines the incentives for would-be reformers of the MMA. This set of mass-level feedbacks shows how the new design of Medicare can be locked in, as the public is hardly agitating for change.

Successful Issue Preemption by the Republicans

Public demobilization feeds into the second feedback effect of the reform: the successful preemption of the prescription drug issue by Republicans. By "issue preemption," we mean pushing an item off the agenda in a way that removes it from the opposition's arsenal. By passing the MMA, Republicans pushed the

Medicare prescription drug issue off the political agenda and undermined Democrats' ability to capitalize on the issue for electoral gain. Given the durability of issue ownership discussed above, it seems that securing issue preemption was the more feasible and ultimately more politically useful goal.

As chapter 5 detailed, in the lead-up to the 2003 reform, Democrats relentlessly pounded on Republicans for the shortcomings and stinginess of their vision of a new drug benefit.[59] Figure 7.4 shows the proportion of House and Senate campaign ads aired in 2002 and 2004 that mentioned the prescription drug issue or, a subset of those ads, Medicare prescription drugs.[60] In 2002, the prescription drug issue was one of the main themes mentioned, outpaced only by taxes and Social Security. But passage of the MMA in 2003 then reduced the significance of prescription drugs as a campaign issue, with steep declines in mentions of both prescription drugs and Medicare prescription drugs in 2004. Mentions declined for both parties (Figure 7.5), for the Democrats apparently because MMA passage had robbed the issue of its political utility, and for the Republicans apparently because there was little credit-claiming advantage for them.

Further evidence of the declining salience of the issue comes from the 2006 House and Senate campaign season. Initially, it appeared that the Democrats would use the Medicare drug benefit as a major campaign issue. As mentioned in chapter 6, political strategists Stan Greenberg and James Carville urged Democrats to hang the flawed drug benefit around the Republicans' necks,[61] and the

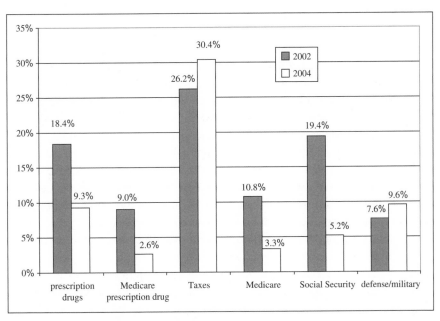

Figure 7.4 Percent of House/Senate Campaign Ads Mentioning Prescription Drugs and Other Topics, 2002 and 2004. Source: Wisconsin Advertising Project.

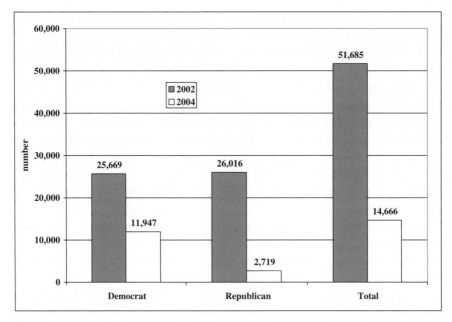

Figure 7.5 Number of House/Senate Campaign Ads Mentioning Medicare Prescription Drugs, by Party. Source: Wisconsin Advertising Project.

Democratic House leadership vowed to do so.[62] Nonetheless, by September 2006, GOP pollster Bill McInturff reassured Republicans that no Democratic candidate had made this a major issue and that the benefit would hardly have any negative impact on Republican candidates.[63] Republicans also did not do much credit-claiming in the 2006 election, as neither the National Republican Congressional Committee nor the National Republican Senate Committee ran ads lauding the new benefit, and few Republican candidates sought to take credit for the reform.[64] For both parties, the issue faded off the political agenda by 2006.

The intensity of opinion on this issue also declined among the American public. On the one hand, there was continued support for possible reforms to the MMA: in our 2007 follow-up survey, more than three-quarters of Medicare beneficiaries continued to support drug re-importation and government price negotiation with pharmaceutical companies. Yet, Kaiser surveys asking respondents what they believe is the "most important health problem" facing the nation showed the waning intensity of opinion about drug costs among seniors, as previously noted in Figure 5.1, which includes the results for senior citizens; the results for the general public are smoother due to the larger number of respondents and show a similar decline. Mentions of a Medicare drug benefit and concern about prescription drug prices first appeared after President Clinton proposed the former in his 1999 State of the Union address, and mentions of both issues subsequently rose, especially in 2003 as the MMA was debated. Once the legislation was passed, however, the percentage of seniors citing either a Medicare drug benefit or prescription drug prices in general as the most important health problem dropped off through August 2006, the last date for which these data are available. Instead, general concerns about the cost of health insurance and the need for universal coverage increased, an effect even more pronounced for people of all ages. We asked in the third wave of the MMA Panel Study administered in early 2009 how important various issues should be as a "priority for the new President and Congress elected in 2008." Medicare prescription drug benefit reform came in dead last, with only 37 percent of respondents deeming it "very important." Medicare beneficiaries were more likely to cite other issues as "very important:" the economy (88 percent), terrorism (62 percent), health care (59 percent), energy policy (53 percent), and Iraq (49 percent).

One beneficiary of issue preemption and the shifting attention to other issues was the much-maligned pharmaceutical industry. In the lead-up to the 2003 law, skyrocketing drug prices and the lack of coverage for senior citizens fueled anger against the industry that was on ample display during each electoral season. The pharmaceutical industry became an easy target for Democrats, and its popularity in the public eye plummeted: the percentage of Americans saying that drug companies "do a good job serving their customers" fell from 60 percent in 2002 to 45 percent

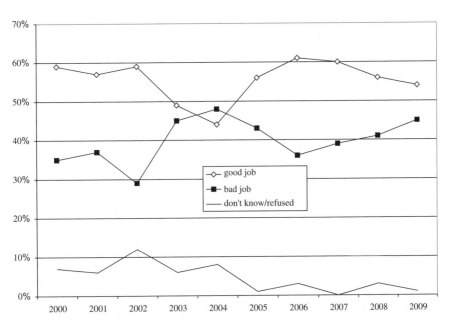

Figure 7.6 Opinions about Pharmaceutical Companies, 2000–2009. Source: Surveys by Harris Interactive, archived by the Roper Center at the University of Connecticut. Note: Responses to question: "Do you think pharmaceutical and drug companies generally do a good job or bad job serving their customers?"

in 2004, a time of particularly fierce partisan jostling over the drug costs (Figure 7.6). Yet by 2006, the "good job" percentage had risen back to 60 percent and then dropped only a few percentage points in 2008 and 2009, despite the fact that the industry made record profits on the MMA due to the influx of customers whose drug purchases were newly subsidized by the government. With public attention moving on to other issues, the industry has largely escaped scrutiny of its profits.

Issue preemption also dampened enthusiasm for changing one aspect of the original MMA—lifting the prohibition on the re-importation of drugs from Canada and other nations. This idea did enjoy considerable bipartisan support, and some expected it to be a "done deal" in 2007 after the Democrats re-took control of the House and Senate.[65] Instead, the drive to allow re-importation failed to muster a sufficient majority in 2007, and issue preemption helped dampen the sense of urgency around this issue. For example, because of the drug benefit, fewer older Americans turned to Canada to fill their prescriptions, and the value of the industry selling Canadian drugs to Americans fell by half between 2004 and May 2007.[66] AARP recognized the shifting political terrain as well: although still formally in favor of drug re-importation, by 2006 the organization watered down its stance, stating that seniors would save more money from the new drug benefit than they would from buying drugs in Canada.[67] The issue also did not get much play in the 2009–2010 health care reform debates, in part because of President Obama's promise to the industry that he would not support any measures that allowed drug re-importation in return for their support for the health reform effort. But once again, the grassroots swell that used to exist around the issue—exemplified by the busloads of seniors crossing the Mexican and Canadian border to buy cheaper pharmaceuticals—was gone.

Conclusion

By testing policy feedback hypotheses with a "live case," we find that some commonly proposed effects of the reform are not upheld, at least not in the short term. For example, the reliance upon competing private plans in Medicare has not changed seniors' opinions about the merits of market-based reform and role of government versus that of the private sector in delivering social welfare programs (although new cohorts of seniors might come to embrace privatization even more, having never experienced Medicare in a pre-MMA world). But while the fears of some MMA critics of conservative ideological conversion have not been realized, the program has entrenched itself in ways that are less overtly ideological but more tangible and ultimately more consequential. The new design of Medicare, with the provision of drug benefits through risk-bearing private insurers and expanded choice of receiving all benefits through Medicare Advantage plans, is the established reality. Beneficiaries are relatively satisfied with Part D and are hardly protesting in the streets for change. And the political agenda moved on to other pressing issues, such as national health care reform and coverage of the uninsured. Lack of beneficiary agitation for change, issue preemption, and agenda change reinforce the new design of Medicare. A delegated program provides just enough to peel off advocates for more direct governmental action, a half solution that undercuts the push for change while nonetheless being marked by significant shortcomings. The consequences for senior citizens' well-being are the subject of the next chapter.

8

Citizens, Consumers, and
the Market Model

The MMA of 2003 introduced a particular form of delegation—the consumer choice model—into Medicare. The theory behind the law was that seniors would now get part of their Medicare benefits from private insurers that compete for the business of customers who shop around for the best value for their dollar. However, the design of the MMA, and the drug benefit in particular, raises a number of questions about the effectiveness of the consumer choice model—questions about how well positioned individuals are to act as consumers, what kinds of incentives shape the behavior of drug plans, and how vulnerable populations such as the poor, the sick, and the cognitively impaired fare.

As chapter 6 showed, Part D has succeeded in many of its goals: as we would expect for a program delivering a 75-percent government subsidy for senior drug purchases, drug utilization has increased, especially among those who previously lacked drug coverage. At the same time, out-of-pocket expenses and cost-related noncompliance with prescribed courses of medications have fallen. Part D is popular among seniors, with favorability toward the law increasing among most seniors over time. Risk adjustment seems to be working, with few plans complaining about dual eligibles and other high-cost beneficiaries.

However, there is also cause for concern. Even though subjective favorability has increased, our panel survey of Medicare beneficiaries shows that those getting their prescription drugs through Part D and Medicare Advantage plans experience far more problems and have lower satisfaction with their drug coverage than those with creditable coverage from former employers and unions, VA/Tricare, or state prescription drug programs. The doughnut coverage gap has caused serious problems with increased expenses and cost-related non-compliance. And yet, disturbingly, there is little switching among plans from year to year, even among those experiencing significant problems and hitting the doughnut, whereas studies show that failing to switch plans can lead to substantially higher out-of-pocket costs over time. Lack of switching among consumers—apparent "satisficing"—undermines competition among plans and encourages increased premiums and cost-sharing. All of these problems are magnified among the poor, the sick, and the aged.

Meanwhile, the Part D market is experiencing consolidation, particularly among plans with more generous coverage. Some of the most popular plans have substantially increased premiums. Although a number of observers have issued quite positive reports on the MMA in recent years, as chapter 6 noted, and although its private-insurer, market-model structure was held up as a successful example during the debate over health care reform in 2009–2010, the coming years will be quite telling of the durability of this program design.

Consumers and the Requirements of the Market Model

Advocates of market reform often assert that government programs are ineffective and unaccountable to the public. Critics on both the Right and Left have long excoriated unresponsive bureaucracies for low levels of effectiveness, equity, quality, and, sometimes, disdain for both clients and taxpayers in programs run by bureaucrats whose salaries are not tied to performance and whose programs face little possibility of elimination. Democratic accountability may be flawed as well: in theory, elected politicians oversee bureaucracies and have an electoral incentive to make bureaucrats attend to the needs of their constituents. But this path of accountability is indirect, and not all constituents are equally situated to make their voices heard through political participation.[1]

Here we evaluate how well market accountability functions. Both the Part D and Medicare Advantage programs were structured around certain assumptions about how a social welfare marketplace would work. First, for-profit firms should compete for customers' business and thus have an incentive to offer the best value they can—the highest quality for the lowest price. Otherwise they will be disciplined by the market as customers depart for plans that offer better value. Second, the market model assumes that well-informed, self-interested, rational consumers will act to maximize their utility,[2] choosing the plan that best fits their needs and maximizes their personal welfare, and updating their choices in light of new information and changing personal circumstances. It is the movement of these knowledgeable customers that exacts market discipline and accountability.

The MMA market commenced on November 15, 2005, as the Part D enrollment window opened (the first benefits became available January 1 of the following year). Senior citizens faced a choice of whether or not to enroll in a Part D plan that would provide drug coverage on top of the hospital and physician services covered by Medicare Parts A and B. Alternatively, they could elect to leave traditional fee-for-service Medicare altogether and enroll in a Medicare Advantage (MA) plan that would cover their health care and (typically) their prescription drugs as well (some MA plans do not cover prescription drugs; those enrollees can sign up for a Part D plan also).[3] Seniors could put off the choice if they wished, but if they did not sign up for a Part D plan by May 15, 2006, when the initial enrollment window closed, they would face a penalty if they signed up later—a one percent increase in premiums for each month they delayed.[4] And they had plenty of choice: despite initial concerns that the insurance industry would not create this new product, in 2006 seniors could choose from among at least 27 plans, and from as many as 52 in some states, a number that grew to between 41 and 55 plans in 2010.[5] With so much choice, the ingredients of the market model appeared to be well in place.

However, research in psychology and behavioral economics suggests that individuals often fall short of the knowledgeable, information-updating, cognitively sharp, and friction-free ideal upon which traditional economic theory—and the MMA—are based. Indeed, both studies of individual-level decision-making and experiences with earlier consumer choice programs, such as the Medicare+Choice program of the 1990s and the prescription drug discount card program in place between 2004 and 2006, suggest that consumers in general and seniors in particular are ill-equipped to make the kinds of discerning choices that enable market accountability mechanisms to work.

As psychologists and behavioral economists have found, many individuals have trouble utilizing information and interpreting data to support their decision-making; innumeracy is widespread in the population as well.[6] According to economist Daniel McFadden, "[B]oth computational and logical skills are limited."[7] Deficits of information and cognition are particularly apparent in situations with a large amount of choice. One reaction to too much choice is paralysis: faced with multiple options, many individuals decline to participate in markets and thus fail to purchase goods, take loans, or enroll in 401(k) retirement plans.[8] Confronted with multiple options, people often choose a default if there is one[9] or copy the choices made by others in their social network.[10] In addition, among those who do make a choice, the size of the choice set affects the quality of decision-making; for example, research shows that workers facing more retirement plan options are more likely to select safer funds (money market or bond funds) rather than riskier but potentially more age-appropriate stock investments.[11] In many instances, individuals are better off when faced with fewer rather than more choices.[12]

Older individuals are even more susceptible to these shortcomings of information utilization, cognition, and decision-making in the face of choice. The cognitive skills needed to make complex decisions, such as executive functioning and working memory, tend to decline with age.[13] After age 60, scores on memory and analysis tasks fall off sharply,[14] while dementia rates double every five years.[15] According to the National Adult Literacy Study, literacy skills are lower among older adults than younger ones.[16] The impact of these limitations and declines has been shown in studies of seniors' personal financial decisions. Compared to middle-aged consumers, seniors pay higher fees and interest rates on credit cards, mortgages, home equity loans, and small business loans.[17] And these shortcomings are quite evident in the health care arena. In one health care literacy study, more than one-third of English speakers over age 65 had inadequate health literacy.[18] In a study of the usage of comparative data on health plan performance as presented in tables, charts, and text, seniors had three times the error rate of those under age 65, with older, sicker, and less-educated seniors performing particularly poorly.[19] When making health care decisions, seniors suffer greater comprehension errors and exhibit more inconsistent preferences than younger people.[20]

Such findings suggest that many senior citizens might have difficulty with the kinds of decisions required by Part D's design. Seniors' experiences with two earlier policy initiatives demonstrated some of the impacts of these limits on older persons' information utilization and cognition. During the 1990s and early 2000s, Medicare managed care plans were available under "Medicare+Choice," as Medicare Part C was known at the time. Studies from this period and beyond found that seniors suffer considerable confusion and lack of knowledge about the various terms associated with Medicare such as "traditional" or "original" Medicare, Medigap, HMOs, PSOs, PPOs, POSs, MSAs, and private FFS plans (confusion only exacerbated when policy-makers alter their terms, such as changing the blanket designation for managed care options from Medicare+Choice to Medicare Advantage).[21] Beyond the confusion over labeling are low levels of health care literacy and information. One study found that only 11 percent of seniors had enough knowledge to make an effective choice between traditional Medicare and Medicare+Choice managed care plans.[22] Consequential for the market model and the ideal of an informed consumer shopping among options, studies found that beneficiaries in Medicare or Medicare+Choice plans knew a fair amount about the particular plan they were in (basic benefits, costs, their right to appeal care decisions), due to direct experience with it, but knew little about other options, thus inhibiting choice or change.[23] As with general studies of senior cognition, knowledge was greater among more educated, affluent, younger, and male subpopulations. Also undermining the market model was consumers' failure to utilize quality information in selecting plans. One study found that although three-quarters of Medicare beneficiaries given quality reports for different health plans said they were somewhat or very easy to understand, more than half declined to use the information in considering alternative health insurance arrangements.[24] Similarly, an experiment in which Medicare beneficiaries were asked to select traditional FFS Medicare or a managed care plan found the same pattern of choices whether subjects were shown quality of care information (in which the managed care plans scored highly) or not.[25] If consumers fail to factor quality information into their insurance choices, plans have little inducement to improve on quality.

A second policy initiative presaged even more directly what might happen when Part D commenced: the temporary prescription drug discount program. Because Part D plans did not begin until January 2006, the 2003 MMA provided for a temporary program beginning in June 2004 in which Medicare beneficiaries could sign up for private Medicare-approved drug discount cards. Those with incomes below 135 percent of the federal poverty level and who had no other drug coverage were also eligible for a federal Transitional Assistance subsidy, which provided $600 annually toward drug costs. Because beneficiaries had a choice among many discount cards—there were 39 national and 33 regional cards available at the beginning of the program[26]—the card program offered a preview of what might happen when Part D began in January 2006.

Senior behavior was not encouraging. Only one-third of beneficiaries who signed up for a discount card considered more than one option when enrolling.[27] Rather than shop around, many people simply chose the card affiliated with the insurance company with which they already had a relationship. Most beneficiaries were passive in their acquisition and use of information, relying on recommendations by physicians, pharmacists, or their insurance company's customer service staff, and not seeking the best card but rather ending their search when they found a card that was "good enough." When asked why they did not seek further, many responded that they were not aware of the variations in discounts and formularies across cards, or that they did not perceive the differences as large or valuable enough to be worth the effort.[28] The very old (those over age 85) had less knowledge of the drug card program.[29] The haphazard way in which most enrollees chose their cards notwithstanding, experiences were positive and satisfaction rates with the program were very high.[30]

Senior Consumers and Part D Decision-making

The discount card program experiences have been repeated almost exactly in Part D. Although most seniors who "should have" signed up for a Part D program did so, they fell short of the rational actor ideal when selecting a plan for themselves.

The Decision to Enroll: Seniors Fare Well

The first choice that seniors faced was whether to enroll in a stand-alone drug program or in an MA-PDP program. As noted in chapter 6, most senior citizens—90 percent—had drug coverage by the summer of the first year, June 2006,[31] and analysis reveals that there was particularly heavy take-up of the new benefit among those who previously had no drug coverage. Those who remained without coverage tended to be healthier and to use fewer or no prescriptions (in the MMA Panel Study, for example, those who remained without drug coverage in the May 2007 follow-up survey did not differ from those who signed up for a Part D plan by age, gender, or income, but had fewer health conditions—1.1 versus 1.6—and took fewer medications—just under two on average, compared to nearly four among the Part D enrollees).[32] There was some evidence early on that seniors were confused about the optimal time to sign up for drug coverage, given their current and likely future drug needs, as against the early enrollment penalty: about 10 percent intended to delay enrollment, though they would have been better off enrolling immediately, and another 19 percent enrolled but would have been better off delaying.[33] It was also the case that older seniors and the cognitively less sophisticated were less likely to enroll, although there were no differences in enrollment across education or income groups. Overall, drug usage was the most significant factor in the decision to join a PDP or MA-PDP.[34] Thus most senior decision-making around whether to enroll in the new drug benefit was rational and driven by economic factors.

Plan Selection: Far Less Rationality

Unfortunately, senior consumers were far less rational when it came to choice of plan, a vastly more difficult decision. Perhaps this is not surprising, given the pattern of low-information, cue-driven plan selection in the earlier discount card program. One might hope that shortcomings in decision-making there could be attributed to the temporary nature of the program, and that seniors would bring more rigorous considerations to bear when the stakes were higher. However, a number of studies, including our own MMA Panel Survey, show that this is not the case.

Seniors faced a daunting array of choice among dozens of plans, which varied on multiple dimensions: different monthly premiums, co-payments, formularies, tiers, use of generics, and coverage in the doughnut hole, among others. Ironically, working aged people face much less choice of prescription drug plans: among those with drug coverage, 37 percent have just one choice; only 20 percent have more than five choices.[35] Indeed, studies have determined that constraining the number of choices to fewer than 10, and even as few as three, heightens senior welfare.[36] And seniors seem to agree that 40 or 50 plans are too many: a 2006 Kaiser Family Foundation poll found that three-fifths of seniors favored Medicare offering only a handful of plans "so seniors have an easier time choosing."[37] In our MMA Panel Survey, the majority of seniors—60 percent—said the optimal number of plans to choose from was 3 to 5; 18 percent said 1 to 2 plans, 17 percent said 6 to 10 plans. Just 0.4 percent said 40 or more, the number of choices that many seniors faced in their states. Thus the design of the MMA requires considerable decision-making prowess from a group perhaps least capable of having it.

One concern with informational and cognitive shortcomings among seniors is that they produce enrollment choices that fail to maximize their welfare. Congruent with studies showing minimalistic information-seeking among individuals, Medicare beneficiaries largely failed to utilize the information resources available to them. As of April 2006, over five months after Part D enrollment commenced, only 12 percent of seniors reported in a national survey that they had ever called the Medicare toll-free phone number, and only 5 percent had utilized the Medicare web site to compare drug plans.[38] Less than 1 percent of pharmacists surveyed in June 2006 felt that their clients understood the drug benefit "very well;" 13 percent said "somewhat well."[39] In selecting plans, beneficiaries tended to use inferior criteria, weighting monthly plan premiums more than overall out-of-pocket costs, or choosing doughnut hole coverage—and therefore paying higher premiums—even though their drug costs were well below the doughnut threshold.[40] Indeed, the proportion of seniors choosing plans with doughnut coverage is virtually the same from the 10th to the 85th percentile of drug costs, which means that a great many were using irrelevant criteria and wasting a lot of money.[41] The power of a default option is seen in the fact that one of the top two plans in 2007 enrollment (and in 2009) was the AARP Medicare Rx plan offered by United Healthcare, suggesting that AARP branding provided a convenient cue for those flummoxed by the large array of choices they faced.[42]

Thus a great many seniors chose sub-optimal plans due to inadequate information collection, the use of inferior criteria, and susceptibility to advertising and branding. Proponents of choice say that it only takes a few well-informed clients to make markets work,[43] but this may be the case more in areas like common consumer items or even school vouchers, where multiple families may be using the same criteria of selection and where "market mavens" and "information seekers" are helpful agents within the population, as opposed to drug plans, where needs are so individualistic and where simple imitation of peers may be less appropriate.[44]

Of particular concern in many seniors' poor Part D choices is their misplaced confidence in them. Seniors not only on average bring a number of cognitive deficits to the health insurance arena, but they are also unaware of their own limitations. Experimental data on health care choices show that older people both make worse choices than younger people and are also more confident that they made the right choice. When asked in an experimental setting to identify the drug plan (from among 3, 10, or 20 alternatives) that would minimize total annual costs, subjects aged 65 and over were less likely than non-seniors to select correctly the cost-minimizing plan, but also were much more likely to feel "very confident" that they had in fact done so.[45]

It may be that senior decision-making will be aided in the future by publicly available data on plan quality. One of the reasons that the AARP plan earned high market share may have been due to the reputation of the sponsor. Beginning with the 2008 open enrollment period, seniors could view plan performance ratings on the "Medicare Prescription Drug Plan Finder" web site,[46] although the continued dominance of the AARP-branded plan into 2009 suggests that reputation continues to matter more than other criteria. There is also the possibility that after several years' experience with Part D, recipients may stop relying so heavily on more visible criteria like monthly premiums and consider overall out-of-pocket costs instead.[47] In the meantime, however, many seniors remain in sub-optimal plans.

Part D Effectiveness and Senior Welfare: Mixed Evidence

Despite the fact that many seniors did not select the best plan for themselves, they have in many ways fared well under Part D. As chapter 6 detailed, utilization of prescription drugs is up, particularly among the previously uninsured,[48] while their drug expenses per day have fallen 69 percent.[49] Cost-related noncompliance—skipping medications, skimping on doses, and so on—has also decreased,[50] although not among the sickest, a point to which we will return. Beyond these objective measures of program effectiveness are positive subjective evaluations of Part D as well. As with the earlier prescription drug discount card, reported favorability is quite high. In the second wave of the MMA Panel Study, majorities of almost every category of seniors had a favorable impression of the new drug benefit, including 63 percent of those in Part D overall and 67 percent who previously did not have drug coverage (Figure 8.1). Overall favorability increased between the first and second survey by 15–17 points among those in Part D, those with creditable coverage, and even those without drug coverage. Among those respondents who remained in the panel survey, favorability increased by ten more points between the second wave in 2007 and the third wave in 2009. [51]

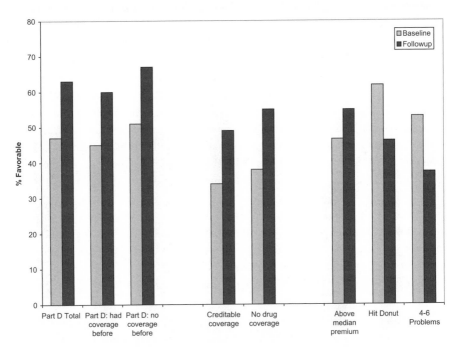

Figure 8.1 Favorability toward Prescription Drug Benefit. Source: MMA Panel Survey.
Note: Figure shows percentage of respondents with a favorable impression of the Medicare prescription drug benefit in the baseline and follow-up surveys.

However, these improvements in utilization, out-of-pocket costs, and subjective evaluations of the reform—not to mention the fairly positive marks given the MMA by economists and other observers mentioned in chapter 6—mask some less positive realities. Those getting their prescription drugs through either Part D or Medicare Advantage plans are actually less satisfied and experience more problems than those with drug coverage from other comparable and "creditable" forms of coverage such as the Veterans Administration or former employers. In the second wave of the MMA Panel Study, conducted 17 months into Part D implementation, we asked respondents how satisfied they are with the plan that provides their prescription drugs. Just 39 percent of Part D enrollees said they were "very satisfied," compared to 76 percent among those with creditable coverage from the Veterans Administration/Tricare for Life, 60 percent among those with coverage from a former employer or union or with some other form of coverage, and 50 percent among those with state pharmaceutical assistance plan coverage (Figure 8.2). Satisfaction with the drug coverage provided by Medicare Advantage plans was low as well, just 45 percent saying they were "very satisfied."[52] We also asked about problems that consumers might have in getting their prescriptions.[53] Again, Part D and MA enrollees reported substantially more difficulties: of the six problems we asked about, respondents with Part D plans experienced 1.5 on average, and Medicare Advantage enrollees 1.4 on average, compared to just 0.9 or less for respondents with creditable coverage (Figure 8.3).[54] Indeed, some subgroups did not become

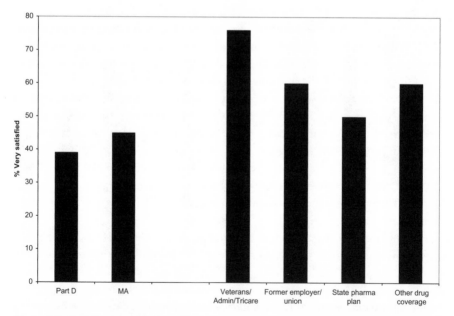

Figure 8.2 Satisfaction with Drug Plan. Source: MMA Panel Survey. Note: Figure shows percentage of respondents very satisfied with their drug coverage.

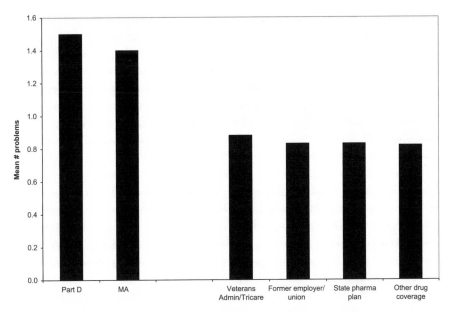

Figure 8.3 Mean Number of Problems with Drug Plan. Source: MMA Panel Survey.
Note: Figure shows average number of problems experienced out of six asked in survey. See text for wording.

more favorable toward the drug benefit over time (Figure 8.1), chiefly those who hit the doughnut and those who experienced four or more problems getting their prescriptions, indicating that there are pockets of seniors facing significant difficulties. The fact that satisfaction is lower and the mean number of problems is higher for Part D and MA-PDP beneficiaries than for those with creditable coverage begs the question of just how good these prescription drug plans are.

A second set of issues about the effectiveness of the Part D drug plans and the market for them concerns lack of plan switching. Together with informed choice, switching is a crucial component of the market model: individuals should review their choices—the law allows them to do so once a year during the annual open enrollment period—and switch if a better plan becomes available or if their needs change and a different plan better suits them. Switching is crucial both in maximizing beneficiary welfare and in incentivizing insurers to provide value for the dollar.

In practice, however, stasis predominates, with beneficiaries staying in their (typically non-optimal) plans year to year. In the MMA Panel Survey, only 9 percent of respondents switched plans between 2006 and 2007, the first and second years of the Part D program; other national surveys have found similarly low rates.[55] Switching rates in the MMA Panel Survey were somewhat higher among those paying above median premiums (12 percent), those hitting the doughnut (17 percent), and those experiencing a high number of problems with their drug plans (21 percent among those with four or more of the six problems we asked about). Although switching rates were somewhat higher among those experiencing difficulties, they are still quite low—note that of those experiencing a high number of problems, a remarkable four-fifths stayed with their plan a second year.[56] Moreover, other national data reveal that about half of those who switched plans between 2006 and 2007 did not do so of their own accord in the search for a better plan; instead, they were dropped by their plans, which had decided no longer to cover low-income beneficiaries. In short, these persons did not leave their plans; their plans left them.[57]

Lack of switching means that the costs of an initial poor choice—or failure to update one's choice given changing circumstances—accumulate over time. Although prescription drug expenditures are steadier for individuals than are other health care expenditures,[58] the particular medications used can shift substantially, and failure to update one's coverage based on such changes can be quite costly. An analysis of Medical Expenditure Panel Survey data comparing initial- and end-of-year drug use and costs found that 43 percent of seniors sampled faced higher out-of-pocket costs at the end of the year, averaging $556, due to changes in medications. The largest average loss was for diabetics, perhaps because of the large number of medications they typically use.[59] One can imagine how much losses would pile up over time if a beneficiary with changing medications failed to update her choice of Part D plan. And insurers seem to be taking advantage of this stickiness in the market: there is a lot of money to be made raising premiums on these cognitively captive populations. The Part D plan that attracted the largest enrollment after AARP Medicare Rx was the Humana PDP Standard plan, probably because it was initially the least expensive plan in most regions. However, its average monthly premium quadrupled between 2006 and 2009, while the weighted average premium across all drug plans increased just 35 percent over the same period, demonstrating the very real cost of plan stickiness.[60] Indeed, between 2007 and 2008, three-quarters of Part D drug plans increased their monthly premiums, and did so by an average of 17 percent, compared to a 3.1 percent increase in the Medicare Part B premium. About a quarter of Part D enrollees who did not switch plans between 2006 and 2008 faced premium increases of at least 50 percent over the three-year period.[61] As Dan Mendelson, president of Avalere Health, said, "Seniors are used to buying insurance and then leaving it there forever. Many of them are approaching the Part D market in that way; I think it would take probably some more dramatic changes to move seniors off [their plans]. So the market is remaining relatively stable."[62] Lack of switching leaves seniors vulnerable to premium increases and accumulating deficits to their welfare.[63]

It may well be the case that Part D enrollees did not switch plans because they did not believe that they could find a better plan. In the third wave of the MMA Panel Study, we asked respondents who had not switched drug plans why they had not done so. Fifty-six percent said that a major reason was that they were "satisfied with my current plan." But 38 percent said a major reason was that they "didn't think there was a better plan for me."[64] High percentages of respondents who had various kinds of negative experiences thought there was no better plan for them: 41 percent of those who fell in the doughnut, 45 percent of those paying above median premiums, and 48 percent of those experiencing four or more problems getting their prescriptions. These survey findings square with behaviors reported in focus groups conducted for the Kaiser Family Foundation in late 2007 asking seniors about their intentions during the 2008 open enrollment period. A number expressed problems with their current plans, such as unexpected costs, having to switch medications, and billing errors, but virtually none said they were considering switching plans for the new year. Many beneficiaries did not want to revisit the complex decision, thought most plans were pretty similar, believed they were already in the best plan for themselves, and feared that switching plans might cause more problems or greater out-of-pocket expenses.[65]

From the patient perspective, it is a very good thing that the 2010 Affordable Care Act promises to reduce the doughnut hole in coverage, as it generates a particularly serious set of problems.[66] Relatively few beneficiaries fell into the doughnut during the first few years of Part D operation—14 percent of enrollees, or 3.4 million individuals, in 2007[67]—but the consequences could be dire for those who did. Monthly out-of-pocket expenses nearly doubled for those entering the gap, and most did not reach the catastrophic threshold when their cost-sharing would have dropped to 5 percent.[68] While a decrease in cost-related noncompliance has been a major benefit of Part D, it tends to shoot up again when people fall in the doughnut. More broadly, the structure of Part D plans with a doughnut—a feature included only for budgetary reasons and which exists nowhere else in the health insurance world—confronts beneficiaries with a series of decisions that force a potentially dangerous trade-off between money and health. In initial choice among plans, enrollees must weigh monthly premiums and co-payments against the generosity of coverage. These trade-offs become even more acute around the doughnut, when beneficiaries must decide "how much to economize in drug use below and above" the doughnut hole and how to finance out-of-pocket expenses when they reach the doughnut threshold.[69] Some respondents in the MMA Panel Survey simply stopped taking their meds, skipped doses, or split pills in half when they reached the doughnut,[70] in line with studies showing that greater cost-sharing generally results in lower drug usage by patients trying to save money.[71] Such economizing can result in hospitalizations and other acute interventions and worse physiological outcomes.[72]

That the doughnut represents such a threat to the well-being of beneficiaries is a particular problem, in that a large and increasing proportion of PDPs do not cover the gap at all, 80 percent in 2010, up from 72 percent in 2007.[73] Not only do plans with gap coverage attract more expensive beneficiaries, but also the design of the benefit is such that covering part of the gap, even with generic drugs, means that the kick-in of catastrophic reinsurance is delayed, increasing the effective cost of such enrollees to the plan.[74] The decrease in gap coverage is emblematic of a number of shifts in the PDP marketplace that may have negative consequences for beneficiaries. The market is already highly concentrated, with 4 percent of the 1,824 plans in operation in 2008 accounting for over half of all enrollment; the top three firms—UnitedHealth Group, Humana, and Universal American—controlled 55 percent of the market.[75] The adverse selection of sicker enrollees into plans that offered brand name drug coverage in the doughnut hole brought about their complete extinction by 2008.[76]

One concern with a market in which beneficiaries select a drug plan from myriad choices is that insurers will have an incentive to cream-skim and try to attract healthier, lower cost enrollees. Plans can do this by setting formularies, for example, that minimize their offerings in classes of drugs consumed at higher rates by high-cost beneficiaries.[77] The MMA seeks to mitigate such risk selection through risk adjustment—adjusting the prospective payment that Medicare pays to Part D plans or Medicare Advantage prescription drug plans for each beneficiary by a risk score calculated from their disease burden. However, the approach used by CMS in administering the program only predicts 12 percent of the variation in future drug costs, and both over-predicts costs for enrollees with low actual costs and under-predicts costs for enrollees with high actual costs.[78]

These flaws in risk adjustment give insurers considerable incentive to cherry pick, incentives that will increase as the "risk corridors" written into the original legislation, which limited financial penalties for providers, widen between 2008 and 2011.[79] Previous studies show how effective insurers are at attracting healthy risks through advertising, how the incentives to do so increase when there is more competition, and how susceptible individuals are to such appeals. For example, where there is greater HMO penetration both cross-sectionally and over time, the more advertising insurers do, especially more risk-selective advertising aimed at attracting healthier beneficiaries.[80] At the same time, however, risk adjustment seems to have been good enough that firms are not complaining about covering dual eligibles,[81] nor have studies found that plans open to beneficiaries with low-income subsidies have more restrictive formularies.[82]

Vulnerable Populations and Redistributive Issues

One concern about marketized public programs is how well vulnerable groups—low-income, older, sicker, cognitively impaired, or isolated senior citizens—are able to navigate a social welfare marketplace. Research suggests that the cognitive requirements of market models can exacerbate underlying inequalities by penalizing such groups more severely. Previous experience did not bode well: general Medicare knowledge is lower among less educated, poorer, older, and female senior citizens,[83] and awareness about and knowledge of the temporary prescription drug discount card program was lower among older seniors.[84] In the Part D choice experiment in which respondents had to choose the cost-minimizing, optimal Part D plan from among multiple options, older seniors were less able to do so.[85] The kinds of informational and cognitive skills needed to negotiate market-model programs are unevenly distributed across the population, and the neediest may be the worst equipped and the most heavily affected.

Low-income beneficiaries are one such group. The MMA instituted a low-income subsidy program (LIS) to help pay premiums and meet the cost-sharing requirements for beneficiaries who qualify. Many LIS recipients are dual eligibles—the 8.8 million seniors (as of 2010) who are eligible for both Medicare and Medicaid (Medicaid pays their Medicare premiums and cost-sharing). In addition, other low-income seniors such as those receiving Supplemental Security Income (SSI) and those enrolled in Medicare Savings Programs (MSPs), who get some Medicaid assistance with their Medicare cost-sharing, could also qualify for LIS subsidies. Some additional seniors can qualify for partial subsidies if they meet certain income and asset requirements.[86] LIS beneficiaries receiving full subsidies do not pay monthly premiums or deductibles for drug coverage, nor do they face a dough-nut coverage gap; however, they do make co-payments for drugs on their plan's formulary and they pay the full cost of drugs not on the formulary.[87]

LIS beneficiaries are randomly assigned to a "benchmark plan" that has monthly premiums below the average premium of all plans in their region offering the basic drug benefit. They are not allowed to enroll in plans offering enhanced benefits, even if the premiums are below the benchmark.[88] If the initial assignment is a poor match for the individual's prescription needs, it is his or her responsibility to make a change; unlike other seniors, who can change plans only once a year during the open enrollment period, LIS beneficiaries have the opportunity to change plans once a month.

There are a number of concerns surrounding the enrollment of LIS beneficiaries into Part D plans. Dual eligibles have more extensive prescription drug and medical needs on average than other Medicare beneficiaries, and are more likely to suffer from mental illness, cognitive impairment, and chronic conditions. Not surprisingly, total health care spending on dual eligibles is double that of other Medicare beneficiaries.[89] And yet, as chapter 6 described, dual eligibles were in many ways the MMA guinea pigs, bearing the brunt of the rocky early months of the program's implementation in 2006. For other Medicare beneficiaries, Part D was voluntary, and the initial enrollment period was six months long, from November 15, 2005, to May 15, 2006. Dual eligibles, by contrast, had their Medicaid drug coverage abruptly terminated on December 31, 2005, and immediately became clients of a Part D plan to which they had been randomly assigned. Some dual eligibles thus confronted many of the problems of the program's early days—including overcharging of beneficiaries, inability to procure medications, and failures to enroll people in plans. Concern about the fate of these vulnerable groups led 37 states to create temporary coverage programs to ensure that their dual eligibles received their prescriptions.[90]

What does the Part D marketplace look like for LIS recipients today? On the one hand, analysis shows that benchmark and non-benchmark plans are quite similar. For example, benchmark plans have slightly smaller formularies in most regions but also employ fewer utilization management restrictions. On the other hand, only about one-quarter of Part D plans qualify as benchmark plans, and the number has fallen over time. From year to year, fewer PDPs are premium-free to LIS beneficiaries as well.[91] There is also considerable regional variation in the number of plans available, ranging from 19 in Illinois to just 2 in Nevada.[92] The LIS market is also characterized by substantial instability. About 40 percent of benchmark plans changed status between 2007 and 2008, either losing their benchmark status or leaving the Part D market altogether;[93] 2.1 million dual eligibles in 2008 and 1.6 million in 2009 were reassigned plans as a result.[94] Moreover, benchmark plans in general have higher co-payments and more restrictive formularies than dual eligibles experienced under Medicaid.

Between having lost what in many cases was more generous Medicaid drug coverage, and now being subject to a churning Part D market, we might wonder how dual eligibles and other low-income subsidy recipients—not to mention other vulnerable populations such as older and sicker seniors—are faring under the MMA. Although our MMA Panel Survey contained relatively few dual eligibles, and probably failed to capture very low income or very sick persons in the sample, the vulnerable respondents who were included in the survey experienced significant difficulties. Dual eligibles, low-income (the bottom quintile), and the sickest respondents (who had three or more chronic conditions out of the seven we asked about) reported about the same level of favorability toward the new drug benefit, and just slightly lower satisfaction with their drug plan, as their non-dual eligible, higher income, and healthier counterparts (Table 8.1). But such respondents reported significantly more problems getting their medications, and sicker respondents were more likely to hit the doughnut hole in coverage as well. They were also more likely to say that the new prescription drug benefit had made them less sure they could afford their medications and made them feel less financially secure.[95] Multivariate analysis (Appendix Table B.5) shows that, all else equal, female, older, sicker, and dually eligible respondents were less likely to switch plans between years 1 and 2.[96] Sicker, less educated, younger, and male respondents reported more problems getting their prescriptions, as did those hitting the doughnut. Those who are older, along with those experiencing more problems and paying higher premiums, said they were now less sure they could afford their prescriptions, and those experiencing more problems and paying higher premiums reported feeling less financially secure. Together with other findings showing that cost-related noncompliance has not fallen among the sickest Medicare beneficiaries,[97] there are real concerns about what the MMA reform means for populations less well equipped to negotiate the drug plan marketplace.

Going forward it will be important to monitor the experience of dual eligibles and other LIS beneficiaries in Part D. There could be further consolidation of

Table 8.1. **Part D Experiences of Vulnerable Populations**

	% of sample	% Favorable toward drug benefit	% Very satisfied with drug plan	Average 2006 premium	Mean # problems (out of 6)	% Hitting donut	% Switched plans	% less sure they can afford drugs	% less financially secure
Dual Eligible	14	51	42*	$45*	1.7*	16.5	9.9	22*	29*
Non-Dual Eligible	86	54	51	$36	1.1	14.8	9.4	11	14
Low Income	20	54	40*	$35	1.7*	15.3	10.7	19*	28*
Non-Low Income	80	54	53	$38	1.1	15.0	8.9	11	14
# Chronic health conditions: 3–7	24	53	49	$43*	1.9*	18.7*	8.5	21*	27*
1–2	56	56	53	$38	1.0	16.3	11.0	10	14
0	20	53	44	$24	0.7	6.8	6.3	8	12

Note: Difference of means test or chi-square test significant at: * p<.05. Difference calculated for zero vs. 3–7 chronic health conditions. Low-income defined as income less than $15,000.

Source: Medicare Modernization Act Panel Study, first follow-up.

benchmark programs, limiting the options—and the formularies—available to these vulnerable populations. In addition, because they pay so little out-of-pocket, LIS beneficiaries' drug use has to be controlled by other methods, such as prior authorization, step therapy (starting patients on the cheapest drug in a class and going to more expense therapies only if necessary), or more restricted formularies.[98] Whether such restrictions have negative effects on their access to medications will be of continuing concern, as is the LIS take-up rate: beyond the dual eligibles who were automatically rolled from Medicaid into Part D, other LIS beneficiaries have to sign up to get the financial assistance, and as of 2009, 20 percent of those eligible for LIS subsidies were not receiving it.[99]

Conclusion

In the consumer choice form of delegated governance, citizens operate in a market environment in which their well-being depends largely on their skills and capacities as consumers. Unfortunately, many individuals fall short of the rational and well-informed ideal assumed by economic models. And senior citizens fare the worst of all, with fewer health literacy skills, lower levels of knowledge, and impaired cognition compared to younger people. And yet the MMA requires seniors to make choices among a far vaster array of options than non-seniors typically face, and to do so in an arena where the stakes are especially high and where money/health trade-offs can be acute. Perhaps even more worrying are seniors' self-evaluations, in which they overrate their abilities as market actors, and their ignorance of superior alternatives; both of these tendencies appear to undermine plan switching. The market model generates little market accountability if the consumers involved fail to search across alternatives or move to new plans when it is advantageous to do so. The daunting level of choice, combined with general human tendencies toward inertia and reluctance to change,[100] have produced considerable stickiness in the MMA that is far from the welfare-maximizing market ideal and that undermines mechanisms of market accountability. This market stickiness advantages providers, who can raise premiums on their immobile clients. The incidence of risk does not bode well for consumers either, since they bear the financial and health risks of poor plan choices and of cream-skimming behavior by insurers.

Markets produce unequal outcomes. The question with the market model is always whether regulation is sufficient to mitigate these inequalities and other negative externalities and to fulfill the societal obligation to protect the vulnerable.[101] Experiences with market model programs suggest that consumers can be let down not just by unaccountable bureaucracies in programs of direct governance, but also by insufficiently regulated market-based programs. Consumers need assistance and protections—assistance in making effective choices and protections from the business practices of firms far more aggressive than they are.

Traditional social insurance programs like Social Security are sometimes criticized for being paternalistic, eliminating choice, and forcing beneficiaries into a prescribed set of behaviors. But the pendulum swings perhaps too far in the other direction with the consumer choice model, especially programs with vast amounts of choice for which citizens are ill-prepared but must pay the price for poor choices.

‖ 9 ‖

Conclusion

Delegated Governance, Past, Present, and Future

The goal of this book is to explore some of the ways in which the American welfare state delegates authority to private actors. It is well-known that the private sector plays a vital role in the delivery of social benefits and services. Many have also written about the indirect way in which American government often achieves its social policy objectives—using tax policy or regulation, for instance, as a way to prod private provision in lieu of direct government action. We have taken this line of inquiry a step further, examining how, even in what seem to be the most "public" of social programs, such as Medicare, considerable authority for the management and delivery of these programs has long been vested with non-state actors. Although many would assume that such practices are a product of neo-liberal political currents that have taken hold since the early 1980s, we instead find delegated governance to be a pervasive feature of the American welfare state, one that predates the coming to power of Ronald Reagan and other market-oriented conservatives. In fact, much of the growth of the American state in the post-1945 period has been achieved through the granting of governing authority over social programs to private entities.

To capture this phenomenon, we develop the concept of delegated governance: the delegation of responsibility for publicly funded social welfare programs to non-state actors. We use this general term to encompass several more specific forms of delegation. The form most common in the earliest development of social programs was one that assigned responsibility for program administration or service delivery to nonprofit organizations or publicly minded professionals. Here, the assumption was that profit motives were not always appropriate when it came to delivering social welfare programs and services, and thus many policy-makers preferred to rely on nonprofits or professionals—such as physicians—as essentially nongovernmental extensions of the government. In later years, however, a growing chorus of advocates favored introducing market competition into the delivery of public programs. This would shape two other variants of delegated governance—a marketized version that shifted governance to risk-bearing, for-profit entities and/or sought to introduce greater competition among all government contractors; and a consumer choice version that, through vouchers and other sub-sidies, delegated more responsibility to individuals themselves, who then select their benefits or services from the marketplace. All three forms are now present within the Medicare program, making it an excellent case for exploring the ori-gins, evolution, and consequences of delegated governance.

What explains the repeated reliance upon delegated governance and the forms that it has taken? Such a large and complex phenomenon defies a mono-causal explanation, but led us to examine the interplay of political institutions, interest groups, and public opinion in the crafting of redistributive policy. First, we empha-size the important role that Congress plays in the policy-making process. Porous, decentralized, and full of risk-averse politicians who feel individually vulnerable to voter wrath, Congress creates high hurdles for the passage of any major reform. The price paid for such legislation has often been administrative incoherence, as deals are cut and compromises made in order to build a majority coalition. Relying on non-state actors to deliver public programs has been one way to build such a coalition, as it blunts assertions that a reform will vastly increase the size of gov-ernment. It also may appease private interests. Although we reject accounts that presume the hegemonic influence of fat-cat lobbyists, there can be no denying that interest groups have weight in the policy-making process. We find that they especially gain clout when they can help bring legislative votes on board, and that delegated governance helps give these groups a stake in a reform either by diluting the influence of government over their arena of interest (in the case of physicians) or by cutting them into the deal (in the case of insurers)—offering potential profit-making opportunities or promises of government subsidies with minimal government interference. We see these interest group dynamics as particularly important in health care, but at times also present in other social policy areas.

For legislators who are notoriously leery of imposing pain on either constitu-ents or powerful interests, delegating administrative responsibilities has an added advantage of shifting difficult decision-making to someone else's shoulders. As Lowi wrote insightfully back in 1969 about why policy-makers prefer to shift au-thority to private actors, "The typical American politician displaces and defers and delegates conflict where possible; he squarely faces conflict only when he must."[1] Particularly in health care, where there may be a need to make difficult determina-tions about how much health care people should access and at what cost, many politicians have preferred to leave such determinations up to private insurers. In fact, the allure of market-based reform of social programs—and health care in particular—lies in part in the cherished hope that private firms can make the tough allocative decisions that government officials would rather not have to make. Thus, if the government ought not be in your medicine cabinet determining what prescriptions you will take and at what cost, the task is then left to HMOs and other private insurers.

Beyond these institutional and interest group factors we see a larger, more fun-damental force at work—the divided and frequently contradictory nature of public opinion when it comes to the welfare state. Significant majorities of Americans clamor for public protections against social risks and needs, yet they often voice skepticism, disdain, or even fear about the federal government, or government in general. Delegated governance represents a way to seemingly respond to both sides of this coin, as the Janus-faced nature of public opinion puts constraints on what both liberals and conservatives can achieve. Outside of Social Security, which was enacted at a time of national crisis and private market collapse, liberals have repeatedly been frustrated in their efforts to enact universal, uniform, and federally administered social programs. Efforts to craft such programs usually run up against a political mobilization decrying "Big Government" that, while marshaled largely by elites, has resonance in popular opinion. Frequently, then, delegated governance has been a compromise solution that takes some of the sting out of claims about Big Government. At the same time, conservatives have found the public less than enthusiastic about market-based reforms, antipathetic toward Big Business, and still desirous of protections against social risks and needs. Unable to push outright privatization, which would fully shed burdens from the public to the private sector, they have instead sought to combine public subsidies and regulations with marketized forms of delivery.

The apotheosis of this policy-making strategy came in the 2003 Medicare Modernization Act, which requires seniors to sign up with a private insurance plan to receive coverage for prescription drug benefits. At first glance, the MMA is puzzling: Why would conservative Republicans who had long been championing cuts in federal entitlements instead enact a major and universalistic expansion of a federal social program? The answer lies in the way in which the new program would be administered, which enabled Republicans to respond to powerful public demand for a drug benefit while still being able to claim they were not simply expanding Medicare but were implanting the seeds of market-based reform in the program. The latter set of claims were vital in providing political cover for Republican House and Senate members, many of whom were deeply skeptical about creating an expensive new entitlement. Yet, the episode shows just how powerful public demand for the welfare state can be, especially when used as a political cudgel by Democrats angling for political advantage. Delegating governance of the new program to private, risk-bearing firms was a way for Republicans to square the circle: to address this public fervor in a way that seemingly limits the growth of government.

Do these kinds of administrative arrangements really matter? Is not the important fact that the programs are created and provide social support to the population, or should we care about how programs are actually run? We argue that there are several reasons that we should be attentive to the governance of the American welfare state. First, we use the case study of Medicare to explore how well these governing arrangements have worked in practice. We find that they mostly serve a political function—enabling the passage of controversial policies and their administration in a context of hostility to expanding the federal civil service—but that this often comes at a price of administrative coherence. The original Medicare program, for instance, delegated so much authority to private actors that policymakers struggled to hold down program costs or ensure sufficient scrutiny of provider claims. Over time, cost control improved through instituting a more direct federal role in running the program, yet other problems would continue, such as difficulties controlling fraud and abuse. We find little evidence that these problems result from inherent governmental incompetence, but instead that they reflect political opposition to the expansion of federal administrative capabilities over health care. In other words, the very hostility to government that led to the delegation of program governance also impeded the growth of effective public agencies to oversee a vast, decentralized, and complex program—arguably one that needs more muscular public administration at the top, not less.

We use the implementation of the 2003 MMA to explore the extent to which market-based arrangements have proven superior to the "old-style" contracting out of the past. Does market-based reform lead to more efficient administration of programs and produce greater accountability, for instance, through the substitution of market forces for democratic processes? In many ways, the MMA has achieved many of its goals, such as assuring broad-based coverage of prescription drug needs and reducing the out-of-pocket costs paid by seniors for these medications. Some argue that it has done so at lower cost than originally anticipated because of the influence of competitive pressures—that competing private insurers are holding down premiums to lure customers and are engaging in tough negotiations with pharmaceutical companies over the prices paid for prescription drugs. We find, however, that the competitive design of the new benefit has had only a limited impact on the overall cost of the program; instead, lower-than-expected enrollments and an overall drop in pharmaceutical prices best explain the seeming "efficiencies" of the program.

Moreover, we find that the market design has many costs—most notably in widespread marketing abuses and other manipulative practices that take advantage of the complexity of the program and, at times, cognitive limitations of the target population. More generally, we find that market forces are not working in the way anticipated—Medicare beneficiaries are not leaving bad plans or using their market power to induce better performance by drug plans. Beneficiaries have instead "satisficed," making do with the plan they have chosen rather than revising this decision, even in the face of poor plan performance. The resulting stickiness of early plan choice was something that insurance plans fully expected, and it is what drove their aggressive efforts to snap up market-share early in the program's implementation (and their aggressive marketing toward new beneficiaries that come into the marketplace). Yet, once again, the hollow administrative agency charged with overseeing this highly complex new marketplace has struggled to rein in manipulative or fraudulent practices.

We also explore some of the political consequences of delegated governance, examining in particular arguments about policy feedback effects. A growing literature argues that public policies have enduring political legacies, as they can remake the interest group, public opinion, and institutional landscape and thus shape future policy reforms. This question had particular salience during the debate over the 2003 MMA, as some argued it represented a "stealth privatization" of Medicare that would create a growing constituency of beneficiaries who favored market-like arrangements in the program. Using a panel study of Medicare beneficiaries before and after the reform, we find no growth in support for market reform of Medicare or the Republican pro-competitive approach to health care. Although the partisan tussles over the MMA appeared to be a fight over issue ownership, with each side jostling to gain credibility on the issue of health care and entitlement reform, Republicans at best achieved some degree of issue preemption in that they addressed a problem before Democrats could. This blunted Democratic attacks and removed an issue from the political field. It also ensured a good deal of entrench-ment of the Republican approach. Although shifts in the partisan control of gov-ernment led to some undermining of the Republican policy architecture, much of the overall structure remains intact. Now, for the first time in the program's history, Medicare beneficiaries must sign up with a private insurance firm in order to receive part of their benefits.

The MMA may generate policy legacies further down the road, providing a road map for future reform of federal entitlements at moments of fiscal crisis. For instance, the privatized structure of the MMA is one apparent precedent for the Republicans' fiscal year 2012 federal budget, which passed the House in April 2011 with no Democratic votes. The budget proposes to replace the traditional Medicare program with a "premium support" model in which seniors would receive a voucher for the purchase of private insurance coverage. Concern about mounting levels of federal debt created an opening for the GOP to revisit the idea of transforming Medicare into a system of competing private plans. It appears that the MMA has been one "template" for this idea, as Senator John Breaux once predicted.

Implications for Thinking about the American State

Our study has implications for ongoing debates about the nature of the American state. These discussions are long-standing: since at least Louis Hartz, scholars have debated the extent to which the United States is exceptional in the character of its bureaucratic apparatus. Few today defend the idea of American "stateless-ness": even in the nineteenth century, when federal administrative capacities were clearly smaller than those found in western Europe by most measures, the federal government achieved a good deal.[2] In the twentieth century, the United States fought and won two major world wars, waged a costly cold war and emerged triumphant from it, and mobilized the political energies to tackle a host of diffi-cult goals, be they putting astronauts in space, dramatically reducing poverty among senior citizens, or racially desegregating schools and other facilities.[3] Clearly, the American state "is more potent as an authoritative rule maker, national standardizer, and manager of the nation's affairs than earlier accounts generally concluded."[4]

Yet, one can quickly go overboard in extolling the great number of things the American state does, sliding inadvertently into presumptions about the strength or weakness of the governing apparatus.[5] Scholars still struggle to arrive at the right vocabulary and set of concepts to describe this strange beast that is the American state.[6] Our approach was to start first with an in-depth empirical study of what the American state actually does and how it goes about it. Instead of asking whether the state is strong or weak, we looked at how public policies actually structure administrative arrangements and try to meet various goals. We then sought to analyze what we saw: Where does administrative power lie? How effectively is the federal government achieving its stated aims? And what do particular governing arrangements mean for politics, redistribution, and accountability?

In answering these questions, we arrived at a view of the American state as a system of delegated and diffused authority in which public and private administrative capacities are pervasively intertwined. Much of the expansion of the American state since the New Deal, and particularly since World War II, has come about through heavy reliance on private actors that are subsidized, regulated, and otherwise encouraged to furnish the goods and services that the state does not directly provide. Private bureaucracies are frequently substituted for public ones. And authority over the management of public programs is delegated to actors who are not only unelected but indirectly accountable to the mass public. When viewed this way, one can say that the American state is vast, as its influence extends well into the many nooks and crannies of our economic and social life. Yet, its influence is indirect, diluted, and masked by a façade of private actors who deliver needed goods and services. When people tell pollsters that they want government to keep its hands off their Medicare or Social Security benefits, they express the very contradiction that lies at the heart of the American state. It is both there and not there, a leviathan of tremendous power but also an enfeebled giant, one incapable at times of managing seemingly basic governmental tasks.

Perhaps most important is to recognize how deliberate these institutional choices have been. It is not as if there is some cultural incapacity among Americans for effective government, or some other inadvertent processes at work. Moreover, when the stakes are high, the federal government can and will directly intervene to achieve its goals. After the attacks on the World Trade Center on September 11, 2001, public disgust with the failings of passenger and baggage screeners led to a rapid overhaul of what had been a contracted-out system of transportation safety. In the Transportation Security Administration (TSA), federal employees screen bags and provide security in airports across the country.

The effectiveness of the TSA continues to provoke controversy and debate, as many Republicans and Democrats disagree about whether a federal workforce should be screening passengers or whether this can be effectively contracted out to private firms.[7] Nonetheless, the TSA represents a clear shift in authority from the private sector to the public one and the construction of centralized bureaucratic authority to address an issue of vital national importance.

More commonly, however, policy-makers tie the hands of administrative officials, limiting their capacity for future intervention by constructing hollowed-out bureaucracies with weak mandates for action. They have done so for political reasons: public ambivalence or hostility toward the federal government has been channeled and amplified through a political system that has repeatedly given weight to anti-statists—first, through the power of Southern Democrats in Congress, and in the more contemporary period through the intense polarization of American politics precisely around questions of state power. By and large, the Republican Party is a fierce advocate of markets over state provision and, if not always able to achieve that vision through outright privatization, has tried to limit the size of government by constricting its fiscal base. They have found allies in the "Blue Dog" or centrist Democrats who are leery of governmental growth and favor private solutions where possible. Faced with the seeming wall of opposition to an expanded federal bureaucracy, and sometimes their own ambivalence about government authority, even liberal policy-makers have repeatedly chosen to delegate governing power to private actors.

We use the language of "delegation" to highlight not only the deliberateness of this act but also the fact that it is governing authority—power—that is being vested in private actors. We are certainly not the first to raise this point, although the study of power in American politics has long been out of fashion. Some of the older, major contributions on this topic, such as classic works by Grant McConnell and Theodore Lowi, insightfully explored the phenomenon of "private power" and its implications for democratic theory and practice. These works principally targeted the then-dominant pluralist school, which tended to view favorably the competitive jockeying of interest groups in American politics as a means of resolving governing dilemmas. As McConnell and Lowi rightly pointed out, delegation of governing authority to these groups would often result and was a way for political elites to avoid having to make difficult decisions themselves. In so doing, politicians could pretend that "the unsentimental business of coercion need not be involved and that the unsentimental decisions about how to employ coercion need not be made at all."[8] In short, through delegations of governing power to private actors, one could pretend that the state, with its monopoly over the use of legitimate force, was not really there.

Many students of the American state have neglected these insights, and instead worked to prove the United States really *does* have a state, and a state that does a good deal. These observations are valid, but just as important are the self-imposed limitations put upon this "uneasy state"[9] and the tremendous reliance upon private authority to achieve public aims. This has a number of implications for American politics. One is that by masking the role of the federal government in providing for Americans' social welfare needs, Americans live with the illusion that they are far more independent of government than they are in reality. Suzanne Mettler has shown this recently with a public opinion survey revealing that individuals who receive various tax credits, for instance, do not see themselves as benefiting from government programs.[10] Schlesinger and Hutchings also found that people in Medicare HMOs tended to view their benefits as coming from the private sector rather than from government.[11] In our panel survey, we do not find any immediate change in perceptions about the role of government from those in privately run drug plans, but our survey captures only a small time period. When public responsibility is so pervasively obscured, for a person's entire life, it is only natural that she or he comes to believe that government is a problem, imposing heavy tax burdens without providing much in return.

Another implication is for democratic theory. Today, it is rather startling to realize that there was a time in American politics when the idea of delegating policy-making power from Congress to executive agencies was a source of grave concern. Now, we readily delegate governing authority and the use of public funds to people who are not even civil servants, charged with the mission of carrying out legislative intent. All of the alarm bells raised about these practices by Lowi and McConnell many decades ago have not been heeded. Further alarms raised around the contracting out of areas of government that lie at the heart of the state—the use of private security forces, for instance, or the private management of prisons—have been largely ignored by policy-makers. In all of these instances, the chain of democratic accountability is potentially weakened. Market theorists hope that profit-making incentives will provide an alternative, and superior, form of accountability, but we find little evidence of that to be the case. Medicare contractors have often been ineffective or engaged in outright fraudulent practices, and consumers who are supposed to be using their market power to exit from bad providers are not using it. They are either showing loyalty or, what appears more likely, indifference to the variable quality of the product being delivered to them. Market accountability appears to be no better than democratic accountability in assuring the quality of public services.

Perhaps most problematic of all is that the ill-well felt toward government impedes the development of the effective public agencies needed to manage privately run programs. Thoughtful market advocates are well aware that it is not enough to contract out service delivery; effective, continual supervision is needed of those private actors to make sure that they perform. However we wish to design our government, with whatever mix of public and private authority, there is no avoiding the need for at least some number of competent, respected, and empowered civil servants. Hostility to government has blinded many to this fact. The result is government ineffectiveness that cannot be rectified simply by the further delegation of governance to the private sector.

The Politics of Entitlements: Off-Center
or Catering to the Mushy Middle?

The political dynamics we have uncovered in this project also have much to say about the future of entitlement politics in this country. We have focused on a central ambiguity in American public opinion—the simultaneous support for public benefits and services coupled with a deep and enduring hostility toward government—that underlies all debates about the American welfare state. We do not argue that one can draw a simple line from public opinion to public policy; to the contrary, our book has examined the interplay of opinion, political institutions, and the power of organized interests. These three factors intermingle and reinforce each other in a way that repeatedly produces the same outcome—a welfare state that responds to a host of social needs yet one in which governmental authority is dispersed and masked through the heavy reliance on private authorities. Given the centrality of this model since at least 1945, the politics of delegated governance are, to a large degree, the politics of the American welfare state and can help us think about current and future debates about social entitlements.

One conclusion is that, although the conflict over federal entitlement policy is often portrayed as being about markets (conservatives) versus the state (liberals), the reality is more often a mushy middle ground in which both sides accept the basic parameters of American politics: that the public wants the government to cushion them from a host of social risks, but that this should be achieved by minimizing the direct role of government. Thus American social welfare policy is not "off center" as Jacob Hacker and Paul Pierson argue, but rather a middle-ground amalgam of compromise features that in fact reflect and conform to the ambiguities of public opinion.[12]

It may well be the case that conservatives sometimes prevail in formulating and implementing policies "that starkly and repeatedly depart from the center of public opinion" in esoteric areas such as financial deregulation or tax reductions for corporations and wealthy individuals.[13] However, that is not what we find in the politics of delegated social policy governance, in two regards. First, the correspondence between public preferences and public policy is much greater on high salience issues such as social welfare policy.[14] Clearly, the public can be bamboozled in complex and seemingly irrelevant issue areas, but on issues that the public cares about, is reasonably knowledgeable about, and monitors, such as many areas of social policy, outcomes reflect public opinion much more closely. Of course giving the public what it wants—social protections but also small government—results in the inefficient modes of delegated governance, but it does conform to the professed desires of the majority, contradictory though they may be.

Second, under delegated governance, politics is not "off center" in that neither conservatives nor liberals completely get their way. Republicans, much as they have tried to privatize Social Security or impose major cuts in entitlement programs, have largely failed in their efforts. The George W. Bush administration's plan to create a system of private accounts within Social Security was dead virtually upon its arrival at Congress's door because it was widely unpopular. Republicans succeeded in implanting some market principles into Medicare through the MMA, but only after they were forced by political realities to recognize that they could not require senior citizens to join HMOs to get health benefits or offer them only means-tested assistance for their prescription drug costs. Instead, Republicans had to swallow many of their long-held beliefs and create a universal benefit. Likewise, there has been significant public opposition to the Republicans' 2012 budget, which would cap the federal government's contribution toward senior health insurance and shift risk onto seniors. There are limits to the degree to which public programs can be cut; at best, marketized elements can be introduced into them, but only with significant subsidies and cushioning of risk by the federal government.

Similarly, Democrats may dream of "Medicare for All" or other systems of government-provided health insurance, but in reality they have reined in their ambitions when it comes to reforming the health care system. The Clinton administration's proposed health care reform in the early 1990s was castigated for threatening a massive expansion of the federal government's role in health care, yet the plan largely relied upon private entities and state governments for its administration. In particular, private insurers (HMOs) were to be the central actors in the new system, and new nonprofit regional health alliances were to be group purchasers of insurance. Conscious of the many objections to the Clinton proposal to have virtually all Americans purchase their insurance through these health alliances, the Obama health care reform was even more moderate, successfully passing Congress in part because it took pages from both the Left and Right playbooks.

The 2010 Health Care Reform:
More Delegated Governance

The recent health care reform is very much in line with the analysis of delegated governance in this book, in both the form of the legislation adopted and the politics leading up to its passage. The Affordable Care Act of 2010 (ACA) is, in many ways, the very portrait of delegated governance, bringing together the three forms of delegation described in earlier chapters. Much as in the MMA, the law provides subsidies to individuals who buy coverage on regulated insurance marketplaces, called American Health Benefit Exchanges. Unlike the MMA, which was voluntary but subsidized all plans, the ACA mandates the purchase of coverage but only subsidizes individuals below a certain income level. Still, both laws create new marketplaces in which individuals will choose from a range of insurance plans. Private insurers offer the plans, including two that will contract with the Office of Personnel and Management (OPM) to put forth multi-state plans. Because the Democrats crafting the legislation were skeptical about the effect of the profit motive on insurer behavior, they sought to revitalize an earlier form of delegation to nonprofit entities. The ACA thus allows grants to flow to nonprofit member-run insurance companies, which can also offer plans, and requires that at least one of the two OPM-contracted plans be nonprofit as well.

The health care reform also engages in a form of delegation that we discussed less in this book but that has always been important in the American welfare state—the shifting of authority over federally funded programs to state governments. Although the law includes significant new federal regulations on insurance policies—particularly on policies offered through health insurance exchanges—state governments will be responsible for their enforcement, reflecting the delegation of insurance regulatory authority to the states since the McCarran-Ferguson Act of 1945.[15] States also bear primary responsibility for setting up temporary high-risk pools and health plan exchanges for individuals and small businesses, although they can choose to opt out and leave this to the federal government. Finally, the ACA directs significant new resources to state Medicaid programs, which will cover more people living above the federal poverty line. This provision expands a multiply delegated system, as many states already contract out their Medicaid programs to managed care firms. These private firms will thus gain new subsidies to cover millions of new claimants.

Contrary then to statements that the ACA is a "massive government takeover of health care,"[16] direct federal government involvement in managing the nation's health care system remains truncated. Certainly, the cost of the legislation over ten years—an eye-popping $1 trillion—signifies an important increase in federal *resources* flowing into the health care system, but this is not accompanied by significant growth in *direct* federal authority over that system. The new federal role is largely limited to writing a copious number of regulations, overseeing the actions of state governments, serving as a fallback if states fail or refuse to perform their assigned tasks, and of course paying much of the bill—a long way from national health insurance, Medicare for all, or even a national public option for the uninsured. As critics have noted, the ACA is limited in tackling the fundamental problems of high cost and variable quality health care that the current system delivers.[17] Attempts to start to address these problems at a federal level—such as the Independent Payment Advisory Board or the push for greater use of comparative effectiveness research in guiding policy decisions—are significant but were considerably watered down in the final legislation.

Politically, many of the same dynamics were at work in the health care reform that had shaped earlier decisions to delegate the governance of public programs. In part, this was because the Obama administration and its Congressional allies sought to learn from past reform initiatives that failed or succeeded.[18] Failed efforts (e.g., under the Clinton administration) stumbled in seeming to assert too much governmental authority over the delivery and cost of medical care. As we noted in chapter 4, claims that the Clinton reform represented a vast governmental take-over of the health care sector were exaggerated, as the system envisioned would have relied heavily upon private entities and state governments for its administration. Nonetheless, even this proposal represented too much government intrusion, particularly the idea of creating a National Health Board to oversee the entire system and a global health spending cap. Interest groups rallied against the reform, spearheading advertising campaigns that mobilized public fears of government-run health care and diminished choice over the doctors they see.

By contrast, reforms that have survived the political process, such as the 2003 Medicare Modernization Act, limited the government's direct role and sought instead to enlist private actors in the delivery of the new benefits. In the case of Part D, this not only brought insurance companies on board once they were assured of profit-making opportunities, but the diffusion of payer power among a large number of insurance companies helped bring the pharmaceutical industry into the pro-reform camp as well. Both recognized that an expanded federal role in health care was likely and decided that, rather than try to block such a development, they should instead seek to gain from whatever new law emerged.

From the start, the Obama administration and Congressional Democrats pursued the latter strategy, designing a bill that built upon the existing system of health care insurance and delivery, infused the system with new subsidies to expand coverage, and kept the role of the federal government relatively minimal. Such a reform design defanged many of the medical interest groups that otherwise might have launched anti-reform campaigns.[19] Insurance companies, who faced a declining pool of insurable "lives" in the employer-sponsored or individual markets, were tempted by profit-making opportunities in the publicly subsidized one, as long as they could be assured that mandates would force both good and bad risks into the insurance market. In fact, if anything, insurers wanted *more* government intervention in the health care sphere, not less, in their insistence upon a government mandate that all individuals be required to have health insurance.[20] Pharmaceutical firms, physicians, hospitals, and other health care providers stood to gain additional sources of revenue through the expanded coverage, a fact that had become ever more important to the medical industry as "Americans were increasingly being priced out of its goods and services."[21] Liberal groups, such as Families USA and organized labor, also liked the overall reform approach, given its promise of near-universal coverage and greater regulation of insurance industry practices. AARP, for instance, strongly backed the various reform bills that promised to reduce or close the doughnut hole in Medicare Part D.

Although there was much in the various reform bills that key medical interest groups opposed—including the public option, which we discuss more below—many seemed to calculate that "[i]f you don't have a seat at the table, you could end up being the meal."[22] With the exception of insurers, which came out strongly against various drafts of the legislation, the other major industry groups maintained a constructive stance toward the reform that aimed to modify or remove objectionable elements as the various bills wended their way through Congress. The American Medical Association (AMA) endorsed early House legislation, although its support hinged on blocking a scheduled large cut in Medicare reimbursement rates to physicians.[23] Still, the endorsement was stunning, coming from a group that had opposed national health reform for decades. The pharmaceutical industry cut a deal with the Obama administration and Senate Finance Committee Chairman Max Baucus limiting to around $80 billion the amount they would contribute to the reform and promising that there would be no measure allowing drug re-importation or government negotiations over Medicare drug prices. Hospitals agreed to contribute $115 billion to the efforts. Both then refrained from openly attacking elements of various reform bills that they did not like, and continued to voice their overall support for reform. By August 2009, a "strange bedfellows" coalition, which included PhRMA, the AMA, Families USA, Federation of American Hospitals (representing for-profit hospitals), and the Service Employees International Union, had agreed to spend as much as $150 million on an advertising campaign in favor of health care reform.[24] As a whole, the surprising coalition of industry lobbyists and liberal advocates was crucial to the passage of the reform.[25]

The delegated design of the bill also sought to overcome potential backlashes in public opinion. This was important, given low levels of public trust in government and skepticism about its ability to improve the health care system.[26] Between the start of 2009 and the passage of the law in 2010, trust in government, which was already low, declined even further, to the lowest levels recorded since trust was first measured in 1958.[27] Moreover, Democratic lawmakers were well aware of how public support for the Clinton health care plan melted away once the package gained the reputation of being a mammoth expansion of government that would take away people's choice of physician. Thus, even though polls frequently showed majorities in favor of reform, they also showed that people were pretty happy with the coverage they had and leery of excessive government interference in the system. In 1994, 84 percent of Americans rated their health insurance coverage as "good" or "excellent"; in August 2009, as the Obama reform was being debated, the figure was 90 percent.[28] In the same 2009 poll, more respondents were worried that under reform "government agencies would play too big a role in deciding what medical procedures people can or can't get" (48 percent) than were worried about what insurance companies do "currently" (38 percent).[29] The reform thus preserved much of the health care status quo, and lawmakers avoided using terms such as "universal health care," which had connotations of a public insurance system of inferior quality.[30] Instead, officials used the phrase "insurance reform" to describe the health care law and periodically sought to direct public animus toward the already unpopular insurance industry, which some Democrats referred to as the "real villains."

Mollifying public concerns about the growth of government and building ties with medical interest groups were essential for getting a reform bill through the policy-making minefield that is Congress. Obama was elected with a large popular majority and came into office with majorities in both chambers, but because the institutional barriers to reform are so high, even these majorities were not enough. In the Senate, the Democrats ultimately lacked a supermajority that could overcome a Republican filibuster, and the Democratic camps in both chambers included a considerable sub-group of centrist Democrats who were leery of federal government growth.[31] These Blue Dog Democrats in the House[32] and centrist or conservative Democrats in the Senate tend to represent Southern and/or rural districts and states in which President Obama lacks electoral pull. They are fiscal conservatives who tend to favor private market or nonprofit solutions over public ones. And they have influence because of the structure of Congressional decision-making. In the Senate, the Finance Committee is crucial to the passage of health care legislation yet contains a number of centrist Democrats who are skeptical of federal government expansion and friendly to key health care industries. The need to gain 60 votes to overcome a filibuster on the Senate floor also necessitated keeping centrists on board. In the House, Speaker Nancy Pelosi also had to draw in some of the Blue Dogs in order to pass the health care reform bill. Like the MMA, the ACA passed with slender majorities that the House and Senate leadership spent months cajoling and arm-twisting into place.[33]

These political forces not only influenced the original conception of the reform but ensured that, as various reform bills wended their way through the legislative process, they lost many of the elements that would have augmented the power of the federal government over the health care system. Nothing better exemplifies this than the fate of the "public option"—a proposal to have a government health care plan available on the health care exchange where uninsured individuals could buy coverage. The three House committee bills all included a public option, and two of those bills—those marked up in the Ways and Means and Labor and Education committees—included a "robust" variant of the public option, one that would pay providers according to Medicare rates.[34] In the Energy and Commerce committee, however, a revolt by Blue Dog Democrats on the committee led to some watering down of the provision. Rather than pay Medicare rates, the federal official overseeing the public option would have to negotiate with private insurers over the rates they would receive. According to the CBO, this negotiated system would save less money—only $25 billion over ten years, compared to $110 billion saved under a system using Medicare rates.[35] Yet, because Speaker Pelosi was unable to pull together the votes around the robust public option, she ultimately accepted the Energy and Commerce committee's version—much to the chagrin of Congressional liberals and their advocacy and interest group allies.[36] Still, the House bill did envision some growth in federal authority over the health care system, as it would have created a national insurance exchange and national public insurance option, both of which would be overseen by federal health administrators.[37]

The Senate adopted a more decentralized approach to reform and ultimately rejected the public option. The Senate Health, Education, Labor and Pensions

Committee passed a bill in mid-July 2009 that envisioned health insurance exchanges and a public option but had states playing the central role in administering the exchanges and public plan.[38] The Senate Finance Committee failed to arrive at agreement on a public option, however, and instead sought to find other nongovernmental alternatives such as nonprofit cooperatives that could offer an alternative to the existing insurance market. Majority Leader Harry Reid also attempted a compromise that would jettison the public option and allow people aged 55–64 to buy into Medicare, but this proposal angered physicians and provider groups who chafe at what they see as unduly low Medicare rates.[39] Senators from rural states, where Medicare reimbursement rates are lower than those in higher-cost urban areas, were also opposed. Reid thus ultimately turned to a watered-down alternative: having the OPM contract with private insurers to offer two plans that would be available on the health insurance exchanges, and providing federal grants for the creation of nonprofit, member-owned insurance companies. In general, the Senate bill left greater responsibility on the shoulders of state governments, and the final bill that passed in March 2010 largely embraced the Senate approach.

What explains the demise of the public option? The clearest cause was lack of support among moderate and conservative Democrats who held crucial institutional levers of power in both chambers. They repeatedly argued that the public option went too far in involving the government in insuring the nonpoor or nonretiree population—groups that had long been cordoned off into public programs because of the difficulty insuring them in private markets. Allowing a government-funded program to cover nonpoor, non-retired people signaled the beginning of the end of private coverage—particularly if the public plan paid Medicare rates lower than what private insurers could pay, inducing these private firms to leave the market. These Democrats instead argued for regulating and reforming the existing market so that it could continue to function as the backbone of the health insurance system. "We don't have to have the government run everything. We most certainly can have the private sector if we put the right framework and regulations and use the power of the market," said one public option–opponent, Senator Mary Landrieu (D-LA).[40] These Democrats had power to block the public option because of the need for a 60-vote supermajority in the Senate to end a filibuster. They also had more leverage than liberals, for whom passing a bill was of utmost importance. Moderate and conservative Democrats, by contrast, were more willing to let the reform die if they did not get what they wanted.[41]

Moreover, because critics attacked the public option as a covert governmental take-over of the health care system, the proposal fed into an anti-statist popular movement that emerged in the spring and summer of 2009. Reacting initially against the bailout of Wall Street and the auto industry, the Tea Party movement entered the political scene, challenging the perceived expansion of federal power under the Obama administration. Their impact on the health care debate came during the August recess, when anti-government activists showed up at the town hall meetings held by members of Congress to discuss the health care reform. Heckling, scuffling with opponents, and burning members of Congress in effigy assured that they would receive wide media coverage. So did their sharp rhetoric about the health care bill—which they labeled "tyranny" or "socialism"—and their embrace of the false rumor that the reform would allow "death panels" that could cut off care from critically ill senior citizens or disabled people.[42] Republicans were initially caught off guard by the movement but then quickly sought to play up some of their themes. As Republican Charles Grassley (R-Iowa) said on CBS's *Face the Nation*, "The federal government is in the process of nationalizing banks, nationalizing General Motors. I'm going to make sure we don't nationalize health insurance and a public option is the first stop to doing that."[43] Some Republicans also did not deny the "death panels" rumor, which gained steam after Sarah Palin claimed on her Facebook page that the plan would create such panels.[44]

It is difficult to evaluate the influence of this anti-statist movement on public opinion and decision-making around the reform. Although a startling 41 percent of respondents surveyed in a September 2009 CNN poll believed that the Democratic health care plans created death panels, these people were disproportionately Republican and already predisposed against the reform, whereas Democrats and Independents were more likely to reject the falsehood.[45] The public option also was not fatally wounded in public opinion: surveys in the fall of 2009 did not show a precipitous drop in support for the public option. If anything, there was some increase in support for the idea during the fall months.[46] Thus, one could interpret the negative rumors and feelings about the reform as the voices of people predisposed to hold negative opinions about the Obama administration. On the other hand, national aggregate opinion ultimately mattered less than the perceptions of lynchpin legislators—moderate Republicans and Democrats who in some cases worried about electoral challenges from Tea Party movements and other conservative groups. They repeatedly claimed that their constituents opposed the public option and for that reason refused to support it.

Finally, lobbyists for the major health care industries worked steadily to gut or eliminate the public option. Virtually all the major industry and provider groups, including the drug makers, insurers, physicians, and hospitals, were leery of or outright against the public option. Yet, while the insurance industry incessantly and publicly beat the drum of opposition, others worked more quietly against it. When House legislation passed that included a public option, many health care lobbyists did not like many of its provisions and made clear that they preferred the Senate bill, yet chose not to push the issue publicly or make it a basis for wholly rejecting health care reform. Some had been assured behind the scenes that a meaningful public option would not make it into the final legislation anyway. For instance, hospital lobbyists negotiating with Senate Finance Committee Chair Max Baucus over the terms of their support were told early on that a robust public option paying Medicare rates would not be in the final bill.[47] In the end, many of the health care interest groups banked on the belief that even if a public option made it into a final bill, it would be considerably defanged and not an immediate threat to them.

In short, the public option came to represent something larger for both sides—an expanded role for government in providing health insurance—and this is precisely what doomed it. It tapped age-old conflicts about the appropriate role of the state versus the marketplace in protecting people against life's risks. It helped mobilize popular fears, worried many medical interest groups, and stiffened the spines of conservatives and centrists in Congress who saw in the proposal a black hole of ever-growing government and future fiscal obligations. As Senator Lindsey Graham (R-SC) put it, "Every big issue gets boiled down to one phrase. The public option in many ways has become to health care what 'amnesty' was to immigration or 'privatization' was to Social Security."[48] Ultimately, the Democratic leadership and the Obama administration accepted that it would have to be sacrificed for the legislation to pass.

In addition to these resonances with the politics of delegated governance that we discuss in this book, the ACA raises some of the implementation issues that have arisen with delegated arrangements in the past. One problem is the lack of attention given to the need for effective arrangements for administering the reform. The new law envisions a complex system of governance in which state governments and an array of federal agencies, including the Internal Revenue Service and the Department of Health and Human Services, have new roles and interlocking responsibilities. Yet, relatively little money was budgeted for the ACA's implementation—too little in the view of the CMS administrator who oversaw the implementation of Medicare Part D, Mark McClellan.[49] Both the MMA and ACA allotted about $1 billion for implementation, but the ACA is a much more complicated reform.[50]

In addition, the law depends heavily upon state governments to do the work of overseeing private insurers, when in fact state capacity for insurance regulation is highly variable and often inversely correlated with the size of their uninsured population. In other words, it is precisely in those states where the new health insurance exchanges will be most needed that the government has been least effective in regulating and overseeing the insurance industry in the past. Similarly, some of the states with the most uninsured also have had the smallest and less well-functioning Medicaid programs.[51] A number of states also have made plain their resistance to the new law. As of July 2010, 21 states sued the federal government to prevent implementation, and the state of Georgia has already refused to set up a high-risk pool, leaving this to the federal government. Such actions do not bode well for the level of federal-state cooperation needed for reform success.[52]

Finally, experience with existing consumer-focused programs (Part D; HSAs) suggests that individuals are not always capable of being the effective consumers that the insurance exchange model assumes.[53] The ACA calls for states to set up insurance exchanges from which small businesses and individuals outside the employer-provided system can buy health care coverage. The law simplified consumer choice by stipulating four benefit categories of plan, ranging from the lowest premium bronze plan, which covers 60 percent of benefit costs, to the most expensive platinum plan, which covers 90 percent of benefit costs.[54] Such standardization has simplified choice in other health insurance areas such as the Medicare Supplemental Insurance market, allowing consumers to comparison shop. However, how much choice consumers will have under the ACA, and along which parameters, depends on how their states set up their exchanges.[55] States will determine how many insurers will be allowed to offer plans. They will also specify whether co-insurance, co-payments, and deductibles will be uniform within each tier, or whether each insurer will set its own actuarially equivalent cost-sharing parameters.[56] Thus consumers could face choice among just a few plans and constellations of parameters, or a great many, a set of trade-offs with which each state must grapple. As the former director of the Massachusetts Insurance Connector has pointed out, "too little choice may conflict with consumers' preferences and stifle innovation in the design of insurance policies and benefits," but "too much choice may confuse consumers and lead to adverse selection," undermining the insurance marketplace.[57]

Improving the Delegated Welfare State

Delegated governance is a long-standing phenomenon, and because its root causes are enduring features of American politics—the contradictory nature of public opinion, the policy-making centrality of a cautious and deal-cutting Congress, and the permeability of the system to interest groups—there is little reason to believe that it will cease to be an important feature of social policy design. Certainly, there are examples of the government taking over roles previously delegated to private actors, such as a 2010 measure that replaced publicly subsidized and privately administered student loans with a system of direct lending, or the assumption of direct federal responsibility for air transportation safety following September 11, 2001. Such acts are more the exception than the norm, however, and often are the result of extraordinary circumstances.[58]

One question then is how to improve delegated governance. We see two main avenues for action. First is the need for greater oversight of private, welfare-providing actors by public authorities, including both Congress and executive branch departments and agencies. Episodic Congressional oversight is likely insufficient by itself, given the pervasiveness and depth of delegated arrangements. Rather, departments and agencies, with their expertise and constant immersion in the issues, are needed for this significant job. However, because Congress has frequently shown itself unwilling to build up bureaucratic capacities, it is essential that members of Congress stop bashing government and recognize the need for a certain amount of effective public administration. As the history of delegated governance demonstrates repeatedly, a hollowed-out state is insufficient to monitor and correct the potential shortcomings, inefficiencies, and even abuses of the non-state entities that administer delegated programs. Contrary to the desires of market thinkers, the state cannot disappear with delegation but instead should take on a different and often vitally important role. The federal government may no longer be directly administering programs, but it still requires the budgets and personnel necessary for muscular oversight.

A second way to improve delegated governance is to help individuals navigate the consumer choice programs that have become increasingly prominent. Clearly, individuals have woeful shortcomings as decision-makers and require considerable information and assistance to help them successfully utilize social welfare marketplaces. The standardization of health care plans in the ACA is a step in the right direction. Within the MMA, Part D drug plans remain un-standardized, and the number of plans offered is enormous. Surveys show that seniors would prefer fewer choices in the program, and so allowing an actor such as CMS to winnow down the number of plans available might help seniors make sound choices.[59] There are limits to standardization, however, as it may undermine contractors' business models—insurers need to be able to offer different formularies if they are going to differentiate themselves from each other. Other consumer aides may be needed as well, such as public advocates. Indeed, the ACA calls on states to create ombudsmen to assist consumers shopping for health insurance plans and to run interference for them with insurers. Unfortunately, as with many state-level features of the law, the ombudsman program is encouraged but not required.

Born of perennial features of American politics, delegated governance has proven a way to provide social protections in a political environment hostile to direct government. It is doubtful that alternative governing arrangements would make the public any happier, as moving toward either more direct governance or diminished social protection would violate one or the other sides of public opinion. Like all compromises, delegated governance fully satisfies no one, but more rigorous oversight and help for consumers can improve this enduring feature of the American welfare state.

Appendix A

DATA SOURCES

Interviews

To reconstruct the legislative process surrounding the creation and passage of the 2003 Medicare Modernization Act, we relied on an array of primary and secondary sources. Supplementing these efforts and aiding in their interpretation were 35 interviews that we conducted with individuals who were either involved in the development of the bill or who were close observers of the process: Congressional staff and several members of Congress; executive branch staff; lobbyists and officers from the pharmaceutical, insurance, and other involved industries; representatives of consumer and senior citizen interest groups; think tank analysts; and other learned observers. Most of these interviews took place during 2006 and 2007. Most of these informants spoke on background; endnotes identify interviewees who were willing to be quoted on the record.

MMA Panel Survey

To measure Medicare beneficiaries' attitudes toward and experiences with the Medicare Modernization Act of 2003, we designed a three-wave panel survey of senior citizens, which was conducted by Knowledge Networks (KN) in December 2005, April–May 2007, and February–March 2009. Knowledge Networks provides an Internet-based nationally representative probability sample by drawing an original sample through Random Digit Dialing (RDD) and then providing WebTV units and free Internet connections to the sample. The sample used for the MMA Panel Survey consisted of KN panel participants aged 65 and over as of December 2005.

We conducted the baseline survey December 15–27, 2005, just prior to the January 1, 2006, beginning of the Part D drug program. The baseline survey included 1,664 respondents. Between April 13 and May 18, 2007, we re-inter-viewed 1,255 of those respondents and asked many of the same attitudinal ques-tions. We also asked those enrolled in Part D drug plans about their experiences in 2006, the first year of the program, as well as their plans for 2007, the second year of the program (whether they had switched plans, what their monthly pre-miums were for 2006 and 2007, and so on). We conducted a third wave from Jan-uary 30 to March 19, 2009, during the fourth year of MMA implementation, during which we asked about experiences during the program's third year, 2008, and their plan elections in 2009. Unfortunately, by this third wave, Knowledge Networks dropped a number of respondents from their national panel—not part of the original plan—and so we were only able to re-interview 675 of the original respondents (570 of whom were still in the KN panel, as well as 105 who had withdrawn but who completed the survey through a personal or public Internet connection after we contacted them).

The baseline December 2005 KN senior sample compares very favorably with June 2005 Census figures on basic demographic characteristics (Table A.1). In addition, the December 2005 sample compares well with a telephone sample of senior citizens surveyed by the Kaiser Family Foundation in October 2005 in terms of demographics, health status, prescription drug usage, and impression of the new drug benefit (Table A.2). We also found the same rate of Part D plan switching as an analysis based on a much larger (16,000 respondent) mail- and telephone-survey, which was itself benchmarked using CMS administrative data.[2] As the third wave differs somewhat demographically, containing a higher propor-tion of younger and higher income respondents than the first two waves, in the text we report data primarily from the first two waves with some findings from the third wave.

Despite the good quality of the baseline sample along these demographic and attitudinal dimensions, there may be concerns that those seniors willing to accept KN's WebTVs and to participate in Internet surveys may be more sophisticated or differ in other ways from other senior citizens. What matters for our purposes is change within persons, and so sample representativeness is less important. More-over, to the degree to which the seniors in our sample are more sophisticated than the population of older Americans in general, this would exert a downward bias on our coefficients. In other words, we would underestimate rather than overestimate changes in attitudes and behaviors due to Part D or Medicare Advantage enrollment.

Wisconsin Advertising Project Data

We analyzed campaign advertising data provided by the Wisconsin Advertising Project, which beginning with the 1998 midterm election has collected infor-mation on television ads run during each biennial election season in the 75 largest media markets, where over 80 percent of the U.S. population lives (beginning in 2002, the data come from the 100 largest media markets; see the Project's web site at http://wiscadproject.wisc.edu/project.php). The Project purchases these data from the Campaign Media Analysis Group, which monitors the four broadcast networks (ABC, NBC, CBS, and Fox) as well as 25 national cable networks, and then employs a team of research assistants to code the ads for content. The existing data set lacked consistent coding of the prescription drug issue, but with the help of a research assistant, we sharpened the coding and thus were able to analyze the use of the Medicare prescription drug benefit as a campaign issue.

Table A.1. **Knowledge Networks 65+ Year-Old Panel vs. Current Population Survey**

		Knowledge Networks 65+ Year Old Panel (Dec 05)	*Adult 65+ Population (June 05 CPS)*
Gender	Male	45.4%	42.6%
	Female	54.6	57.4
Race	White only	89.3	87.2
	Black only	6.9	8.4
	Other	3.8	4.4
Hispanic		4.2	6.4
Employment	In labor force	13.7	13.8
	full-time	7.3	7.8
	part-time	6.4	5.9
	Not in labor force	87.3	86.2
Marital	Married	63.1	56.2
	Not married	36.9	43.8
Education	< HS	21.7	25.2
	HS grad	37.2	36.6
	Some college	16.2	13.6
	Assoc degree	3.6	5.3
	Bachelor's +	21.3	19.2
Income	< $10,000	5.5	10.1
	$10–24.9K	26.4	32.2
	$25–49.9K	38.9	31.9
	$50K+	29.3	25.9
Census region	Northeast	18.0	21.2
	Midwest	23.4	23.1
	South	37.0	35.3
	West	21.6	20.4

Sources: Knowledge Networks.

Table A.2. **MMA Panel Survey (Internet) vs. Kaiser Family Foundation Survey (Telephone)**

Item	Response Category	KFF Survey Phone	MMA Baseline Survey Internet
Age	65–69	29%	29%
	70–74	21	24
	75–79	19	21
	80–84	18	17
	85+	9	9
Gender	Male	43	43
	Female	57	57
Marital status [a]	Married	45	57
	Not married	55	43
Race/Ethnicity	White, Non-Hispanic	80	82
	Black, Non-Hispanic	8	8
	Hispanic	6	5
Education	HS or less	62	61
	Some college	19	19
	College +	19	20
Income	< $20K	33	24
	$20–50K	27	49
	$50K+	15	27
AARP	Member	54	60
Health	Excellent	10	6
Status	Very good	24	25
	Good	28	39
	Fair	26	24
	Poor	11	6
Health	Heart disease	30	23
Conditions	Hypertension	47	54
	Diabetes	23	17
	Asthma	15	14
	Physical disability	21	14
	Cancer	18	17
	Other chronic	22	21
Take drugs	Yes	81	85
How many	1	11	10
	2	18	17
	3	15	16
	4	15	16

Continued

Item	Response Category	KFF Survey Phone	MMA Baseline Survey Internet
	5	9	14
	6	9	9
	7+	21	17
Ever not filled prescription b/c of cost?	Yes	14	15
Current plans that help pay for prescriptions	Former employer/union	45	47
	Medicaid/Medi-Cal	11	4
	State Rx assistance program	7	7
	Medigap plan	31	16
	Veterans' Administration	15	15
	Medicare HMO or PPO	18	17
	Rx drug discount card	23	12
Impression of new Medicare prescription drug benefit [a]	Favorable	45	40
	Unfavorable	55	60
Party identification[a]	Republican	31	31
	Independent	27	30
	Democrat	42	40

Note: [a] Of those giving an answer in the KFF poll, which allowed for don't know responses and refusals.

Sources: Kaiser Family Foundation/Harvard School of Public Health, "The Medicare Drug Benefit: Beneficiary Perspectives Just Before Implementation," telephone survey of Americans aged 65 and over, October 13–31, 2005; MMA Panel survey, Internet survey of Americans aged 65 and over, first wave, December 15–27, 2005.

Appendix B

SUPPLEMENTARY TABLES

Table B.1 **Effects of Part D or Medicare Advantage Enrollment on Group Consciousness and Attitudes toward State and Market Roles, December 2005, May 2007, February 2009, among Respondents Who Remained in Third Wave**

		Part D		*Medicare Advantage*		
		Not in Part D	*In Part D*	*Never in private plan*	*MA now; private plan before*	*MA now; not private plan before*
Group Consciousness						
To encourage good Medicare reforms, it is important for elders to stick together in the messages they send Washington: % disagree	Baseline	4%	5%	4%	6%	5%
	First Follow-up	3	3	3	2	4
	Second Follow-up	3	6	5	5	3
My views about Medicare are based mostly on how reforms would affect me, not how they would affect other people covered by Medicare: % agree	Baseline	55	49	59	47	41
	First Follow-up	49	50	48	52	50
	Second Follow-up	50	49	49	54	46

Continued

		Part D		Medicare Advantage		
		Not in Part D	In Part D	Never in private plan	MA now; private plan before	MA now; not private plan before
State vs. Market Attitudes						
The federal government has a basic responsibility to guarantee that elderly persons have adequate health insurance: % disagree	Baseline	15	15	19	14	9
	First Follow-up	19	14	19	13	22
	Second Follow-up	20	13	21	11	15
Individuals should be responsible for setting aside enough money to pay for their health care in retirement: % agree	Baseline	31	27	32	27	30
	First Follow-up	30	28	33	20	28
	Second Follow-up	34	32	35	31	27
For health insurance rely on fed government or private insurance: mean score on 1–7 scale, private health insurance is high	Baseline	3.8	3.6	3.6	4.0	3.8
	First Follow-up	3.9	3.7	3.8	3.7	4.0
	Second Follow-up	3.9	3.8	3.9	3.7	3.8
Fed spending on Medicare: % increase	Baseline	59	61	56	68	56
	First Follow-up	59	64	60	62	55
	Second Follow-up	52	52	49	59	54
Social Security privatization: % support	Baseline	29	35	29	27	34
	First Follow-up	36	35	38	29	37
	Second Follow-up	21	32	26	25	20
Ideology: % conservative	Baseline	40	41	39	36	47
	First Follow-up	38	32	37	36	35
	Second Follow-up	37	36	36	34	41

Table B.1. (Continued)

		Part D		Medicare Advantage		
		Not in Part D	*In Part D*	*Never in private plan*	*MA now; private plan before*	*MA now; not private plan before*
Trust in government: % only some of the time	Baseline	74	77	77	78	68
	First Follow-up	83	81	83	86	82
	Second Follow-up	74	76	79	68	69

Note: Table contains responses for the 675 respondents who survived into the third wave (February 2009). Compare to Table 7.1, which shows results for the 1,255 respondents in the second wave (May 2007).

Source: MMA Panel Study, baseline (December 2005), first follow-up (May 2007), and second follow-up (February 2009) waves.

Table B.2 **Effects of Part D or Medicare Advantage Enrollment on Group Consciousness and Attitudes toward State and Market Roles: Multivariate Analysis**

	Elders should stick together	How reforms affect me	Fed govt Guarantee Elder ins	Indivs set aside $ for health care in retirement	Gov/Priv Ins Scale	Fed Spend Medicare	SS Priv	Ideology	Trust
a. Effect of Part D Enrollment									
Baseline attitude	3.516*	1.296*	2.355*	1.898*	.532*	1.942*	2.963*	3.022*	2.099*
Education	-.398*	-.014	-.017	.074	-.002	-.185*	.112	-.040	-.010
Age	-.023	.018	.015	.026*	.037	-.010	-.041*	.010	-.058*
Female	.660	-.130	.027	-.018	-.036	.320*	-.363*	-.084	-.167
Income	.001	.000	-.005	.001	-.023	.000	-.002	-.001	.004
Dual eligible	-.035	.223	.763*	-.225	-.034	.974*	.659*	-.226	.230
# Health problems	-.322	.037	.004	-.182*	-.051	-.008	-.091	.078	-.047
# Meds taken	.105	.000	.044	.088*	-.035	.032	.025	-.071	.016
Republican	.077	-.108	-.864*	.349*	.063*	-.784*	.548**	1.542*	-.254
Independent	-.282	-.221	-.018	.157	.049	-.398*	.339	.483	.280

In Part D	.612	-.029	.033	.116	-.002	.126	-.133	-.052*	.275
Constant	2.697	-2.006*	-.758	-3.858*		.393	.981	-3.004*	4.146*
N	1196	1191	1190	1180	1193	1200	1203	1173	1195
Cox & Snell R^2	.07	.10	.18	.17	.31	.26	.34	.43	.18
% correctly predicted	96.3	65.5	84.8	75.5		75.5	84.1	84.1	79.8
b. Effect of MA Enrollment (vs. those not in MA)									
Baseline attitude	3.485*	1.231*	2.347*	1.854*	.532*	1.935*	3.038*	2.953*	2.132*
Education	-.381*	.023	-.027	.125	.006	-.250*	.079	-.090	.015
Age	-.024	.021*	.015	.027*	.047	-.013	-.040*	.003	-.060*
Female	.715*	-.093	.011	.016	-.034	.320*	-.323	-.142	-.131
Income	.001	.000	-.005	.000	-.022	.000	-.002	-.001	.004
Dual eligible	-.052	.217	.775*	-.173	-.051*	1.025*	.517*	.120	.251
# Health problems	-.314	.050	.013	-.175*	-.044	-.01	-.098	.025	-.054
# Meds taken	.102	.008	.045	.087*	-.031	.014	.020	-.081*	.025

Continued

247

	Elders should stick together	How reforms affect me	Fed govt Guarantee Elder ins	Indivs set aside $ for health care in retirement	Gov/Priv Ins Scale	Fed Spend Medicare	SS Priv	Ideology	Trust
b. Effect of MA Enrollment (vs. those not in MA)									
Republican	.019	-.084	-.854*	.371*	.067*	-.792*	.546*	1.461*	-.279
Independent	-.338	-.200	-.042	.100	.052	-.310	.428*	.417	.195
In MA	.659	.108	-.057	.002	-.054*	.149	-.047	-.203	.166
Constant	2.737	-2.410*	-.673	-4.316*		.829	.932	-2.953*	4.195*
N	1199	1194	1194	1184	1194	1206	1209	1178	1200
Cox & Snell R²	.07	.10	.18	.17	.31	.26	.34	.42	.19
% correctly predicted	96.1	64.7	84.9	75.4		76.2	84.5	83.8	80.5
c. Effect of MA Enrollment (vs. those Never in a Private Plan)									
Baseline attitude	3.791*	1.243*	2.440*	2.084*	.557*	1.857*	3.266*	2.933*	2.053*
Education	-.655*	.129	-.045	-.018	-.005	-.223*	-.064	-.089	.071
Age	-.056	.014	.005	.019	.046	-.007	-.056*	-.002	-.084*
Female	.406	-.162	.195	-.238	-.022	.333*	-.675*	-.137	-.014

Income	.001	.001	-.002	.001	-.048	.002	-.003	-.001	.004
Dual eligible	.713	.713*	.783	-.065	-.044	1.227*	.422	-.105	.784*
# Health problems	.050	.021	.017	-.140	-.064	-.148	-.048	.072	-.090
# Meds taken	.074	.020	.056	.069	-.033	.088*	.014	-.064	.047
Republican	.059	-.100	-.631*	.280	.053	-.722*	.796*	1.515*	-.342
Independent	.779	-.257	.211	.039	.016	-.533*	.751*	.518*	.165
In MA	.559	.161	-.311	.153	-.019	.185	.150	-.470*	.433*
Constant	5.492	-2.176*	-.457	-3.595*		.173	2.391	-1.870	5.827*
N	867	863	864	859	856	873	874	855	870
Cox & Snell R^2	.09	.11	.19	.19	.34	.24	.38	.42	.21
% correctly predicted	97.5	65.8	83.9	76.4		74.6	85.6	84.0	81.4

Note: Cells contain logit coefficients, except for Gov/Priv insurance scale, where cells contain standardized OLS coefficients. Dependent variable coding: Gov/Priv Ins Scale (private insurance = high); Federal spending on Medicare (increase = high); Social Security privatization (support = high); Ideology (conservative = high); Trust in government (only some of the time = high). *p <.05; *p <.10.

Source: Medicare Modernization Act Panel Survey.

Table B.3 Issue Ownership among Wave 3 Respondents

	Democratic Party	Republican Party
1. Which party controlled Congress when prescription drug legislation passed?		
Wave 2 (24% not sure)	5%	71%
Wave 3 (40% not sure)	14	46
2. Which party deserves the most credit for the drug benefit?		
Wave 2 Overall	42	58
Wave 3 Overall	49	51
Wave 2 Republicans	11	89
Independents	43	57
Democrats	66	34
Wave 3 Republicans	25	75
Independents	43	57
Democrats	73	27
3. Which party more likely to make the right decisions about Medicare?		
Baseline Overall	60	40
Wave 2 Overall	64	36
Wave 3 Overall	64	36
Baseline Republicans	11	89
Independents	63	37
Democrats	94	6
Wave 2 Republicans	16	84
Independents	68	32
Democrats	95	5
Wave 3 Republicans	18	82
Independents	71	29
Democrats	94	6
4. Which party more likely to make the right decisions about govt?		

Table B.3. (Continued)

	Democratic Party	Republican Party
Baseline Overall	57	43
Wave 2 Overall	58	42
Wave 3 Overall	59	41
Baseline Republicans	6	94
Independents	57	43
Democrats	96	4
Wave 2 Republicans	9	91
Independents	58	42
Democrats	93	7
Wave 3 Republicans	16	84
Independents	59	41
Democrats	91	9
5. Which party better manage prescription drug issue in the future?		
Wave 2 Overall	63	37
Wave 3 Overall	64	36
Wave 2 Republicans	11	89
Independents	63	37
Democrats	94	6
Wave 3 Republicans	17	83
Independents	68	32
Democrats	95	5

Note: Table contains responses among the 675 respondents who survived into the third wave of the panel survey in February 2009. Independent category includes independent leaners. Questions 1, 2, and 5 not included in baseline survey.

Source: MMA Panel Study, baseline (December 2005), wave 2 (May 2007), and wave 3 (February 2009).

Type of Drug Coverage	Baseline Dec 2005	Wave 2 May 2007	Wave 3 Feb 2009	% change Wave 1–3
Part D	.67	.65	.53	-21%
Through MA	.63	.46	.43	-32%
Other creditable coverage	.60	.55	.44	-27%
No drug coverage	.27	.35	.27	0%

Note: Figures in cells are mean number of Medicare-related participatory acts (out of 3). Table contains participation rates among the 675 respondents who survived into the third wave of the panel survey in February 2009.

Source: Medicare Modernization Act Panel Survey.

Table B.5 **Predicting Drug Plan Switching, Problems, Affordability, and Financial Security, May 2007**

	Switched plans between Years 1 and 2 (1=Yes, 0=No)	# Problems (0–6 point scale)	Now less able to afford drugs (3-point scale; less able = high)	Now less secure financially (3-point scale; less secure=high)
Hit doughnut	.506	1.555*	.007	.052
# Problems	.218#	—	.102*	.126*
Premium	.019*	.003	.003*	.004*
# Health problems	-.320*	.419*	-.046	-.057*
Education	-.275	-.150*	.000	-.029
Age	-.075*	-.041*	.013*	.002
Female	-1.132*	-.285*	.012	-.090
Income	.003	-.001	.000	-.001
Dual eligible	-1.199*	.130	.094	.079
Constant	3.635	3.998*	.556	-1.632*
N	437	464	458	461
R^2	.10	.32	.09	.18
% Predicted	90.5			

Note: Cells contain unstandardized OLS coefficients, except for switching, which are logistic regression coefficients. *$p < .05$; #$p < .10$.

Source: MMA Panel Survey, Wave 2 (May 2007).

NOTES

Chapter 1

1. Ricardo Alonso-Zaldivar, "RNC Chairman: Obama's health care is socialism," *Associated Press*, July 20, 2010, http://www.breitbart.com/article.php?id=D99I9EAO1, accessed October 18, 2010; Newt Gingrich "Kill the Bill," *Human Events,* March 10, 2010, http://www.humanevents.com/article.php?id=35962, accessed October 18, 2010; Michael D. Shear and Dan Balz, "Obama offers new health-care plan: GOP slams it as 'government takeover,'" *Washington Post,* February 22, 2010.

2. Since 2010, the federal government has taken control over student lending back from banks and now directly provides loans to college students and their parents.

3. Elisabeth S. Clemens, "Lineages of the Rube Goldberg State: Building and Blurring Public Programs, 1900–1940," in *Rethinking Political Institutions: The Art of the State*, eds. Ian Shapiro, Stephen Skowronek, and Daniel Galvin (New York: New York University Press, 2006), 187–215.

4. See, for instance, Lester M. Salamon, "Rethinking Public Management: Third-Party Government and the Changing Forms of Government Action," *Public Policy* 29, 3 (Summer 1981): 255–275; Donald F. Kettl, *Government by Proxy: (Mis?)Managing Federal Programs* (Washington DC: CQ Press, 1988); John J. DiIulio, Jr., "Government by Proxy: A Faithful Overview," *Harvard Law Review* 116 (2003): 1271–1284; Paul Starr, "The Meaning of Privatization," in *Privatization and the Welfare State*, eds. Sheila B. Kamerman and Alfred J. Kahn (Princeton: Princeton University Press, 1989), 15–48; Milward H. Brinton, "Symposium on the Hollow State," *Journal of Public Administration Research & Theory* 6, 2 (April 1996): 193–195.

5. Steven Rathgeb Smith and Michael Lipsky, *Nonprofits for Hire: The Welfare State in the Age of Contracting* (Cambridge, MA: Harvard University Press, 1993).

6. Lester M. Salamon, "Rethinking Public Management: Third-Party Government and the Changing Forms of Government Action," *Public Policy* 29, 3 (Summer 1981): 255–275; Donald F. Kettl, *Government by Proxy: (Mis?)Managing Federal Programs* (Washington DC: CQ Press, 1988); Kettl, *Sharing Power: Public Governance and Private Markets* (Washington, DC: Brookings 1993); Paul C. Light, *The True Size of Government* (Washington, DC: Brookings, 1999).

7. Theda Skocpol and Kenneth Finegold, "State Capacity and Economic Intervention in the Early New Deal," *Political Science Quarterly* 97, 2 (Summer 1982): 255–278.

8. William J. Novak, "The Myth of the 'Weak' American State," *American Historical Review* 113 (2008): 752–772.

9. Jacob S. Hacker, *The Divided Welfare State: The Battle over Public and Private Social Benefits in the United States* (Cambridge: Cambridge University Press, 2002); Jennifer Klein, *For All These Rights: Business, Labor, and the Shaping of America's Public-Private Welfare State* (Princeton: Princeton University Press 2003).

10. Christopher Howard, *The Hidden Welfare State: Tax Expenditures and Social Policy in the United States* (Princeton: Princeton University Press, 1997).

11. Christopher Howard, *The Welfare State Nobody Knows: Debunking Myths About US Social Policy* (Princeton: Princeton University Press 2007); Suzanne Mettler, "Reconstituting the

Submerged State: The Challenges of Social Policy Reform in the Obama Era." *Perspectives on Politics* 8, 3 (September 2010): 803–824.

12. People are counted as being in Part D if they have purchased stand-alone Part D drug plans or if they are in Medicare Advantage programs, most of which also offer drug coverage. Thus, in 2010, of the 27.7 million people with Part D coverage, 9.9 million were in Medicare Advantage plans while 17.7 million had stand-alone coverage. Kaiser Family Foundation, "The Medicare Prescription Drug Benefit," October 2010, accessed October 18, 2010, http://www.kff.org/medicare/upload/7044-11.pdf.

13. Hacker, *Divided Welfare State*.

14. Lawrence R. Jacobs, *The Health of Nations: Public Opinion and the Making of American and British Health Policy* (Ithaca, NY: Cornell University Press, 1993).

Chapter 2

1. In 46 states, more than half of Medicaid enrollees are in managed care as of 2010. Overall, 70 percent of Medicaid beneficiaries receive some or all of their health care through managed care programs. Kaiser Family Foundation, "Medicaid and Managed Care: Key Data, Trends, and Issues," February 2010, accessed October 18, 2010, http://www.kff.org/medicaid/upload/8046.pdf.

2. See Joe Soss, Richard C. Fording, and Sanford F. Schram, *Disciplining the Poor: Neoliberal Paternalism and the Persistent Power of Race,* forthcoming, University of Chicago Press.

3. Rosemary Stevens, "Can the Government Govern? Lessons from the Formation of the Veterans Administration," *Journal of Health Politics, Policy and Law* 16, 2 (1991): 281–305.

4. E. S. Savas, "Privatization and Public-Private Partnerships," accessed October 18, 2010, http://www.cesmadrid.es/documentos/Sem200601_MD02_IN.pdf.

5. Edgar Kiser, "Comparing Varieties of Agency Theory in Economics, Political Science, and Sociology: An Illustration from State Policy Implementation," *Sociological Theory* 17, 2 (July 1999): 146–170; Cass R. Sunstein, "Nondelegation Canons," *University of Chicago Law Review* 67, 2 (Spring 2000): 315–343.

6. Dru Stevenson, "Privatization of Welfare Services: Delegation by Commercial Contract," *Arizona Law Review* 45 (2003): 83–131.

7. Jody Freeman, "The Private Role in Public Governance," *New York University Law Review* 75 (June 2000): 543. See Stevenson, "Privatization of Welfare Services," for a contrary view.

8. Gillian E. Metzger, "Privatization as Delegation," *Columbia Law Review* 103 (2003): 1367–1502.

9. R.A.W. Rhodes, "The New Governance: Governing without Government," *Political Studies* 44, 3 (1996): 652–667; Mary Daly, "Governance and Social Policy," *Journal of Social Policy* 32, 1 (2003): 113–128; Carolyn J. Hill and Laurence E. Lynn Jr., "Is Hierarchical Governance in Decline? Evidence from Empirical Research," *Journal of Public Administration Research and Theory* 15, 2 (2005): 173–195; H. George Frederickson, "Whatever Happened to Public Administration? Governance, Governance Everywhere," in *The Oxford Handbook of Public Management*, eds. Ewan Ferlie, Laurence E. Lynn, Jr., and Christopher Pollitt (Oxford: Oxford University Press, 2005), 282–304.

10. Freeman, "Private Role"; Mark Considine, *Enterprising States: The Public Management of Welfare-to-Work* (Cambridge: Cambridge University Press, 2001); Janet Newman, "Modernising the State: A New Style of Governance?" in *Welfare State Change: Towards a Third Way?* eds. Jane Lewis and Rebecca Surrender (Oxford: Oxford University Press, 2004), 69–88; Jon Pierre and B. Guy Peters, *Governing Complex Societies: Trajectories and Scenarios* (Houndmills: Palgrave, 2005); Frederickson, "Whatever Happened," 285.

11. Ted Kolderie, "The Two Different Concepts of Privatization," *Public Administration Review* 46, 4 (July/August 1986): 285–291; Starr, "Privatization"; Paul Seidenstat, "Theory and Practice of Contracting Out in the United States," in *Contracting Out Government Services*, ed. Seidenstat (Westport, CT: Praeger, 1999), 3–25.

12. Metzger, "Privatization," 1395.

13. Starr, "Privatization"; Savas, "Public-Private Partnerships."
14. Still other terms include "purchase-of-service" (Harold W. Demone, Jr., and Margaret Gibelman, eds., *Services for Sale: Purchasing Health and Human Services* [New Brunswick, NJ: Rutgers University Press, 1989]) and "public-private partnerships" (Pauline Vaillancourt Rosenau, ed., *Public-Private Policy Partnerships* [Cambridge: MIT Press, 2000]).
15. Metzger, "Privatization," 1395–1396.
16. Grant McConnell, *Private Power and American Democracy* (New York: Alfred A. Knopf, 1966).
17. Martin Rein and Lee Rainwater, "From Welfare State to Welfare Society," in *Stagnation and Renewal in Social Policy: The Rise and Fall of Policy Regimes*, eds. Rein, Rainwater, and Gøsta Esping-Andersen (Armonk, NY: M. E. Sharpe, 1987), 143–159; Beth Stevens, "Blurring the Boundaries: How the Federal Government Has Influenced Welfare Benefits in the Private Sector," in *The Politics of Social Policy in the United States*, eds. Margaret Weir, Ann Shola Orloff, and Theda Skocpol (Princeton: Princeton University Press, 1988), 123–148; Gøsta Esping-Andersen, *The Three Worlds of Welfare Capitalism* (Princeton: Princeton University Press, 1990).
18. Howard, *Hidden Welfare State*; Howard, *Welfare State Nobody Knows*.
19. Hacker, *Divided Welfare State*; Klein, *For All These Rights*.
20. Mettler, "The Submerged State"; Dalton Conley and Brian Gifford, "Home Ownership, Social Insurance, and the Welfare State," *Sociological Forum* 21, 1 (March 2006): 55–82.
21. Clemens, "Rube Goldberg State."
22. Theda Skocpol, *Protecting Soldiers and Mothers* (Cambridge: Belknap Press, 1992); Joe Soss, *Unwanted Claims: The Politics of Participation in the U.S. Welfare System* (Ann Arbor: University of Michigan Press, 2000); Andrea Louise Campbell, *How Policies Make Citizens: Senior Political Activism and the American Welfare State* (Princeton: Princeton University Press, 2003); Mettler, "Submerged State."
23. Salamon, "Rethinking Public Management"; Kettl, *(Mis?)Managing Federal Programs*; Brinton, "Hollow State"; DiIulio, "Government by Proxy."
24. There has, however, been some important work on the role of nonprofit organizations in delivering social welfare services, including Ralph M. Kramer, *Voluntary Agencies in the Welfare State* (Berkeley: University of California Press, 1981), Smith and Lipsky, *Nonprofits for Hire*; Lester M. Salamon, *Partners in Public Service: Government-Nonprofit Relations in the Modern Welfare State* (Baltimore: Johns Hopkins University Press, 1995); and Andrew Morris, *The Limits of Voluntarism: Charity and Welfare from the New Deal to the Great Society* (Cambridge: Cambridge University Press, 2008). Much of this research focuses on the consequences of contracting out service provision to non-profits, but Morris explores the origins, evolution, and political dynamics around this process.
25. There have been publicly funded voucher programs in a handful of cities and states since the early 1990s, as well as several privately funded voucher initiatives. Selection into either is typically by lottery.
26. Byrna M. Sanger, *Welfare Marketplace: Privatization and Welfare Reform* (Washington, DC: Brookings Institution, 2003); Colleen M. Grogan and Michael K. Gusmano, "Political Strategies of Safety-Net Providers in Response to Medicaid Managed Care Reforms," *Journal of Health Politics, Policy and Law* 34 (February 2009): 5–35.
27. In traditional fee-for-service Medicare, individuals choose their own doctor and hospital with a kind of virtual voucher from the government. But Medicare differs from a true voucher program in that there is no fixed subsidy within which individuals have to work: they choose a physician, and the physician is reimbursed as much as the government is willing. Risk then is borne to some extent by the physician, who must be satisfied with current reimbursement levels, but ultimately by the federal government, which pays the cost when beneficiaries use more care than expected. This is FFS Medicare in its original incarnation, in contrast with the use of private managed care firms to deliver Medicare benefits, which do not pay on a FFS basis, but instead receive capitated payments and then negotiate with providers over reimbursement, and try to "manage" beneficiary care so as to hold down utilization and cost.

28. Jason T. Abaluck and Jonathan Gruber, "Choice Inconsistencies among the Elderly: Evidence from Plan Choice in the Medicare Part D Program." NBER Working Paper 14759 (February 2009), accessed October 18, 2010, www.nber.org/papers/w14759; Yaniv Hanoch, Thomas Rice, Janet Cummings, and Stacey Wood, "How Much Choice is Too Much? The Case of the Medicare Prescription Drug Benefit," *Health Services Research* 44, 4 (August 2009): 1157–1168; Thomas Rice, Janet Cummings, and Daniel Kao, "Reducing the Number of Drug Plans for Seniors: A Proposal and Analysis of Three Case Studies," unpublished manuscript, UCLA.

29. Abaluck and Gruber, "Choice Inconsistencies."

30. Originally, landlords who took one Section 8 voucher holder were mandated by law to accept all others who came along, and there was an "endless lease" provision that prohibited the termination of a lease with a Section 8 client except for good cause. These "risks" to landlords limited the supply of housing, and both were eliminated in 1998 legislation. Morton J. Schussheim, *Housing the Poor: An Overview* (New York: Novinka Press, 2003).

31. Metzger, "Privatization," 1387.

32. Beryl Radin, "When Is a Health Department Not a Health Department? The Case of the US Department of Health and Human Services," *Social Policy & Administration* 44, 2 (April 2010): 142–154.

33. Teppo Kröger, "The Dilemma of Municipalities: Scandinavian Approaches to Child Day-Care Provision," *Journal of Social Policy* 26, 4 (1997): 485–507; Elizabeth Docteur and Howard Oxley, "Health System Reform: Lessons from Experience," in *Towards High-Performing Health Systems*, eds. Docteur and Oxley (Paris: OECD 2004). Norway is somewhat exceptional in that the nonprofit sector has long played a significant role in delivering child care and other services. Benjamin Gidron, Ralph M. Kramer, Lester M. Salamon, "Government and the Third Sector in Comparative Perspective: Allies or Adversaries?" in *Government and the Third Sector: Emerging Relationships in Welfare States*, eds. Gidron, Kramer, and Salamon (San Francisco: Jossey-Bass Publishers, 1992), 22–23; Bente Blanche Nicolaysen, "Voluntary Service Provision in a Strong Welfare State," Working Paper 35 (Mannheim, Germany: Mannheimer Zentrum für Europäische Sozialforschung, 2001).

34. Docteur and Oxley, "Health System Reform."

35. Maurizio Ferrera, "The 'Southern Model' of Welfare in Southern Europe," *Journal of European Social Policy* 6, 1 (February 1996): 17–37.

36. In the original incarnation of these systems, individuals could not even choose their physician or hospital; they would use that which was locally available to them (much as the Veterans Administration health care system works in the United States).

37. Hal Pawson, 2006, "Restructuring England's Social Housing Sector Since 1989: Undermining or Underpinning the Fundamentals of Public Housing?" *Housing Studies* 21, 5 (September): 767–783.

38. Gidron, Salamon, and Kramer, "Third Sector"; Birgit Fix, *The Institutionalization of Family Welfare: Division of Labour in the Field of Child Care in Austria and Germany* Working Paper 24 (Mannheim, Germany: Mannheimer Zentrum für Europäische Sozialforschung, 1998).

39. Paul Dekker, "The Netherlands: From Private Initiatives to Non-Profit Hybrids and Back?" in *The Third Sector in Europe*, eds. Adalbert Evers and Jean-Louis Laville (Cheltenham, UK: Edward Elgar, 2004), 144–165.

40. Esping-Andersen, *Three Worlds*; Giuliano Bonoli, "Classifying Welfare States: A Two-Dimensional Approach," *Journal of Social Policy* 26, 3 (1997): 351–372.

41. Colin Crouch, cited in Bernard Ebbinghaus, "Reforming Bismarckian Corporatism: The Changing Role of Social Partnership in Continental Europe," in *A Long Goodbye to Bismarck? The Politics of Welfare Reform in Continental Europe*, ed. Bruno Palier (Amsterdam: Amsterdam University Press, 2010), 255–278.

42. Paul V. Dutton, *Differential Diagnoses: A Comparative History of Health Care Problems and Solutions in the United States and France* (Ithaca, NY: Cornell University Press, 2007); Rémi Lenoir, "Family Policy in France since 1938," in *The French Welfare State: Surviving Social and Ideological Change*, ed. John S. Ambler (New York: New York University Press 1991), 144–186.

43. Ebbinghaus, "Bismarckian Corporatism."
44. David Wilsford, "The Continuity of Crisis: Patterns of Health Care Policymaking in France, 1978–1988," in *The French Welfare State: Surviving Social and Ideological Change*, ed. John S. Ambler (New York: New York University Press, 1991), 94–143; Dutton, *Differential Diagnoses*, 23.
45. Annette Zimmer, "Corporatism Revisited—The Legacy of History and the German Non-profit Sector," *Voluntas: International Journal of Voluntary and Nonprofit Organizations* 10, 1 (1999): 41.
46. Rudolph Bauer, "Voluntary Welfare Associations in Germany and the United States: Theses on the Historical Development of Intermediary Systems," *Voluntas* 1, 1 (1990): 97–111.
47. Wolfgang Seibel, "Government-Nonprofit Relationships in a Comparative Perspective: The Cases of France and Germany," in *The Nonprofit Sector in the Global Community: Voices from Many Nations*, eds. Kathleen D. McCarthy, Virginia A. Hodgkinson, Russy D. Sumariwalla and Associates (San Francisco: Jossey-Bass Publishers, 1992), 205–229.
48. Maria Brenton, "Changing Relationships in Dutch Social Services," *Journal of Social Policy* 11, 1 (1982): 68,
49. Ralph M. Kramer, "The Use of Government Funds by Voluntary Social Service Agencies in Four Welfare States," in *The Nonprofit Sector in International Perspective*, ed. Estelle James (New York: Oxford University Press 1989), 218–219.
50. Christa Altenstetter, "Insights from Health Care in Germany," *American Journal of Public Health* 93, 1 (January 2003): 38–44; Ebbinghaus, "Bismarckian Corporatism"; Bruno Palier, "The Dualization of the French Welfare System," in *A Long Goodbye to Bismarck? The Politics of Welfare Reform in Continental Europe*, ed. Palier (Amsterdam: Amsterdam University Press, 2010), 73–99.
51. Rhodes, "New Governance"; Bob Jessop, "The Changing Governance of Welfare: Recent Trends in Its Primary Functions, Scale, and Modes of Coordination," *Social Policy and Administration* 33, 4 (December 1999): 348–359; Paula Blomqvist, "The Choice Revolution: Privatization of Swedish Welfare Services in the 1990s," *Social Policy & Administration* 38, 2 (April 2004): 139–155; Neil Gilbert, *Transformation of the Welfare State: The Silent Surrender of Public Responsibility* (Oxford: Oxford University Press, 2004).
52. Pawson, "England's Social Housing."
53. Emmanuele Pavolini and Costanzo Ranci, "Restructuring the Welfare State: Reforms in Long-Term Care in Western European Countries," *Journal of European Social Policy* 18, 3 (2008): 254.
54. Daly, "Governance," 120,*
55. Pavolini and Ranci, "Reforms in Long-Term Care," 254.
56. Kimberly J. Morgan, *Working Mothers and the Welfare State: Religion and the Politics of Work-Family Policies in Western Europe and the United States* (Palo Alto: Stanford University Press, 2006).
57. Gilbert, *Transformation of the Welfare State*, 112.
58. Blomqvist, "Choice Revolution"; Michael Baggesen Klitgaard, "Do Welfare State Regimes Determine Public Sector Reforms? Choice Reforms in American, Swedish and German Schools," *Scandinavian Political Studies* 30, 4 (2007): 444–682.
59. Karen M. Anderson and Ellen M. Immergut, "Sweden: After Social Democratic Hegemony," in *The Handbook of West European Pension Politics*, eds. Immergut, Anderson and Isabelle Schultze (Oxford: Oxford University Press, 2007), 349–395.
60. Monica Prasad, *The Politics of Free Markets: The Rise of Neoliberal Economic Policies in Britain, France, Germany, and the United States* (Chicago: University of Chicago Press, 2006).
61. Vivien Schmidt, *Democratizing France: The Political and Administrative History of Decentralization* (New York: Cambridge University Press 1990); Claire F. Ullman, *The Welfare State's Other Crisis: Explaining the New Partnership between Nonprofit Organizations and the State in France* (Bloomington: University of Indiana Press, 1999).
62. Zimmer "Corporatism Revisited," 43–44; Ingo Bode, "Disorganized Welfare Mixes: Voluntary Agencies and New Governance Regimes in Western Europe," *Journal of European Social Policy* 19, 4 (2006): 346–359.

63. Wilsford, "Health Care Policy-Making in France"; Patrick Hassenteufel and Bruno Palier, "Towards Neo-Bismarckian Health Care States? Comparing Health Insurance Reforms in Bismarckian Welfare Systems," *Social Policy and Administration* 41, 6 (December 2007): 574–596.

64. Walter J.M. Kickert, "Expansion and Diversification of Public Administration in the Postwar Welfare State: The Case of the Netherlands," *Public Administration Review* 56, 1 (1996): 89.

65. Certainly, some analysts forecast that the privatization and marketization of welfare programs and services will accelerate in the years ahead due to fiscal constraints and the strains brought by demographic aging. See Wolfgang Streeck, "The Fiscal Crisis Continues: From Liberalization to Consolidation," *Comparative European Politics* 8, 4 (2010): 505–514.

66. James A. Morone, "Citizens or Shoppers? Solidarity under Siege," *Journal of Health Policy, Politics and Law* 25, 5 (October 2000): 959–968; Jacob S. Hacker, "Review Article: Dismantling the Health Care State? Political Institutions, Public Policies and the Comparative Politics of Health Reform," *British Journal of Political Science* 343 (October 2004): 693–724.

67. Hassenteufel and Palier, "Neo-Bismarckian Health Care States," 591.

68. Eddy van Doorslaer and Frederik T. Schut, "Belgium and the Netherlands Revisited," *Journal of Health Politics, Policy and Law* 25, 5 (2000): 881–882.

69. Hassenteufel and Palier, "Neo-Bismarckian Health Care States," 591–592.

70. Geoff Fougere, "Transforming Health Sectors: New Logics of Organizing in the New Zealand Health System," *Social Science & Medicine* 52 (2001): 1236.

71. Todd A. Krieble, "New Zealand," *Journal of Health Politics, Policy and Law* 25, 5 (2000): 925–930.

72. Alan Jacobs, "Seeing Difference: Market Health Reform in Europe," *Journal of Health Politics, Policy and Law* 23, 1 (February 1998): 21.

73. Doorslaer and Schut, "Belgium and the Netherlands," 886.

74. Hacker, "Dismantling the Health Care State?" 701.

75. The following paragraph is based on Yvette Bartholomée and Hans Maarse, "Health Insurance Reform in the Netherlands," *Eurohealth* 12, 2 (2006): 7–9; Jan-Kees Helderman, *Bringing the Market Back In? Institutional Complementarity and Hierarchy in Dutch Housing and Healthcare,* PhD dissertation, Erasmus University Rotterdam 2007; Pauline Vaillancourt Rosenau and Christiaan J. Lako, "An Experiment with Regulated Competition and Individual Mandates for Universal Health Care: The New Dutch Health Insurance System," *Journal of Health Politics, Policy and Law* 33, 6 (2008): 1031–1055; Kieke G. H. Okma, "Commentary on Rosenau and Lako," *Journal of Health Politics, Policy and Law* 33, 6 (2008): 1057–1071; Uwe E. Reinhardt, "The Swiss Health System: Regulated Competition without Managed Care," *JAMA* 292, 10 (2004): 1227–1231.

76. Okma, "Commentary," 1059.

77. Okma, "Commentary," 1060.

78. Okma, "Commentary"; Helderman, *Bringing the Market Back In?*

79. Reinhardt, "Swiss Health System," 1227.

80. Reinhardt, "Swiss Health System," 1230.

81. Paul Pierson, "Increasing Returns, Path Dependence, and the Study of Politics," *American Political Science Review* 94, 2 (2000): 251–267.

82. Gøsta Esping-Andersen, "Power and Distributional Regimes," *Politics & Society* 14, 2 (1985): 223–256.

83. Jill Quadagno, *The Color of Welfare: How Racism Undermined the War on Poverty* (New York: Oxford University Press 1996).

84. Jacob S. Hacker and Paul Pierson, "Business Power and Social Policy: Employers and the Formation of the American Welfare State," *Politics and Society* 30 (2002): 277–325; Peter A. Swenson, "Varieties of Capitalist Interests: Power, Institutions, and the Regulatory Welfare State in the United States and Sweden," *Studies in American Political Development* 18 (Spring 2004): 1–29; Jill Quadagno, *One Nation, Uninsured: Why the U.S. Has No National Health Insurance* (New York: Oxford University Press 2005).

85. Howard, *Welfare State Nobody Knows*; Howard, *Hidden Welfare State*; Julian E. Zelizer, *Taxing America: Wilbur D. Mills, Congress, and the State, 1945–1975* (Cambridge: Cambridge University Press, 1998); Hacker, *Divided Welfare State*.

86. Lloyd A. Free and Hadley Cantril, *The Political Beliefs of Americans* (New Brunswick: Rutgers University Press, 1967).

87. Free and Cantril,*The Political Beliefs of Americans*, 30; 12–15.

88. Benjamin I. Page and Lawrence R. Jacobs, *Class War? What Americans Really Think about Economic Inequality* (Chicago: University of Chicago Press, 2009).

89. Stanley Feldman and John Zaller, "Political Culture of Ambivalence: Ideological Responses to the Welfare State," *American Journal of Political Science* 36 (1992): 268–307; see also Herbert McClosky and John Zaller, *The American Ethos: Public Attitudes toward Capitalism and Democracy* (Cambridge, MA: Harvard University Press 1984), and Jennifer Hochschild, *What's Fair?* (Princeton: Princeton University Press 1981).

90. This figure is from 2000, the last time it was included in the ANES.

91. These figures are from 2008 except for homeless and financial aid for college (1996) and food stamps (2000).

92. Robert J. Blendon and John M. Benson, "Public Opinion at the Time of the Vote on Health Care," *New England Journal of Medicine*, e55(2). See also Mollyann Brodie, Drew Altman, Claudia Deane, Sasha Buscho, and Elizabeth Hamel, "Liking the Pieces, Not the Package: Contradictions in Public Opinion During Health Reform," *Health Affairs* 29, 6 (2010): 1125–1130.

93. Blendon and Benson, "Public Opinion at the Time of the Vote on Health Care," p. e55(3).

94. McClosky and Zaller, *The American Ethos*.

95. Feldman and Zaller, "Political Culture."

96. John Zaller, *The Nature and Origins of Mass Opinion* (New York: Cambridge University Press, 1992).

97. Jacobs, *Health of Nations*.

98. Marcia Angell, *The Truth about the Drug Companies* (New York: Random House 2004).

99. David Vogel, *Fluctuating Fortunes: The Political Power of Business in America* (New York: Basic Books 1989); Steven M. Teles, *The Rise of the Conservative Legal Movement: The Battle for Control of the Law* (Princeton: Princeton University Press, 2008).

100. Frank R. Baumgartner and Beth Leech, *Basic Interests: The Importance of Groups in Politics and in Political Science* (Princeton: Princeton University Press, 1998).

101. Jacob S. Hacker, "The Historical Logic of National Health Insurance: Structure and Sequence in the Development of British, Canadian, and U.S. Medical Policy," *Studies in American Political Development* 12, 1 (April 1998): 57–130; Sven Steinmo and Jon Watts, "It's the Institutions, Stupid! Why Comprehensive National Health Insurance Always Fails in America," *Journal of Health Politics, Policy and Law* 20, 2 (1995): 329–372.

102. Some exceptions include Zelizer, *Taxing America*; Howard, *Welfare State Nobody Knows*; Howard, *Hidden Welfare State*; and Jonathan Oberlander, *The Political Life of Medicare* (Chicago: University of Chicago Press, 2003).

103. Quadagno, *Color of Welfare*.

104. Theodore R. Marmor, *The Politics of Medicare*, 2nd ed. (New York: Aldine de Gruyter, 2002); Zelizer, *Taxing America*.

105. Ellis W. Hawley, "Social Policy and the Liberal State in Twentieth-Century America," in *Federal Social Policy: The Historical Dimension*, eds. Donald T. Crichlow and Ellis W. Hawley (University Park: Pennsylvania State University Press, 1988), 125–127; Barry D. Karl, *The Uneasy State: The United States from 1915 to 1945* (Chicago: University of Chicago Press, 1983), 236–238.

106. R. Kent Weaver, "The Politics of Blame Avoidance," *Journal of Public Policy* 6 (October–December 1986): 371–398.

107. Matthew A. Crenson and Francis E. Rourke, "By Way of Conclusion: American Bureaucracy since World War II," in *The New American State: Bureaucracies and Policies since World War II*, ed. Louis Galambos (Baltimore: Johns Hopkins University Press, 1987), 149; see Theodore J. Lowi, *The End of Liberalism* (New York: W.W. Norton & Company 1969).

108. James C. Robinson, "The Commercial Health Insurance Industry in an Era of Eroding Employer Coverage," *Health Affairs* 25, 6 (November/December 2006): 1484.

109. William Niskanen, *Bureaucracy and Representative Government* (Chicago: Aldine-Atherton, 1971).

110. Anthony H. Pascal, "Clients, Consumers, and Citizens: Using Market Mechanisms for the Delivery of Public Services," Rand Corporation Research Paper P-4803 (1972); Savas, *Privatizing the Public Sector: How to Shrink Government* (Chatham, NJ: Chatham House Publishers, 1982).

111. Savas, *Privatizing the Public Sector*; Stephen Moore, "Contracting Out: A Painless Alternative to the Budget Cutter's Knife," *Proceedings of the Academy of Political Science* 36, 3 (1987): 60–73; Simon Domberger and Paul Jensen, "Contracting Out by the Public Sector: Theory, Evidence, Prospects," *Oxford Review of Economic Policy* 13, 4 (1997): 67–78.

112. Steve H. Hanke, "Privatization: Theory, Evidence, and Implementation," *Proceedings of the Academy of Political Science* 35, 4 (1985): 101–113; Seidenstat, "Contracting Out."

113. Julien Le Grand, "Quasi-Markets and Social Policy," *The Economic Journal* 101, no. 408 (September 1991): 1256–1267; Michael Lipsky, and Steven Rathgeb Smith, "Nonprofit Organizations, Government, and the Welfare State," *Political Science Quarterly* 104, 4 (1989–1990): 633–634.

114. Milton Friedman, *Capitalism and Freedom* (Chicago: University of Chicago Press, 1962); Pascal, "Clients, Consumers and Citizens."

115. Smith and Lipsky, *Nonprofits for Hire*.

116. David M. Van Slyke, "The Mythology of Privatization in Contracting for Social Services," *Public Administration Review* 63, 3 (May/June 2003): 296–315; Stevenson, "Privatization of Welfare Services," 129.

117. Steven Rathgeb Smith and Judith Smyth, "Contracting for Services in a Decentralized System," *Journal of Public Administration and Theory* 6, 2 (April 1996): 277–297.

118. Peter F. Drucker, "The Sickness of Government," *Public Interest* 14 (Winter 1969): 3–23; James A. Morone, "Hidden Complications: Why Health Care Competition Needs Regulation," *American Prospect* 10 (1992): 40–48; Kettl, *Sharing Power*; Lawrence D. Brown and Lawrence R. Jacobs, *The Private Abuse of the Public Interest: Market Myths and Policy Muddles* (Chicago: University of Chicago Press, 2008).

119. Smith and Lipsky, *Nonprofits for Hire*, 243–244.

120. Frederick C. Mosher, "The Changing Responsibilities and Tactics of the Federal Government," *Public Administration Review* 40, 6 (November/December 1980): 541–548.

121. Mathew McCubbins, "The Legislative Design of Regulatory Structure," *American Journal of Political Science* 29, 4 (1985): 721–748; Mathew McCubbins, Roger Noll, and Barry Weingast, "Administrative Procedures as Instruments of Political Control," *Journal of Law, Economics, and Organization* 3, 2 (1987): 243–277.

122. Pascal, "Clients, Consumers, and Citizens."

123. Pascal, "Clients, Consumers, and Citizens."

124. Donald F. Kettl, "The Transformation of Governance: Globalization, Devolution, and the Role of Government," *Public Administration Review* 60, 6 (November/December 2000): 494.

125. Albert O. Hirschman, *Exit, Voice and Loyalty* (Cambridge, MA: Harvard University Press, 1970).

126. John E. Chubb and Terry M. Moe, *Politics, Markets, and America's Schools* (Washington, DC: Brookings, 1990); Le Grand, "Quasi-Markets."

127. Smith and Lipsky, *Nonprofits for Hire*, 249.

128. For a vivid account of the consequences of the delegation of welfare programs to for-profit firms, see Joe Soss, Richard C. Fording, and Sanford F. Schram, *Disciplining the Poor: Neoliberal Paternalism and the Persistent Power of Race* (forthcoming, University of Chicago Press).

129. McConnell, *Private Power*, 51.

130. Novak, "'Weak' American State."

131. Louis Galambos, "By Way of Introduction," in *The New American State: Bureaucracies and Policies since World War II*, ed. Galambos (Baltimore: Johns Hopkins University Press, 1987),

1–20; Stephen Skowronek, *Building a New American State: The Expansion of National Administrative Capacities, 1877–1920* (Cambridge: Cambridge University Press, 1982).

132. Skocpol and Finegold, "State Capacity"; Daniel P. Carpenter, *The Forging of Bureaucratic Autonomy: Reputations, Networks, and Policy Innovation in Executive Agencies, 1862–1928* (Princeton: Princeton University Press, 2001).

133. Data are from 2006; the American figure is even further from the European Union average, which is 39.8 percent of GDP. *OECD in Figures* (Paris: OECD, 2009).

134. Laura S. Jensen, "Government, the State, and Governance," *Polity* 40, 3 (July 2008): 379–385.

135. Skocpol, *Protecting Soldiers and Mothers*; Kimberly J. Morgan and Monica Prasad, "The Origins of Tax Systems: A French-American Comparison," *American Journal of Sociology* 114, 5 (March 2009): 1350–1394.

136. Aaron L. Friedberg, "American Antistatism and the Founding of the Cold War State," in *Shaped by War and Trade: International Influences on American Political Development*, eds. Ira Katznelson and Martin Shefter (Princeton: Princeton University Press, 2002), 239–266.

137. Peter Baldwin, "Beyond Weak and Strong: Rethinking the State in Comparative Policy History," *Journal of Policy History* 17, 1 (2005): 12–33; Desmond King and Robert C. Lieberman, "Ironies of State Building: A Comparative Perspective on the American State," *World Politics* 61, 3 (July 2009): 547–588.

138. Lowi, *End of Liberalism*, xi.

139. We are grateful to Ann Orloff for her insights on this.

140. Clemens, "Rube Goldberg State"; Kimberley S. Johnson, *Governing the American State: Congress and the New Federalism, 1877–1929* (Princeton: Princeton University Press, 2007).

141. Mosher, "Tactics of the Federal Government"; DiIulio, "Government by Proxy."

142. Paul C. Light, "The New True Size of Government," *Organizational Performance Initiative Research Brief No. 2* (New York University Wagner School, 2006).

143. Mosher, "Tactics of the Federal Government," 543.

Chapter 3

1. Theodore J. Lowi, *The End of Liberalism: Ideology, Policy and the Crisis of Public Authority* (New York: W. W. Norton, 1969).

2. Frederick C. Mosher, "The Changing Responsibilities and Tactics of the Federal Government," *Public Administration Review* 40, 6 (November/December 1980): 541–548; Lester M. Salamon, "Rethinking Public Management: Third-Party Government and the Changing Forms of Government Action," *Public Policy* 29, 3 (Summer 1981): 255–275.

3. Jacobs, *Health of Nations*, 158.

4. James A. Morone, *The Democratic Wish: Popular Participation and the Limits of American Government* revised edition (New Haven: Yale University Press, 1998).

5. Grant McConnell, *Private Power and American Democracy* (New York: Alfred A. Knopf, 1966), 91.

6. Louis Galambos, "By Way of Introduction," in *The New American State: Bureaucracies and Policies since World War II*, ed. Galambos (Baltimore: Johns Hopkins University Press, 1987), 13; see also Aaron L. Friedberg, "American Antistatism and the Founding of the Cold War State," in *Shaped by War and Trade: International Influences on American Political Development*, eds. Ira Katznelson and Martin Shefter (Princeton: Princeton University Press, 2002), 241.

7. Stephen Skowronek, *Building a New American State: The Expansion of National Administrative Capacities, 1877–1920* (Cambridge: Cambridge University Press, 1982).

8. Galambos, "Introduction," 9–10.

9. Barry D. Karl, *The Uneasy State: The United States from 1915 to 1945* (Chicago: University of Chicago Press, 1983), 25.

10. Theda Skocpol and Kenneth Finegold, "State Capacity and Economic Intervention in the Early New Deal," *Political Science Quarterly* 97, 2 (Summer 1982): 255–278; Daniel P. Carpenter, *The*

Forging of Bureaucratic Autonomy: Reputations, Networks, and Policy Innovation in Executive Agencies, 1862–1928 (Princeton: Princeton University Press, 2001).

11. Karl, *Uneasy State*.

12. Karl, *Uneasy State*, 46.

13. Hawley, Ellis W. 1974. "Herbert Hoover, the Commerce Secretariat, and the Vision of an 'Associative State,' 1921–28," *Journal of American History* 61, 1 (June): 116–140; McConnell, *Private Power*.

14. Elisabeth S. Clemens, "Lineages of the Rube Goldberg State: Building and Blurring Public Programs, 1900–1940," in *Rethinking Political Institutions: The Art of the State,* eds. Ian Shapiro, Stephen Skowronek, and Daniel Galvin (New York: New York University Press, 2006), 196.

15. Nina Bernstein, *The Lost Children of Wilder: The Epic Struggle to Change Foster Care* (New York: Vintage Books, 2002).

16. Clemens, "Rube Goldberg State."

17. Steven Rathgeb Smith and Michael Lipsky, *Nonprofits for Hire: The Welfare State in the Age of Contracting* (Cambridge, MA: Harvard University Press, 1993), 48–49.

18. Suzanne Mettler, *Dividing Citizens: Gender and Federalism in New Deal Public Policy* (Ithaca, NY: Cornell University Press, 1998).

19. Mettler, *Dividing Citizens,* 67.

20. Jacob S. Hacker, *The Divided Welfare State: The Battle over Public and Private Social Benefits in the United States* (Cambridge: Cambridge University Press, 2002), 96–97.

21. Jennifer Klein, *For All These Rights: Business, Labor, and the Shaping of America's Public-Private Welfare State* (Princeton: Princeton University Press, 2003), 87–90.

22. Peter A. Swenson, "Varieties of Capitalist Interests: Power, Institutions, and the Regulatory Welfare State in the United States and Sweden," *Studies in American Political Development* 18 (Spring 2004): 1–29.

23. Theodore J. Lowi, "American Business, Public Policy, Case-Studies, and Political Theory" *World Politics* 16, 4 (1964): 677–715.

24. Edwin E. Witte, *The Development of the Social Security Act* (Madison: University of Wisconsin Press, 1963), 75–99.

25. Smith and Lipsky, *Nonprofits for Hire,* 48–49.

26. Andrew Morris, *The Limits of Voluntarism: Charity and Welfare from the New Deal to the Great Society* (Cambridge: Cambridge University Press, 2008), 17–19.

27. Morris, *Limits of Voluntarism,* 190.

28. Morris, *Limits of Voluntarism,* 19–23.

29. Elizabeth Wickenden, "Social Security and Voluntary Social Welfare," *Industrial and Labor Relations Review* 14 (1960–1): 102–103.

30. Charles Gilbert, "Welfare Policy," in *Handbook of Political Science.* Vol. 6: *Policies and Policy-making,* eds. Fred I. Greenstein and Nelson W. Polsby (Reading, MA: Addison-Wesley, 1975), 117–119; Lowi, *End of Liberalism,* 224–225.

31. Karl, *Uneasy State,* 145–146.

32. Alan Brinkley, *The End of Reform: New Deal Liberalism in Recession and War* (New York: Alfred A. Knopf 1995), 17.

33. Karl, *Uneasy State*; George B. Shepherd, "Fierce Compromise: The Administrative Procedure Act Emerges from New Deal Politics," *Northwestern University Law Review* 90, 4 (1996): 1557–1683.

34. Mack C. Shelley II, *The Permanent Majority: The Conservative Coalition in the United States Congress* (University of Alabama Press, 1983).

35. Karl, *Uneasy State,* 181.

36. Friedberg, "American Antistatism," 242.

37. Paul C. Light, *The True Size of Government* (Washington DC: Brookings, 1999), 99–100.

38. Light, *True Size,* 119–122.

39. Daniel Guttman and Barry Willner, *The Shadow Government: The Government's Multi-Billion-Dollar Giveaway of Its Decision-Making Powers to Private Management Consultants, "Experts," and Think Tanks* (New York: Pantheon Books 1976); Light, *True Size*.

40. Guttman, "Inherently Governmental Functions and the New Millennium: The Legacy of Twentieth Century Reform," in *Making Government Manageable: Executive Organization and Management in the Twenty-First Century* (Baltimore: Johns Hopkins University Press, 2004), 41.

41. Murray Weidenbaum, *The Modern Public Sector: New Ways of Doing the Government's Business* (New York: Basic Books, 1969).

42. Milward H. Brinton, "Symposium on the Hollow State," *Journal of Public Administration Research & Theory* 6, 2 (April 1996): 193–195.

43. Presidential Papers of Dwight D. Eisenhower, Document #1147, Letter to Edgar Newton Eisenhower. Available on-line at http://www.eisenhowermemorial.org/presidential-papers/first-term/documents/1147.cfm, accessed November 15, 2010.

44. Skocpol and Finegold, "State Capacity and Economic Intervention."

45. Salamon, "Rethinking Public Management."

46. Matthew A. Crenson and Francis E. Rourke, "By Way of Conclusion: American Bureaucracy since World War II," in *The New American State: Bureaucracies and Policies since World War II*, ed. Louis Galambos (Baltimore: Johns Hopkins University Press, 1987), 148.

47. Martha Derthick, *Uncontrollable Spending for Social Services Grants* (Washington, DC: Brookings, 1975), 20; Morris, *Limits of Voluntarism*, 198.

48. Gilbert, "Welfare Policy," 165.

49. Elizabeth Wickenden, "A Perspective on Social Services: An Essay Review," *The Social Science Review* 50, 4 (December 1976): 579.

50. Morris, *Limits of Voluntarism*, 186–187.

51. Gilbert, "Welfare Policy," 165.

52. Arnold Gurin, "Governmental Responsibility and Privatization: Examples from Four Social Services," in *Privatization and the Welfare State*, eds. Sheila B. Kamerman and Alfred J. Kahn (Princeton: Princeton University Press, 1989), 182; Ralph M. Kramer, "The Future of the Voluntary Agency in a Mixed Economy," *Journal of Applied Behavioral Science* 21, 4 (1985): 386.

53. Morris, "The Voluntary Sector's War on Poverty," *Journal of Policy History* 16, 4 (2004): 280–282.

54. Crenson and Rourke, "By Way of Conclusion," 151–152.

55. Nicole P. Marwell, "Privatizing the Welfare State: Nonprofit Community-Based Organizations as Political Actors," *American Sociological Review* 69 (April 2004): 268.

56. Alan Pifer, quoted in Morris, *Limits of Voluntarism*, 185.

57. Derthick, *Uncontrollable Spending*, 20.

58. Derthick, *Uncontrollable Spending*; Morris, *Limits of Voluntarism*, 199–200.

59. Smith and Lipsky, *Nonprofits for Hire*, 55–56; Kramer, "Future of the Voluntary Agency," 379.

60. Cited in Gilbert, "Welfare Policy," 166.

61. Gilbert, "Welfare Policy," 167; Ralph M. Kramer, "The Use of Government Funds by Voluntary Social Service Agencies in Four Welfare States," in *The Nonprofit Sector in International Perspective*, ed. Estelle James (New York: Oxford University Press, 1989), 223.

62. Morris, *Limits of Voluntarism*, 207–208.

63. Marmor, *Politics of Medicare*, 17.

64. Robert Ball, *Reflections on Implementing Medicare* (Washington, DC: National Academy of Social Insurance, 2001), 2.

65. Beatrix Hoffman, *The Wages of Sickness: The Politics of Health Insurance in Progressive America* (Chapel Hill: University of North Carolina Press, 2001); Paul Starr, *The Social Transformation of American Medicine* (New York: Basic Books, 1982).

66. Peter Corning, *The Evolution of Medicare . . . From Idea to Law* (Washington, DC: US Dept. of Health, Education and Welfare, Research Report No. 29, 1969), 29–41.

67. Rick Mayes, *Universal Coverage: The Elusive Quest for National Health Insurance* (Ann Arbor: University of Michigan Press, 2004), 23.

68. Jill Quadagno, *One Nation, Uninsured: Why the U.S. Has No National Health Insurance* (New York: Oxford University Press, 2005); Colin Gordon, *Dead on Arrival: The Politics of Health Care in Twentieth Century America* (Princeton: Princeton University Press, 2004).

69. American Medical Association, quoted in Gordon, *Dead on Arrival*, 134.

70. Paul B. Magnuson, "Medical Care for Veterans," *Annals of the American Academy of Political and Social Science* 273 (January 1951): 76–83.

71. Rosemary Stevens, "Can the Government Govern? Lessons from the Formation of the Veterans Administration," *Journal of Health Politics, Policy and Law* 16, 2 (Summer 1991): 293.

72. Starr, *Social Transformation*, 289; Stevens, "Veterans Administration."

73. Gordon, *Dead on Arrival*, 132–133.

74. John K. Iglehart, "Reform of the Veterans Affairs Health Care System," *New England Journal of Medicine* 335, 18 (October 31, 1996): 1407–1411.

75. Starr, *Social Transformation*, 345, 351.

76. Starr, *Social Transformation*, 311–320; Beth Stevens, "Blurring the Boundaries: How the Federal Government Has Influenced Welfare Benefits in the Private Sector," in *The Politics of Social Policy in the United States*, eds. Margaret Weir, Ann Shola Orloff, and Theda Skocpol (Princeton: Princeton University Press, 1998), 123–148; Hacker, *Divided Welfare State*; Klein, *For All These Rights*.

77. Melissa A. Thomasson, "From Sickness to Health: The Twentieth-Century Development of U.S. Health Insurance," *Explorations in Economic History* 39 (2002): 238–239.

78. Thomasson, "Sickness to Health," 241; Melissa A. Thomasson, "The Importance of Group Coverage: How Tax Policy Shaped U.S. Health Insurance," *American Economic Review* 93, 4 (September 2003): 1373–1384; Hacker, *Divided Welfare State*, 217–218.

79. Thomasson, "Group Coverage," 1374–1375.

80. Starr, *Social Transformation*, 348–351; Lawrence R. Jacobs, "Politics of America's Supply State: Health Reform and Technology," *Health Affairs* 14, 2 (Summer 1995): 143–157.

81. Starr, *Social Transformation*, 338–351.

82. Starr, *Social Transformation*, 340–344.

83. Michael A. Dowell, "Hill-Burton: The Unfulfilled Promise," *Journal of Health Politics, Policy and Law* 12, 1 (Spring 1987): 153–175.

84. Jacobs, "Supply State."

85. Theda Skocpol, *Protecting Soldiers and Mothers* (Cambridge: Belknap Press, 1990); Louis Galambos, "By Way of Introduction," in *The New American State: Bureaucracies and Policies since World War II*, ed. Galambos (Baltimore: Johns Hopkins University Press, 1987), 9.

86. In his careful evaluation of public opinion toward various social welfare policies, Michael Schiltz finds that the issue of NHI is of surprisingly low salience—only 56 percent of respondents in a March 1949 Gallup poll had heard of the national health insurance proposal, for example. Generally Schiltz finds that support for national health insurance appears to drop, from 58 to 36 percent from November 1945 to November 1949. The penetration of the AMA publicity campaigns is evidenced in the March 1949 Gallup poll that found that among those who had heard of the proposal, 70 percent knew that physicians were opposed to it. Michael E. Schiltz, *Public Attitudes Toward Social Security 1935–1965*, Research report no. 33 (Social Security Administration, 1970), 134.

87. Richard Harris, *A Sacred Trust* (New York: Penguin Books, 1966); Quadagno, *One Nation Uninsured*.

88. Robert Cunningham III and Robert M. Cunningham Jr., *The Blues: A History of the Blue Cross and Blue Shield System* (De Kalb: Northern Illinois Press, 1997), 137; Hacker, *Divided Welfare State*, 238.

89. Cunningham and Cunningham, *The Blues*, 121–129.

90. Wickenden "Voluntary Social Welfare," 103.

91. Sheri I. David, *With Dignity: The Search for Medicare and Medicaid* (Westport, CT: Greenwood Press, 1985), 35; Colleen M. Grogan and Vernon K. Smith, "From Charity Care to Medicaid: Governors, States, and the Transformation of American Health Care," in *A Legacy of Innovation: Governors and Public Policy*, ed. Ethan G. Sribnick (Philadelphia: University of Pennsylvania Press, 2008), 209.

92. Edward D. Berkowitz, *Disabled Policy: America's Programs for the Handicapped; a Twentieth Century Fund Report* (New York: Cambridge University Press, 1987), 71; Quadagno, *One Nation Uninsured*, 54.

93. Hacker, *Divided Welfare State*, 242.

94. Cunningham and Cunningham, *The Blues*, 147.

95. David, *Search for Medicare*, 3–5.

96. Corning *Evolution of Medicare*, 78, 102.

97. Jacobs, *Health of Nations*, 91–94.

98. Jacobs, *Health of Nations*, 98–99.

99. Jacobs, *Health of Nations*, 137–140, 143–44.

100. Schiltz, *Attitudes toward Social Security*, 140.

101. James L. Sundquist, *Politics and Policy: The Eisenhower, Kennedy, and Johnson Years* (Washington, DC: The Brookings Institution, 1968), 290, 297–299.

102. Jacobs, *Health of Nations*, 89–90.

103. Karlyn Bowman, "Attitudes toward the Federal Government," AEI Public Opinion Study (June 2008), 15, 27.

104. Bowman, "Attitudes toward the Federal Government," 7.

105. Monte M. Poen, *Harry S. Truman versus the Medical Lobby: The Genesis of Medicare* (Columbia and London: University of Missouri Press, 1979); Quadagno, *One Nation Uninsured*.

106. Judith M. Feder, *Medicare: The Politics of Federal Hospital Insurance* (Lexington, MA: Lexington Books, 1977).

107. Timothy Stoltzfus Jost, "Medicare and the Joint Commission on Accreditation of Healthcare Organizations: A Healthy Relationship?" *Law and Contemporary Problems* 57, 4 (Autumn 1994): 15–45.

108. Sallyanne Payton, "Professionalism as Third-Party Governance: The Function and Dysfunction of Medicare," pp. 112–140 in Thomas H. Stanton and Benjamin Ginsberg, eds., *Making Government Manageable: Executive Organization and Management in the Twenty-First Century* (Baltimore: JHU Press, 2004); Richard A. Posner, "Regulatory Aspects of National Health Insurance Plans," *University of Chicago Law Review* 39, 1 (Autumn 1971): 1–29.

109. Jaap Kooijman, . . . *and the Pursuit of National Health: The Incremental Strategy Toward National Health Insurance in the United States of America* (Amsterdam Monographs in American Studies 9, 1999), 174.

110. Neil Hollander and Bruce L.R. Smith, "The Framework of Medicare Administration," in *The Administration of Medicare: A Shared Responsibility*, eds. Smith and Hollander (Washington, DC: National Academy of Public Administration Foundation, 1973), 2.

111. Richard A. Posner, "Regulatory Aspects of National Health Insurance Plans," *University of Chicago Law Review* 39, 1 (Autumn 1971): 18.

112. Jacobs, *Health of Nations*, 156–157.

113. Arthur Hess, Oral History Interview with Edward Berkowitz, Charlottesville, VA: July 8, 1996.

114. Edward D. Berkowitz, *Robert Ball and the Politics of Social Security* (Madison: University of Wisconsin Press, 2003), 128.

115. Jacobs, *Health of Nations*, 158–159.

116. p. 22.

117. Feder, *Medicare*, 37; Kooijman, *Incremental Strategy*, 171.

118. quoted in Sundquist, *Politics and Policy*, 300.

119. Corning, *Evolution of Medicare*, 83; Sundquist, *Politics and Policy*, 301–305; David, *With Dignity*, chap. 5.

120. Kooijman, *Incremental Strategy*, 172–173; Hale Champion, Oral History Interview with Edward Berkowitz, Cambridge, MA: August 9, 1995.

121. Sylvia Law, *Blue Cross: What Went Wrong?* (New Haven: Yale University Press, 1974), 34.

122. David, *With Dignity*.

123. Herman Miles Somers and Anne Ramsay Somers, *Medicare and the Hospitals: Issues and Prospects* (Washington, DC: The Brookings Institution, 1967), 34.

124. Hess, oral history interview.
125. Marmor, *Politics of Medicare*. As Hale Champion said in his oral history interview: "One of the big management problems in terms of bringing Medicare closer to Medicaid were the commitments that were made at the time that Medicare was passed . . . that is, 'Hey, if you'll let us get Medicare, we'll let you decide how the payment system runs.' In other words, it was pretty much left to the hospitals and the docs, primarily the docs in that case and to some extent the insurance companies, 'You decide the payment system. You let us have Medicare' . . . And this is the thing that Wilbur [Cohen] and I have had arguments about over the years: did you have to go as far as you went in just giving up on the ability to be a prudent buyer? I've always said you didn't have to give away so much. I said Johnson always wants to win 410 to 5, and you guys should have won this one 285 to 243 or whatever numbers."
126. Marmor, *Politics of Medicare*, 34–35.
127. Kooijman, *Incremental Strategy*, 156.
128. U.S. House of Representatives, Committee on Ways and Means, *Medical Care for the Aged: Executive Hearings*, 89th Cong., 1st session, on H.R. 1, and Other Proposals, January 27, 1965, 60–67, 135–137, 200–205, 215–216.
129. Committee on Ways and Means, *Medical Care for the Aged*, 163.
130. Ways and Means, *Medical Care for the Aged*, 216.
131. Lawrence D. Brown, "Capture and Culture: Organizational Identity in New York *Blue Cross*," *Journal of Health Politics, Policy and Law* 16, 4 (1991): 654.
132. Committee on Ways and Means, *Medical Care for the Aged*, part 2, 491. Ultimately a number of state governments chose Blue/Cross and Blue Shield to serve as the fiscal intermediaries to run their Medicaid programs as well. This was not something that was present in the Medicaid statute, which required that states "provide such methods of administration . . . as are found by the Secretary to be necessary for the proper and efficient operation of the plan" (cited in Law, *Blue Cross*, 46). But Blue Cross/Shield plans lobbied states for a role in administering the program, and by 1968, they were involved in 23 states. There were no real federal standards on how this should be done, nor much supervision (Law, *Blue Cross*, 46–47).
133. Hollander and Smith, "Framework of Medicare Administration," 5.
134. Quoted in Somers and Somers, *Medicare and the Hospitals*, 41.
135. Payton, "Third Party Governance," 113.
136. Payton, "Third Party Governance," 119.
137. Matthew A. Crenson and Francis E. Rourke, "By Way of Conclusion: American Bureaucracy since World War II," in *The New American State: Bureaucracies and Policies since World War II*, ed. Louis Galambos (Baltimore: Johns Hopkins University Press, 1987), 159.

Chapter 4

1. Christopher Howard, *The Welfare State Nobody Knows: Debunking Myths About US Social Policy* (Princeton: Princeton University Press 2007).
2. Jeffrey R. Henig, "Privatization in the United States: Theory and Practice," *Political Science Quarterly* 104, 4 (1989–90): 649–670.
3. David Vogel, *Fluctuating Fortunes: The Political Power of Business in America* (New York: Basic Books, 1989).
4. David O. Sears and Jack Citrin, *Tax Revolt: Something for Nothing in California* (Cambridge, MA: Harvard University, 1982); Martin Gilens, *Why Americans Hate Welfare: Race, Media, and the Politics of Antipoverty Policy* (Chicago: University of Chicago Press, 1999).
5. Larry Bartels, *Unequal Democracy: The Political Economy of the New Gilded Age* (Princeton: Princeton University Press, 2007).
6. Nolan McCarty, Keith Poole, and Howard Rosenthal, *Polarized America: The Dance of Ideology and Unequal Riches* (Cambridge, MA: MIT Press, 2006).
7. John W. Kingdon, *Agendas, Alternatives, and Public Policies*. 2nd ed. (New York: Longman, 1995).

8. Kimberly J. Morgan, "Constricting the Welfare State: Tax Policy and the Political Movement against Government," in *Remaking America: Democracy and Public Policy in an Age of Inequality*, eds. Joe Soss, Suzanne Mettler, and Jacob Hacker (New York: Russell Sage, 2007), 27–50.

9. Henig, "Privatization."

10. Paul Pierson, *Dismantling the Welfare State? Reagan, Thatcher, and the Politics of Retrenchment* (Cambridge: Cambridge University Press, 1994); Steven M. Teles and Martha Derthick, "Social Security from 1980 to the Present: From Third Rail to Presidential Commitment—and Back?" in *Conservatism and American Political Development*, eds. Brian J. Glenn and Steven M. Teles (New York: Oxford University Press 2009), 261–290.

11. Michael E. Schiltz, *Public Attitudes Toward Social Security 1935–1965*, Research report no. 33 (Social Security Administration, 1970), 36.

12. Jennifer Baggette, Robert Y. Shapiro, and Lawrence R. Jacobs, "Poll Trends: Social Security—An Update," *Public Opinion Quarterly* 59 (Fall 1995): 420–442.

13. 74 percent in 2001; Greg M. Shaw and Sarah E. Mysiewicz, "The Polls—Trends: Social Security and Medicare," *Public Opinion Quarterly* 68, 3 (Fall 2004): 406–406.

14. Shaw and Mysiewicz, "Social Security and Medicare," 415–416.

15. Programs for "the poor" are typically more popular in surveys than "welfare" programs. Greg M. Shaw and Robert Y. Shapiro, "Trends: Poverty and Public Assistance," *Public Opinion Quarterly* 66 (2002): 105–128; Fay Lomax Cook and Edith J. Barrett, *Support for the American Welfare State: Views of Congress and the Public* (New York: Columbia University Press 1992).

16. Virginia P. Reno and Joni Lavery, "Economic Crisis Fuels Support for Social Security: Americans' Views on Social Security," (Washington, DC: National Academy of Social Insurance, August 2009), 6.

17. Reno and Lavery, "Support for Social Security," 15.

18. Teles and Derthick, "Social Security from 1980."

19. Karlyn Bowman, "Attitudes toward the Federal Government," *AEI Public Opinion Study* (June 2008), 28.

20. Bowman, "Attitudes," 10.

21. Karlyn Bowman and Adam Foster, "Taking Stock of Business," *AEI Public Opinion Study* (April 6, 2009), 11.

22. Bowman and Foster, "Taking Stock," 6. In decreasing order by "a great deal of confidence," the institutions ranked: the military (45 percent), small business (28), the police (28), the church or organized religion (26), the medical system (16), public schools (16), U.S. Supreme Court (13), the presidency (13), banks (11), television news (11), newspapers (10), organized labor (10), criminal justice system (8), big business (7), HMOs (6), Congress (6).

23. Bowman and Foster, "Taking Stock," 4.

24. Bowman and Foster, "Taking Stock," 17.

25. Bowman and Foster, "Taking Stock," 35–36.

26. David Mechanic, "The Rise and Fall of Managed Care," *Journal of Health and Social Behavior* 45 (2004): 76–86; Robert J. Blendon, Mollyann Brodie, John M. Benson, Drew E. Altman, Larry Levitt, Tina Hoff, and Larry Hugick, "Understanding the Managed Care Backlash," *Health Affairs* 17 (1998): 80–94.

27. Anonymous, "United States: Managed Retreat," *Economist* 353, 8145 (November 13, 1999): 32.

28. Robert J. Blendon and John M. Benson, "Americans' Views on Health Policy: A Fifty-Year Historical Perspective," *Health Affairs* 20, 2 (2001): 33–46.

29. Kaiser/Harvard School of Public Health Survey, June 20–July 9, 1996. Accessed November 14, 2010, from the iPoll database at the Roper Center at the University of Connecticut, item number USPSRA.073096.R15.

30. Andrea Louise Campbell and Ryan King, "Social Security: Political Resilience in the Face of Conservative Strides," in *The New Politics of Old-Age Policy,* 2nd ed., ed. Robert Hudson (Baltimore: Johns Hopkins University Press, 1989).

31. Howard, *Hidden Welfare State.*
32. Stuart M. Butler, "Changing the Political Dynamics of Government," *Proceedings of the Academy of Political Science* 36, 3 (1987): 4–13; Henig, "Privatization."
33. Stephen Moore, "Contracting Out: A Painless Alternative to the Budget Cutter's Knife," *Proceedings of the Academy of Political Science* 36, 3 (1987): 60.
34. Teles and Derthick, "Social Security from 1980."
35. Stuart M. Butler, *Why Conservatives Need a National Health Plan,* Heritage Lecture #442 (Washington, DC: Heritage, March 22, 1993).
36. "Speaker of the House Newt Gingrich (R-GA) Remarks to Blue Cross/Blue Shield Conference," Federal News Service, October 24, 1995.
37. Peter F. Drucker, "The Sickness of Government," *Public Interest* 14 (Winter 1969): 22.
38. See also Robert A. Levine, "Rethinking Our Social Strategies," *Public Interest* 10 (Winter 1968): 86–96.
39. Frederick C. Mosher, "The Changing Responsibilities and Tactics of the Federal Government," *Public Administration Review* 40, 6 (November/December 1980): 541–548.
40. Paul Terrell, "Private Alternatives to Public Human Services Administration," *Social Services Review* 53 (March 1979): 56–74; Mosher, "Changing Responsibilities and Tactics"; Ira Sharkansky, "Policy Making and Service Delivery on the Margins of Government: The Case of Contractors," *Public Administration Review* 40 (March/April 1980): 116–123; Lester M. Salamon, "Rethinking Public Management: Third-Party Government and the Changing Forms of Government Action," *Public Policy* 29, 3 (Summer 1981): 255–275.
41. Vogel, *Fluctuating Fortunes.*
42. Drucker, "Sickness of Government," 20.
43. Jon F. Hale, "The Making of the New Democrats," *Political Science Quarterly* 110, 2 (Summer 1995): 207–232; Stephen K. Medvic, "Old Democrats in New Clothing? An Ideological Analysis of a Democratic Party Faction," *Party Politics* 13, 5 (2007): 587–609.
44. Hale, "New Democrats," 208, 222.
45. David Osborne and Ted Gaebler, *Reinventing Government: How the Entrepreneurial Spirit is Transforming the Public Sector* (New York: Penguin Press, 1992).
46. Medvic, "Old Democrats in New Clothing."
47. Kenneth J. Arrow, "Uncertainty and the Welfare Economics of Medical Care," *American Economic Review* 53, 5 (December 1963): 951.
48. Evan M. Melhado, "Competition versus Regulation in American Health Policy," in *Money, Power, and Health Care,* eds. Melhado, Walter Feinberg, and Harold M. Swartz (Ann Arbor, MI: Health Administration Press, 1988), 15–102.
49. Starr, *Social Transformation.*
50. Clark C. Havighurst, "The Changing Locus of Decision Making in the Health Care Sector," *Journal of Health Politics, Policy and Law* 11, 4 (1986): 697–735.
51. Mark V. Pauly, "Is Medical Care Different?" in *Competition in the Health Care Sector,* ed. Warren Greenberg (Germantown, MD: Aspen Systems Corporation), 11–42; Clark C. Havighurst, "Decentralizing Decision Making: Private Contract versus Professional Norms," in *Market Reforms in Health Care: Current Issues, New Directions, Strategic Decisions,* ed. Jack A. Meyer (Washington, DC: American Enterprise Institute Press, 1983), 34–45.
52. Theodore R. Marmor, Richard Boyer, and Julie Greenberg, "Medicare Care and Procompetitive Reform," in *Political Analysis and American Medicare Care,* ed. Marmor (Cambridge: Cambridge University Press, 1983), 239–261; Melhado, "Competition versus Regulation."
53. Martin Feldstein, "A New Approach to National Health Insurance," *Public Interest* 23 (Spring 1971): 93–105; Pauly, "Is Medical Care Different?."
54. Feldstein, "New Approach."
55. Jacob S. Hacker, *The Road to Nowhere: The Genesis of President Clinton's Plan for Health Security* (Princeton: Princeton University Press, 1997), 45.
56. Alain C. Enthoven, *Health Plan: The Only Practical Solution to the Soaring Cost of Medical Care* (Reading, MA: Addison-Wesley Publishing, 1980); Hacker, *Road to Nowhere,* 47–49.

57. I. S. Falk, "Medical Care in the USA: 1932–1972; Problems, Prospects, and Programs from the Committee on the Costs of Medical Care to the Committee for National Health Insurance," *Milbank Memorial Fund Quarterly* 51, 1 (Winter 1973): 23.

58. James C. Robinson, "The Politics of Managed Competition: Public Abuse of the Private Interest," *Journal of Health Politics, Policy and Law* 28, 2–3 (April–June 2003): 341–353.

59. Enthoven, *Health Plan*, chap. 6; William J. Baumol, "Containing Medical Costs: Why Price Controls Won't Work," *Public Interest* 93 (Fall 1988): 37–53.

60. Harry P. Cain, II, "Moving Medicare to the FEHBP Model, Or How to Make an Elephant Fly," *Health Affairs* 18, 4 (July/August 1999): 25–39.

61. Mancur Olson, "Introduction," *A New Approach to the Economics of Health Care*, ed. Olson (Washington, DC: American Enterprise Institute Press, 1981).

62. Enthoven, *Health Plan*; McClure 1981, 122–125.

63. Enthoven, *Health Plan*, 95.

64. Enthoven, *Health Plan*, 112.

65. Havighurst, "Changing Locus."

66. Havighurst, "Changing Locus," 723.

67. James A. Morone, "American Political Culture and the Search for Lessons from Abroad." *Journal of Health Politics, Policy and Law* 15, 1 (Spring 1990): 129–143.

68. Arrow, "Welfare Economics of Medical Care," 965.

69. Mark Schlesinger, Theodore R. Marmor, and Richard Smithey, "Nonprofit and For-Profit Medicare Care: Shifting Roles and Implications for Health Policy," *Journal of Health Politics, Policy and Law* 12, 3 (Fall 1987): 434.

70. Schlesinger, Marmor and Smithey, "Nonprofit and For-Profit."

71. Carolyn Hughes Tuohy, *Accidental Logics: The Dynamics of Change in the Health Care Arena in the United States, Britain, and Canada* (New York: Oxford University Press, 1999).

72. Harvey M. Sapolsky, "Empire and the Business of Health Insurance," *Journal of Health Politics, Policy and Law* 16, 4 (1991): 747–760; Starr, *Social Transformation*.

73. Lawrence D. Brown, *Politics and Health Care Organization: HMOs as Federal Policy* (Washington, DC: Brookings Institution, 1983), 35–41.

74. Bradford H. Gray, "The Rise and Decline of the HMO: A Chapter in U.S. Health-Policy History," in *History and Health Policy in the United States: Putting the Past Back In*, eds. Rosemary A. Stevens, Charles E. Rosenberg, and Lawton R. Burns (New Brunswick, NJ: Rutgers University Press, 2006), 313–316.

75. Rick Mayes and Robert A. Berenson, *Medicare Prospective Payment and the Shaping of U.S. Health Care* (Baltimore: Johns Hopkins University Press, 2006).

76. Beth Fuchs, Bob Lyke, Jennifer O'Sullivan, and Richard Price, *Medicare: The Restructuring Debate in the 104th Congress* (Washington, DC: Congressional Research Service, 1997), 3.

77. For an overview see Robert H. Miller and Harold S. Luft, "HMO Plan Performance Update: An Analysis of the Literature, 1997–2001," *Health Affairs* 21, 4 (2002): 63–86.

78. Baumol, "Containing Medical Costs."

79. Harry P. Cain, II. "Privatizing Medicare: A Battle of Values," *Health Affairs* 16, 2 (March/April 1997): 182.

80. Paul B. Ginsburg, "Medicare Vouchers and the Procompetition Strategy," *Health Affairs* 1, 1 (Winter 1981): 39–52; Glenn R Markus, *Health Insurance: The Medicare Voucher Proposals*, (Washington, DC: Congressional Research Service, 1983).

81. Stuart M. Butler and Robert E. Moffitt, "The FEHBP as a Model for a New Medicare Program," *Health Affairs* 14, 4 (Winter 1995): 47–61.

82. Hacker, *Divided Welfare State*, 242–243.

83. Butler and Moffitt, "The FEHBP as a Model for a New Medicare Program"; Cain, "Moving Medicare."

84. Henry J. Aaron and Robert D. Reischauer, "The Medicare Reform Debate: What Is the Next Step?" *Health Affairs* 14, 4 (Winter 1995). Payments to beneficiaries would be adjusted for things such as risk factors, income, and geographic location.

85. Butler and Moffitt, "FEHBP as a Model."

86. Scott Wenger, "IRAs Are Seen as Model for Health Care: Accounts Are Proposed for Funding Medical Costs," *Wall Street Journal,* October 23, 1992, A5.

87. Peter Ferrera, *How to Avert the Medicare Crisis* (Washington DC: Heritage Foundation, 1984); John Goodman and Richard W. Rahn, "Salvaging Medicare With an IRA," *Wall Street Journal,* March 20, 1984.

88. Wenger, "IRAs Are Seen as Model."

89. Posner, "National Health Insurance Plans."

90. Butler and Moffitt, "FEHBP as a Model," 52.

91. See Joe Soss, Richard C. Fording, and Sanford F. Schram, *Disciplining the Poor: Neoliberal Paternalism and the Persistent Power of Race* (forthcoming, University of Chicago Press).

92. Henig, "Privatization."

93. Paul I. Posner, *The Politics of Unfunded Mandates: Whither Federalism?* (Washington, DC: Georgetown University Press, 1998), 2.

94. Henig, "Privatization," 658.

95. Colleen M. Grogan, "The Medicaid Managed Care Policy Consensus for Welfare Recipients: A Reflection of Traditional Welfare Concerns," *Journal of Health Politics, Policy and Law* 22, 3 (June 1997): 817–818.

96. Elicia J. Herz, *Medicaid Managed Care: An Overview and Key Issues for Congress* (Congressional Research Report, October 26, 2006).

97. Mark Duggan, "Does Contracting Out Increase the Efficiency of Government Programs? Evidence from Medicaid HMOs," *Journal of Public Economics,* 88, 2 (December 2004): 2549–2572.

98. Gillian E. Metzger, "Privatization as Delegation," *Columbia Law Review* 103 (2003): 1381–1382.

99. Mechanic, "Rise and Fall"; Blendon et al. 1998.

100. Kaiser Family Foundation, *Medicaid and Managed Care: Key Data, Trends, and Issues* (February 2010).

101. Grogan, "Medicaid Managed Care Policy."

102. Federal regulations stipulate that as long as a state provides at least two choices, it can mandate managed care enrollment.

103. Henry Freedman, Mary R. Mannix, Marc Cohan, and Rebecca Scharf, "Uncharted Terrain: The Intersection of Privatization and Welfare," 35 *Clearinghouse Review* 557 (January–February 2002).

104. Michele Estrin Gilman, "Legal Accountability in an Era of Privatized Welfare," *California Law Review* 89 (2001): 569–642.

105. Richard Fording, Sanford Schram, and Joe Soss, "Race and Discretion in the Implementation of Welfare Reform: An Analysis of Local Variation in TANF Sanctioning in Florida," Presented at the Annual Meeting of the Midwest Political Science Association, Chicago, IL (2005); Fording, Soss, and Schram, "Devolution, Discretion and the Impact of Local Political Values on TANF Sanctioning," *Social Services Review* 81, 2 (2007): 285–316.

106. Terry M. Moe, *Schools, Vouchers, and the American Public* (Washington, DC: Brookings Institution Press, 2001).

107. Teles and Derthick, "Social Security from 1980."

108. Campbell and Ryan, "Social Security."

109. Jonathan Oberlander, *The Political Life of Medicare* (Chicago: University of Chicago Press, 2003), 183.

110. Theodore R. Marmor, Donald A. Wittman, and Thomas C. Heagy, "The Politics of Medical Inflation," *Journal of Health Politics, Policy and Law* 1, 1 (1976): 69–84.

111. Mayes and Berenson, *Medicare Prospective Payment,* 19; Kaiser Family Foundation, "Health Care Spending in the United States and OECD Countries," Exhibit 5. Available: http://www.kff.org/insurance/snapshot/chcm010307oth.cfm.

112. Lawrence D. Brown, "Technocratic Corporatism and Administrative Reform in Medicare," *Journal of Health Politics, Policy and Law* 10, 3 (1985): 587.

113. Brown, "Technocratic Corporatism."

114. HMOs had been allowed to contract with Medicare since the program's inception, but due to provider opposition, they could only be paid through Fee-for-Service reimbursements. The 1972 law allowed them to be paid on a capitated basis, but only older HMOs were allowed to do this, and they were still subject to retrospective payments adjustments so as to limit their profits, but not their losses. Given these barriers, few HMOs participated in the program. Jonathan Oberlander "Managed Care and Medicare Reform," *Journal of Health Politics, Policy and Law* 22, 2 (1997): 597–598.

115. Brown, *Health Care Organization*.

116. David A. Stockman, "Premises for a Medical Marketplace: A Neoconservative's Vision of How to Transform the Health System," *Health Affairs* 1, 1 (Winter 1981): 5–18.

117. Richard A. Gephardt, "Do We Need Competition Legislation? The View of an Advocate," *Health Affairs* 1, 2 (Spring 1982): 53–68.

118. Ginsburg, "Medicare Vouchers"; Markus, *Medicare Voucher Proposals*; Thomas R. Oliver, "Health Care Market Reform in Congress: The Uncertain Path from Proposal to Policy," *Political Science Quarterly* 106 (1991): 453–477.

119. Payments were set at 95 percent of the estimated adjusted average per capita cost (AAPCC) of providing Medicare under the fee-for-service system. The AAPCC differs by county and certain demographic characteristics.

120. Richard Himelfarb, *Catastrophic Politics: The Rise and Fall of the Medicare Catastrophic Coverage Act of 1988* (University Park: Pennsylvania State University Press, 1995).

121. Uwe E. Reinhardt, "The Clinton Plan: A Salute to American Pluralism," *Health Affairs* 13, 1 (Spring 1994): 162.

122. Oliver, "Health Care Market Reform"; Oberlander *Political Life*, 122–125; Mayes and Berenson, *Medicare Prospective Payment*.

123. R. Douglas Arnold, "The Politics of Reforming Social Security," *Political Science Quarterly* 113, 2 (Summer 1998): 213–240.

124. Margaret H. Davis and Sally T. Burner, "Three Decades of Medicare: What the Numbers Tell Us," *Health Affairs* 14, 4 (Winter 1995): 234.

125. Theda Skocpol, Boomerang: Clinton's Health Security Effort and the Turn against Government in U.S. Politics (New York: W. W. Norton, 1995); Paul Starr, "What Happened to Health Care Reform?" *The American Prospect* 20 (Winter 1995): 20–31; James A. Morone, "Nativism, Hollow Corporations, and Managed Competition: Why the Clinton Health Care Reform Failed," *Journal of Health Politics, Policy and Law* 20, 2 (Summer 1995): 391–398; Mark A. Peterson, "The Health Care Debate: All Heat and No Light," *Journal of Health Politics, Policy and Law* 20, 2 (Summer 1995): 425–430; Sven Steinmo and Jon Watts, "It's the Institutions, Stupid! Why Comprehensive National Health Insurance Always Fails in America," *Journal of Health Politics, Policy and Law* 20, 2 (1995): 329–372; Hacker, *Road to Nowhere*; Marie Gottschalk, *The Shadow Welfare State: Labor, Business and the Politics of Health Care in the United States* (Ithaca, NY: Cornell University Press, 2000).

126. Skocpol, *Boomerang*.

127. Hacker, *Road to Nowhere*.

128. Lawrence D. Brown and Theodore R. Marmor, "The Clinton Reform Plan's Administrative Structure: The Reach and the Grasp," *Journal of Health Politics, Policy and Law* 19, 1 (Spring 1994): 193–199; James A. Morone, "The Administration of Health Care Reform," *Journal of Health Politics, Policy and Law* 19, 1 (Spring 1994): 233–237.

129. Brown and Marmor, "Clinton Reform Plan."

130. Morone, "Administration of Health Care Reform."

131. Thomas H. Stanton, "The Administration of Medicare: A Neglected Issue," *Washington & Lee Law Review* 60 (Fall 2003).

132. Cited in Skocpol, *Boomerang*, 75.

133. Raymond L. Goldsteen, Karen Goldsteen, James H. Swan, and Wendy Clemeña, "Harry and Louise and Health Care Reform: Romancing Public Opinion," *Journal of Health Politics, Policy and Law* 26, 6 (2001): 1325–1352.

134. Jacobs, *Health of Nations*.

135. Robert J. Blendon, Mollyann Brodie, and John Benson, "What Happened to Americans' Support for the Clinton Health Plan," *Health Affairs* 14, 2 (Summer 1995): 13. The trust in government question asks about "how much of the time you can trust the government in Washington to do the right thing." The response of 77 percent is only some of the time or never, while 23 percent believe it is "just about most of the time."

136. The original House GOP proposal for Medicaid entirely eliminated the federal entitlement to the program, but after Senate opposition, an entitlement was maintained for pregnant women, children under the age of 13, and the disabled.

137. Smith, *Entitlement Politics*, 93–94.

138. Smith, *Entitlement Politics*, 101–102.

139. Robert J. Blendon and John M. Benson, "Americans' Views on Health Policy: A Fifty-Year Historical Perspective," *Health Affairs* 20, 2 (2001): 40.

140. Sarah A. Binder, "The Disappearing Political Center: Congress and the Incredible Shrinking Middle," *The Brookings Review* 14, 4 (Fall 1996): 36–39.

141. Morris P. Fiorina, *Culture War? The Myth of a Polarized America* (New York: Pearson Longman, 2005).

142. Oberlander, *Political Life*.

143. National Journal's *CongressDaily* June 28, 1995, reporting on recent interview with Gingrich in *Atlanta Journal and Constitution*. See also Smith 2002, 71–72.

144. Linda Killian, *The Freshmen: What Happened to the Republican Revolution?* (Boulder, CO: Westview Press, 1998).

145. Laurie McGinley, "Gingrich's Many Parleys, Long Days on Medicare Link His Political Health to an 'Explosive Issue,'" *Wall Street Journal*, June 29, 1995, A18.

146. Smith *Entitlement Politics*, 128.

147. Killian, *The Freshmen*.

148. Butler, "Changing the Political Dynamics."

149. Laurie McGinley, "GOP Overhaul Of Medicare Could Be a Windfall for Insurance Firms Because of Voucher System," *Wall Street Journal*, August 4, 1995, A10.

150. Smith *Entitlement Politics*, 79.

151. Thomas Rosenstiel and Bill Turque, "Buying Off the Elderly," *Newsweek* 126, 14 (October 2, 1995); Bara Vaida, "AARP's Big Bet," *National Journal* 36, 11 (March 13, 2004): 796–802.

152. Smith, *Entitlement Politics*, 175.

153. Oberlander, *Political Life*, 182–183.

154. Eric Weissenstein, "Survey Casts Doubt on Medicare Fix," *Modern Healthcare* 28, 43 (October 26, 1998): 16–18.

155. Matthew Miller, "Premium Idea: A Medicare Fix that Can Really Work," *New Republic* 220, 15 (April 12, 1999): 24–27.

156. Bruce C. Vladeck, "Plenty of Nothing: A Report from the Medicare Commission," *New England Journal of Medicine* 340, 19 (May 13, 1999): 1503–1506.

157. Smith, *Entitlement Politics*, 73.

Chapter 5

1. Christopher Howard, *The Welfare State Nobody Knows: Debunking Myths About US Social Policy* (Princeton: Princeton University Press, 2007).

2. People dually eligible for Medicare and Medicaid receive a full subsidy of their premiums, as do people with incomes below 135 percent of the poverty level and assets that do not exceed $6,000 for single people ($9,000 for a couple) (as of 2006; the amount is indexed to the CPI). People with incomes below 150 percent of the poverty line and assets below $10,000 for a single person ($20,000 for a couple) also could get a premium subsidy according to a sliding scale. Dual eligibles and people with incomes/assets below certain thresholds also receive subsidies for deductibles, co-payments, and out-of-pocket costs in the doughnut hole.

3. Kaiser Family Foundation, *Low-Income Assistance under the Medicare Drug Benefit* (December 2009).

4. MedPAC, *Report to Congress: Medicare Payment Policy* (March 2009).

5. MedPAC, *Report to Congress,* 252.

6. In MSAs, only employees of small businesses or the self-employed could enroll. HSAs are open to all who purchase a high deductible health insurance plan ($1,000 for individual coverage and at least $2,000 in family coverage).

7. Kaiser Family Foundation, *The Coverage Gap,* November 2009.

8. US Federal News Service, "Medicare Part B Premiums to Increase in 2008," October 1, 2007.

9. http://www.ssa.gov/pubs/10161.html#premium. In 2010 the standard monthly premium was actually $110.50, but because Social Security checks contained no cost-of-living adjustment for 2010 due to low inflation, and the Social Security Act prevents pension benefits from decreasing due to an increase in Part B premiums, those seniors who have their Part B premiums deducted from their Social Security checks continued to pay the 2009 premium of $96.40. See www.medicare.gov/Publications/Pubs/pdf/11444.pdf.

10. Timothy Stoltzfus Jost, "The Most Important Health Care Legislation of the Millennium (So Far): The Medicare Modernization Act," *Yale Journal of Health Policy, Law & Ethics* 437, 5 (2005): 445–446.

11. Sarah A. Binder, "The Disappearing Political Center: Congress and the Incredible Shrinking Middle," *The Brookings Review* 14, 4 (Fall 1996): 36–39.

12. Jeffrey M. Stonecash, *Class and Party in American Politics* (Boulder, CO: Westview Press, 2000); Larry Bartels, *Unequal Democracy: The Political Economy of the New Gilded Age* (Princeton: Princeton University Press, 2007).

13. Jeffrey M. Stonecash and Andrew E. Milstein, "Parties and Taxes: The Emergence of Distributive Divisions, 1950–2000," paper presented at the Midwest Political Science Association Conference (Chicago, IL: April 27–30, 2000); Jacob S. Hacker and Paul Pierson, *Off Center: The Republican Revolution and the Erosion of American Democracy* (New Haven: Yale University Press, 2005).

14. Nolan McCarty, Keith Poole, and Howard Rosenthal, *Polarized America: The Dance of Ideology and Unequal Riches* (Cambridge, MA: MIT Press, 2006).

15. Sarah A. Binder, "The Dynamics of Legislative Gridlock, 1947–96," *The American Political Science Review* 93, 3 (September 1999): 519–533.

16. Nicol C. Rae, "Be Careful What You Wish For: The Rise of Responsible Parties in American National Politics," *Annual Review of Political Science* 10 (2007): 169–191.

17. John H. Aldrich and David W. Rohde, "The Logic of Conditional Party Government: Revisiting the Electoral Connection," in *Congress Reconsidered,* 7th ed., eds. Lawrence C. Dodd and Bruce I. Oppenheimer (Washington, DC: CQ Books, 2000), 269–292.

18. David W. Rohde, *Parties and Leaders in the Postreform House* (Chicago: University of Chicago Press, 1991); Barbara Sinclair, *Legislators, Leaders, and Lawmaking: The U.S. House of Representatives in the Postreform Era* (Baltimore: Johns Hopkins University Press, 1995).

19. As Teles and Derthick point out, the polarized context made it more difficult to pass something more threatening like Social Security privatization, which needed greater bipartisan support. Steven M. Teles and Martha Derthick, "Social Security from 1980 to the Present: From Third Rail to Presidential Commitment—and Back?" in *Conservatism and American Political Development,* eds. Brian J. Glenn and Steven M. Teles (New York: Oxford University Press, 2009), 261–290.

20. Jonathan Oberlander, *The Political Life of Medicare* (Chicago: University of Chicago Press, 2003).

21. Bruce C. Vladeck, "Democrats and the Struggle over Medicare," *Dissent* 51, 3 (Summer 2004): 67.

22. Marmor, *Politics of Medicare,* 175–176.

23. David G. Smith, Entitlement Politics: Medicare and Medicaid 1995–2001 (New York: Aldine de Gruyter, 2002).

24. Oberlander, *Political Life*; Bruce C. Vladeck, "The Struggle for the Soul of Medicare," *Journal of Law, Medicine and Ethics* (Fall 2004): 410–415.

25. Smith, *Entitlement Politics*; Mark A. Peterson, "The Politics of Health Care Policy: Overreaching in an Age of Polarization," in *The Social Divide: Political Parties and the Future of Activist*

Government, ed. Margaret Weir (Washington, DC: Brookings Institution Press/Russell Sage Foundation, 1998), 203.

26. Mary A. Laschober, et al., "Trends in Medicare Supplemental Insurance and Prescription Drug Coverage, 1996–1999," *Health Affairs,* Web Exclusive (February 27, 2002): W127–W138.

27. Robert Pear and Robin Toner, "Despite High Hopes, Drug Plan May Be Disappointing to Elderly," *New York Times,* July 22, 2001, A1.

28. Robert Pear, "Clinton's Plan to Have Medicare Cover Drugs Means a Big Debate Ahead in Congress," *New York Times,* January 24, 1999, A24; Robin Toner, "The Nation: The Prescription Drug Debate; Why the Elderly Wait . . . and Wait," *New York Times,* June 23, 2002, D1.

29. M. B. Rosenthal, et al., *Demand Effects of Recent Changes in Prescription Drug Promotion.* Henry J. Kaiser Foundation, 2003.

30. General Accounting Office, *Prescription Drugs: Improvements Needed in FDA's Oversight of Direct-to-Consumer Advertising* (2006).

31. Milt Freudenheim, "Insurers Push Rates Higher for Medigap," *New York Times,* February 8, 2001, C1.

32. Kaiser Family Foundation, *Current Trends and Future Outlooks for Retiree Health Benefits: Findings from the Kaiser/Hewitt 2004 Survey on Retiree Health Benefits* (Kaiser Family Foundation, December 2004), v.

33. Robert Kuttner, "The American Health Care System: Health Insurance Coverage," *New England Journal of Medicine,* 340, 2 (January 14, 1999): 163–168.

34. Marsha Gold, "Medicare+Choice: An Interim Report Card," *Health Affairs* 20, 4 (2001): 120–138.

35. The 2010 health care reform again reduces those reimbursements to 95 percent in many areas; it remains to be seen whether this results in insurer exit from those markets.

36. Robert Pear, "Medicare H.M.O.'s to End Free Drugs, Report Says," *New York Times,* September 22, 1999, A22.

37. John W. Kingdon, *Agendas, Alternatives, and Public Policies.* 2nd ed. (New York: Longman, 1995).

38. The premiums would be $24 per month in the beginning, rising to $44 in a few years. The plan would pay for half the cost of prescription drugs, with the maximum federal payment rising from $1,000 per year initially to $2,500 when the program was fully implemented. Robert Pear, "Drug Benefits up to $2,500 are in Plan for Medicare," *New York Times,* June 29, 1999, A17.

39. The Clinton plan also contained features that became central to the policy debate for the next three years: the program would be voluntary (premiums were intentionally set low to maximize enrollment); would include all seniors rather than low-income or those without supplemental coverage; would use pharmacy benefit managers, private firms that government would hire to manage the new benefit; would not include full catastrophic coverage (the maximum federal payment would remain $2,500 no matter what the beneficiaries' total expenditures); contained no explicit price controls; introduced price competition among HMOs (but not traditional Medicare); and subsidized employers to continue retiree health benefits including drug coverage at least as generous as the proposed program. The poor (incomes under $17,000 for a couple) would have no out-of-pocket costs. Robert Pear, "Clinton Lays Out Plan to Overhaul Medicare System," *New York Times,* June 30, 1999, A1.

40. Robert Pear, "Budget Office Says Clinton Underestimated Cost of Drug Plan," *New York Times,* July 23, 1999, A17.

41. Note that when prescription drugs for seniors were first mentioned in responses to the surveys' open-ended questions, the responses were coded together with general Medicare, April 2000 to August 2000. But starting in August 2000, prescription drugs for seniors were coded as a separate issue. In neither case was concern over these issues greater than more long-standing issues like health care costs and general insurance costs/availability.

42. Robin Toner, "Drug Coverage Dominates Fight Brewing on Medicare," *New York Times,* June 16, 1999, A1.

43. Toner, "The 2000 Campaign: The Medicare Issue; Basic Differences in Rival Proposals on Drug Coverage," *New York Times*, October 1, 2000, A1.

44. Robert H. Binstock, "Older Voters and the 2004 Election," *The Gerontologist* 46, 3 (2006), 384.

45. Robin Toner, "Shift by Older Voters to G.O.P. Is Democrats' Challenge in 2000," *New York Times*, May 31, 1999, A1; Sue Kirchhoff, "Parties Tailor Hill Agendas to Win Seniors' Loyalty," *CQ Weekly Report*, September 18, 1999.

46. The Commission met between 1998 and 1999 and was unable to reach the required supermajority to agree on any one proposal for Medicare reform. A majority on the committee did support the premium support model of reform.

47. Dean Rosen, personal interview, Washington, DC, November 16, 2006.

48. Robert Pear, "Politically and Technically Complex, Medicare Defies a Sweeping Redesign," *New York Times*, March 18, 1999, A23.

49. Charles Cook, "Prescription Drugs Could Be Candidates' Cure," *National Journal*, April 11, 2000.

50. The data in figure 5.2 were obtained from the University of Wisconsin Advertising Project that includes media tracking data from TNSMI/Campaign Media Analysis Group in Washington, DC. The UW Advertising Project was sponsored by a grant from The Pew Charitable Trusts; opinions expressed in this book are those of the authors and do not necessarily reflect the views of the UW Advertising Project or The Pew Charitable Trust."

51. Mary Agnes Carey, "Prescription Drug Coverage Dragged Quickly into the Fray," *Congressional Quarterly Weekly Report*, February 26, 2000.

52. Thomas Scully, telephone interview, April 3, 2007.

53. Juliet Eilperin, "Insurance Man's Medicare Drug Plan Draws GOP Interest," *Washington Post*, February 18, 2000, A14. The Republican Leadership Coalition was a 527 political organization that sought to achieve private-sector solutions to social and economic problems. It appears now to be defunct, but during its existence it received large donations from the Golden Rule Insurance Company that promoted medical savings accounts.

54. Helen Dewar and Juliet Eilperin, "GOP Majority Is Poised for Action When Congress Returns," *Washington Post*, January 23, 2000, A4.

55. Adam Clymer, "The 2000 Campaign: Political Memo; G.O.P. Follows 'Script' on Prescription Drugs," *New York Times*, June 16, 2000, A28.

56. Shailagh Murray, "Bush Camp Shrugs Off Lack of Health Plan, But Some in GOP Worry as Gore Assault Grows," *Wall Street Journal*, May 16, 2000, A28.

57. Scully, telephone interview.

58. This was a remark made by many interviewees who were advocates of this approach.

59. Scully, telephone interview.

60. Smith, *Entitlement Politics*, 93–94.

61. Congressional Budget Office, *Issues in Designing a Prescription Drug Benefit for Medicare* (Washington, DC: 2002); Elizabeth J. Fowler, personal interview, Washington DC, October 25, 2006.

62. CBO, *Prescription Drug Benefit*, 26.

63. Fowler, personal interview.

64. Gardiner Harris, "Prescription for Gridlock: A Look at the Competing Players in the Medicare Drug Debates Shows Why It Will Be Hard to Get Legislation Passed," *Wall Street Journal*, February 21, 2001, R5.

65. Jill Wechsler, "The New 'War on Drugs'" *Pharmaceutical Executive* 20, 6 (June 1, 2000): 22–28.

66. Shailagh Murray and Lucette Lagnado, "Drug Companies Face Assault on Prices—Pressure Rises for Price Controls, But Pharmaceutical Firms Aren't Ready to Dial 911 Yet," *Wall Street Journal*, May 11, 2000, B1.

67. Tony Fong, "PBMs to the Rescue?" *Modern Healthcare* 35, 48 (November 28, 2005): 26–30.

68. Elyse Tanouye, "TV Ad against Medicare Drug Plan Puts Clinton and the Industry at Odds," *Wall Street Journal*, September 9, 1999, B6.

69. Elyse Tanouye, "Clinton Medicare Drug Plan Encourages Businesses to Drop Retirees, Group Says," *Wall Street Journal*, September 21, 1999, A4

70. Robert Pear, "Drug Makers Drop Their Opposition to Medicare Plan," *New York Times*, January 14, 2000, A1.

71. Wayne Koberstein, "The Inner Merck," *Pharmaceutical Executive* 20, 1 (January 2000).

72. Lucette Lagnado, Laurie McGinley, and Elyse Tanouye, "Dose of Reality: Idea of Having Medicare Pay for Elderly's Drugs Is Roiling the Industry," *Wall Street Journal*, February 19, 1999, A1; Howard Cohen, personal interview, Washington, DC, January 26, 2007; Ian Spatz, personal interview, Washington DC, February 2, 2007.

73. Aaron Zitner, "Leaders Meet over Senior Drug Benefit Plan," *The Boston Globe*, January 21, 2000, C2.

74. "House Republicans Return to A Shifting Landscape on Medicare Drug Coverage," *The White House Bulletin*, January 24, 2000.

75. Juliet Eilperin, "Division among Foes Could Aid Drug Plan for Elderly," *Washington Post*, February 17, 2000, A04; Jim VandeHei and Shailagh Murray, "GOP Feels Ill Side Effects from Prescription-Drug Issue," *Wall Street Journal*, September 8, 2000, A20.

76. Juliet Eilperin, "Division among Foes Could Aid Drug Plan for Elderly," *Washington Post*, February 17, 2000, A4.

77. "House Republicans Return to a Shifting Landscape on Medicare Drug Coverage," *The White House Bulletin*, January 24, 2000.

78. Bob Cusack, "Norwood Drug Plan Gathers Momentum," *The Hill*, May 21, 2003, 23.

79. Jim VandeHei and Shailagh Murray, "GOP Feels Ill Side Effects From Prescription-Drug Issue," *Wall Street Journal*, September 8, 2000, A20.

80. Tom Hamburger, "Drug Industry Raises Spending for Ads, Lobbyists to Fight Critics," *Wall Street Journal*, September 22, 2000, A24.

81. Jim VandeHei and Tom Hamburger, "Drug Firms Underwrite U.S. Chamber's TV Ads," *Wall Street Journal*, October 6, 2000, A24.

82. Tom Hamburger and Laurie McGinley, "Drug Lobby Wins Big with Massive Spending against Medicare Plan," *Wall Street Journal*, November 9, 2000, B1.

83. Thomas B. Edsall, "High Drug Prices Return as Issue That Stirs Voters; New Challenges for a Lobby Used to Spending—and Winning," *Washington Post*, October 15, 2002, A8.

84. See http://www.opensecrets.org/lobbyists/index.asp?txtindextype=i.

85. Steven H. Landers and Ashwini R. Sehgal, "Health Care Lobbying in the United States," *The American Journal of Medicine* 116 (2004): 474–477.

86. Spatz, personal interview; Shailagh Murray, "Merck Plays Role In GOP Proposal On Drug Benefits," *Wall Street Journal*, June 30, 2000, A2.

87. Murray, "Merck Plays Role."

88. Mary Agnes Carey, "Parties Fighting Toward a Standoff over Prescription Drug Benefits," *Congressional Quarterly Weekly Report*, June 24, 2000.

89. Spatz, personal interview.

90. Mary Agnes Carey, "Insurers' Queasiness about Costs Helped Sink GOP Prescription Drug Bill," *Congressional Quarterly Weekly Report*, October 28, 2000.

91. Robert Pear, "House Republicans to Draft Bill on Medicare Prescription Drugs," January 27, 2000, A18.

92. Robert Pear, "Drug Makers and Insurers Lock Horns over Medicare," *New York Times*, February 21, 2000, A10.

93. Rebecca Adams, "House GOP Proposal on Seniors' Drug Coverage Taking Shape," *CQ Monitor*, March 22, 2000.

94. Gardiner Harris, "Prescription for Gridlock: A Look at the Competing Players in the Medicare Drug Debates Shows Why It Will Be Hard to Get Legislation Passed," *Wall Street Journal*, February 21, 2001, R5.

95. Mary Agnes Carey, "Complex Drug Bill May Prove More Difficult for GOP to Sell," *CQ Weekly Report*, June 22, 2002.

96. Michael Waldholz, Laurie McGinley, and David Rogers, "Bill Advances in Congress—Benefits Managers, Insurers Are Leery on Profitability; Drug Makers Applaud Plan," *Wall Street Journal*, June 27, 2003, A3.

97. Robert Pear, "Drug Makers Drop Their Opposition to Medicare Plan," *New York Times*, January 14, 2000, A1.

98. That being said, even if Bush administration policy suggestions were often neither appreciated nor heeded by Republicans on the Hill, the administration's support for the legislation was very important in keeping it alive and holding Congressional Republicans together around it. For a good telling of the White House perspective on the bill, see David Blumenthal and James A. Morone, *The Heart of Power: Health and Politics in the Oval Office* (Berkeley: University of California Press, 2009), chap. 11.

99. A budget point of order can be raised in either the House or Senate against any measure that exceeds the terms of that year's budget resolution setting revenues and spending targets. In the Senate, a point of order can only be waived with 60 votes, whereas in the House it requires only a simple majority.

100. Robert Pear, "G.O.P. Drug Coverage Plan Is to Include Private Insurers," *New York Times*, April 12, 2000, A24.

101. The measure would charge seniors monthly premiums on a sliding scale and cover half their drug costs up to $5,000. Beneficiaries would then pay all of the next $1,500 out of pocket, after which the government would pay all additional costs. Sheryl Gay Stolberg, "The 2000 Campaign: The Medicare Issue; No Simple Answers to Rising Cost of Drugs for the Elderly," *New York Times*, September 3, 2000, A26.

102. Mike Allen, "Gore Vows to Reduce Seniors' Drug Costs," *Washington Post*, August 29, 2000, A1.

103. The government would pay the entire cost for low-income elderly while subsidizing costs for the near-poor. Out-of-pocket health care spending would be capped at $6,000 per year. Alison Mitchell, "The 2000 Campaign: The Texas Governor; Bush Spells out Major Overhaul in Medicare Plan," *New York Times*, September 6, 2000, A1.

104. Mary Agnes Carey, "Drug Plan's Low-Key Launch Signals Bush May Be Open to Deal," *CQ Weekly Report*, February 3, 2001, 281.

105. Cohen, personal interview.

106. Robert Pear, "Panel Won't Take Up Bush's Medicare Plan," *New York Times*, February 15, 2001, A24.

107. Mary Agnes Carey, "Medicare Prescription Drug Debate Likely to Play Key Role in Campaigns," *CQ Weekly Report*, April 27, 2002, 1076.

108. Robin Toner, "Party Battles Looming over Costly Old Issue: Health Care Coverage," *New York Times*, January 11, 2002, A16.

109. Samuel Goldreich, "GOP Medicare Bill Near Completion as Groups Sign Off," *CQ Monitor*, May 31, 2002. Notably, higher subsidies to providers were contrary to the initial aims of the House Ways and Means Chairman Bill Thomas, who originally had cuts in provider payments as a way to save money in the bill, as well as creating a co-payment for use of Medicare home health services. Thomas faced a "quiet rebellion" by some members of Congress anxious about voting for provider payment cuts in an election year. Robert Pear, "House Republican Plan Would Increase Medicare Payments to Providers," *New York Times*, June 5, 2002, A18.

110. Samuel Goldreich, "House Passes GOP-backed Medicare Prescription Drug Bill," *CQ Today*, June 28, 2002.

111. Amy Goldstein and Juliet Eilperin, "House Backs GOP Drug Plan for Seniors," *Washington Post*, June 29, 2002, A1.

112. Mary Agnes Carey, "Senate Vote on Medicare Drugs Yields More Blame but No Bill," *CQ Weekly Report*, August 3, 2002, 2111.

113. Edsall, "High Drug Prices Return."

114. Ceci Connolly, "Medicare Drug Plan Likely to Move," *Washington Post*, November 16, 2002, A8.

115. Morton M. Kondracke, "Phase-in Idea May Be Key to Passing Medicare Drug Plan," *Roll Call*, February 17, 2003.
116. Robert Pear and Robin Toner, "Bush Medicare Proposal Urges Switch to Private Insurers," *New York Times*, March 5, 2003, A19.
117. Jonathan Blum, *A History of Creating the Medicare Prescription Drug Benefit* (Washington, DC: Avalere, August 2006), 7.
118. Blum, *Prescription Drug Benefit*, 7.
119. Robin Toner and Robert Pear, "House and Senate Pass Measures for Broad Overhaul of Medicare," *New York Times*, June 27, 2003, A1.
120. Sheryl Gay Stolberg, "Revamping Medicare: The Voting; In the Wee Hours, Votes Change as Arms Twist," *New York Times*, June 28, 2003, A8.
121. Bob Cusack, "How Tide Turned on Medicare Policy," *The Hill*, June 17, 2003, 1.
122. Rebecca Adams and Mary Agnes Carey, "GOP Bids to Claim Victory on Democrats' Signature Issue," *Congressional Quarterly Weekly Report*, June 14, 2003.
123. Melissa Seckora, "Conservatives Swipe at Medicare bill," *The Hill*, June 24, 2003, 7. David Nather, "Conservatives See Shades of LBJ in Bush Medicare Overhaul," CQ Weekly Report, June 21, 2003, 1540.
124. Blum, *Prescription Drug Benefit*, 2.
125. Rebecca Adams, "Grueling Medicare Conference Will Bring Leaders Face to Face," *Congressional Quarterly Weekly Report*, July 12, 2003.
126. Mary Agnes Carey, "Players in the Medicare Conference," *CQ Weekly Report*, September 20, 2003, 2291.
127. Dean Rosen, personal interview, Washington, DC, November 16, 2006; Chris Hansen, personal interview, Washington, DC, January 3, 2007.
128. Marilyn Werber Serafini and Bada Vaida, "AARP's Big Bet," *National Journal* 36, 11 (March 13, 2004).
129. Serafini and Vaida, "AARP's Big Bet."
130. Mary Agnes Carey, "Medicare Drug Deal At Hand," *CQ Weekly*, November 15, 2003, 2827.
131. Jonathan E. Kaplan, "Blunt Plans War Room: GOP Effort to Pass Medicare Bill Hits High Gear," *The Hill*, November 18, 2003, 1.
132. Rother said they would be "opening up the stops to get this thing through," using telephone lobbying, a grassroots mobilization, television and print media advertising, etc. Kate Schuler and Mary Agnes Carey, "GOP Leaders Prepare Full-Court Press on Medicare Bill as AARP Endorses It," *CQ Today*, November 17, 2003.
133. Hansen, personal interview; Kristen Sloan, personal interview, Washington, DC, 2007; William D. Novelli, "Why AARP Said 'Yes' to Medicare Prescription Drug Bill," News Release by the AARP, December 1, 2003.
134. Mary Agnes Carey, "Medicare Deal at Hand," *CQ Weekly Report*, November 15, 2003, 2827.
135. Mary Agnes Carey, "GOP Wins Battle, Not War," *CQ Weekly Report*, November 29, 2003, 2956.
136. John K. Iglehart, "The New Medicare Prescription-Drug Benefit: A Pure Power Play," *New England Journal of Medicine* 350, 8 (February 19, 2004): 826–833.
137. Kaplan, "War Room."
138. Kaplan, "War Room."
139. Thomas Medvetz, "The Strength of Weekly Ties: Relations of Material and Symbolic Exchange in the Conservative Movement," *Politics and Society* 34, 3 (2006): 356–357.
140. Robert E. Moffit, personal interview, Washington, DC, October 3, 2006.
141. Gebe Martinez, "Long Back-and-Forth House Vote Ran Afoul of Democrats, Not Rules," *CQ Weekly*, November 29, 2003.
142. Jackie Koszczuk and Jonathan Allen, "Late-Night Medicare Vote Drama Triggers Some Unexpected Alliances," *CQ Weekly*, November 29, 2003.
143. *Congressional Record*, November 24, 2003, S15766.

144. Rosen, personal interview; the Democrats voting for the conference report were Baucus (MT), Breaux (LA), Carper (DE), Conrad (ND), Dorgan (ND), Feinstein (CA), Landrieu (LA), Lincoln (AR), Z. Miller (GA), Ben Nelson (NE), and Wyden (OR).

145. Tom Daschle, personal interview, August 15, 2007.

146. Don Devine, "GOP the Party of the Welfare State as Conservative Heroes Fight Back," American Conservative Union, December 10, 2003.

Chapter 6

1. Sallyanne Payton, "Professionalism as Third-Party Governance: The Function and Dysfunction of Medicare," in *Making Government Manageable: Executive Organization and Management in the Twenty-First Century,* eds. Thomas H. Stanton and Benjamin Ginsberg (Baltimore: Johns Hopkins University Press, 2004), 112–140.

2. Timothy Stoltzfus Jost, "Medicare and the Joint Commission on Accreditation of Healthcare Organizations: A Healthy Relationship?" *Law and Contemporary Problems* 57, 4 (Autumn 1994): 15–45.

3. Neil Hollander and Bruce L. R. Smith, "The Framework of Medicare Administration," in *The Administration of Medicare: A Shared Responsibility*, eds. Smith and Hollander (Washington DC: National Academy of Public Administration Foundation, 1973), 1–15.

4. Jost, "Medicare and the Joint Commission."

5. Robert Ball, *Reflections on Implementing Medicare* (Washington, DC: National Academy of Social Insurance, 2001), 28.

6. Elizabeth Cusick, personal interview, Baltimore, MD, May 18, 2009.

7. Hollander and Smith, "Framework of Medicare Administration," 2–3.

8. Jost, "Medicare and the Joint Commission," 27.

9. Eleanor D. Kinney, "Private Accreditation as a Substitute for Direct Government Regulation in Public Health Insurance Programs: When Is It Appropriate?" *Law and Contemporary Problems* 57, 4 (Autumn 1994): 49.

10. The associations involved were the American College of Surgeons, American College of Physicians, American Hospital Association, American Medical Association (AMA), and the Canadian Medical Association (CMA).

11. General Accounting Office, *HCFA Needs Better Assurance That Hospitals Meet Medicare Conditions of Participation*, T-HRD-90-44 (June 21, 1990), 4.

12. General Accounting Office, *HCFA Needs Better Assurance*, 5.

13. Lawrence D. Brown, "Political Evolution of Federal Health Care Regulation," *Health Affairs* (Winter 1992):17–37.

14. Jost, "Medicare and the Joint Commission."

15. Feder, *Medicare*, 8–9; Clark C. Havighurst, "The Place of Private Accrediting among the Instruments of Government," *Law and Contemporary Problems* 57, 4 (Autumn 1994): 9; General Accounting Office, *Medicare: CMS Needs Additional Authority to Adequately Oversee Patient Safety in Hospitals*, GAO-04-850 (2004).

16. Jost, "Medicare and the Joint Commission," 36.

17. For example, see Elliott S. Fisher, David E. Wennberg, Thérèse A. Stuken, Daniel J. Gottlieb, F. L. Lucas, and Étoile L. Pinder, "The Implications of Regional Variations in Medicare Spending. Part 1: The Content, Quality, and Accessibility of Care," *Annals of Internal Medicine* 138, 4 (February 18, 2003): 273–287.

18. Jost, "Medicare and the Joint Commission," 31–32.

19. Marlene R. Miller, Peter Pronovost, Michele Donithan, Scott Zeger, Chunliu Zhan, Laura Morlock, and Gregg S. Meyer, "Relationship Between Performance Measurement and Accreditation: Implications for Quality of Care and Patient Safety," *American Journal of Medical Quality* 20, 5 (September/October 2003): 239–249; David Greenfield and Jeffrey Braithwaite, "Health Sector Accreditation Research: A Systematic Review," *International Journal for Quality in Health Care* 20, 3 (2008): 172–183.

20. U.S. Congress, Senate, Committee on Finance, *Medicare and Medicaid: Problems, Issues, and Alternatives; Report of the Staff,* 91st Congress, 1st Session (1970); it is important to note some political background on this Senate Finance Committee report. Jay Constantine was the main staffer behind this investigation and he previously had worked for Senator McNamara on the Subcommittee on Aging. McNamara felt slighted by the way in which Wilbur Mills and the Ways and Means Committee had ignored the work of this subcommittee on Medicare. Moreover, both the Senate Finance Committee and its chair, Russell Long, felt that Mills had had too much power over the program. Arguably, then, the report was a way for Constantine and Long to get back at Mills by highlighting program shortcomings. Edward D. Berkowitz, *Robert Ball and the Politics of Social Security* (Madison: University of Wisconsin Press, 2003), 140–141, 157–158.

21. Hollander and Smith, "Framework of Medicare Administration," 1.

22. There were reports of physician "gang visits" to nursing homes and hospitals, with a doctor seeing as many as 50 patients a day at a particular facility, whether or not those individuals needed to see a physician. Senate Finance Committee, *Medicare and Medicaid,* 9–10; Marmor, *Politics of Medicare,* 98.

23. Theodore R. Marmor, Donald A. Wittman, and Thomas C. Heagy, "The Politics of Medical Inflation," *Journal of Health Politics, Policy and Law* 1, 1 (1976): 69–84.

24. Hale Champion, Oral History Interview with Edward Berkowitz, Cambridge, MA, August 9, 1995.

25. Senate Finance Committee, *Medicare and Medicaid* 114: 117–119.

26. Erwin Witkin, *The Impact of Medicare* (Springfield, IL: Charles C. Thomas, 1971), 74–77.

27. Because providers could choose to directly contract with the federal government for Medicare payments, a division within the Social Security Administration processed these claims and could serve as the basis of the comparison.

28. There is controversy about how to measure Medicare administrative costs, although most estimates do put it lower than private insurers' costs. The CBO, for example, calculates them at about 3 percent, compared with 5–10 percent of premiums going to overhead costs in large-company self-insured plans. Cathy Schoen, Karen Davis, and Sara R. Collins, "Building Blocks for Reform: Achieving Universal Coverage with Private and Public Group Health Insurance," *Health Affairs* 27(May/June 2008): 647. Administrative costs among other private insurers are likely even higher.

29. National Academy of Social Insurance, *Improving Medicare's Governance and Management* (Washington, DC, 2002) 10; Centers for Medicare and Medicaid Services, Improper Medicare Fee-For-Service Payments Report (November 2007), https://www.cms.gov/apps/er_report/preview_er_report.asp?from=public&which=long&reportID=7, accessed April 18, 2011.

30. Gregg Blesch, "Medicare Fee-For-Service Payment Error Rate More Than Doubles, White House Says," *Modern Healthcare* (2009). Between 1996 and 2002, OIG calculated the error rate, but since November 2003, CMS has been producing its own measurement of, and regular reports on, the error rate.

31. U.S. General Accounting Office, *Medicare: Existing Contract Authority Can Provide for Effective Program Administration* (1986); U.S. General Accounting Office, *Health Insurance: Medicare and Private Payers Are Vulnerable to Fraud and Abuse* (1992); General Accounting Office, *Inadequate Review of Claims Payments Limits Ability to Control Spending* (1994).

32. U.S. General Accounting Office, *Inadequate Review of Claims Payments;* U.S. General Accounting Office, *Medicare Fraud, Waste, and Abuse: Challenges and Strategies for Preventing Improper Payments.* Statement before the Subcommittee on Health and Oversight, Committee on Ways and Means, House of Representatives, GAO-10-844T (2010), 6.

33. U.S. General Accounting Office, *Medicare: Improprieties by Contractors Compromised Medicare Program Integrity* (1999), 10; U.S. General Accounting Office, *Medicare Contractors: Despite Its Efforts, HCFA Cannot Ensure Their Effectiveness and Integrity* (1999).

34. U.S. General Accounting Office, *Medicare Fraud, Waste, and Abuse: Challenges and Strategies for Preventing Improper Payments,* Statement before the Subcommittee on Health and Oversight, Committee on Ways and Means, House of Representatives, GAO-10-844T (2010).

35. U.S. General Accounting Office, *Medicare Contractors;* Stanton, "Administration of Medicare"; Payton, "Third Party Governance"; U.S. General Accounting Office, *Centers for Medicare and Medicaid Services: Pervasive Internal Control Weaknesses Hindered Effective Contract Management* GAO-10-637T (2010); U.S. General Accounting Office, *Medicare Fraud, Waste, and Abuse: Challenges and Strategies for Preventing Improper Payments*, Statement before the Subcommittee on Health and Oversight, Committee on Ways and Means, House of Representatives, GAO-10-844T (2010).

36. Stanton, "Administration of Medicare," 1380.

37. Centers for Medicare and Medicaid Services, *Justification of Estimates for Appropriations Committees* (2010), 6.

38. John K. Iglehart, "Doing More with Less: A Conversation with Kerry Weems," *Health Affairs* web exclusive (June 18, 2009), w690.

39. http://www.socialsecurity.gov/budget/FY10KeyTables.pdf. The table reports 60,744 FTEs working for the SSA in FY 2008 and 583 for the Office of Inspector General. The number of FTEs enacted for 2009 also went up to 63,469 FTEs in SSA and 604 in the OIG, whereas in the CMS the budgeted FTEs for FY 2009 declined to 4,461.

40. For comparison, in 2001, nine of the largest private insurers in the US, with 71 million enrollees, had 168,000 employees, or 16.8 employees per 10,000 clients. By contrast, the Saskatchewan and Ontario Health Plans have 1.4 and 1.2 employees per 10,000 beneficiaries, respectively. Steffie Woolhandler, Terry Campbell, and David U. Himmelstein, "Costs of Health Care Administration in the United States and Canada," *New England Journal of Medicine* 349 (August 21, 2003), 773.

41. Stuart Butler, et al., "Crisis Facing HCFA & Millions of Americans," *Health Affairs* 18, 1 (January/February 1999): 8–10; U.S. General Accounting Office, *Medicare: 21st Century Challenges Prompt Fresh Thinking about Program's Administrative Structure* GAO/T-HEHS-00/108GAO (2000); National Academy of Social Insurance, *Medicare Governance;* Iglehart, "Conversation with Kerry Weems."

42. Butler et al., "Crisis Facing HCFA," 8.

43. U.S. General Accounting Office, *Medicare: Improvements Needed in Provider Communications and Contracting Procedures*, GAO-01-1141T (2001).

44. U.S. General Accounting Office, *Medicare: 21st Century Challenges Prompt Fresh Thinking about Program's Administrative Structure*, GAO/T-HEHS-00/108 (2000).

45. General Accounting Office, *Medicare: Existing Contract Authority Can Provide for Effective Program Administration* (1986); National Academy of Social Insurance, *Medicare Governance;* Stanton, "Administration of Medicare."

46. Iglehart, "Conversation with Kerry Weems."

47. Stanton, "Administration of Medicare."

48. Michael Birnbaum, "A Conversation with Bruce Vladeck," *Journal of Health Policy, Politics and Law* 34, 3 (June 2009): 408.

49. Quoted in Stanton, "Administration of Medicare."

50. Stanton, "Administration of Medicare"; Payton, "Third Party Governance."

51. U.S. General Accounting Office, *Medicare Contracting Reform: Opportunities and Challenges in Contracting for Claims Administration*, GAO-01-918T (2001).

52. U.S. GAO, "Medicare: Existing Contract Authority," 12–13.

53. Posner, "National Health Insurance Plans."

54. Cusick, personal interview.

55. U.S. General Accounting Office, *Improprieties by Contractors*, 20.

56. Cusick, personal interview.

57. Bruce C. Vladeck, "The Political Economy of Medicare," *Health Affairs* 18, 1 (January/February 1999), 29.

58. Centers for Medicare and Medicaid Services, *Medicare Contracting Reform: A Blueprint for a Better Medicare* (2005).

59. There also are four regional home health intermediaries and four regional durable medical equipment intermediaries.

60. Iglehart, "Conversation with Kerry Weems."

61. U.S. General Accounting Office, *Medicare: Contingency Plans to Address Potential Problems with the Transition of Dual-Eligible Beneficiaries from Medicaid to Medicare Drug Coverage*, GAO-06-278R (December 16, 2005).

62. U.S. General Accounting Office, "Medicare: Contingency Plans"; Medicare Rights Center, *MMA and Dual Eligibles: A Transition in Crisis* (March 2005).

63. Ceci Connolly, "The States Step in as Medicare Falters," *Washington Post*, January 14, 2006, A1; Susan Levine, "Stability of Mentally Ill Shaken by Medicare Drug Plan Problems," *Washington Post*, February 6, 2006, A1; Robert Pear, "Medicare Woes Take High Toll on Mentally Ill," *New York Times*, January 21, 2006, A1; Kate Schuler, "New Medicare Drug Plan Gets Off to Rocky Start," *CQ Weekly* (January 30, 2006): 267.

64. Schuler, "Medicare Drug Plan."

65. Kaiser Family Foundation, *Medicare Prescription Drug Plan Information, by State, 2006*, http://www.kff.org/medicare/upload/74261.pdf; Jack Hoadley, Juliette Cubanski, Elizabeth Hargrave, Laura Summer, and Tricia Neuman, *Part D Plan Availability in 2010 and Key Changes since 2006*, Kaiser Family Foundation (November 2009), http://www.kff.org/medicare/upload/7986.pdf.

66. Based on their negotiations with manufacturers, for example, two Part D plans might offer the same drug in different tiers at different co-payment amounts.

67. Kaiser Family Foundation, "Public Opinion on Medicare Part D—the Medicare Prescription Drug Benefit," *Kaiser Public Opinion Spotlight* (2006), http://www.kff.org/spotlight/medicarerx/index.cfm.

68. In April 2006, the Kaiser Family Foundation reported that although six out ten seniors had heard about 1-800-MEDICARE and Medicare.gov, only 12 percent had called the toll-free number and 9 percent sought out information on the web site ("Public Opinion on Medicare Part D").

69. U.S. Senate, Subcommittee on Aging, *Meeting the Challenges of Medicare Drug Benefit Implementation*, S. Hrg. 109–389, (US GPO, 2006), 8.

70. Michael A. Fletcher, "Medicare Drug Benefit Works, Bush Says," *Washington Post*, March 15, 2006, A4.

71. Democracy Corps, *Alert: Prescription Drug Plan; Prospect of a Voter Revolt* (2006) http://www.greenbergresearch.com/articles/1666/1847_Democracy_Corps_February_10_2006_Alert.pdf.

72. Jeffrey H. Birnbaum and Claudia Deane, "Most Seniors Enrolled Say Drug Benefit Saves Money," *Washington Post*, April 12, 2006, A1; Robert Pear, "For Some Who Solve Puzzle, Medicare Drug Plan Pays Off," *New York Times*, March 26, 2006, A1.

73. Michael Perry, Adrianne Dulio, and Juliette Cubanksi, *Voices of Beneficiaries: Medicare Part D Insights and Observations One Year Later* (Kaiser Family Foundation 2006); Adrianne Dulio, Michael Perry and Juliette Cubanksi, *Voices of Beneficiaries: Attitudes Toward Medicare Part D Open Enrollment for 2008* (Kaiser Family Foundation 2007).

74. Gwen Glazer, "Poll Track," *National Journal* 38, 18 (May 6, 2006); Washington Post-ABC News Poll, available at http://www.washingtonpost.com/wp-dyn/content/graphic/2006/04/12/GR2006041200154.html.

75. Mark Duggan, Patrick Healy, and Fiona Scott Morton, "Providing Prescription Drug Coverage to the Elderly: America's Experiment with Medicare Part D," *Journal of Economic Perspectives* 22, 4 (Fall 2008): 69–92; Dana P. Goldman and Geoffrey F. Joyce, "Medicare Part D: A Successful Start with Room for Improvement," *Journal of the American Medical Association* 299, 16 (April 23/30, 2008): 1954–1955; Florian Heiss, Daniel McFadden, and Joachim Winter, "Regulation of Private Health Insurance Markets: Lessons from Enrollment, Plan Type Choice, and Adverse Selection in Medicare Part D," NBER Working Paper 15392 (2009); Patricia Neuman and Juliette Cubanski, "Medicare Part D Update—Lessons Learned and Unfinished Business," *New England Journal of Medicine* 361, 4 (July 23, 2009): 406–414; David Wessel, "The Lessons of Medicare Part D," *Wall Street Journal*, January 7, 2010.

76. Bill Frist and John Breaux, "Medicare Part D: A Health Care Success," *Politico* (November 16, 2009); Mark McClellan, personal interview, Washington, DC, June 8, 2007.

77. Benjamin E. Sasse, "Why Medicare Part D is the Answer to Health Reform," *US News & World Report*, December 15, 2009.

78. Kaiser Family Foundation, *Medicare: The Medicare Prescription Drug Fact Sheet* (October, 2010), http://www.kff.org/medicare/upload/7044-11.pdf.

79. Jack Hoadley, *Medicare's New Adventure: The Part D Drug Benefit* (The Commonwealth Fund, 2006).

80. Helen Levy and David Weir, "Take-Up of Medicare Part D: Results from the Health and Retirement Study," NBER Working Paper 14692 (2009).

81. Frank R. Lichtenberg and Shawn X. Sun, "The Impact of Medicare Part D on Prescription Drug Use by the Elderly," *Health Affairs* 26, 6 (November/December 2007): 1735–1744; Yin et al. 2008.

82. Sebastian Schneeweiss, Amanda R. Patrick, Alex Pedan, Laleh Varasteh, Raisa Levin, Nan Liu, and William H. Shrank, "The Effect of Medicare Part D Coverage on Drug Use and Cost Sharing among Seniors without Prior Drug Benefits," *Health Affairs* web exclusive (February 3, 2009): w305–16.

83. Jack Hoadley, Elizabeth Hargrave, Juliette Cubanski, and Tricia Neuman, *The Medicare Part D Coverage Gap: Costs and Consequences in 2007* (Kaiser Family Foundation: August 2008).

84. Yuting Zhang, Julie Marie Donohue, Joseph P. Newhouse, and Judith R. Lave, "The Effects of the Coverage Gap on Drug Spending: A Closer Look at Medicare Part D," *Health Affairs* web exclusive (February 3, 2009): w317–325.

85. See Jeanne M. Madden, Amy J. Graves, Fang Zhang, et al., "Cost-Related Medication Non-adherence and Spending on Basic Needs Following Implementation of Medicare Part D," *JAMA* 299 (April 23/30, 2008): 1922–1928.

86. Geoffrey F. Joyce, Dana P. Goldman, William B. Vogt, Eric Sun, and Anupam B. Jena, "Medicare Part D after Two Years," *American Journal of Managed Care* 15, 8 (August 2009): 536–544.

87. Kaiser Family Foundation, *Medicare: A Primer* (Kaiser Family Foundtion: 2010), http://www.kff.org/medicare/upload/7615-03.pdf.

88. PiperReport, *Medicare Drug Plans and Risk Mitigation: Risk Corridors, Risk Adjustment, and Federal Reinsurance* (April 5, 2006), available at http://www.piperreport.com/archives/2006/04/risk_mitigation.html

89. Martin Sipkoff, "Health Plans Undaunted by Medicare Part D," *Managed Care Magazine* (May 2005).

90. Russ Banham, "Prescription for Malaise?" *CFO Magazine* (June 1, 2005).

91. Sarah Lueck and Vanessa Fuhrmans, "Golden Oldies: New Medicare Drug Benefits Sparks an Industry Land Grab," *Wall Street Journal*, January 25, 2006, A1.

92. Michael McCaughan, "The Part D Bubble: Why Everyone Wants to Be a PDP," *RPM Report* (November 2006): 32–38; James C. Robinson, "The Commercial Health Insurance Industry in an Era of Eroding Employer Coverage," *Health Affairs* 25, 6 (November/December 2006): 1475–1486.

93. "Humana Embarks on National MA Strategy as Medicare MCOs Report Solid Earnings," *Medicare Advantage News* (May 12, 2005).

94. MedPAC, *Report to the Congress: Medicare Payment Policy* (March 2010), 260.

95. MedPAC, *Report to the Congress*, 260.

96. Milt Freudenheim, "Medicare Drug Plan Feeds More Profitable Managed Care," *New York Times*, March 31, 2006, C1.

97. Freudenheim, "Medicare Drug Plan."

98. Howard Gleckman, "Plan A: Hook Them with Part D," *Business Week*, January 30, 2006, 96.

99. Kaiser Family Foundation, *Pitching Private Medicare Plans: An Analysis of Medicare Advantage and Prescription Drug Plan Advertising* (September 2008), available at http://www.kff.org/medicare/upload/7805.pdf.

100. Jonathan Blum, Ruth Brown, and Miryam Frieder, *An Examination of Medicare Private Fee-for-Service Plans*, Kaiser Family Foundation Issue Brief (March 2007).
101. Heiss, McFadden, and Winter, "Private Health Insurance Markets."
102. Charles N. ("Chip") Kahn III, personal interview, Washington, DC, February 22, 2007.
103. Frist and Breaux, "Medicare Part D"; Mark Duggan and Fiona Scott Morton, *The Effect of Medicare Part D on Pharmaceutical Prices and Utilization*, NBER working paper no. 13917 (2009).
104. Duggan and Morton, *Effect of Medicare Part D*.
105. Murray Aitken, Ernst R. Berndt, and David M. Cutler, "Prescription Drug Spending Trends in the United States: Looking beyond the Turning Point," *Health Affairs* web exclusive (December 16, 2008): w151–60; Micah Hartman, Anne Martin, Patricia McDonnell, Aaron Catlin, and the National Health Expenditure Accounts Team, "National Health Spending in 2007: Slower Drug Spending Contributes to Lowest Rate of Overall Growth Since 1998," *Health Affairs* 28, 1 (January/February 2009): 246–261.
106. Douglas Holtz-Eakin, *Estimating the Cost of the Medicare Modernization Act*, Testimony before the House Committee on Ways and Means (Washington, DC: Congressional Budget Office, March 24, 2004), 4.
107. "Study Asserts Total 10-Year Cost of Medicare Modernization Act Overestimated," *Drug Week*, February 18, 2005.
108. Aitken, Berndt, and Cutler, "Prescription Drug Spending."
109. Marc Steinberg and Kim Bailey, *No Bargain: Medicare Drug Plans Deliver High Prices* (Washington, DC: Families USA, 2007).
110. Walid F. Gellad, Sebastian Schneeweiss, Phyllis Brawarsky, Stuart Lipsitz, and Jennifer S. Haas, "What if the Federal Government Negotiated Pharmaceutical Prices for Seniors? An Estimate of National Savings," *Journal of General Internal Medicine* 23, 9 (2008): 1435–1440.
111. Richard G. Frank and Joseph P. Newhouse, "Should Drug Prices Be Negotiated Under Part D of Medicare? And If So, How?" *Health Affairs* 27, 1 (2008): 33–43. Incentives to bargain are also undercut by regulations stipulating that most drugs in "protected classes" must be offered. Frank and Newhouse found that the prices of brand-name drugs used heavily by the elderly increased after MMA implementation more than did those with few elderly users.
112. Fiona Scott Morton, Testimony before the Senate Finance Committee hearing, *Prescription Drug Pricing and Negotiation: An Overview and Economic Perspectives for the Medicare Prescription Drug Benefit*, January 11, 2007.
113. Kelly McCormack, "Fred, Ethel, Drug-Plan Shills," *The Hill*, December 6, 2005.
114. McCormack, "Drug-Plan Shills."
115. Robert Pear, "Insurers' Tactics in Marketing Drug Plans Draw Complaints," *New York Times*, November 27, 2005, A33; Elizabeth Williamson and Christopher Lee, "Abuses in Enrollment Tactics Found for Private Medicare," *Washington Post*, May 16, 2007, A3.
116. Robert Pear, "Troubles Linger in Regulation of Medicare Customer Service," *New York Times*, June 25, 2006, A17.
117. Daniel R. Levinson, *Memorandum Report: Medicare Part D Prescription Drug Plan Sponsor Internet Web Sites: Content and Accessibility*, OEI-06-06-00340 (October 2007), available at http://oig.hhs.gov/oei/reports/oei-06-06-00340.pdf.
118. Daniel R. Levinson, *Marketing Materials for Medicare Prescription Drug Plans*, OEI-01-06-00050 (2008), available at http://oig.hhs.gov/oei/reports/oei-01-06-00050.pdf.
119. Kaiser Family Foundation, *Pitching Private Medicare Plans: An Analysis of Medicare Advantage and Prescription Drug Plan Advertising* (Kaiser Family Foundation, September 2008), available at http://www.kff.org/medicare/upload/7805.pdf.
120. David Lipschutz, Paul Precht, and Bonnie Burns, *After the Goldrush: The Marketing of Medicare Advantage and Part D Plans* (California Health Advocates and the Medicare Rights Center, January 2007), 11.
121. Levinson, *Marketing Materials*.
122. Tom Lauricella, "Open Season for Drug-Insurance Swindlers," *Wall Street Journal*, December 9, 2007, 3.

123. The MMA regulatory preemption clauses stipulate that federal standards for MA and PDP plans supersede state regulations other than state laws on licensing or solvency. Hence state regulators have no jurisdiction over the marketing or other practices of MA and PDP plans.

124. Robert Pear, "Medicare Audits Show Problems in Private Plans," *New York Times*, October 7, 2007, A1.

125. Government Accounting Office, *Medicare Part D: Complaint Rates Are Declining, but Operational and Oversight Challenges Remain*, GAO-08-719 (June 2008).

126. General Accounting Office, *Medicare Part D: CMS Oversight of Part D Sponsors' Fraud and Abuse Programs Has Been Limited, but CMS Plans Oversight Expansion*, GAO-10-481T (March 3, 2010), 1.

Chapter 7

1. Suzanne Mettler, *Dividing Citizens: Gender and Federalism in New Deal Public Policy* (Ithaca, NY: Cornell University Press, 1998).

2. Martha Derthick, *Policymaking for Social Security* (Washington, DC: Brookings Institution Press, 1979).

3. Paul Pierson, *Politics in Time: History, Institutions, and Social Analysis* (Princeton: Princeton University Press, 2004).

4. On displacement and layering, see James Mahoney and Kathleen Thelen, "A Theory of Gradual Institutional Change," in *Explaining Institutional Change: Ambiguity, Agency, and Power*, eds. Kathleen Thelen and James Mahoney (New York: Cambridge University Press, 2010).

5. Pierson, *Politics in Time*.

6. Andrea Louise Campbell, *How Policies Make Citizens: Senior Citizen Activism and the American Welfare State* (Princeton: Princeton University Press, 2003).

7. Staffan Kumlin, *The Personal and the Political: How Personal Welfare State Experiences Affect Political Trust and Ideology* (New York: Palgrave Macmillan, 2004).

8. Elisabeth S. Clemens, "Lineages of the Rube Goldberg State: Building and Blurring Public Programs, 1900–1940," in *Rethinking Political Institutions: The Art of the State*, eds. Ian Shapiro, Stephen Skowronek, and Daniel Galvin (New York: New York University Press, 2006), 380–443.

9. Christopher Howard, *The Hidden Welfare State: Tax Expenditures and Social Policy in the United States* (Princeton, NJ: Princeton University Press, 1997); Christopher Howard, *The Welfare State Nobody Knows: Debunking Myths about US Social Policy* (Princeton, NJ: Princeton University Press, 2007); Suzanne Mettler, "Visible Lessons: How Experiences of Higher Education Politics Influence Participation in Politics," unpublished manuscript, Cornell University, November 2, 2009.

10. Beth Stevens, "Blurring the Boundaries: How the Federal Government Has Influenced Welfare Benefits in the Private Sector," in *The Politics of Social Policy in the United States*, eds. Margaret Weir, Ann Shola Orloff, and Theda Skocpol (Princeton: Princeton University Press, 1988), 123–148; Jacob S. Hacker, "Review Article: Dismantling the Health Care State? Political Institutions, Public Policies and the Comparative Politics of Health Reform," *British Journal of Political Science* 343 (2004): 693–724.

11. Mark Schlesinger and Vincent L. Hutchings, "Affiliation, Collective Identification and Public Policy: Medicare Privatization and Elders' Attitudes toward Federal Involvement in Medical Care," unpublished manuscript, Yale University, 2003.

12. Andrea Louise Campbell and Theda Skocpol, "Down Goes Their Clout: The New Medicare Law Could Leave the AARP Toothless and the Elderly Upstaged by Business Lobbies," *Newsday*, November 30, 2003, A28–29; Theodore R. Marmor and Jerry L. Mashaw, "Understanding Social Insurance: Fairness, Affordability, and the 'Modernization' of Social Security and Medicare," *Health Affairs* March 21, 2006: W114–W134; Theda Skocpol, "A Bad Senior Moment," *The American Prospect*, (January 2004): 26–29.

13. Because individuals select into Part D or MA, the "treatment" is not random, and we might worry that those individuals are different to begin with. However, the differences-in-differences analysis in Table 7.1 shows that the treatment and control groups are quite similar in baseline attitudes. Moreover, having panel data allows us to condition on pre-treatment attitudes, as in the multivariate analysis in Table B.2, a key tactic in ensuring that observational data approximate experimental benchmarks (see Thomas D. Cook, William R. Shadish, Jr., and Vivian C. Wong, "Within-Study Comparisons of Experiments and Non-Experiments," unpublished manuscript, Northwestern University, 2007). By including pre-treatment attitudes from the baseline survey, we are controlling for all of the prior factors that would influence respondents' attitudes, in addition to the other demographic and experiential variables we measured in our survey. Having pre-treatment attitudes also allows us to avoid the Heckman selection models that we would have to rely on if we only had cross-sectional data and had to model respondents' selection into Part D or MA after the fact. Such models are useful when only post-treatment data are available, but also have a number of pitfalls, such as sensitivity to specification, need for a valid instrument, and heavy reliance on distributional assumptions.

14. Gøsta Esping-Andersen, *Politics against Markets: The Social Democratic Road to Power* (Princeton: Princeton University Press, 1985).

15. Ken Wang, "Policy Feedback, Cultural Change and Party Systems: Understanding the Continued Dominance of the LDP in Japan," unpublished manuscript, University of Hong Kong, 2005.

16. Theda Skocpol, *Boomerang: Health Care Reform and the Turn against Government* (New York: W.W. Norton, 1996).

17. Skocpol, "A Bad Senior Moment."

18. On issue ownership, see John R. Petrocik, "Issue Ownership in Presidential Elections, with a 1980 Case Study," *American Journal of Political Science* 40 (1996): 825–850.

19. Other measures show little shift in issue ownership as well. As in Figures 7.1 and 7.2, respondents were more likely to say the Democratic Party was more likely to make prescription drugs for the elderly more affordable by large margins between October 2000 and September 2006. Also, except for a brief period in early 2003, Americans were more likely to disapprove than to approve of President Bush's handling of the prescription drug benefit, and his approval rating on prescription drugs was even lower than his overall job approval rating throughout this period (although the latter declined more dramatically over time). Various polls archived by the Roper Center, University of Connecticut.

20. On policy learning, see Michael Gusmano, Mark Schlesinger, and Tracey Thomas, "Policy Feedback and Public Opinion: The Role of Employer Responsibility in Social Policy," *Journal of Health Politics, Policy, and Law* 27 (2002): 731–772.

21. Note that in this and other multivariate analyses carried out, and in tables showing results for chi-square or difference of means tests, we note a single level of statistical significance.

22. We asked respondents whether they experienced any of the following six problems in getting their prescriptions: left the pharmacy without their prescription because one of the drugs they were taking wasn't covered by their plan; left the pharmacy without their prescription because they couldn't afford it; had to switch medications because one of the drugs they were taking wasn't covered by their plan; had to switch from a brand-name drug to a generic drug; had to deal with a billing mistake for a prescription or a premium; or had to pay costs they hadn't expected—either for a prescription or a premium.

23. We tested interactions between favorability and party ID; these were not statistically significant except that among Part D enrollees, Republicans with favorable experiences were even more likely to say the Republican Party makes the right decisions about government.

24. Drew Armstrong, "An Insurers' Network Grows Into a Constituency," *CQ Weekly Report*, February 4, 2008.

25. Cole Werble, "Follow the Money: Why the Democrats Won't Kill Private Medicare Plans," *RPM Report* 2, 1 (December 2006): 27–32.

26. Bennett Roth, "Industries See Reform as Victory," *Roll Call*, March 23, 2010.

27. Kaiser Family Foundation, *Medicare Advantage Chartpack 2007*, available at http://www.kff. org/medicare/upload/7646.pdf, accessed November 28, 2010.

28. MedPAC, *Report to Congress: Medicare Payment Policy* (March 2009), 252.

29. Jerome L. Sherman, "Blue Cross Warns of Medicare Cuts," *Pittsburgh Post-Gazette*, February 28, 2007.

30. Rosa Rosales, Letter to Members of Congress, March 14, 2007.

31. Ways and Means Minority Staff, "Democrats' Plan to Slash Medicare Advantage Would Hurt Minorities Most," Ways and Means Press Office, July 25, 2007.

32. Fawn Johnson, "Stark Accuses GOP of Peddling 'Propaganda' on Medicare," *CongressDaily*, March 9, 2007; Jeffery Young, "NAACP May Temper Support for Medicare Advantage," *The Hill*, May 15, 2007.

33. Sarah Lueck, "Health-Care Plans Set to Collide in Congress," *Wall Street Journal*, July 25, 2007.

34. David Espo, "Democrats Slowed in Efforts on Medicare," *Newsday.com*, April 15, 2007.

35. Alex Wayne, "Pros, Cons of Private Medicare Plans Weighed as Lawmakers Assess Program," *CQ Today*, April 11, 2007.

36. Senate Finance Committee, *Examination of the Medicare Advantage Program*, 110th Congress, First Session, S. Hrg. 110–428, April 11, 2007.

37. MedPAC analyses show that payment to PFFS plans averaged 119 percent of traditional Medicare FFS spending. HMO payments averaged 110 percent.

38. The bill also eliminated payments to MA plans for indirect medical expenses, a subsidy to teaching hospitals.

39. Congressional Budget Office, *H.R. 6331, Medicare Improvement for Patients and Providers Act of 2008*, July 8, 2008, http://www.cbo.gov/ftpdocs/95xx/doc9550/hr6331GreggLtr.pdf, accessed November 28, 2010.

40. The Staff of the Washington Post, *Landmark: America's New Health-Care Law and What It Means for Us All* (New York: Public Affairs, 2010), pp. 117–118.

41. Bennett Roth, "Health Insurers Attack Public Option, Cuts," *Roll Call*, October 28, 2009.

42. Senate Finance Committee, *Executive Committee Meeting to Consider Health Care Reform*, September 22–4, 2009.

43. Under current policy, CBO had projected enrollment would rise from 10.6 million in 2009 to13.9 million people in 2019. CBO, *Comparison of Projected Enrollment in Medicare Advantage Plans and Subsidies for Extra Benefits Not Covered by Medicare under Current Law and under Reconciliation Legislation Combined with H.R. 3590 as Passed by the Senate* (March 19, 2010).

44. David M. Drucker, "Moderate Democrats Staying In Line," *Roll Call*, January 19, 2010. Senator Jim Webb (D-VA), for instance, opposed the cuts but supported the reform bill, as did Senator Bill Nelson (D-FL). Ron Wyden (D-OR), whose state has a large proportion of MA beneficiaries and who opposed cuts to the program in the past, supported the effort to reduce overpayments. The ACA gives bonus payments to high-quality MA plans and, not coincidentally, Oregon is a state with a lot of high-quality plans.

45. Jonathan Oberlander, *The Political Life of Medicare* (Chicago: University of Chicago Press, 2003).

46. Senate Finance Committee, *Executive Committee Meeting to Consider Health Care Reform*, September 23, 2009.

47. The reduction in the extra MA subsidies will take place over three years beginning in 2011, although may take longer in some localities. MA payments will differ by area, depending on FFS rates, with higher MA reimbursement in areas with low FFS rates, and lower MA subsidies—95%—in areas with high FFS rates. MA programs that earn high-quality ratings will be rewarded with higher reimbursements. Kaiser Family Foundation, *Summary of New Health Reform Law*, March 26, 2010, http://www.kff.org/healthreform/upload/8061.pdf.

48. Medicare Advantage plans may offer benefits that traditional Medicare does not, such as vision and dental, and may have lower cost-sharing, although the latter may depend on individual situations. MA plans are allowed to impose daily co-payments for hospital stays,

home health visits, and the early part of skilled nursing facility stays that are not required under traditional Medicare. See Patricia Neuman, "Medicare Advantage: Key Issues and Implications for Beneficiaries," Statement before the House Budget Committee, June 28, 2007, http://budget.house.gov/hearings/2007/06.28neuman_testimony.pdf.

49. Senate Finance Committee, *Executive Committee Meeting to Consider Health Care Reform*, September 22, 2009.

50. Senate Finance Committee, *Executive Committee Meeting to Consider Health Care Reform*, September 24, 2009.

51. James Mahoney and Kathleen Thelen, "A Theory of Gradual Institutional Change."

52. Donald R. Kinder and David O. Sears, "Public Opinion and Political Action," in *Handbook of Social Psychology*, 3rd ed., eds. Gardner Lindzey and Elliot Aronson (New York: Random House, 1985); Donald Green, Bradley Palmquist, and Eric Schickler, *Partisan Hearts and Minds* (New Haven: Yale University Press, 2002).

53. Mark A. Smith, *The Right Talk: How Conservatives Transformed the Great Society into the Economic Society* (Princeton: Princeton University Press, 2007); Larry M. Bartels, *Unequal Democracy: The Political Economy of the New Gilded Age* (New York: Russell Sage and Princeton University Press, 2008).

54. John Breaux, telephone interview, June 28, 2007. Some other interviewees remarked upon the way in which the MMA laid the foundation for transforming Medicare into a system more like the FEHBP. Yet, some conservatives remained skeptical that there was sufficient reform in the bill.

55. Seventy-three percent of seniors agreed that the Medicare drug benefit is "too complicated;" 68 percent favored reducing the number of plans available, 65 percent favored spending more federal money to close the doughnut hole, 81 percent favored government negotiation power on drug prices, 66 percent wanted to get drugs directly from Medicare, and 79 percent of adult Americans supported re-importation of drugs from Canada. See Kaiser Family Foundation, "Seniors and the Medicare Drug Benefit," December 2006, available at www.kff.org/kaiserpolls/upload/7604.pdf; and Kaiser Family Foundation, "The Public's Health Care Agenda for the New Congress and Presidential Campaign," December 2006, available at www.kff.org/kaiserpolls/upload/7597.pdf.

56. Campbell, *How Policies Make Citizens*.

57. Richard Himelfarb, *Catastrophic Politics: The Rise and Fall of the Medicare Catastrophic Coverage Act of 1988* (University Park: Pennsylvania State Press, 1995).

58. Herbert A. Simon, *Reason in Human Affairs* (Stanford: Stanford University Press, 1983).

59. Mary Agnes Carey, "Prescription Drug Coverage Dragged Quickly into the Fray," *CQ Weekly Report*, February 26, 2000); Robin Toner, "The 2000 Campaign: the Issues; Bitter Partisan Fight Brewing over Medicare Drug Benefits," *New York Times*, April 5, 2000, A1; Peter Marks, "The 2000 Campaign: Advertising; Costly Prescriptions: One Issue That Fits All," *New York Times*, October 1, 2000, A22; Robert Pear, "Drug Plans for Elderly Are Unveiled by 2 Parties," *New York Times*, May 2, 2002, A21.

60. The data in Figures 7.4 and 7.5 were obtained from the University of Wisconsin Advertising Project that includes media tracking data from TNSMI/Campaign Media Analysis Group in Washington, DC. The UW Advertising Project was sponsored by a grant from The Pew Charitable Trusts; opinions expressed in this book are those of the authors and do not necessarily reflect the views of the UW Advertising Project or The Pew Charitable Trust.

61. Democracy Corps, "Alert: Prescription Drug Plan. Prospect of a Voter Revolt," Washington, DC, unpublished report, February 10, 2006.

62. Douglas Waller, "Cold Shoulder," *Time*, January 15, 2006; Shailagh Murray and Charles Babbington, "New Offensive on Medicare Drug Benefit," *Washington Post*, February 28, 2006, A13. Some races that raised this theme were Clay Shaw's reelection bid in a Florida district with a high proportion of Medicare recipients; Bob Casey's drive to unseat Senator Rick Santorum in Pennsylvania, where nearly 15 percent of voters are seniors; and the reelection campaigns of Nancy Johnson (R-CT), Jim Talent (R-Mo.), and John Kyl (R-AZ). See Jeffrey Young, "Drug Benefit Is Popular, but Not Touted Much by GOP," *The Hill*, November 15, 2006. Shaw, Santorum, Johnson, and Talent lost their races.

63. Medical News Today, "Medicare Drug Benefit Unlikely to Determine 2006 Congressional Elections, According to GOP Pollster," September 26, 2006, www.medicalnewstoday.com.

64. Young, "Drug Benefit is Popular."

65. Maria Bartiromo, "Should Business Be Worried?" *Business Week,* November 6, 2006.

66. Barrie McKenna, "U.S. Demand for Canadian Drugs Dwindles," *Globe and Mail,* May 24, 2007, B13; Warren Wolfe, "Prescription Drugs: Last Bus to Canada," *Star Tribune,* July 1, 2007, 1B.

67. Kelly McCormack and Bob Cusack, "AARP Edges Away from Drug Imports," *The Hill,* January 4, 2006, 1.

Chapter 8

1. Sidney Verba, Kay Lehman Schlozman, and Henry E. Brady, *Voice and Equality: Civic Voluntarism in American Politics* (Cambridge, MA: Harvard University Press, 1995).

2. Jason T. Abaluck and Jonathan Gruber, "Choice Inconsistencies among the Elderly: Evidence from Plan Choice in the Medicare Part D Program," NBER Working Paper 14759 (February 2009), www.nber.org/papers/w14759.

3. In 2010, 79 percent of MA plans also covered prescription drugs. Kaiser Family Foundation, "Medicare Advantage" (September 2010), http://www.kff.org/medicare/upload/2052-14.pdf

4. For those turning 65 and therefore becoming eligible for Medicare in subsequent years, the initial eligibility period during which they must sign up for Part D to avoid late enrollment penalties is seven months long: the month they turn 65 and the three months before and after. See http://www.medicare.gov/new-to-medicare/new-beneficiary.aspx.

5. Kaiser Family Foundation, "Part D Plan Availability in 2010 and Key Changes since 2006," (November 2009), available at http://www.kff.org/medicare/upload/7986.pdf.

6. Ellen Peters, Daniel Vastfjall, Paul Slovic, C. K. Mertz, Ketti Mazzocco, and Stephan Dickert, "Numeracy and Decision Making," *Psychological Science* 17 (2006): 407–413.

7. Daniel McFadden, "Free Markets and Fettered Consumers," *American Economic Review* 96 (2006): 5–29.

8. Sheena S. Iyengar, and Mark R. Lepper, "When Choice is Demotivating: Can One Desire Too Much of a Good Thing?" *Journal of Personality and Social Psychology* 79 (2000): 995–1006; Marianne Bertrand, Dean S. Karlan, Sendhil Mullainathan, Eldar Shafir, and Jonathan Zinman, "What's Psychology Worth: A Field Experiment in Consumer Credit Markets," Yale University Economic Growth Center Discussion Paper 918, 2005; Shlomo Benartzi and Richard H. Thaler, "Naïve Diversification Strategies in Defined Contribution Saving Plans," *American Economic Review* 93 (2001): 193–215; Sheena S. Iyengar, Wei Jiang, and Gur Huberman, "How Much Choice Is Too Much? Contributions to 401(k) Retirement Plans," in *Pension Design and Structure: New Lessons from Behavioral Finance,* eds. Olivia S. Mitchell and S. Utkus (Oxford: Oxford University Press, 2004), 83–96.

9. Eric J. Johnson, John Hershey, Jacqueline Meszaros, and Howard Kunreuther, "Framing, Probability Distortions, and Insurance Decisions," *Journal of Risk and Uncertainty* 7 (1993): 35–51; Donald A. Redelmeier, "Medical Decision Making in Situations That Offer Multiple Alternatives," *Journal of the American Medical Association* 273, 4 (January 25, 1995): 302–305.

10. Charles F. Manski, "Dynamic Choice in Social Settings: Learning from the Experiences of Others," *Journal of Econometrics* 58 (1993): 121–136.

11. Sheena S. Iyengar and Emir Kamenica, "Choice Overload and Simplicity Seeking," University of Chicago Graduate School of Business Working Paper, 2006.

12. Barry Schwartz, *The Paradox of Choice: Why More Is Less* (New York: Harper Collins, 2004).

13. Sarah E. MacPherson, Louise H. Phillips, and Sergio Della Sala, "Age, Executive Function, and Social Decision Making: A Dorsolateral Prefrontal Theory of Cognitive Aging," *Psychology of Aging* 17 (2002): 598–609.

14. T. A. Salthouse, "The Processing-Speed Theory of Adult Age Differences in Cognition," *Psychological Review* 103 (1996): 403–428.

15. L. Fratiglioni, D. DeRonchi, and H. A. Torres, "Worldwide Prevalence and Incidence of Dementia," *Drugs & Aging* 15 (1999): 365.

16. L. Kirsch, A. Jungeblut, L. Jenkins, et al., *Adult Literacy in America: A First Look at the Findings of the National Adult Literacy Survey.* 3rd ed., Vol. 201 (Washington, DC: U.S. Department of Education, National Center for Education, 2002).

17. Sumit Agarwal, John C. Driscoll, Xavier Gabaix, and David Laibson, "The Age of Reason: Financial Decisions over the Lifecycle," (October 21, 2008) http://ssrn.com/abstract=973790.

18. Julie A. Gazmararian, David W. Baker, Mark V. Williams et al., "Health Literacy among Medicare Enrollees in a Managed Care Organization," *Journal of the American Medical Association* 281, 6 (1999): 541–551.

19. Interestingly, only lack of education, not age or illness, had adverse effects on the information processing of non-seniors. See Judith H. Hibbard, Paul Slovic, Ellen Peters, Melissa L. Finucane, and Martin Tusler, "Is the Informed-Choice Policy Approach Appropriate for Medicare Beneficiaries?" *Health Affairs* 20, 3 (2001): 199–203.

20. Melissa L. Funicane, Paul Slovic, Judith H. Hibbard, Ellen Peters, C. K. Mertz, and Donald G. MacGregor, "Aging and Decision-making Competence: An Analysis of Comprehension and Consistency Skills in Older versus Younger Adults Considering Health-plan Options," *Journal of Behavioral Decision Making* 15 (2002): 141–164.

21. Precisely because seniors do not understand terms like "PPO," health plans tend to use trade names like "Golden Choice" and leave out "PPO," which probably perpetuates seniors' lack of understanding of such terms. See Leslie M. Greenwald, Lauren A. McCormack, Jennifer D. Uhrig, and Nathan West, "Measures and Predictors of Medicare Knowledge: A Review of the Literature," *Health Care Financing Review* 27, 4 (2006): 1–12.

22. Judith H. Hibbard, Jacquelyn J. Jewett, Siegfried Englemann, and Martin Tusler, "Can Medicare Beneficiaries Make Informed Choices?" *Health Affairs* 17, 6 (1998): 181–193.

23. Greenwald et al. "Measures and Predictors of Medicare Knowledge." We observed a similar phenomenon in the pilot study for the second wave of our MMA Panel Survey. We tried asking those who had chosen to remain in traditional Medicare why they did not enroll in a Medicare Advantage plan (and vice versa), but found that respondents knew so little about the path not taken that they were unable to articulate reasons (and we dropped the question from the final survey).

24. Pamela Farley Short, Lauren McCormack, Judith H. Hibbard et al., "Similarities and Differences in Choosing Health Plans," *Medical Care* 40, 4 (2002): 289–302.

25. Jennifer D. Uhrig and Pamela Farley Short, "Testing the Effect of Quality Reports on the Health Plan Choices of Medicare Beneficiaries," *Inquiry* 39 (2002/2003): 355–371.

26. Kaiser Family Foundation, "Medicare Drug Discount Cards: A Work in Progress," (July 2004).

27. Andrea Hassol, Marian V. Wrobel, and Teresa Doksum, "Medicare's Drug Discount Card Program: Beneficiaries' Experience with Choice," *Health Care Financing Review* 28, 1 (2007): 1–13.

28. Hassol et al., "Medicare's Drug Discount Card Program."

29. Noemi V. Rudolph and Sunyna S. Williams, "Medicare Beneficiary Knowledge of and Experience with Prescription Drug Cards," *Health Care Financing Review* 29, 1 (Fall 2007): 87–101.

30. G. A. Fergusson, "Public Opinion Regarding the New Medicare Benefit," *Healthcare Leadership Council* (October 2004); Andrea Hassol, Susan Jureidini, Teresa Doksum, and Louise Hadden, "Evaluation of the Medicare-Approved Prescription Drug Discount Card and Transitional Assistance Program," Final Report to the Centers for Medicare and Medicaid Services, May 2006; J. Love, "Filling the Rx: An Analysis of the Perceptions and Attitudes of Medicare Rx Discount Card Holders," AARP Knowledge Management, December 2004.

31. Patricia Neuman and Juliette Cubanski, "Medicare Part D Update—Lessons Learned and Unfinished Business," *New England Journal of Medicine* 361, 4 (July 23, 2009): 406–414.

32. Patricia Neuman, Michelle Kitchman Strollo, Stuart Guterman, William H. Rogers, Angela Li, Angie Mae C. Rodday, and Dana Gelb Safran, "Medicare Prescription Drug Benefit Progress Report: Findings from a 2006 National Survey of Seniors," *Health Affairs* 26, 5 (2007):

W630–643; Florian Heiss, Daniel McFadden, and Joachim Winter, "Mind the Gap! Consumer Perceptions and Choices of Medicare Part D Prescription Drug Plans," National Bureau of Economic Research Working Paper 13627 (2007).

33. McFadden, "Free Markets and Fettered Consumers," 22.

34. Helen Levy and David Weir, "Take-Up of Medicare Part D: Results from the Health and Retirement Study," National Bureau of Economic Research Working Paper 14692 (2009).

35. Yaniv Hanoch and Thomas Rice, "Can Limiting Choice Increase Social Welfare? The Elderly and Health Insurance," *Milbank Quarterly* 84 (2006): 37–73.

36. Abaluck and Gruber, "Choice Inconsistencies among the Elderly;" Yaniv Hanoch, Thomas Rice, Janet Cummings, and Stacey Wood, "How Much Choice Is Too Much? The Case of the Medicare Prescription Drug Benefit," *HSR: Health Services Research* 44, 4 (August 2009): 1157–1168; Thomas Rice and Janet Cummings, "Reducing the Number of Drug Plans for Seniors: A Proposal and Analysis of Three Case Studies," *Journal of Health Politics, Policy and Law* 35, 6 (2010): 961–997.

37. Kaiser Family Foundation, "Seniors and the Medicare Drug Benefit," December 2006. www. kff.org/kaiserpolls/upload/7604.pdf.

38. Kaiser Family Foundation, "Seniors' Early Experiences with the Medicare Prescription Drug Benefit," April 2006, www.kff.org/kaiserpolls/upload/7502.pdf.

39. Kaiser Family Foundation, "National Survey of Pharmacists and National Survey of Physicians: Findings on Medicare Part D," June 2006, available: www.kff.org/kaiserpolls/upload/7556.pdf. On pharmacists' experiences with the MMA implementation, see Tara Sussman, "Polarized Politics, Public Opinion and Health Reform," PhD dissertation, Harvard University, 2009.

40. Abaluck and Gruber, "Choice Inconsistencies among the Elderly"; Jeffrey Kling, Sendhil Mullainahan, Eldar Shafir, Lee Vermeulen, and Marian V. Wrobel, "Misperception in Choosing Medicare Drug Plans," NBER, October 2009, available at www.nber.org/~kling/choosing.pdf.

41. Abaluck and Gruber, "Choice Inconsistencies among the Elderly."

42. Jack Hoadley, Jennifer Thompson, Elizabeth Hargrave, Katie Merrell, Juliette Cubanski, and Tricia Neuman, "Medicare Part D 2008 Data Spotlight: Premiums," November 2007, Kaiser Family Foundation publication number 7706; Elizabeth Hargrave, Jack Hoadley, Juliette Cubanski, and Tricia Neuman, "Medicare Prescription Drug Plans in 2009 and Key Changes since 2006," Kaiser Family Foundation publication number 7917, June 2009, www. kff.org/medicare/upload/7917.pdf.

43. Mark V. Pauly, *Markets Without Magic: How Competition Might Save Medicare* (Washington, DC: AEI Press, 2008). For examples from consumer marketing, see Lawrence F. Feick and Linda L. Price, "The Market Maven: A Diffuser of Marketplace Information," *Journal of Marketing* 51 (January 1987): 83–97; Hans B. Thorelli and Jack L. Engledow, "Information Seekers and Information Systems: A Policy Perspective," *Journal of Marketing* 44 (Spring 1980): 9–24.

44. McFadden, "Free Markets and Fettered Consumers."

45. Hanoch, et al., "How Much Choice Is Too Much?"

46. Mark Duggan, Patrick Healy, and Fiona Scott Morton, "Providing Prescription Drug Coverage to the Elderly: America's Experiment with Medicare Part D," *Journal of Economic Perspectives* 22 (Fall 2008): 69–92.

47. Duggan, Healy, and Morton, "Providing Prescription Drug Coverage to the Elderly."

48. Sebastian Schneeweiss, Amanda R. Patrick, Alex Pedan, Laleh Varasteh, Raisa Levin, Nan Liu, and William H. Shrank, "The Effect of Medicare Part D Coverage on Drug Use and Cost Sharing among Seniors without Prior Drug Benefits," *Health Affairs* 28 (2009): w305–w316; Yuling Zhang, Julie M. Donohue, Judith R. Lave, Gerald O'Donnell, and Joseph P. Newhouse, "The Effect of Medicare Part D on Drug and Medical Spending," *New England Journal of Medicine* 361 (July 2, 2009): 52–61.

49. Duggan, Healy, and Morton, "Providing Prescription Drug Coverage to the Elderly."

50. Jeanne M. Madden, Amy J. Graves, Fang Zhang, Alyce S. Adams, Becky A. Briesacher, Dennis Ross-Degnan, Jerry H. Gurwitz, Marsha Pierre-Jacques, Dana Gelb Safran, Gerald S.

Adler, and Stephen B. Soumerai, "Cost-Related Medication Nonadherence and Spending on Basic Needs Following Implementation of Medicare Part D," *Journal of the American Medical Association* 299, 16 (2008): 1922–1928.

51. Favorability toward the new prescription drug benefit among those respondents who survived into the third wave was 38 percent in the December 2005 baseline survey, 55 percent in the second May 2007 wave, and 65 percent in the third February 2009 wave.

52. The differences in satisfaction between Part D and MA on the one hand and creditable coverage on the other are statistically significant at *p* <.001.

53. The six experiences were: left the pharmacy without their prescription because one of the drugs they were taking wasn't covered by their plan; left the pharmacy without their prescription because they couldn't afford it; had to switch medications because one of the drugs they were taking wasn't covered by their plan; had to switch from a brand-name drug to a generic drug; had to deal with a billing mistake for a prescription or a premium; or had to pay costs they hadn't expected—either for a prescription or a premium.

54. The differences in the average number of problems between Part D and MA on the one hand and creditable coverage on the other are statistically significant at *p* <.001.

55. Patricia Neuman, Michelle Kitchman Strollo, Stuart Guterman, William H. Rogers, Angela Li, Angie Mae C. Rodday, and Dana Gelb Safran, "Medicare Prescription Drug Benefit Progress Report: Findings from a 2006 National Survey of Seniors," *Health Affairs* 26, 5 (2007): W630–643.

56. In the third wave of our panel survey, 18 percent of the respondents who remained in the sample switched plans between 2008 and 2009. These were mostly new switchers—only one of those individuals had also switched between 2006 and 2007. Switching rates were also a bit higher among those with various negative experiences. The 2008–2009 switching rates were 19 percent among those paying above median premiums, 20 percent for those hitting the doughnut, and 33 percent among those with four or more problems getting their prescriptions. Keep in mind that the respondents remaining in the panel in wave three were younger and higher income than those who dropped out, which may contribute to these high switching rates.

57. Michael McCaughan, "Making Part D Stick: Lessons from the First Year of Medicare Rx," *RPM Report* 2, 4 (March 207): 26–32.

58. Mark V. Pauly, and Y. Zeng, "Adverse Selection and the Challenges to Stand-Alone Prescription Drug Insurance," *Frontiers in Health Policy Research* 7 (2004): 55–74; M. V. Wrobel, J. Doshi, B. C. Stuart, et al., "Predictability of Prescription Drug Expenditures for Medicare Beneficiaries," *Health Care Financing Review* 25, 2 (2003): 37–46.

59. Marisa Elena Domino, Sally C. Stearns, Edward C. Norton, and Wei-Shi Yeh, "Why Using Current Medications to Select a Medicare Part D Plan May Lead to Higher Out-of-Pocket Payments," *Medical Care Research and Review* 65, 1 (2008): 114–126.

60. The AARP Medicare Rx plan annual premium increased 41 percent over the same period. See Elizabeth Hargrave, Jack Hoadley, Juliette Cubanski, and Tricia Neuman, "Medicare Prescription Drug Plans in 2009 and Key Changes since 2006," Kaiser Family Foundation publication number 7917 (June 2009), www.kff.org/medicare/upload/7917.pdf.

61. Jack Hoadley, Jennifer Thompson, Elizabeth Hargrave, Katie Merrell, Juliette Cubanski, and Tricia Neuman, "Medicare Part D 2008 Data Spotlight: Premiums," Kaiser Family Foundation publication number 7706, November 2007.

62. Ramsey Baghdadi, "Tilting the Contracting Scales: Part D Plans Have Advantages over Manufacturers in 2008," *RPM Report* 2, 4 (March 2007): 36.

63. Consumers Union, "Cha-Ching! Seniors Enrolled in Medicare Prescription Drug Plans Might Be in for Sticker Shock Next Year," (November 9, 2007), www.consumersunion.org/pub/core_health_care/005184.html.

64. The percentage citing other options as a "major reason" they did not switch plans were "it was too difficult to select a new plan" (16 percent), "I was not aware that I could switch plans" (6 percent), "I couldn't get help to select a new plan" (5 percent), "I forgot to switch before the deadline" (2 percent), and "my pharmacist asked me not to switch plans" (<1 percent).

65. Adrianne Dulio, Michael Perry, and Juliette Cubanski, "Voices of Beneficiaries: Attitudes toward Medicare Part D Open Enrollment for 2008," Washington, DC: Kaiser Family Foundation (December 2007), www.kff.org/medicare/upload/7722.pdf.

66. The health care reform plan that President Obama signed in March 2010 makes several changes to the coverage gap. In 2010, those hitting the doughnut will receive a $250 rebate. Beginning in 2011, those in the gap will receive a 50 percent discount on brand-name drugs from manufacturers. Between 2011 and 2020, co-insurance in the gap will be reduced so that eventually seniors will only pay 25 percent of drug costs rather than the current 100 percent. Kaiser Family Foundation, "Explaining Health Care Reform: Key Changes to the Medicare Part D Drug Benefit Coverage Gap," March 2010, www.kff.org/healthreform/upload/8059.pdf.

67. Jack Hoadley, Laura Summer, Elizabeth Hargrave, Juliette Cubanski, and Tricia Neuman, "The Coverage Gap," November 2009, Kaiser Family Foundation.

68. Patricia Neuman and Juliette Cubanski, "Medicare Part D Update—Lessons Learned and Unfinished Business," *New England Journal of Medicine* 361, 4 (July 23, 2009): 406–414.

69. John Graham and Jianhui Hu, "The Risk-Balance in the United States: Who Decides?" *Health Affairs* 26 (2007): 625–635.

70. In the second wave of the MMA Panel Survey, we asked respondents who faced a gap in which they had no coverage what they did during that period. Eight-seven percent said they bought drugs with their own money, 34 percent stopped taking some or all of their prescription drugs, 21 percent skipped doses, 20 percent asked a relative to pay for their prescriptions, 13 percent split pills in half, and 13 percent bought medicines from a pharmacy outside the United States (respondents could choose multiple answers).

71. Geoffrey F. Joyce, Dana P. Goldman, Pinar Karaca-Mandic, and Yuhui Zheng, "Pharmacy Benefit Caps and the Chronically Ill," *Health Affairs* 26 (September/October 2007): 1333–1344; C. W. Tseng, "Cost-Lowering Strategies Used by Medicare Beneficiaries Who Exceed Drug Benefit Caps and Have A Gap in Drug Coverage," *Journal of the American Medical Association* 292, 8 (2004): 952–960.

72. John Hsu, Mary Price, Jie Huang, Richard Brand, et al., "Unintended Consequences of Caps on Medicare Drug Benefits," *New England Journal of Medicine* 354, 22 (2006): 2349–2359; U. D. Patel and M. M. Davis, "Falling into the Doughnut Hole: Drug Spending among Beneficiaries with End-Stage Renal Disease under Medicare Part D Plans," *Journal of the American Society of Nephrology* 17, 9 (2006): 2546–2553.

73. Hoadley et al., "The Coverage Gap."

74. Heiss, McFadden, and Winter, "Mind the Gap!" The point at which Catastrophic coverage begins depends on the enrollee's out-of-pocket costs. Plans that cover part of the doughnut effectively slow the rate at which those costs accrue, delaying the onset of catastrophic reinsurance and making those enrollees even more expensive to the insurer. See Duggan, Healy, and Morton, "Providing Prescription Drug Coverage to the Elderly" at page 73.

75. Duggan, Healy, and Morton, "Providing Prescription Drug Coverage to the Elderly," 72.

76. Neuman and Cubanski, "Medicare Part D—Lessons Learned and Unfinished Business."

77. Duggan, Healy, and Morton, "Providing Prescription Drug Coverage to the Elderly," 87.

78. John Hsu, Jie Huang, Vicki Fung, Mary Price, Richard Brant, Rita Jui, Bruce Fireman, William Dow, John Bertko, and Joseph P. Newhouse, "Distributing $800 Billion: An Early Assessment of Medicare Part D Risk Adjustment," *Health Affairs* 28, 1 (2009): 215–225.

79. Hsu et al., "Distributing $800 Billion," recommend incorporating prior-year drug use to improve risk adjustment; doing so increases the variation in drug costs that can be predicted from 12 percent to more than 40 percent.

80. Ateev Mehrotra, Sonya Grier, and R. Adams Dudley, "The Relationship between Health Plan Advertising and Market Incentives: Evidence of Risk-Selective Behavior," *Health Affairs* 25, 3 (May/June 2006): 759–765.

81. Duggan, Healy, and Morton, "Providing Prescription Drug Coverage to the Elderly."

82. Medicare Payment Advisory Commission (MedPAC), "A Data Book: Healthcare Spending and the Medicare Program," June 2007.

83. Leslie M. Greenwald, Lauren A. McCormack, Jennifer D. Uhrig, and Nathan West, "Measures and Predictors of Medicare Knowledge: A Review of the Literature," *Health Care Financing Review* 27, 4 (2006): 1–12.

84. Rudolph and Williams, "Medicare Beneficiary Knowledge of and Experience with Prescription Drug Cards."

85. Hanoch et al., "How Much Choice is Too Much?"

86. In 2009, there were 6.3 million dual eligibles who received the low-income subsidy, 1.8 million MSP and SSI recipients, and an additional 1.5 million people who successfully applied to receive it. Laura Summer, Jack Hoadley, and Elizabeth Hargrave, *The Medicare Part D Low-Income Subsidy Program: Experience to Date and Policy Issues for Consideration*, Henry J. Kaiser Family Foundation, September 2010.

87. Jack Hoadley, Elizabeth Hargrave, and Juliette Cubanski, "Medicare Part D 2008 Data Spotlight: Low-Income Subsidy Plan Availability," Kaiser Family Foundation, April 2008.

88. Hoadley, Hargrave, and Cubanski, "Medicare Part D 2008 Data Spotlight: Low-Income Subsidy Plan Availability."

89. MedPAC, "A Data Book: Healthcare Spending and the Medicare Program."

90. Vernon Smith, Kathleen Gifford, Sandy Kramer, and Linda Elam, "The Transition of Dual Eligibles to Medicare Part D during Implementation: Results from a 50-State Snapshot," Kaiser Family Foundation, February 2006.

91. MedPAC, *Report to Congress 2009*.

92. Hoadley, Hargrave, and Cubanski, "Medicare Part D 2008 Data Spotlight: Low-Income Subsidy Plan Availability."

93. Hoadley, Hargrave, and Cubanski, "Medicare Part D 2008 Data Spotlight: Low-Income Subsidy Plan Availability."

94. Julie M. Donohue, Haiden A. Huskamp, and Samuel H. Zuvekas, "Dual Eligibles with Mental Disorders and Medicare Part D: How Are They Faring?" *Health Affairs* 28, 3 (2009): 746–759.

95. We also examined Part D experiences by education, gender, and age. Seniors with the lowest education levels (the quarter of the sample with less than high school educations) were less favorable toward the drug benefit (44 percent very favorable versus 58 percent of those with high school educations and above), had more problems (1.6 versus 1.1), and were more likely to say that the new program had made them less sure they can afford their drugs (20 percent versus 10 percent) and made them feel less financially secure (27 percent versus 13 percent among the more educated). In multivariate analyses (Table B.5), the effect of education is mostly absorbed by other variables. We also looked at Part D experiences by gender and age, but found few differences at the bivariate level. As we expected, women were less likely to switch plans (just 6 percent switched between the first and second years of the program compared to 16 percent of men who switched), but it was men who were more likely to say that the reform had made them feel less financially secure (13 percent of women but 24 percent of men said so), the opposite of expectations. Differences by gender along other dimensions were small and not statistically significant. By age, bivariate differences in Part D experiences were small and statistically insignificant as well, with two exceptions. The oldest fifth of the sample (aged 80 and above) did pay higher monthly premiums in 2006 ($45, compared to $35 among those aged 65 to 79). The other statistically significant difference by age was not in the expected direction: older respondents reported fewer problems getting their medications than younger respondents (0.9 versus 1.2).

96. Those with more problems getting their prescriptions and paying higher monthly premiums were more likely to switch than those with fewer problems and lower premiums, while hitting the doughnut made no difference in switch rates, ceteris paribus.

97. Madden et al. "Cost-Related Medication Nonadherence and Spending on Basic Needs Following Implementation of Medicare Part D."

98. Duggan, Healy, and Morton, "Providing Prescription Drug Coverage to the Elderly."

99. Neuman and Cubanski, "Medicare Part D Update—Lessons Learned and Unfinished Business."

100. McFadden, "Free Markets and Fettered Consumers."

101. McFadden, "Free Markets and Fettered Consumers."

Chapter 9

1. Theodore J. Lowi, *The End of Liberalism: Ideology, Policy and the Crisis of Public Authority* (New York: W. W. Norton, 1969), 76.
2. Richard R. John, "Rethinking the Early American State," *Polity* 40, 3 (July 2008): 332–339; Laura S. Jensen, "Government, the State, and Governance," *Polity* 40, 3 (July 2008): 379–385.
3. Aaron L. Friedberg, "American Antistatism and the Founding of the Cold War State," in *Shaped by War and Trade: International Influences on American Political Development,* eds. Ira Katznelson and Martin Shefter (Princeton: Princeton University Press, 2002), 239–266.
4. Desmond King and Robert C. Lieberman, "Finding the American State: Transcending the 'Statelessness' Account," *Polity* 40, 3 (July 2008): 368.
5. William J. Novak, "The Myth of the 'Weak' American State," *American Historical Review* 113 (2008): 752–772.
6. Peter Baldwin, "Beyond Weak and Strong: Rethinking the State in Comparative Policy History," *Journal of Policy History* 17, 1 (2005): 12–33; King and Lieberman, "American State."
7. Members of Congress have disagreed about the merits of federal versus private screeners since the creation of the TSA, and since 2004 airports have been allowed to opt-out of relying on federal security screeners. A small number have done so, and some Republicans have sought to encourage this practice. In the words of Representative John Mica (R-FL), Chairman of the House Transportation and Infrastructure Committee, "When the TSA was established, it was never envisioned that it would become a huge, unwieldy bureaucracy which was soon to grow to 67,000 employees. As TSA has grown larger, more impersonal, and administratively top-heavy, I believe it is important that airports across the country consider utilizing the opt-out provision provided by law." Byron York, "Amid Airport Anger, GOP Takes Aim at Screening." *Washington Examiner* November 15, 2010, http://www.washingtonexaminer.com/politics/Amid-airport-anger_-GOP-takes-aim-at-screening-1576602–108259869.html, accessed November 18, 2010. See also Bartholomew Elias, *A Return to Private Security Screening At Airports?: Background and Issues Regarding the Opt-Out Provision of the Aviation and Transportation Security Act,* Congressional Research Service Report, May 14, 2004.
8. Lowi, *End of Liberalism,* 85.
9. Barry D. Karl, *The Uneasy State: The United States from 1915 to 1945* (Chicago: University of Chicago Press, 1983).
10. Suzanne Mettler, "Reconstituting the Submerged State: The Challenges of Social Policy Reform in the Obama Era," *Perspectives on Politics* 8, 3 (September 2010): 803–824.
11. Mark Schlesinger and Vincent L. Hutchings, "Affiliation, Collective Identification and Public Policy: Medicare Privatization and Elders' Attitudes toward Federal Involvement in Medical Care." Unpublished manuscript, Yale University. 2003.
12. Jacob S. Hacker and Paul Pierson, *Off-Center: The Republican Revolution and the Erosion of American Democracy* (New Haven: Yale University Press, 2005).
13. Hacker and Pierson, *Off-Center,* 16.
14. For overviews of the public opinion-public policy literature, see Paul Burstein, "The Impact of Public Opinion on Public Policy: A Review and an Agenda," *Political Research Quarterly* 56 (2003): 29–40; Carroll J. Glynn, Susan Herbst, Garrett J. O'Keefe, Robert Y. Shapiro, and Lawrence R. Jacobs, "Public Opinion and Policy Making," in *Public Opinion,* eds. Glynn, Herbst, O'Keefe, and Shapiro (Boulder, CO: Westview Press, 1999), 299–340; Jeff Manza and Fay Lomax Cook, "A Democratic Polity? Three Views of Policy Responsiveness to Public Opinion in the United States," *American Politics Research* 30 (2002): 630–667.
15. Len Nichols, "Implementing Insurance Market Reforms under the Federal Health Reform Law," *Health Affairs* 29, 6 (2010): 1152–1157.
16. John Boehner, "Why Republicans Will Fight to Repeal Health-Care Takeover," *Des Moines Register,* March 24, 2010, accessed November 22, 2010, http://www.desmoinesregister.com/article/20100324/OPINION01/3250323/Guest-opinion-Why-Republicans-will-fight-to-repeal-health-care-takeover.

17. William G. Weissert and Carol S. Weissert, "Why Major Health Reform in 2009–10 Won't Solve Our Problems," *The Forum* 18, 1 (2010): Article 9.

18. Jackie Calmes, "A Policy Debacle and Its Lessons," *New York Times*, September 6, 2009, A1; Lawrence R. Jacobs and Theda Skocpol, *Health Care Reform and American Politics: What Everyone Needs to Know* (Oxford: Oxford University Press, 2010).

19. Jacobs and Skocpol, *Health Care Reform*, 67–75.

20. Jacobs and Skocpol, *Health Care Reform*, 73.

21. Jacob S. Hacker, "The Road to Somewhere: Why Health Reform Happened," *Perspectives on Politics* 8, 3 (September 2010): 865.

22. Jeffrey Young, "GOP Uneasy as Allies Stray on Healthcare," *The Hill*, March 17, 2009, 1.

23. Jeffrey Young, "Doctors Like Healthcare," *The Hill*, July 17, 2009, 1; Amy Goldstein, "Influential AMA's Support for Reform Is Far from Certain: Medicare Fee Cuts Are Crux of Issue, Policy Analysts Say," *Washington Post*, October 16, 2009, A4.

24. Katharine Q. Seelye, "Ad Campaign Counterattacks against Overhaul's Critics," *New York Times*, August 14, 2009, A12.

25. Jonathan Oberlander, "Long Time Coming: Why Health Reform Finally Passed," *Health Affairs* 29, 6 (2010): 1112–1116.

26. Mollyann Brodie, Drew Altman, Claudia Deane, Sasha Buscho, and Elizabeth Hamel, "Liking the Pieces, Not the Package: Contradictions in Public Opinion during Health Reform," *Health Affairs* 29, 6 (2010): 1125–1130.

27. Pew Research Center for the People and the Press, "Public Trust in Government: 1958–2010," accessed November 22, 2010, http://people-press.org/trust/.

28. ABC News/Money Poll, July 27–August 7, 1994; Kaiser Health Tracking Poll, August 4–11, 2009. Both polls accessed from the iPoll archive of the Roper Center at the University of Connecticut.

29. Kaiser Health Tracking Poll, August 4–11, 2009. Along these lines, a March 2009 Gallup/USAToday poll found that Americans preferred "maintaining the current system based mostly on private health insurance" to "replacing the current health care system with a new government run health care system" by 56 to 39 percent. Gallup Poll, March 27–29, 2009. Accessed from the iPoll archive of the Roper Center at the University of Connecticut.

30. Drew Westen, "Selling Health Care? Watch What You Say," *Washington Post*, June 28, 2009, B03.

31. At the start of the Obama administration, there were 57 Democrats in the Senate plus two independents who caucused with the Democrats, until Al Franken was declared the winner of the Minnesota Senate race. That brought the number of Democrats and Independents up to 60. However, the victory of Republican Scott Brown in a Massachusetts special election to replace Edward Kennedy then lowered their majority to 59.

32. During the reform debate, 52 House Democrats belonged to this group.

33. The House passed the Senate bill on March 21 by a vote of 219 to 212—only a few votes above the 216 needed and with 34 Democrats voting against it. The House then approved changes to the Senate bill by a vote of 220 to 211.

34. Hinda Chaikind, Bernadette Fernandez, Chris L. Peterson, and Paulette C. Morgan, *Private Health Insurance Provisions of H.R. 3200*, Congressional Research Service report R40724 (August 31, 2009).

35. Helen A. Halpin and Peter Harbage, "The Origins and Demise of the Public Option," *Health Affairs* 29, 6 (June 2010): 1117–1124.

36. Richard Cohen, "Pelosi's Bill: How She Did It," *National Journal* (November 14, 2009): 20.

37. Lori Montgomery and Peter Slevin, "States Likely to Shape Health Reform," *The Washington Post*, November 1, 2009, A03.

38. Hinda Chaikind, Bernadette Fernandez, Chris L. Peterson, and Paulette C. Morgan, *Private Health Insurance Provisions of S.1679*, Congressional Research Service report R40861 (October 15, 2009).

39. Shailagh Murray and Lori Montgomery, "Senate Groups Satisfied with Deal; but Groups Representing Hospitals and Doctors Oppose Medicare Buy-in," *Washington Post*, December 10, 2009, A1.

40. Michel Martin, "Democrat Sen. Mary Landrieu Concerned about Health Care Overhaul," Interview on NPR News, October 22, 2009.

41. Jacobs and Skocpol, *Health Care Reform*, 62–63.
42. Jim Rutenberg and Jackie Calmes, "Getting to the Source of the 'Death Panel' Rumor," *New York Times*, August 14, 2009, A1.
43. Kathleen Silvassy, "Senators Debate 'Public Plan' Health Care Option," *CQ Today Online News*, July 5, 2009.
44. Brendan Nyhan, "Why the 'Death Panel' Myth Wouldn't Die: Misinformation in the Health Care Reform Debate," *The Forum* 8, 1 (2010): Article 5.
45. Nyhan, "'Death Panel' Myth."
46. Dan Balz and John Cohen, "Public Option Gains Support: Clear Majority Now Backs Plan," *Washington Post*, October 20, 2009.
47. David Kirkpatrick, "Obama Taking an Active Role in Health Talks," *New York Times*, August 13, 2009, A1.
48. Ezra Klein, "Outspoken: A Conversation with Lindsey Graham Dealmaker," *Washington Post*, August 9, 2009, B2.
49. Marilyn Werber Serafini, "Writing the Rules for the Health Law," *National Journal*, May 1, 2010, 6.
50. James A. Barnes, "The Next Health Care Fight," *National Journal*, March 20, 2010, 1.
51. Montgomery and Slevin, "Health Care Reform."
52. Len Nichols, "Implementing Insurance Market Reforms under the Federal Health Reform Law," *Health Affairs* 29, 6 (2010): 1152–1157.
53. Jason T. Abaluck and Jonathan Gruber, "Choice Inconsistencies among the Elderly: Evidence from Plan Choice in the Medicare Part D Program," NBER Working Paper 14759 (February 2009). Available: www.nber.org/papers/w14759.
54. Under each plan, individuals' out-of-pocket costs are limited to the current Health Savings Account out-of-pocket limit ($5,950 for individuals and $11,900 for families in 2010).
55. The law allows regional exchanges as well. States may opt out of establishing an exchange and rely on a federally operated exchange instead. Jon Kingsdale and John Bertko, "Insurance Exchanges under Health Reform: Six Design Issues for the States," *Health Affairs* 29, 6 (2010): 1158–1163.
56. Kingsdale and Bertko, "Insurance Exchanges."
57. Kingsdale and Bertko, "Insurance Exchanges," 1160.
58. For instance, the student loan measure was included with health care reform in the 2010 reconciliation bill that requires only a simple majority to pass in the Senate, and this was done because of the need for cost savings in the bill. The push for health care reform thus helped get this highly contested piece of legislation through the legislative gauntlet. Mettler, "Submerged State."
59. Thomas Rice, Janet Cummings, and Daniel Kao, "Reducing the Number of Drug Plans for Seniors: A Proposal and Analysis of Three Case Studies," unpublished manuscript, UCLA; Yaniv Hanoch and Thomas Rice, "Can Limiting Choice Increase Social Welfare? The Elderly and Health Insurance," *Milbank Quarterly* 84 (2006): 37–73.

Appendices

1. On KN's samplng mechanism, see Karol Krotki and J. Michael Dennis, "Probability-Based Survey Research on the Internet," presented at the 53rd Conference of the International Statistical Institute, Seoul, South Korea, 2001. On the representativeness of the KN sample, see Jon A. Krosnick and Lin Chiat Chang, "A Comparison of the Random Digit Dialing Telephone Survey Methodology with Internet Survey Methodology as Implemented by Knowledge Networks and Harris Interactive," unpublished manuscript, Ohio State University, 2001. The authors find the KN sample to be representative of the U.S. population on both demographic characteristics and political attitudes).
2. Patricia Neuman, Michelle Kitchman Strollo, Stuart Guterman, William H. Rogers, Angela Li, Angie Mae C. Rodday, and Dana Gelb Safran, "Medicare Prescription Drug Benefit Progress Report: Findings from a 2006 National Survey of Seniors," *Health Affairs* 26, 5 (2007): W630–643.

INDEX

Aaron, Henry, 92
AARP
    cultivation by Republican lawmakers, 104,
      136–37
    and the Medicare Modernization Act, 108,
      136–37, 140
    opposition to Social Security privatization, 97,
      183
    Part D prescription drug plan, 206
    political effects of support for MMA, 183, 186
    stance on prescription drug reimportation, 198
    support for Affordable Care Act of 2010, 229
Affordable Care Act of 2010, 3
    Center for Medicare and Medicaid Innovation
      in, 148
    consumer choice in, 234–35
    "death panel" rumors, 233
    delegated governance in, 17, 227–35
    implementation of, 234
    Medicare Advantage changes in, 16, 187–88,
      287n47
    Medicare Modernization Act as model for, 171,
      229
    Office of Personnel Management (OPM)
      contracts with private insurers in, 228, 232
    and prescription drug reimportation, 198
    public opinion toward, 43, 230, 233
    public option, 231–34
    role of states in, 228, 234
    Tea Party protests and, 232–33
Agency for Healthcare Research and Quality, 148
Aid to Families with Dependent Children (AFDC).
    See welfare
America's Health Insurance Plans (AHIP), 128,
    186, 187
American Association of Health Plans (AAHP), 128
American Association of Retired Persons. *See* AARP
American Medical Association (AMA)
    and Affordable Care Act of 2010, 230
    capitalizing on anti-government sentiment
      among public, 72
    and Medicare, 73–74
    opposition to national health insurance, 69–70
    opposition to Veterans Health Administration,
      67–68
American state

before twentieth century, 58
    delegated governance and, 222–25
    expansion of, 59–63
    nature of, 9, 16–17, 52–55
Armey, Richard K., 101
Arrow, Kenneth, 88

Balanced Budget Act of 1995, 102–4, 122
Balanced Budget Act of 1997, 11, 95, 104–5, 109,
    110, 115, 122, 161
Ball, Robert, 67, 147
Bartels, Larry, 189
Baucus, Max, 130, 131, 134–36, 230, 233
Bipartisan Commission on the Future of Medicare,
    105, 115, 118, 122
Bliley, Thomas, 120
Blue Cross/Blue Shield
    changes in business practices of, 91
    as early private insurers, 68, 70
    and health care providers, 88, 146, 149–50
    as Medicaid payment administrator, 266n132
    as Medicare payment administrator, 11, 22,
      73–77, 149
    role in Federal Employees Health Benefits
      program creation, 70
Breaux, John, 105, 135–36, 189–90, 222
Bush, George W.
    and the Medicare Modernization Act, 107, 133,
      140, 142, 157, 187
    prescription drug proposals of, 129, 130, 132
    role in Medicare Modernization Act versus
      Congress's, 13, 108, 132
    Social Security private accounts proposal of, 84,
      97, 183, 227
Butler, Stuart M., 84, 93

campaign ads, on prescription drug reform,
    118–19, 131, 195–96
campaign contributions, 45, 51, 84, 126–28,
    137–39
Centers for Medicare and Medicaid Services, 85,
    112, 147–48, 150, 154, 162
    as underfunded agency, 151–52, 165
Chamber of Commerce, 127, 137

Champion, Hale, 149, 266n125
child support enforcement, administrative
   arrangements of, 22–26
Citizens for Better Medicare, 125, 127
Clemens, Elisabeth, 9, 21, 54
Clinton, Bill, 87, 103–5
   health care reform effort of, 99–102, 176,
      228–30
   Medicare prescription drug proposals of,
      114–15, 118, 120, 123, 125–27, 274n39
Children's Health Insurance Program (CHIP),
   186–87
Clinton, Hillary, 157
Coalition for Medicare Choices, 187
Cohen, Wilbur, 73, 74, 266n125
Committee on Economic Security, 11, 59
Community Action Agencies, 64
Congress
   and Affordable Care Act of 2010, 230–32
   as cause of delegated governance, 7, 35, 46–48,
      56–57, 62–63, 78, 117, 141, 219, 224
   as central force behind Medicare Modernization
      Act, 13, 108, 129, 132
   and health care interests, 12, 69, 90, 121, 127,
      133, 138–39, 188, 233
   and Medicare, 66, 71–72, 74–76, 98–99, 142,
      187–88
   and New Deal, 60, 62, 67
   oversight role in delegated governance, 149–50,
      151–52, 154, 165, 235–36
   polarization in, 103, 112–13
   and Veterans Health Administration, 68
Congressional Budget Office
   scoring of health reform proposals, 186–88, 231
   scoring of prescription drug proposals, 118,
      122–23, 159, 162
conservative movement
   barriers to agenda of, 80–84
   conditions behind rise of, 80
   think tanks, 12, 45, 80, 84, 93, 102, 135, 140,
      142, 151
consumer choice reforms, 6, 8–9, 26, 88–91
   Affordable Care Act of 2010 as example of,
      234–35
   information usage in, 205–6
   international examples of, 28, 31, 34
   and Medicare Modernization Act, 11, 13, 110
   requirements on consumers, 201, 216–17
   risk bearing in, 27, 110
   senior citizen shortcomings as consumers in,
      202–6
consumer-directed health care
   Health Savings Accounts, 15, 93, 110, 133, 134,
      135, 140, 297n54
   Medical Savings Accounts, 93, 102, 104, 273n6,
      275n53
contracting out
   versus "delegated governance," 20–21

Daschle, Tom, 131, 140
delegated governance. *See also* consumer choice
   reforms.
   accountability in, 4, 8–9, 21–22, 49, 50–52, 153,
      201–2, 209–10, 221, 225
   Affordable Care Act of 2010 as example of,
      227–35
   ambiguous nature of, 141–42
   appeal of, to centrist and conservative
      Democrats, 87, 92, 98, 102, 120, 122, 224, 231
   causes of, 4, 6–8, 35–48, 56–57, 63–64, 73–74,
      77–78, 116–17, 219–22
   compared with "contracting out," 20–21
   compared with "governance," 20
   compared with "privatization," 20–21
   consequences of, 8–10, 48–55, 146–54, 220–22
   decision-making in, 26, 219, 234–35
   definition of, 4, 19–22
   effects on public opinion, 223, 225
   eligibility determinations in, 52
   forms of, 5–6, 23, 218–19
   "hollow state" created by, 72, 166, 224
   hypothesized policy feedback effects of,
      168–70, 172, 176, 183, 190–91, 194–95
   implications for American state of, 222–25
   improvements to functioning of, 235–36
   inefficient administration in, 145–54, 166–67,
      221
   interest groups in, 51, 141
   international examples of, 8, 28–35
   within Medicare, 11, 22–25, 66, 72–73,
   Medicare Modernization Act as example of,
      108–9, 141–42
   motivation behind, during 1950s and 1960s, 65
   motivation behind, since 1980s, 84–87, 219–20
   as "mushy middle," not "off center," 226–27
   nonprofits as object of, 23–25, 63–65
   path dependence arising from, 198–99, 222
   policy effectiveness in, 49–50
   redistributive concerns in, 51, 212–16
   regulatory shortcomings in, 166
   reluctance of nonprofits to engage in
      historically, 64
   Republican party use of, 84, 120–23, 141, 220
   rise of, during 1950s, 62
   risk bearing in, 26–27, 87
   social welfare programs with elements of, 22–27
   state and local government use of, 94–95
   within welfare, 96
Democratic party
   Blue Dog coalition within, 87, 231
   Centrists and conservatives within, 66, 87, 98,
      102, 105, 120, 122, 135, 224, 231
   Congressional Budget Office scoring of
      proposals, 123
   incentives to pass Affordable Care Act of 2010,
      230–31
   and the MMA, 130–36, 140, 142

prescription drug proposals of, 114, 118, 120–21
public opinion limits on goals of, 227
Southern Democrats in, 35, 36, 46, 59, 61–62, 66, 69, 78, 80, 224
Devine, Don, 142
Dole, Bob, 103
Drucker, Peter, 86, 87
Dual eligibles. *See* Medicare Prescription Drug Improvement and Modernization Act of 2003

electoral competition
around entitlement programs, 103, 105, 112–14, 119, 123, 129–31
for senior citizen votes, 117, 131
Enthoven, Alain, 90

Feder, Judith, 137
Federal Acquisition Regulation, 112
Federal Emergency Relief Administration (FERA), 61
Federal Employees Health Benefits Program (FEHBP), 70, 92, 288n54
Feldstein, Martin, 88–89
free market movement, 4–6, 21, 31, 56, 77, 80–81
and Democrats, 99–100
in health care, 12, 33–34, 88–94
limits of Reagan administration reform efforts, 98–99
Frist, Bill, 118, 131, 134, 136,

Gephardt, Richard, 103
Gilmartin, Raymond V., 125, 126, 128
Gingrich, Newt, 85, 103, 104, 113, 140
Goodman, John, 92, 93
Gore, Al
prescription drug proposal of, 129
Graham, Lindsey, 234
Grassley, Charles (Chuck), 134, 135, 186, 233

Hacker, Jacob, 226
Hastert, Dennis, 119–20, 132, 134, 136
Health Care Financing Administration. *See* Centers for Medicare and Medicaid Services
Health Insurance Association of America, 128
Health Insurance Portability and Accountability Act of 1996 (HIPAA), 104, 110
Health maintenance organizations (HMOs). *See* managed care
Health Savings Accounts. *See* consumer-directed health care
Health Security Act. *See* Clinton health care reform
Hess, Arthur, 73, 74
hidden welfare state, 9, 21, 172

Hill-Burton Act. *See* Hospital Construction Act of 1946
Hopkins, Harry, 61
hospitals. *See also* interest groups
accreditation of, 5, 72, 75, 146–48
and Affordable Care Act of 2010, 229–30, 233
delegation to, 146
as health care interest group, 69, 90, 131
importance of Medicare to, 10
intermediary selection by, 76
Medicare payments to, 149
as recipients of federal research funds, 69
rise of non-profit, 91
wariness of federal government interference, 46, 72
Hospital Construction Act of 1946, 69
housing vouchers. *See* Section 8 housing vouchers

Ignagni, Karen, 128
insurance industry. *See also* interest groups
early growth of, 68–69
"enroll-and-migrate" strategy of, 161
fears would not enter Part D market, 155, 159
Humana, 160–61, 163, 210, 212
incentives to support Affordable Care Act of 2010, 229
Part D marketing campaigns of, 163–64
Part D subsidies to, 159
policy feedback effects of MMA on, 186–89
role in Affordable Care Act of 2010, 227–28, 230
skepticism about prescription drug benefit, 127–28
interest groups
as cause of delegated governance, 7, 45–46, 73, 219
capture of regulating bureaucracies by, 90
in health care, 10, 46–47, 66–70, 71, 76, 78, 100, 104
K Street, 126, 137
policy feedback effects of MMA on, 183–89
role in Medicare Modernization Act of 2003, 123–29, 131, 137, 138–39
issue ownership, 9, 16, 189, 286n19
of Medicare Modernization Act, 169, 176–83, 222
of prescription drugs, 119
issue preemption, 9, 16
effect of Medicare Modernization Act on, 170, 194–98, 222

JOBS program
administrative arrangements of, 22–26
Joint Commission (JC), 147, 148. *See also* hospitals, accreditation of
Joint Commission on Accreditation of Hospitals (JCAH). *See* Joint Commission

Joint Commission on Accreditation of Healthcare
Organizations (JCAHO). *See* Joint
Commission

Kahn, Charles N. ("Chip"), III, 128, 131–32, 161
Kennedy, Edward M., 126, 130–31, 134, 140, 157,
187
Kennedy, John F., 63, 71
Kristol, William, 176
Krugman, Paul, 142

Landrieu, Mary, 232
League of United Latin American Citizens, 186
Lowi, Theodore, 53, 219, 224, 225

managed care. *See also* Medicare managed care,
Medicare Advantage
confusion over labels for, 203
emergence and spread of, 91–92
as free-market reform, 12, 47, 89–90
HMO Act of 1973, 97
in Medicaid, 18, 95–96
public opinion toward, 83, 118
risk contracts in Tax Equity and Fiscal
Responsibility Act of 1982 (TEFRA), 98
McCarran-Ferguson Act of 1945, 228
McConnell, Grant, 52, 224, 225
McClellan, Mark, 234
McFadden, Daniel, 202
Medicaid. *See also* Medicare Prescription Drug
Improvement and Modernization Act of 2003
(MMA); dual eligibles
administrative arrangements of, 23–27
Affordable Care Act of 2010 and, 228, 234
attempted cuts to, 81, 102, 272n136
managed care in, 18, 95–96, 160, 254n1
Medical Savings Accounts. *See* consumer-directed
health care
Medicare, 10
administrative arrangements of, 11, 22–27, 72,
146–48
cost of, 97, 99, 149
creation of, 71–77
delegated governance within, 11–12, 66–77,
146–54
federal workforce, 11, 151
interest group role in during creation, 66–67
intermediaries for Parts A and B in, 66, 72–77,
93, 109–10, 112, 145–47, 149–54, 225
lack of prescription drug benefit in, 114
managed care enrollment, 99, 159, 186, 187,
188
Medicare Savings Programs, 213
non-interference clause, 76–77, 146
Part B premiums, 112, 136, 160, 273n9

premium support, 34, 92, 93, 105, 118, 122,
124, 126, 189–90, 222, 275n46
private fee-for-service plans (PFFS), 11, 161,
164, 187, 287n37
private plans within, 11. *See* Medicare
Advantage; Medicare managed care
prospective payment, 13, 99, 188
public opinion in creation of, 71
public opinion toward, 81, 83–84
resource-based relative value scale, 99
senior citizens as focus of, 71
vouchers. *See* Medicare premium support
Medicare Advantage
cuts to, in Affordable Care Act of 2010, 187–88,
287n47
cost of, compared to FFS Medicare, 110, 145,
160
as delegated governance, 23–24, 26–27
Democratic support for, 186–87
"enroll-and-migrate" strategy, 161
enrollment in, 11, 159, 254n12
enrollment procedure, 201–3
marketing of, 164
in the Medicare Modernization Act, 109–11
number of plans available, 159
political support for, 186–89
prescription drug coverage in, 111
risk adjustment in, 212
satisfaction with, 208–9
Medicare Catastrophic Coverage Act, 98–99,
190–91
as lesson for MMA framers, 191
Medicare managed care, 13. *See also* Medicare
Advantage
MedicarePlus, 102, 122
Medicare + Choice, 104, 110, 128, 172, 183,
202–3
Medicare Prescription Drug Improvement and
Modernization Act of 2003 (MMA), 11. *See
also* Medicare Advantage; Part D drug plans
attitudinal acquiescence toward, 191–94
AARP role in passing, 136–37
agenda-setting moment, 115
beneficiary confusion, 156–57
budget for, 132
costs of, 145, 159, 160, 162
Democratic vision for, 120–21
difficulty in regulating market practices around,
164–65
doughnut hole in, 111, 120, 132–33
dual eligibles, 111, 135, 155–57, 181, 184, 193,
200, 213–15, 272n2
final vote, 140
health savings accounts in, 133
implementation of, 155–57
income-tested Part B premiums in, 112, 136
low-income subsidy in, 109, 213–16
Medicare Administrative Contractor, 112, 153

Medicare spending trigger in, 135
as model for health care reform, 157,171,
    189–90, 229
non-interference clause, 111, 142
political participation concerning, 191–92
prescription drug benefit as carrot in Medicare
    reform, 118
prescription drug price negotiation, 163
premium support in, 133, 136, 140
private fee-for-service plans (PFFS), 161, 187
provisions, 108–9
Republican vision for, 121–23
role of interest groups in, 123–29, 137
subsidies to insurers, 159
temporary prescription drug discount program,
    203–04
Medicare Modernization Act (MMA) Panel Survey,
    170–71
Mendelson, Dan, 210
Mills, Wilbur, 75–76, 280n20
Moffit, Robert E., 93
Moore, Stephen, 136
Morton, Fiona Scott, 163
Mosher, Frederick, 54

NAACP, 186
Nelson, Bill, 188
Neo-liberalism. *See* free market movement
New Deal
    administration in programs of, 61
    issue ownership effects of, 176
    rejection of national health insurance during, 67
non-delegation doctrine, 20
non-interference clause
    in Medicare, 76–77, 146
    in Medicare Modernization Act, 111, 142
Novak, William, 53
Novelli, Bill, 136

Obama health care reform. *See* Affordable Care Act
    of 2010

Palin, Sarah, 233
Part D drug plans. *See also* Medicare Modernization
    Act of 2003
    beneficiary costs, 158
    doughnut hole in, 26, 43, 158–59, 161, 181–82,
        184, 191, 194, 205–6, 209, 211–14, 229,
        293n74
    dual eligibles in, 213–15
    effects on prescription drug utilization, 158
    enrollment, 158, 159, 254n12
    enrollment procedure, 201–2
    enrollment decisions, 204–5
    favorability toward, 194, 207

low-income subsidy in, 213–16
market consolidation, 212
marketing of, 163–64
number of plans available, 156, 202
plan selection, 205–6
plan switching, 209–11
problems with, compared to creditable coverage,
    209
risk adjustment, 212
satisfaction with, compared to creditable
    coverage, 208
vulnerable populations in, 212–16
Payton, Sallyanne, 77, 146, 152
Patient Protection and Affordable Care Act of 2010.
    See Affordable Care Act of 2010
Pelosi, Nancy, 133, 140, 231
pharmacy benefit managers (PBMs), 110, 125,
    127–28
    in Congressional Budget Office scoring, 122–23
    as intermediaries in Democratic prescription
        drug proposals, 120–21, 125
pharmaceutical manufacturers. *See also* interest
    groups
    and Affordable Care Act of 2010, 229–30
    Amgen, 125, 126
    campaign and lobbying expenditures of, 127,
        131, 137–39
    and Clinton prescription drug proposals,
        120–21, 125–26
    Merck 125–29
    opposition to government formularies and price
        setting, 108, 124
    Pfizer, 124, 126
    PhRMA, 126, 137, 230
    public opinion toward, 197–98
pharmacists, 156, 204, 206
physicians. *See also* interest groups
    Affordable Care Act of 2010 and, 229, 233
    delegation to, 57, 88, 146, 218
    as healthcare interest group, 67, 69, 90
    importance of Medicare to, 10
    intermediaries for, 66
    as market rationalists, 87–88
    Medicare Modernization Act subsidies to, 137
    Medicare payments to, 149, 188, 230, 232
    utilization review by, 97
    wariness of federal government interference,
        46, 72
Pierson, Paul, 226
policy feedbacks, 16, 22
    attitudinal acquiescence effects of MMA, 192–93
    challenges of studying, 169
    interest group power effects of MMA, 183–88
    issue ownership effects of MMA, 176–83, 222
    limits to, 189
    of the Medicare Modernization Act, 168–70,
        221–22
    political participation effects of MMA, 191–92

policy feedbacks (*continued*)
  of Social Security, 168
  state-market attitude effects of MMA, 172–76
political polarization, 102–3, 112
  and Congress, 113
Prasad, Monica, 86
prescription drugs
  costs of, 114, 162–63
  coverage, among senior citizens, 114–15
  direct-to-consumer advertising of, 114, 125
  use, among senior citizens, 114, 158
private prisons
  administrative arrangements concerning,
    23–27
privatization
  versus "delegated governance," 20–21
Professional Standards Review Organizations
  (PSROs), 97
public opinion
  on Affordable Care Act of 2010, 43, 230, 233
  ambiguous nature of, 37–45, 81–84,
    226–27
  as barrier to conservative movement, 81–84
  as cause of delegated governance, 6–7, 37–45,
    220
  demobilization of, by MMA, 190–94
  effects of delegated governance on, 223, 225
  effects of MMA enrollment on seniors' attitudes,
    172–76
  effects of MMA enrollment on seniors'
    perceptions of parties,176–83
  on health maintenance organizations (HMOs),
    102
  as influence on design of Social Security, 60
  on issue ownership of prescription drugs, 119,
    286n19
  and issue preemption, 197–98
  on Medicare creation, 71
  on Medicare prescription drug coverage, 115–16,
    190
  on national health insurance during the 1940s,
    264n86
  on Part D prescription drug plans, 157, 190, 207,
    288n55
  toward privatization, vouchers, and premium
    support, 83–84, 105
Public Welfare Amendments of 1962, 64

Quality Improvement Organizations, 148

Reid, Harry, 232
reimportation (of prescription drugs from abroad),
  125, 190, 198
Reinhardt, Uwe, 99
Reischauer, Robert, 92, 129
Republican party

doubts of conservatives on prescription drug
  proposals of, 130, 133, 141
failure to gain issue ownership on health,
  176–83
fiscal year 2012 budget, 189, 222
incentives to pursue delegated governance, 13,
  84–85, 107–8, 220
issue preemption with MMA passage,
  194–98
Medicaid and Medicare proposals after 1994
  election, 102, 104
prescription drug proposal of 2000, 120–22,
  128, 129
prescription drug proposal of 2002,
  130–31
public opinion limits on goals of, 226–27
risk bearing
  in consumer choice reforms, 27
  in delegated governance, 26–27, 87
  in Democratic prescription drug proposals, 121
  in managed care, 93
  in Medicare Modernization Act, 109–10, 142,
    159
  in Medicare premium support, 93
  in Republican prescription drug proposals,
    121
Roosevelt, Franklin Delano, 59, 62, 67
Ryan, Paul, 189

Sasse, Benjamin E., 157
Savas, A. E., 86
school vouchers, 96–97
  administrative arrangements of, 23–27
Schultze, Charles, 86, 89
Schumer, Charles, 188
Section 8 housing vouchers
  administrative arrangements of, 23–27
Shaw, Clay, 131
Simon, Herbert, 191
Smith, Mark, 189
Social Security
  administrative arrangements of, 11, 14, 19
  as example of direct federal governance, 60
  influence of public opinion in design of, 60
  privatization, 84, 97,153, 227
  public opinion toward, 81
Social Security Act Amendments of 1950
  direct state payment of providers in, 70
Social Security Act Amendments of 1967
  nonprofit contracting in, 64–65
Social Security Act Amendments of 1974
  nonprofit contracting in, 65
Social Security Disability Insurance program, 70,
  107
Social welfare programs
  delegation of to nonprofits during 1950s and
    1960s, 63–65

early state and local responsibility for, 59
federal responsibility for, 59
Starr, Paul, 91
Stockman, David, 98
Supplemental Security Income, 213
Switzer, Mary, 64

Tauzin, Billy, 132
Tax Equity and Fiscal Responsibility Act of 1982 (TEFRA)
HMO risk contracts in, 98
Tea Party Movement, 232–33
Thomas, Bill, 105, 120, 122, 127, 135–36
Thompson, Tommy, 133
Transitional Assistance to Needy Families (TANF). *See* welfare
Transportation Safety Administration, 233–34, 295n7
trust in government, 8, 43–44, 71–72, 82, 101, 230
effect of delegated governance on, 225

Veterans Health Administration
administrative arrangements of, 14, 19, 22
as "socialized medicine" exception in US, 57, 67–68
prescription drug benefit in, 200, 208–9, 241
prescription drug costs compared to Part D, 162
Vladeck, Bruce, 152
Vocational Rehabilitation Agency, 64
Vouchers. *See* Medicare premium support; school vouchers; Section 8 housing vouchers

War on Poverty, 64
Watts, John C., 75
Weems, Kerry, 151, 152
welfare
administration of, 18, 22–27
delegated governance in, 96
public opinion toward, 38–39, 44, 81
1996 reform of, 94, 96
Whitten Amendment, 62